To Alan McLaren
with warm regards
from a fellow bibliophile,
Mike Parrish

With thanks for a
delightful evening,
Sylvia Frank

BROTHERS IN GRAY

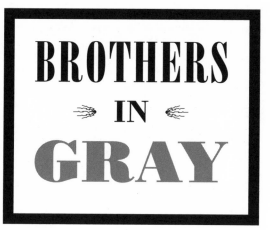

BROTHERS
≫ IN ≪
GRAY

THE CIVIL WAR
LETTERS OF THE
PIERSON FAMILY

Edited by

THOMAS W. CUTRER

and

T. MICHAEL PARRISH

LOUISIANA STATE UNIVERSITY PRESS
BATON ROUGE AND LONDON

Designer: Amanda McDonald Key
Typeface: Adobe Garamond
Typesetter: Impressions Book and Journal Services, Inc.
Printer and binder: Thomson-Shore, Inc.

Grateful acknowledgment is made to the Tulane Manuscripts
Department for permission to reproduce the Pierson letters herein.
Most of the letters are located in the Rosemonde E. and Emile Kuntz
Collection, Manuscript Collection 600, Manuscripts Department,
Howard-Tilton Memorial Library, Tulane University, New Orleans.

Library of Congress Cataloging-in-Publication Data

Brothers in gray : the Civil War letters of the Pierson family /
edited by Thomas W. Cutrer and T. Michael Parrish.
        p.   cm.
    Includes index.
    ISBN 0-8071-2134-7 (alk. paper)
    1. Pierson, David — Correspondence.   2. Pierson, Reuben —
Correspondence.   3. Pierson, James — Correspondence.   4. Pearson
family — Correspondence.   5. Soldiers — Louisiana — Bienville Parish —
Correspondence.   6. United States — History — Civil War, 1861–1865 —
Personal narratives, Confederate.   7. Louisiana — History — Civil
War, 1861–1865 — Personal narratives.   8. Bienville Parish (La.) —
Biography.   I. Cutrer, Thomas W.   II. Parrish, T. Michael.
E605.B87   1997
973.7'84'0922763 — dc21
    [B]   97-11123
                                        -                  CIP

To Norman and Betty Brown with gratitude and affection

⇒ CONTENTS ⇐

6

THE DEMON LOUISIANANS / 183

7

TELL THE GIRLS TO WAIT / 219

⇛ ILLUSTRATIONS ⇚

following page 142

➢ PREFACE ➣

David, Reuben, and James Pierson, whose letters are reproduced here, were well-educated men for their time and place, and their grammar, usage, and spelling are remarkably good considering the circumstances under which they wrote. We have chosen, therefore, to transcribe their letters exactly as written, using [*sic*] only occasionally to mark departures from standard usage. The reader will notice that at least one of the brothers consistently spells *Bowie* as "buoyie," *brigade* as "briggade," *brigadier* as "briggadier," *coarse* as "course," *Culpeper* as "Culpepper," *Rappahannock* as "Rhappahannock," *measles* as "measels," and *mumps* as "mumphs." These and other such variations are reproduced without comment, although misspellings that can be rectified by the injection of a letter or two in brackets are so corrected, and misspellings of proper names are generally corrected silently in the annotations. Words and phrases accidentally omitted by the writer or missing because of the deterioration of the original letters have been added in brackets where possible. In addition to the Piersons' letters, four related letters written by other individuals are included.

The Pierson brothers mention scores of individuals in their correspondence, some of whom are well known to Civil War historians, and many of whom have been obscured or even obliterated from the historical record by the passage of time. On first reference we have provided biographical information on every individual whom we could identify. We have cited in the notes the principal sources of this information, except for such standard reference volumes as Mark M. Boatner's *Dictionary of the Civil War*, Richard N. Current's *Encyclopedia of the Confederacy*, Patricia L. Faust's *Historical Times Illustrated Encyclopedia of the Civil War*, Francis Bernard Heitman's *Historical Register and Dictionary of the United States Army*, Robert K. Krick's *Lee's*

Colonels: A Biographical Register of the Field Officers of the Army of Northern Virginia, E. B. Long's *The Civil War Day by Day: An Almanac, 1861–1865,* Dumas Malone's *Dictionary of American Biography,* Jon L. Wakelyn's *Biographical Dictionary of the Confederacy,* Ezra J. Warner's *Generals in Gray* and *Generals in Blue,* and Ezra J. Warner and W. Buck Yearns's *Biographical Register of the Confederate Congress.*

Unfortunately, the 1860 census for Bienville Parish, Louisiana, has disappeared, and all but three issues of the local newspaper, the *Louisiana Baptist,* are no longer extant, making identifications difficult or, in some cases, impossible. These handicaps were more than offset, however, by the enthusiastic assistance of Wilbur E. Meneray, Assistant University Librarian for Special Collections, Howard-Tilton Memorial Library, Tulane University; Faye Phillips, Assistant Dean for Special Collections, Hill Memorial Library, Louisiana State University; Mary Linn Wernet, University Archivist, Eugene P. Watson Memorial Library, Northwestern State University of Louisiana; Florence M. Jumonville, Head Librarian, Louisiana and Special Collections, Earl K. Long Library, University of New Orleans; Kate Adams, Assistant Director of the Center for American History, University of Texas at Austin; and Dennis Isbell, Assistant Librarian, Fletcher Library, Arizona State University West. For their help and friendship, we are truly grateful. We also extend our gratitude to our University of Texas comrade and classmate Gary W. Gallagher for his intelligent, informed, and conscientious reading and critique of our manuscript, as well as for his old and valued friendship.

The letters reproduced herein are now housed in the Rare Books, Manuscripts, and University Archives division of Tulane University's Howard-Tilton Memorial Library.

BROTHERS IN GRAY

➣ INTRODUCTION ≼

In 1860 the north Louisiana parish of Bienville was, in the words of tourist J. W. Dorr, "very much in the woods and everything is in keeping with that style." Moreover, Dorr observed, Bienville Parish was "largely laid out but thinly populated," and worse, it was based on "a regular old-fashioned sand-bed." Given the relatively unsettled condition and poor soils of the frontier community, it was scarcely surprising that few large planters were in the parish, "the people being mostly small farmers with but few slaves."[1]

With only a modest commitment to the slave economy, Bienville Parish was at best lukewarm on the issue of secession in 1861. Although its delegates to the secession convention, Robert Hodges and Felix Lewis, ultimately voted in favor of the secession ordinance, many of the parish's citizens objected to the dismemberment of the Union. Of the twenty-one north Louisiana parishes, in fact, eight chose Unionist delegates. Nevertheless, Bienville and its region contributed greatly to the Confederate war effort, with north Louisiana mustering more than fifty thousand troops for military service. Among these were four of the sons of William H. Pierson of Mount Lebanon.[2]

Pierson was born in the Edgefield district of South Carolina on November 14, 1808, the son of John P. and Temperance Cranfield Pierson. Both of his parents died in the same week, when he was yet a child of five or six, and

1. Bienville Parish was organized on March 14, 1848, from a portion of Claiborne Parish. See Walter Prichard, ed., "A Tourist's Description of Louisiana in 1860," *Louisiana Historical Quarterly,* XXI (October, 1938), 1187. See also Gerald Pollard, "The History of Mount Lebanon University, 1852–1912" (M.Ed. thesis, Louisiana State University, 1971).

2. *Official Journal of the Proceedings of the Convention of the State of Louisiana* (New Orleans, 1861), rpr. in *Louisiana History,* II (Winter, 1961), 3, 4, 233, hereinafter cited as *OJ.*

young Pierson was sent to live with an uncle with whom he did not get along. At the age of twelve or thirteen, therefore, he left home and soon became a plantation overseer in Georgia. By 1826 or 1827, according to family tradition, he had saved enough money to purchase a farm in Stewart County, Georgia, and a single slave to assist him. There, on December 13, 1829, he married Mary Collins, and there the first six of the ten Pierson children were born. In 1841 or 1842 William Pierson moved his family to Pike County, Alabama. In 1847 he emigrated with his wife, six surviving sons, and two daughters to the Bienville Parish community of Mount Lebanon, the oldest settlement in the parish and the second largest after the parish seat at Sparta.[3]

Mary Collins Pierson died the year after the family's move to Louisiana, on November 11, 1848. Before the end of the year, Pierson married her younger sister, Nancy Collins. They had one child, Joseph H. Pierson, born in Bienville Parish on August 28, 1849.

At the time of the family's move to Louisiana, William H. Pierson owned four slaves and no more than $2,000 in other assets. By 1850, he owned ten slaves and one of the largest plantations in the parish, having 150 acres under cultivation and an additional 490 in timber. The value of his land was assessed at $2,500, with an additional $500 worth of machinery and equipment and $495 worth of livestock. The Pierson plantation produced that year 600 bushels of corn, 18 bales of cotton, and 100 bushels of sweet potatoes. Although small by the standards of the opulent rice and sugarcane plantations of south Louisiana and the cotton plantations along the Mississippi River, this was an excellent yield for the relatively poor soils and primitive transportation facilities of Bienville Parish. The increase in the family's fortune, wrote the author of a biographical sketch in 1890, offered "a good illustration of how rapidly money could be accumulated in Louisiana at that day, his being an average increase of the prosperity of the settlers from 1847 up to the opening of the Rebellion."[4]

3. Mary Collins was born in Stewart County on August 16, 1808, the daughter of Dennis and Joyce Collins. Her children born in Georgia were Henry Lewis (born on November 3, 1832); Martha A. Miranda Pierson (June 20, 1833); Reuben Allen Pierson (September 23, 1834); Samuel Pierson (May 18, 1836), who died in infancy; David Pierson (August 30, 1837); and William (April 29, 1839), who died at the age of two. Four more children were born to the family in Pike County, Alabama: Mary Catherine Pierson (May 17, 1841); Jonathan Pierson (October 21, 1842), who was mentally retarded; James F. Pierson (October 3, 1844); and Stephen (May 7, 1846), who died in October, 1849.

4. In 1860 William H. Pierson sold his plantation to Hodge Raburn (or Rabun) for thirty thousand dollars and moved to Mount Lebanon. During the Civil War he served as a member of the Bienville Parish police jury. In 1868 he moved to Sparta and in 1883 to Natchitoches, where he died on November 3, 1885. See "Some Large Landholders of Bienville Parish, 1850," *Louisiana History,* XXIV (Summer, 1983),

So, too, did Mount Lebanon prosper during the antebellum years. With what Judge Henry Bry referred to in *De Bow's Review* as its strong "colony of wealthy and intelligent Baptists" as its principal asset, the frontier community was able to form religious and educational institutions seemingly beyond its capacity. The first settlers established Rehobeth (Baptist) Church on July 8, 1837, for years "the leading congregation of the denomination in the state." Significantly, the first pastor of the Mount Lebanon church was a freeborn black named Henry Adams, who had accompanied the original settlers from South Carolina and was generally respected in the community as "a man of education and ability." He was followed in the pulpit in 1845 by George Washington Baines, the great-grandfather of Lyndon Baines Johnson.[5]

In 1848, the Louisiana Baptist Convention was founded at Mount Lebanon. In 1852, owing to the community's "healthiness and accessibility, as well as the high state of social and moral culture among its citizens," the convention established there Mount Lebanon University, the first college in Louisiana; the following year a consort academy, the Mount Lebanon Female Institute, was organized.[6] The presence of these two institutions and their few outstanding faculty members made Mount Lebanon the center of cultural affairs for much of north Louisiana.[7]

The coming of the Civil War, however, saw the beginning of Mount Lebanon's decline and collapse.[8] Following the election of Abraham Lincoln

---

288; *Biographical and Historical Memoirs of Northwest Louisiana* (Nashville, 1890), 364; Bienville Parish Historical Society, *History of Bienville Parish* (N.p., 1964), 23; James F. Pierson to [?], April 9, 1922, Typescript in Pierson Family Papers, Cammie G. Henry Research Center, Eugene P. Watson Library, Northwestern State University of Louisiana.

5. Bry, quoted in W. E. Paxton, *A History of the Baptists of Louisiana from the Earliest Times to the Present* (St. Louis, 1888), 241–42.

6. *Ibid.*, 433; Prichard, ed., "A Tourist's Description," 1188; Pollard, "History of Mount Lebanon University"; Kent Keeth, "The Luring of William Carey Crane," *Baylor Line* (November–December, 1991), 48.

7. William A. Poe, "Religion and Education in North Louisiana, 1800–1865," in B. H. Gilley, ed., *North Louisiana: Essays on the Region and Its History, Vol. I: To 1865* (Ruston, La., 1984), 119, 121, 124. With the upgrading of ministerial education as a basic goal of the Baptist Convention, the college's board of trustees especially wanted the chair of theology to be filled by a prominent clergyman. The board, however, chose to limit the search for new faculty to southern men—or at least those with sectional sympathies—and thus greatly reduced the school's ability to attract first-class teachers. Despite this obstacle to hiring, Jesse Hartwell and William Carey Crane, both Baptist clergymen of great stature in the region, successively occupied this chair. Hartwell, unfortunately, died in 1859 after a brief tenure. Crane, having become involved in a dispute at the university and with the local church, moved to Texas, where he became president of Baylor University (Paxton, *History of Louisiana Baptists,* 479–80).

8. The war devastated Mount Lebanon. The university, seized for use by Confederate authorities in September, 1863, as a hospital and laboratory, never quite recovered. The institution lost its endowment, which had been invested in Confederate bonds, and when the Vicksburg-Shreveport railway failed to

to the presidency, Louisiana's governor and legislature authorized a special election for January 7, 1861, to choose delegates to a secession convention to meet in Baton Rouge on January 23. David Pierson, the third surviving son of William H. Pierson, was elected to represent Winn Parish—like neighboring Bienville, a Unionist stronghold with few large plantations. The youngest delegate at age twenty-three, Pierson was one of only five to vote "nay" on the resolution approving Governor Thomas Overton Moore's seizure of the Federal forts, arsenals, and munitions in Louisiana; one of the seventeen who voted "nay" to the ordinance of secession; and one of only five who refused to sign the ordinance after it was adopted by the convention. His other votes included opposition to the reopening of the African slave trade and to the formation of a southern Confederacy.[9]

The exact cause of Pierson's strong unionism cannot now be ascertained, but it is reasonable to assume that, like Catahoula Parish's delegate, James G. Taliaferro, he believed that no state had the constitutional right to secede and predicted that economic chaos and bloody war would inevitably follow disunion. Conservative planters often considered their interests far better served by remaining in the Union and taking their chances.[10]

Many other "cooperationists" believed that the slave states should demand of the Lincoln administration a pledge to enforce the Fugitive Slave Law, as well as a guarantee of the perpetuation of slavery in the District of Columbia, protection of the interstate slave trade, and creation of a slave code for the western territories. With these demands met, at least a fraction of the delegates believed, secession would not be necessary. Louisiana's powerful senator Judah P. Benjamin, himself a "conditional unionist," observed, however, that the cooperationists were unable to "stem the wild torrent of passion which is carrying everything before it. . . . It is a revolution . . . of the most intense character . . . and it can no more be checked by human effort, for the time, than a prairie fire can be checked by a gardener's watering pot."[11] With Pierson's and all other such resistance to disunion quickly overwhelmed, on January 26, 1861, Louisiana's convention voted for imme-

---

pass through the town, the institution was further weakened. At length, it was reorganized and moved to Pineville, to become Louisiana College. The Mount Lebanon Female Institute had also closed by 1867. At the end of the 1930s, the community was almost entirely abandoned (Paxton, *History of Louisiana Baptists,* 479–80: Poe, "Religion and Education in North Louisiana," 128–30).

9. *Biographical and Historical Memoirs of Northwest Louisiana,* 364; *OJ,* 20, 24, 34–35, 42–44.

10. *OJ,* 71; John D. Winters, "Secession and Civil War in North Louisiana," in Gilley, ed., *North Louisiana,* I, 161.

11. Quoted in James M. McPherson, *Battle Cry of Freedom: The Civil War Era* (New York, 1988), 235–39.

diate secession, 113–17, with nearly all of the "nay" votes cast by delegates from the northern part of the state.

Despite its overt resistance to abandoning the Union, north Louisiana contributed its share to the Confederate war effort. From a white population of approximately 350,000, nearly 1,000 military companies were organized, and some 56,000 north Louisiana troops served in the Confederate army.[12]

Four of William H. Pierson's nine sons swelled this number, rendering outstanding service in Arkansas, Maryland, Mississippi, Missouri, Pennsylvania, and Virginia, and leaving one of the richest collections of Civil War letters composed by Louisiana soldiers. Educated and articulate, three of the brothers became officers and one a sergeant. The letters of three of the brothers reproduced here reveal the life and duties of the private soldier, the noncommissioned officer, the company grade officer, and the field-grade officer of the Confederate States Army. They range in subject from the little-known early battles of the Trans-Mississippi to the epic battles of the Army of Northern Virginia, and from the brutal trenches of Vicksburg to provost guard duty in the relative backwater of north Louisiana in the waning days of the war. Of equal importance to these military matters, the Pierson letters reflect upon the social history of the South at war, disclosing, among other things, much fascinating detail about the importance of the extended family, attitudes toward religion and the role of Providence in shaping the Confederacy's destiny, and the idealized view of southern womanhood as the guardian of the embattled republic. Romantic and patriotic, the Piersons excoriate prostitutes, profiteers, draft dodgers, and all else whom they see as polluters of their country and its righteous cause.

The first to volunteer, and the one to achieve the highest rank, was David Pierson. Born in Stewart County, Georgia, on August 30, 1837, he spent three years at Mount Lebanon University and then began to study law. He gained admission to the Louisiana bar in 1859. The same year, he moved to nearby Winnfield, Louisiana, where by 1860 he had accumulated a modest estate of $100 worth of real property and $2,000 in personal property.[13] Despite his political opposition to the Union's dismemberment, Pierson was granted a leave of absence from the secession convention on March 14, 1861, to raise an infantry company. He was mustered into Confederate service at New Orleans on May 17, 1861, as captain of Company C—locally designated as the Winn Rifles—Third Louisiana Infantry. Organized and taught

---

12. Winters, "Secession and Civil War," 162.
13. U.S. Census, 1860, for Winn Parish, Louisiana, 843.

the rudiments of drill at Camp Walker, the Third Louisiana was ready to march by May 20.

In response to Governor Moore's fears that his state was in peril of invasion by way of Forts Cobb and Washita in the Indian Territory, Confederate Secretary of War Leroy Pope Walker assured Moore of the strength of Brig. Gen. Ben McCulloch to halt such an incursion but called upon Louisiana for a regiment of infantry. Moore designated the Third Louisiana to join McCulloch's army in northwest Arkansas. The regiment had anticipated being ordered to Virginia, and on learning that they were to be shipped to Fort Smith, their morale suffered a staggering blow. Nevertheless, a Louisiana sergeant recalled that the men "were eager to see their future leader, already so famed as a Ranger on the Texas frontier." Soon this regiment was to become the Old Guard of the Army of the West, one with which McCulloch shared a mutual love and respect comparable to the relationship Robert E. Lee enjoyed with Hood's Texas Brigade or Thomas J. Jackson with the old "Stonewall Brigade."[14]

Capt. John J. Good, a Texas artillery officer, characterized the regiment's officers as "very clever gentlemen," although he saw the men as "turbulent" and "desperately fond of whiskey." Yet "there was not a braver regiment in the entire Confederate Army than the Third Louisiana," wrote an Arkansas soldier. Good admitted that "all are good fighters," and that in battle he would "rather be with them than any regiment in the service."[15] The Third Louisiana's first colonel was Louis Hébert; Samuel M. Hyams was its first lieutenant colonel; and William F. Tunnard was its first major.

David Pierson and his company distinguished themselves at the battle of Wilson's Creek (or Oak Hills, as the Confederates called it) fought in southwest Missouri on August 10, 1861, routing a battalion of U.S. Army regulars and overrunning a battery of Federal artillery. Seven months later, however, the regiment was severely crippled at Pea Ridge (or Elkhorn Tavern), Arkansas, in a disastrous battle that saw McCulloch and his second-in-command, Brig. Gen. James McQueen McIntosh, killed and the Third Louisiana's Colonel Hébert captured, along with many of his men.

14. John Tyler, Jr., to Thomas Overton Moore, May 14, 1861, in *The War of the Rebellion: A Compilation of the Official Records of the Union and Confederate Armies* (130 parts in 70 vols.; Washington, D.C., 1880–1901), Ser. I, Vol. LIII, 682; Willie H. Tunnard, *A Southern Record: The Story of the Third Regiment Louisiana Infantry* (1866; rpr. Dayton, Ohio, 1970), 32, 37. See also William Watson, *Life in the Confederate Army, Being the Observations and Experiences of an Alien in the South During the American Civil War* (1887; rpr. Baton Rouge, 1995).

15. John D. Cater, *"As It Was": Reminiscences of a Soldier of the Third Texas Cavalry and Nineteenth Louisiana Infantry*, ed. T. Michael Parrish (Austin, 1990), 117; Lester N. Fitzhugh, ed., *Cannon Smoke: The Letters of Captain John J. Good* (Hillsboro, Tex., 1971), 102.

The Third Louisiana never again enjoyed the full measure of glory it had achieved at Oak Hills. After Pea Ridge, it accompanied Maj. Gen. Earl Van Dorn to Corinth in April, 1862, and participated in the battles of Farmington on May 9 and Iuka on September 19. At Iuka, the regiment bore the brunt of the Federal assault, sustaining 40 percent casualties—more than one hundred men—including David Pierson, who received a serious shrapnel wound to the head. Left for dead on the field, Pierson was captured by Union forces. For its action at Iuka, Maj. Gen. Sterling Price reported that the Third Louisiana "had already fought under my eyes at the Oak Hills and at Elkhorn. No men have ever fought more bravely or more victoriously than they, and he who can say hereafter, 'I belonged to the Third Louisiana . . .' need never blush in my presence."[16]

After his almost miraculous recovery and exchange at Vicksburg on October 18, 1862, David Pierson was granted a convalescent leave for sixty days. On October 3 and 4, while he was still in Louisiana, the Third Louisiana took part in the battle of Corinth, another Confederate disaster. On October 6, after suffering more than four thousand casualties, Van Dorn marched with the remnants of his Army of the West to garrison Vicksburg.[17]

Pierson rejoined his regiment and was promoted to major on December 20, 1862. He was in command of the Third Louisiana during much of the siege of Vicksburg. The regiment occupied the Louisiana Redan, or Fort Hill, considered "the most dangerous post" along the beleaguered city's line of works. There the regiment's trenches were twice undermined and exploded by massive charges of black powder laid by Federal sappers, first on June 25 and then on July 1, 1863. These bombings were followed by sharp Union infantry attacks, but the Louisianians quickly rallied and repelled both. In the attack of June 25, Pierson was again severely wounded, this time in the chest by the explosion of a hand grenade. During the siege, the Third Louisiana suffered 45 killed and 126 wounded.

The regiment was paroled soon after the city's surrender on July 4, and Pierson was promoted to lieutenant colonel on August 22, 1863. Seriously reduced in numbers, the Third Louisiana was posted to Natchitoches, Louisiana, for exchange (which came late in 1864) and then assigned to Brig. Gen. Henry Watkins Allen's brigade as provost guards at the Shreveport prisoner-of-war camp. With the end of the war, the Third Louisiana dis-

16. Oran M. Roberts, *Texas* (Atlanta, 1899), 161, Vol. IX of Clement A. Evans, ed., *Confederate Military History*, 12 vols.

17. Robert G. Hartje, *Van Dorn: The Life and Times of a Confederate General* (Nashville, 1967), 214–46; Albert Castel, *General Sterling Price and the Civil War in the West* (1968; rpr. Baton Rouge, 1993), 108–19.

banded—largely spontaneously—on May 19 and 20, 1865. Pierson was paroled on June 15, 1865.[18]

The eldest of the brothers and the second to volunteer was Reuben Allen Pierson. He was born in Stewart County, Georgia, on September 23, 1834, attended Mount Lebanon University, and on the eve of Louisiana's secession, was teaching school in Bienville Parish. On July 7, 1861, at age twenty-nine, Al (as he was known to his brothers and sisters) was mustered into Company C, Ninth Louisiana Infantry, and appointed the company's first sergeant on December 28, 1861. The Ninth Louisiana—like the Third, composed largely of yeomen farmers from north Louisiana—earned a reputation as one of the finest regiments of Robert E. Lee's Army of Northern Virginia. Originally comprising 949 officers and men, the regiment was organized at Camp Moore on July 6, 1861, and elected as its colonel Richard Taylor, the son of "Old Rough and Ready"—the late president Zachary Taylor. Receiving orders to go to Virginia and "packed like sardines in box and platform cars," the Ninth arrived at Manassas Junction on July 22, too late to take part in the battle of July 21.

On February 5, 1862, at Camp Carondelet, Virginia, Al Pierson, together with almost all of his regiment, reenlisted for the duration of the war. He was elected captain of his company on April 15, 1862. As part of the Louisiana Brigade (with the Sixth, Seventh, and Eighth Louisiana regiments and the notorious First Special Battalion of Louisiana Volunteers—better known as the Tiger Rifles), the Ninth gained fame in Stonewall Jackson's Shenandoah Valley campaign in 1862, taking a conspicuous role in action at Middletown, Winchester, Strasburg, and Port Republic. During the Seven Days' Battles around Richmond, the Ninth saw action at Gaines' Mill and at Malvern Hill.

When the Louisiana troops were reorganized on July 26, 1862, the Ninth, along with the First, Second, Tenth, and Fifteenth Louisiana infantries, was transferred to the newly constituted Second Louisiana Brigade. At Second Manassas, the regiment suffered nearly one hundred casualties but gained lasting fame, hurling stones at John Pope's assaulting Union line when its ammunition supply was exhausted. Again heavily engaged at Sharpsburg, the Ninth suffered an additional eighty-two casualties. On October 5, the

18. Tunnard, *A Southern Record*, 547; Arthur W. Bergeron, Jr., *Guide to Louisiana Confederate Military Units, 1861–1865* (Baton Rouge, 1989), 76–79; Andrew B[radford] Booth, comp., *Records of Louisiana Confederate Soldiers and Louisiana Confederate Commands* (3 vols.; New Orleans, 1920), Vol. III, Pt. 2, p. 145; John D. Winters, *The Civil War in Louisiana* (1963; rpr. Baton Rouge, 1991), 423–24. For an authoritative description of the duties of the provost guard, see Kenneth Radley, *Rebel Watchdog: The Confederate States Army Provost Guard* (Baton Rouge, 1989).

regiment was again attached to the First Louisiana Brigade when the Fourteenth Louisiana joined the Second Brigade and it remained with that unit until the war's end.[19]

The Ninth Louisiana was part of Lee's reserve at Fredericksburg but was once again heavily engaged at Chancellorsville, defending Marye's Heights and ferociously attacking John Sedgwick's column at Salem Church on May 4, 1863. During the Gettysburg campaign, the Ninth was crucial to the capture of the Union garrison at Winchester on June 14–15, 1863. At Gettysburg, it took part in the attack on July 1 that broke the Union XI Corps. In an assault on Cemetery Hill on July 2, the regiment briefly overran an enemy battery before being forced back for lack of support.

At Rappahannock Station, on November 7, 1863, the regiment was sadly depleted when 130 officers and men were captured in an attempt to recover the guns of the Louisiana Guard Artillery battalion, unwisely posted on the north bank of the Rappahannock River. Reuben A. Pierson was wounded in the right hand at the battle of the Wilderness on May 5, 1864, and treated at Richmond's General Hospital Number Four. Upon leaving the hospital on May 10, he was granted a thirty-day furlough to recuperate at the home of relatives at Thomasville, Georgia.

After service at the battles of the Wilderness and Spotsylvania, the Ninth Louisiana was transferred to the Shenandoah Valley, where Pierson rejoined it in time to participate in the battle of Monocacy, Maryland, and in Jubal A. Early's famed raid on Washington from June 23 through July 12, 1864. Checked by the Union capital's defenses, Early recrossed the Potomac on July 14 and fell back through Snicker's Gap in the Blue Ridge Mountains. "The enemy followed and some fighting of no great importance took place on the 18th and 19th," wrote Maj. Henry Kyd Douglas of Early's staff.[20] Ironically, after seeing some of the most severe fighting of the war—at Manassas, Sharpsburg, Chancellorsville, Gettysburg, and the Wilderness— Reuben A. Pierson was killed on July 18, 1864, in a nameless picket skirmish at Snicker's Gap, a meaningless incident in the halfhearted Federal pursuit of Early's army back into the Valley.[21]

Thereafter, the Ninth Louisiana saw heavy action against Philip H. Sheridan's powerful Army of the Shenandoah at the battles of Fisher's Hill, the disastrous Third Winchester, and Cedar Creek. The remnant of the Ninth

19. Henry E. Handerson, *Yankee in Gray: The Civil War Memoirs of Henry E. Handerson with a Selection of His Wartime Letters* (Cleveland, 1962), 32.

20. Henry Kyd Douglas, *I Rode With Stonewall: The War Experiences of the Youngest Member of Jackson's Staff* (Chapel Hill, 1940), 296.

21. Booth, comp., *Records*, Vol. III, Pt. 2, p. 146.

returned to Lee's army in December, 1864, and served in the trenches of Petersburg until the evacuation of the city on April 2, 1865. When the regiment surrendered at Appomattox, only 4 officers and 64 enlisted men remained. Of the estimated 1,474 men to have served with the Ninth Louisiana, 233 were killed or mortally wounded in action, 349 died of disease, and 4 died in accidents. This was the highest death rate of any of Louisiana's regiments in Lee's army. One hundred and fifteen of the regiment are thought to have deserted, and three of its commanders—Richard Taylor, Leroy A. Stafford, and William R. Peck—became Confederate generals.[22]

Two other Pierson brothers also served the Confederacy, although neither so conspicuously. James F. Pierson, born in Pike County, Alabama, on October 3, 1844, attended Mount Lebanon University from 1859 to 1861 and then enlisted as a private in his brother David's Company C of the Third Louisiana Infantry at New Orleans on May 17, 1861. On October 11, he was detailed as a nurse in the hospital at Camp Jackson, Arkansas, but returned to his company during November. He was furloughed on February 11, 1862, but was back with his company in May and remained through July 16 of that year, when he was discharged as beneath the minimum age for military duty, thus missing the battles of Oak Hills and Pea Ridge. He returned to the army in the fall of 1862, however, and was captured at Vicksburg. After parole he served in Henry Watkins Allen's brigade at Natchitoches and Shreveport, Louisiana. With the collapse of the trans-Mississippi Confederacy, he was paroled as a sergeant at Shreveport on June 15, 1865.

In November, 1865, James Pierson married Amanda J. Thomas of Sparta, Louisiana, the sister of James Monroe Thomas of Reuben Allen Pierson's company. He studied law and was admitted to the Natchitoches bar in August, 1869. James Pierson died in New Orleans in 1930.[23]

Henry Lewis Pierson, the eldest of the Pierson children and the last to volunteer, was born in Stewart County, Georgia, on November 3, 1832. At the beginning of the war, he was practicing law in Sparta. On April 24, 1862, at age thirty, he enlisted as a private in the "Sparta Guards," Company E of the Twenty-seventh Louisiana Infantry. This regiment was organized at Camp Moore in April, 1862, and departed for Vicksburg on June 1, constituting a part of the city's garrison until its fall on July 4, 1863. Pierson was paroled at Vicksburg and reported to Shreveport for exchange before April 1, 1864. After its parole, the regiment went into camp at Enterprise, Louisiana,

22. Bergeron, *Guide*, 93–95; Terry L. Jones, *Lee's Tigers: The Louisiana Infantry in the Army of Northern Virginia* (Baton Rouge, 1987), 242–44.

23. *Biographical and Historical Memoirs of Northwest Louisiana*, 227–28; Booth, comp., *Records*, Vol. III, Pt. 2, pp. 145, 146.

until six of its companies reorganized at Alexandria in the summer of 1864. The reduced regiment remained at nearby Pineville until it was disbanded at Mansfield, Louisiana, on about May 19, 1865. Henry Pierson was paroled at Shreveport on June 12, 1865, as second lieutenant of Company E. Leon D. Marks was the regiment's first colonel, L. L. McLaurin its first lieutenant colonel, and George Tucker its first major. Marks and McLaurin both were killed in action during the siege of Vicksburg.

Henry Pierson was defeated in a race for judge against William B. G. Egan in March, 1865. After the war, Pierson emigrated to Lower Lake in Lake County, California, where he died on May 7, 1878.[24]

With the collapse of the Confederacy, David Pierson returned to Winnfield and his law practice. In 1866, he was elected district attorney of the Ninth Judicial District, comprising Natchitoches, Rapides, Sabine, and Winn parishes. On December 27 of that year, he married Sidney Amanda Pipes of Baton Rouge at Natchitoches.[25] Pierson remained in office until the adoption of the state constitution of 1868 removed him as "an impediment to Reconstruction." He then formed a partnership with W. H. Jack and returned to private practice in Natchitoches. In 1876, with the end of Reconstruction in Louisiana, he was elected judge of the Seventeenth Judicial District—the parishes of DeSoto, Red River, Natchitoches, and Sabine—and served until the adoption of the constitution of 1880. He was then elected judge of the newly formed Eleventh Judicial District and was reelected in 1884 and 1888. He retired in 1892, after nearly sixteen consecutive years on the bench.

In 1874, David Pierson served as president of the executive committee of the White League of Natchitoches Parish and was said to have been instrumental in returning the region to "home rule"; in 1884, he was elected president of the Fourth Congressional District's Democratic convention; and he was a delegate to the Democratic national convention at St. Louis in 1888 that nominated Grover Cleveland. He was also president of the first board of administrators of the State Normal School at Natchitoches (now Northwestern State University of Louisiana), established in 1884, and was credited with much of the school's early success. In 1900, he was appointed by the governor as a member of the Louisiana State Board of Pensions under a statute re-

24. Napier Bartlett, *Military Record of Louisiana* (1875; rpr. Baton Rouge, 1964); Bergeron, *Guide,* 136–37.

25. Sidney Amanda (Pipes) Pierson was the daughter of David Pipes and Mary (Oswalt) Pipes of West Baton Rouge Parish. She was born on April 27, 1847, and died at Pineville, Louisiana, on April 23, 1934. See New Orleans *Times-Picayune,* April 23, 1934; Sidney A. Pierson, "Widow's Application for Pension," Board of Pension Commissioners, Confederate Pension Applications, Louisiana State Archives.

quiring three Confederate veterans "of established war record." On September 28, 1900, David Pierson died of heart failure at Baton Rouge while attending a meeting of the board. He is buried in Natchitoches' American Cemetery.[26]

Among his four children was Clarence Pierson, who, upon graduation from the Tulane University School of Medicine in 1894, began practice in New Iberia, Louisiana. As a noted specialist in mental and nervous disorders, in 1895 he was appointed superintendent of the Central Louisiana State Hospital for the mentally ill at Pineville, and in 1901 he took charge of the state's principal mental institution located at Jackson, Louisiana. Clarence Pierson was also responsible for the purchase of the Louisiana Hot Wells near Alexandria, where he established a sanitarium for the insane.[27]

26. *Biographical and Historical Memoirs of Northwest Louisiana,* 364-65; John Dimitry, *Louisiana* (Atlanta, 1899), 550, Vol. X of Evans, ed., *Confederate Military History;* Pierson, "Widow's Application for Pension"; Lucile Keator Prud'homme and Fern Christensen, *The Natchitoches Cemeteries* (New Orleans, 1977), 16.

27. Henry E. Chambers, *A History of Louisiana* (3 vols.; Chicago, 1925), III, 16–17.

⇒ 1 ⇐

UPON THE ALTAR OF HIS
COUNTRY'S GLORY

⇒ ⇐

DAVID PIERSON TO WILLIAM H. PIERSON
Shreveport, La., April 22ᵈ, 1861

W*ᵐ* H. Pierson

Dear Father,

By the time this will reach you I will be on my way to New Orleans to join the Army. We have a meeting here tomorrow to make up a company of young men from this parish—all the best young men from this place will go. I have some prospect of being elected an officer of the company but will go as a private if not. We will doubtless get a hundred men.

I hope you will not be disturbed about my leaving so suddenly. I am not acting under any excitement whatever but have resolved to go after a calm and thoughtful deliberation as to all the duties, responsibilities, and dangers which I am likely to encounter in the enterprise. Nor do I go to gratify an ambition as I believe some others do, but to assist as far as in my power lies in the defense of our Common Country and homes which is threatened with invasion and annihilation. I was opposed to secession, it is true, and it was because I thought it would lead to the present difficulties and then in my opinion there was room to hope for a pacific settlement to the difficulties between the two sections that I voted and voted as I did on the secession question. However, it is the privilege of every citizen of free Government, when a political question is open and before the people for settlement to advocate whichever side, in his judgment and honest conviction, is right, just, and proper. Now the question is settled. A majority of the free people of the South have through the ballot box and their chosen representatives have resolved to throw off their alligence to their once-cherished Government and enact another suited to their wants and desires. For me there is but two alternatives left: either to take up arms against the South or in her defense. And between them I am not slow to choose. It would be a violation of my very natural feeling and impulse for me or any other man to rise up against the Government in which we live & under whose care we are protected. I have volunteered because I thought it my duty to do so. Much is the sacrifice of personal interest that I make, with an office full of business and a hundred clients depending upon my labor for the maintenance of their rights, but if those situated as I am do not go, who will? I am young, able-bodied, and have a constitution that will bear me up under any hardships, and above all, there is no one left behind when I am gone to suffer for the necessities of life because of my absence. Hundreds have left their families and their infant helpless children and enlisted in their Country's service, and am I who have none of their dependents better than they? If I loose [sic] all I have and survive, I can make again, and if I perish it will be but a sacrifice which duty impells every patriot to make upon the altar of his Country's Glory. Good bye.

Your faithful son,
David Pierson

⇒ ⇐

DAVID PIERSON TO REUBEN ALLEN PIERSON

Camp Walker[1]
Near N.O., May 14th 1861

R. A. Pierson

Dr Bro.

I have just time to drop you a line. My Company is uniformed after a long time and will get their arms tomorrow (Rifles)[.] We are in the famous 3d Regiment and have been ordered to Richmond Va.—Will leave here in less than 4 days, taking the Jackson Rail road. I am getting used to Camp life and hard work and am in excellent health. You would not know me on account of my sunburnt face. After today no more volunteers will be received except they enlist for the

1. Camp Walker, Louisiana, also known as Camp Metairie or Camp Smith, was located on the Metairie Race Course near New Orleans. Named for Confederate secretary of war Leroy Pope Walker, the camp is now the site of Metairie Cemetery. The camp was opened to receive, organize, and train recruits in April, 1861, and remained the principal Confederate camp of instruction in Louisiana until May 12, 1861, when Camp Moore was established in Tangipahoa Parish. After that date, only the Third Louisiana was housed at Camp Walker, where it remained until May 20 (Powell A. Casey, *Encyclopedia of Forts, Posts, Named Camps, and Other Military Installations in Louisiana, 1700–1981* [Baton Rouge, 1983], 241–42).

war. Write me & direct to D. Pierson of Winn Rifles, 3ᵈ Regiment, Col Hébert's[2] care.

Love & c.

D. Pierson

⇒ ⇐

DAVID PIERSON TO WILLIAM H. PIERSON

Vicksburg, May 25ᵗʰ 1861

Wᵐ H. Pierson

Dear Father,

I have just time to drop you a line from this place. We are stopping here a few hours to await the arrival of our ammunition which has been ordered from Montgomery. It will get here at 3 Oclock this evening and then we start for Fort Smith, Ark.[3] So far our trip has been a pleasant one—the fare is so much better than it was at Camp Walker that it seems a perfect paradise. The officers have most excellent quarters, plenty to eat & drink free of charge, but the men have to stay on deck & cook their own meals as in camp. This I do not like for no distinction should be made between officers & men. I am spending a larger part of my time with my boys on deck, eating with them frequently. Last night I gave my stateroom up to a sick man and was grinned at for it. The men take everything cheerful. It is astonishing to see how soon young men tenderly raised will accustom themselves to a Soldier's life and how cheerful they perform the very irksome tasks imposed upon them. We are the worst sun burnt set you ever beheld. My face is as yellow as pumpkin, so oppressively hot was the sun at Camp Walker.

It is rumored here that we are likely to have to fight our way up Arkansas river with the famous Montgomery[4] of Kansas who is said to be making a raid

2. Louis Hébert was the first colonel of the Third Louisiana Infantry. He fought at Wilson's Creek in August, 1861, and was captured with a large part of his regiment at Elkhorn Tavern in March, 1862. Promoted to brigadier general, Hébert was given command of a brigade of Sterling Price's Army of North Mississippi. After being exchanged following his capture at Vicksburg, Hébert was assigned to duty as chief of heavy artillery at Fort Fisher, North Carolina.

3. Fort Smith, on the Arkansas River near the mouth of the Poteau, was then a city of about twenty-five hundred inhabitants. Near the old fort, on slightly rising ground in the middle of a large prairie, McCulloch's men constructed at Camp Walker rows of wooden barracks around a parade ground featuring "a very high flag pole, carrying an enormous Confederate flag" (Edwin C. Bearss and A. M. Gibson, *Fort Smith: Little Gibraltar on the Arkansas* [Norman, Okla., 1969], 238–69).

4. James Montgomery raised and assumed command of a regiment of cavalry in James Henry Lane's self-styled "Army of the Western Border" but never held a U.S. army commission (Jay Monaghan, *Civil War on the Western Border, 1854–1865* [Boston, 1955], 81, 182).

on Ark. with 3,000 men. Our Regiment belongs to Gen. Ben McCulloch's[5] division and will no doubt see some of the fun, if fun it might be called. I suppose about fifteen thousand troops will be concentrated near Fort Smith to sustain Northern Ark. and assist Missouri. It is expected that there will be much fighting in or about St. Louis and Cairo. Large armies of men are moving in that direction. A Tennessee Regiment passed here two days ago on its way to Fort Smith, and Ben McCulloch is said to have about 300 Texas rangers[6] on route, many of whom are mounted. He is at this time in Ark. arranging a plan for his future operations.

I am well and resigned to anything that may come.

Yours Truly,
David Pierson

⇒ ⇐

DAVID PIERSON TO REUBEN ALLEN PIERSON

On board Steamer Indian N°. 2
Ark. River Near Pine Bluff
May 27th 1861

R. A. Pierson

Dear Brother,

Having some time here which I don't expect to have when we land, I had as well make use of it in writing letters. Up to this time I have heard nothing from home except what the boys from Bienville told me at New Orleans and have thought a little hard of it because I know you have plenty of time, and if you had written me as early as you ought I should have gotten your letters before I

---

5. Ben McCulloch was a veteran of the Texas Revolution and the Mexican War as well as a famed Texas Ranger, "forty-niner," and U.S. marshal. On May 11, 1861, Jefferson Davis appointed McCulloch a brigadier general, the second-ranking brigadier general in the Confederate army and the first general-grade officer to be commissioned from the civilian community. Assigned to the command of Indian Territory, he built the Army of the West with regiments from Arkansas, Louisiana, and Texas (Thomas W. Cutrer, *Ben McCulloch and the Frontier Military Tradition* [Chapel Hill, 1993]).

6. Among the southern sympathizers of the region, one of Greer's troopers wrote, "The best feeling prevails toward Texas and Texians, and everywhere on the road thousands of questions were asked about the Texas Rangers." The name "Texas Ranger" carried a magic of its own, according to Missourian H. Clay Neville, coming as it did "from the Indian frontier with the fame and paraphernalia of the resistless hero." Tales of the ranger's prowess and skill in fighting "the wily savage on the Western plains" were enhanced in the eyes of southern partisans by "the marvelous feats of horsemanship exhibited by the bold Texan as he dashed about camp." None doubted that "the knight of the lasso would perform new wonders in driving back the 'hireling foe'" (Henry Clay Neville, "Wilson's Creek," *Southern Historical Society Papers,* XXXVIII [1910], 370–71).

left New Orleans. I had the pleasure to learn from Dr. James Egan[7] that you had joined a company and started with it before you received the proclamation that no more troops were needed. I am sorry that your gallant company were disappointed, but you will no doubt have a chance to show your valor before the end of the strife.

We are traveling very slow in this river in consequence of low water. The river is falling fast, and I believe we will have to march from Little Rock to Fort Smith, a distance of 180 miles. We have just passed Pine Bluff, a considerable town on a high pine ridge which snakes into the river. These are the first pine trees we have seen since we left home and was a cheering sight to all. The people along the banks of the river continue to cheer us vociferously. At Pine Bluff a few minutes ago the banks were lined for half a mile with human beings, shouting and waving flags & handkerchiefs. But the enthusiasm of the people is exceeded by that of the boy on and of these boats. The whole way the woods and banks fairly roar with the shouts of the 3rd Regiment for Jeff Davis & the South. I never saw so much excitement and so much enthusiasm before.

I was awake this morning just about sun up by the cry from a hundred voices of "man overboard" and on rushing out of my stateroom beheld a man floating down the river just astern of the boat. A Winn Rifleman[8] was in the deep, rapid current struggling for his life. I looked below and twenty men were standing by the yawl boat not making an effort to get it afloat and screamed at

7. James Cronan Egan was a pioneer physician in Mount Lebanon. He was elected first sergeant of Company C when the Ninth Louisiana was organized at Camp Moore and promoted to second lieutenant at Camp Bienville on September 5, 1861. On January 23, 1862, Richard Taylor appointed Egan medical director of his brigade, and on April 26, 1862, he was named medical director of Ewell's division. In January, 1863, Egan requested a leave of absence "for personal reasons." On January 23, 1863, he was relieved of his duties in Virginia and assigned as director of the Confederate hospital at Monroe, Louisiana. On August 16, 1864, he was appointed inspector of hospitals and medical director for North Louisiana, a position from which he resigned on December 19, 1864. After the war, Egan served several terms in the Louisiana State Senate. He was the son of Bartholomew W. Egan, founder and first professor of moral and mental science at Mount Lebanon University, superintendent of a laboratory established on the campus to produce medicines for the Confederacy, and surgeon general of Louisiana. See Andrew B[radford] Booth, comp., *Records of Louisiana Confederate Soldiers and Louisiana Confederate Commands* (3 vols.; New Orleans, 1920), II, 760; Bienville Parish Historical Society, *History of Bienville Parish* (N.p., 1964), 93–94; Egan Family Collection, Cammie G. Henry Research Center, Eugene P. Watson Library, Northwestern State University of Louisiana; *Dictionary of Louisiana Biography,* I, 282; W. E. Paxton, *A History of the Baptists of Louisiana from the Earliest Times to the Present* (St. Louis, 1888), 549–54.

8. "Winn Rifles" was the local designation of Company C, Third Louisiana Infantry, the company David Pierson commanded. Upon his promotion to major on November 5, 1862, N. M. Middlebrooks became the company's second and final commander (Arthur W. Bergeron, Jr., *Guide to Louisiana Confederate Military Units, 1861–1865* [Baton Rouge, 1989], 93).

them to throw it over into the water, but they were too badly frightened to do anything and it was not until two deck hands came up that the yawl could be got afloat. In the mean time, down the river went the man until we could scarcely see his head above the water. At length the boat stopped and the yawl with two deck hands and the mate pulling at the oars swept down the current. All eyes were turned upon the little crew and every heart beat with anxiety for the safety of the unfortunate man. For myself, I was breathless for about five minutes. At a distance of half a mile down the river or more the yawl stopped, and I saw the Mate make a grab with his hands. The man was safe. He had sunk several times after the boat had gotten near him. The Mate seized him by the hair just as he was sinking, perhaps the last time. He was brought into the boat and warmed by the fire and has since been the universal favorite of the Company.

I am well satisfied, & so are most of the men, though our fare is hard & our duties irksome. Write to me and state all you know about everything. Your letters will reach me no matter where I go.

Yours Truly
D. Pierson

⇒ ⇐

DAVID PIERSON TO REUBEN ALLEN PIERSON

Little Rock, Ark., May 30th 1861

R. A. Pierson, Esq.

Dear Brother,

We are stopped here a few days to await orders from our commander, Gen. Ben McCulloch. He is expected here hourly. We would have gone up to Fort Smith and not stopped here at all, but the river got too low for navigation, and as it was expected the enemy were in the state and marching upon this place, we placed ourselves at the service of the Gov. of this state for the time being. Three days ago we expected to have a fight. By this time Harney[9] & Lane[10] had sent

9. Although he seems to have been sincerely devoted to the Union cause, Brig. Gen. William Selby Harney, commander of the Department of the West with headquarters in St. Louis, was made suspect by his Louisiana birth and Democratic political views. In 1861, he was relieved of command and given an unsought leave of absence. Orders never came, and in 1863 he resigned from the army as a major general (Richmond L. Clow, "William S. Harney," in Paul Andrew Hutton, ed., *Soldiers West: Biographies from the Military Frontier* [Lincoln, 1987], 42–58).

10. James Henry Lane, after service in the Mexican War, was elected lieutenant governor of Indiana in 1849, to a seat in the House of Representatives in 1853, and to the Senate from Kansas in 1861. With the outbreak of the war, he was sent to Kansas to organize a brigade for the Union. At its head, he invaded Missouri and so devastated the slaveholding counties along the Kansas border that his name became a byword for terrorism.

word down here that they would take breakfast in Little Rock Friday morning (tomorrow), but the rumor that they were in the state is now discredited. The people here are all ablaze with excitement. Cavalry Companies are forming in every neighborhood and riding all over the country after suspicious characters. A whole regiment of cavalry leaves here tomorrow for the interior of the state.[11] They are all able-bodied young men, well mounted. I do not know as yet where Old Ben McCulloch will take us or what the plan of his operations are, but I can give a guess and will do so. It is my opinion still that we are intended for Missouri and that we will be ordered hence as soon as our division is ready for marching. The people of Missouri, it is said, are willing to join the South but are afraid to do so having no arms and a Lincoln army being stationed in her limits. Our camp at this place is situated in the arsenal grounds about half a mile from the river. We have most excellent cool well water to drink, and the prettiest cool, shady oak grove I ever saw to drill under. In all respects, we are much better situated here than at Camp Walker.

Our Regiment is improving rapidly in infantry exercises. At first we were an awful green set but have improved so far that we do pretty well. We drill six hours every day which, of course, fatigues us very much and makes us sleep soundly at night.

I have a good wall tent which turns the rain equal to a house roof. My furniture is a small, narrow mattress, a blanket, and my cooking utensils. One of my men cooks for me. Two officers tent with me, viz.: Lieut. Emanuel[12] & Strother.[13] They are both clever and agreeable young men. Our cook can make as good biscuits as anybody, and now and then we buy a plate of butter which, as you know, makes quite a fine breakfast. We are not very choice, however,

11. The Third Texas Cavalry, also known as the South Kansas-Texas Regiment, was raised in and around Dallas County in the spring of 1861. It was commanded by Col. Elkhana Greer, a Marshall, Texas, merchant and planter who had served under Jefferson Davis in the First Mississippi Rifles during the Mexican War and been grand commander of the Knights of the Golden Circle in Texas. The regiment served with distinction at the battle of Wilson's Creek (Oak Hills), routed disaffected Cherokees under Chief Hopothleyahola at the battle of Chustenahlah, and was present (although not heavily engaged) at Elkhorn Tavern. Thereafter, it was transferred east of the Mississippi River, where, after the battles of Iuka and Corinth, it was assigned to Brig. Gen. Lawrence Sullivan Ross's famed Texas cavalry brigade (Douglas Hale, *The Third Texas Cavalry in the Civil War* [Norman, Okla., 1993]).

12. Asa Emanuel, known to his friends as "Ace," was elected first lieutenant of Company C on May 17, 1861, at New Orleans. He was captured at the battle of Pea Ridge on March 7, 1862, and incarcerated at Gariot Street Military Prison in St. Louis until July 13, when he was transferred to the military prison at Alton, Illinois. He was exchanged at Aiken's Landing, Virginia, on November 11, 1862, only to be recaptured with the fall of Vicksburg. He returned to his regiment at Natchitoches, Louisiana, for exchange at some time prior to April 1, 1864 (Booth, comp., *Records,* II, 774).

13. William Strother was elected second lieutenant of Company C at New Orleans on May 17, 1861. He died at Jackson, Mississippi, on October 18, 1861 (*ibid.,* Vol. III, Pt. 3, p. 728).

about diet, for after we over the morning drill and parade, we can eat any thing that comes to hand. While in New Orleans I was exposed to many cases of measles, but have not taken them and the time is now passed. My health continues good, though I believe every other man in the Company has been sick but myself.

Write me soon and give me all the news.

Yours Truly,
D. Pierson

⇒ ⇐

DAVID PIERSON TO WILLIAM H. PIERSON
On board Steamer Countess
Ark. River, June 6th 1861

W^m. H. Pierson
Mt. Lebanon
La.

Dear Father,

As we are off from Little Rock, I thought you might like to hear from us and I therefore write you though this craft shakes and totters so that I can scarce make a letter. We have had extraordinary good luck in getting water transportation from Little Rock to Fort Smith. Just as our quartermaster had employed wagons and teams and they had arrived at our camp to take us up and we had begun to pack up our camp property for a march of 180 miles over a mountainous country covered with rock (the idea of which we all dreaded very much) a rise came down in the river. The rise was so rapid that in less than 15 hours the river had rose about 20 feet—over 1½ feet to the hour. In a few hours the river was in good boating order. And as it happened, four small boats were lying at the landing which we pressed into service and compelled to bring us up the river. We are suffering much inconvenience on board these boats—the men are crowded together like Sardines in a box—have nothing to cook on except a small stove which for 200 men is as good as nothing. Besides, the weather is very hot and we suffer much with heat. All this will soon be over with and I had rather take it for 3 days than to have marched up and down mountains for fifteen days on rocks, half the time, perhaps, without water. It was a fortunate thing for us that we got water transportation, for I do not believe one half the men in the Regiment could have stood the march. Well, we will get to Fort Smith tomorrow. What next I am unable to say at this time. The report that Lane & Montgomery of Kansas were about to invade Ark. is entirely false. I don't believe they will even try to retake Fort Smith, which is on the line of Ark. and the Indian Territory.

In all probability we will be sent into the Indian Country where it is said that Lane intends to concentrate an army in order to control the tribes for the North and raise regiments for the war. The Indians are divided. Half the Cherokee Nation is with the North and half with us. The Choctaws are with us to a man. If we are not sent to the Indian Country, there is but one other place which I can imagine, and that is Missouri. There is no particle of use in our staying at Fort Smith, and I cannot believe that it is intended for us to do so. Ark. is strong enough to hold it against any force with the assistance of the Indians in the neighborhood. Our brave and daring Gen. "Ben McCulloch" will no doubt lead us where ever the sharpest work is to be done, and I can have no doubt but that we will have a fight before the summer is over. Our Regiment is made up of the best material for a fight: all young men, able-bodied, and such a dare devil set of fellows I never saw before. The success of the 2^d Regiment of La. Vol. in Virginia is freely talked of among the boys, and all are determined that ours shall not be less distinguished than they for their courage and valor.[14] We had an agreeable time in Little Rock: a cool shady oak grove, plenty of the best well water, and high dry ground. My health continues good though I have been exposed to Measles for more than 3 weeks. I hardly believe that I will take them at all now. About 8 of my Company have them now but are getting along well. My pay in the Army is $130 per month which will defray my expenses handsomely. I will get a month's wages soon. I have no desire to quit—am well contented, & c.

Yours truly,
David Pierson

14. The Second Louisiana Infantry was organized at Camp Walker on May 11, 1861, under the command of Col. Lewis G. DeRussy. Ordered to Virginia, the regiment took part in the defense of Yorktown and Williamsburg during the Peninsula campaign and played a conspicuous role in the Confederate attack at Malvern Hill, losing 182 men killed and wounded, including its colonel and major. Thereafter, it fought in virtually every engagement of the Army of Northern Virginia. When the Second Louisiana surrendered at Appomattox, only 3 officers and 41 men remained of the 1,297 who had served in the regiment (Bergeron, *Guide,* 75–76).

> ⤜

REUBEN ALLEN PIERSON TO MARY CATHERINE PIERSON
[FRAGMENT OF LETTER]

[Camp Moore, La.][15]
[June 20, 1861]

[Miss M. C. Pierson] [16]
[Mt. Lebanon, La.]

About 8 oclock in the morning we arrived at the point of destination, in full sight of the tents which constitute the scene at Camp Moore. Before disbanding we were sworn into the service of the State. The following is as near the oath as I can remember. You and each of you do solemnly swear true and faithful allegiance to the state of La., that you will defend her, that you will obey all orders in camp and will be subject to the orders of the Confederate States when formed into a regiment and having elected officers for the same so help you God. We then went to work and soon cleared away a place for our tents, the officers in the mean time having procured them, and soon, very soon we found ourselves encamped as soldiers. The camp is one of the filthiest places I have ever been permitted to see. There are more flies in and around Camp Moore than there are in all Bienville Parish. Still there are about 20 or 30 men daily employed removing the filth from the camp. It would turn the stomach of any other being except a soldier to go into one of the eating houses kept on this encampment. The flies are so thick until you have to be careful in carrying a mouthful from your plate to your mouth lest a fly should alight upon it before it is received. This is no exaggerated statement but well received testimony for its truth from all who have visited the camp. I have often heard and as often repeated an old saying that there is nothing that a man cannot accustom himself to, and here this saying is verified for you will seldom hear anyone mention the flies after he has been in camp three days; but of all the grumbling of the world it is heard the first few days. Excuse the length of my letter. I am sitting in the woods under a large beech tree, upon a pine log about a quarter [mile] from the

15. Camp Moore, located at the village of Tangipahoa, some seventy-eight miles above New Orleans, was the principal camp of instruction for Louisiana Confederates. When Camp Walker in Metairie proved inadequate for housing and training the large number of volunteers, Camp Moore (named for Louisiana governor Thomas Overton Moore) was established, with the new regiments moving to the camp May 13–15, 1861 (Powell A. Casey, *The Story of Camp Moore and Life at Camp Moore Among the Volunteers* [N.p., 1985]).

16. Mary Catherine Pierson, known to her family as "Cassie," was born on May 17, 1841, in Pike County, Alabama. Little is now known about her except that she taught school, at least for a time before and during the war. She died on November 17, 1909, near Coushatta, Louisiana.

camp where there is not a single thing to disturb me. Well Cassie, we are separated for a year sure and perhaps forever but if I should fall a victim on the battle field while fighting for Justice and Liberty my only grief will be about the welfare of you and my dear old father and Aunt. The little cripple or I may say cripple man will ever find protection from those who have a single spark of humanity within their bosom, but you a non-suspecting innocent woman may find deceiving friends who will seek to destroy your peace for life.

I beg your forgiveness for this solemn warning and must endeavor to impress on your mind the importance of looking out for yourself for no one else will watch as those most interested. Overlook mistakes and pardon all amiss. I send my best regards to you and all the family. Give my love to all enquiring friends and especially to those of the tender sex. I remain your Brother. Wishing you success through life.

Direct your letter as follows
Tangipahoa, La.
Care of
B. W. Pearce [17]
Commander, Bienville Blues [18]
R. A. Pierson

>€

REUBEN ALLEN PIERSON TO WILLIAM H. PIERSON
Camp Moore, La.
June 21st, 1861

[W. H. Pierson]
[Mt. Lebanon, La.]
Dear Father,

I arrived at Camp Moore yesterday morning about 8 Oclock and was mustered into the service of La. subject to the order of the Confederate States. We had quite a pleasant trip down and all the boys are as jovial as a party of youths

17. Benjamin W. Pearce, captain of Company C, Ninth Louisiana Infantry, enrolled in the Confederate service on July 7, 1861, at Camp Moore. A resident of Sparta, he was fifty years old, married, and listed his occupation as farmer. He was also a local politician of some repute, having represented Bienville Parish in the state legislature. On April 24, 1862, upon reorganization of the Army of Northern Virginia, he was dropped from the service on account of ill health (Booth, comp., *Records,* Vol. III, Pt. 2, p. 91; Bergeron, *Guide,* 93).

18. "Bienville Blues" was the popular designation of Company C, Ninth Louisiana Infantry (Bergeron, *Guide,* 93).

at a wedding. Everything is not so bad down in this camp as has been represented by many of those who returned from here. We were cheered by every
one with whom we met from the time we started till our arrival at the camp.
Our provision is course and our beds are hard yet I enjoy it much better than I
could have expected. We have not drilled any up to this time but will begin tomorrow. We have been clearing off our tent ground yesterday and today and
have now the prettiest ground on the encampment. Old Lang Lewis's[19] company will leave in a day or two for Virginia. They are in the 8th regiment. I have
no news to write; have not seen a paper since I arrived on the camp ground. My
mess is made up and consists of the following men viz. Cawthon,[20] Melvin,[21] 2
Theuses,[22] Collins,[23] Rhodes,[24] Pittman,[25] Tarkington,[26] Sanders,[27] Johnson,[28]
making in all ten. We have two tents and are well fixed for living. All the company is well except young Stall[29] and two others who spreed all the way down. I
have met with a few of my old friends and school mates since I have been in
camp. I will try to write again Sunday evening and send it to Vicksburg by one
of the Minden company.[30] It is doubtful when we will get off from this place. It

19. John Langdon Lewis, captain of Company G, Eighth Louisiana Infantry, enrolled on June 23,
1861, at Camp Moore. He resigned from the service on December 9, 1861 (Booth, comp., *Records,* Vol.
III, Pt. 1, p. 752; Bergeron, *Guide,* 90).

20. Thomas J. Cawthon, an Iverson, Louisiana, farmer, enlisted in Company C, Ninth Louisiana
Infantry, at Camp Moore on July 7, 1861. He was elected corporal in April, 1862, was wounded at the
first battle of Winchester on May 25, 1862, and was killed in action at Chancellorsville on May 4, 1863
(Booth, comp., *Records,* II, 299).

21. George W. Melvin of Ringgold, Louisiana, enlisted in Company C, Ninth Louisiana Infantry, at
Camp Moore on July 7, 1861. He was elected third lieutenant of his company on September 23, 1862, and
was captured at the battle of Rappahannock Station, Virginia, on September 7, 1863. Melvin spent the
remainder of the war at the Old Capitol Prison in Washington and at Johnson's Island, Ohio (*ibid.,* Vol.
III, Pt. 1, p. 946).

22. Hezekiah P. Theus, a Ringgold resident, enlisted in Company C, Ninth Louisiana Infantry, at
Camp Moore on July 7, 1861. He was severely wounded at the battle of Sharpsburg and was discharged as
unfit for service. His brother, John C. Theus of Mount Lebanon, enlisted at the same time and place. He
was elected first lieutenant on September 5, 1861, but was not reelected when the company was reorganized and thereafter left the service. He is most likely the J. C. Theus who enlisted in Company E, Thirteenth Battalion, Louisiana Partisan Rangers, on January 1, 1863 (*ibid.,* Pt. 2, p. 799).

23. Philip L. Collins, an Iverson farmer, enlisted in Company C, Ninth Louisiana Infantry, at Camp
Moore on July 7, 1861. He was captured at Rappahannock Station on November 7, 1863, and confined at
Point Lookout, Maryland, until paroled on March 10, 1864. He was again taken prisoner at the third
battle of Winchester, September 19, 1864, and was returned to Point Lookout, where he was held until
the war's end (*ibid.,* II, 391). Collins was the nephew of Mary and Nancy (Collins) Pierson. A number of
his letters are included in this collection.

is now believed by many of the soldiers that the war will close by fall. I will close by saying excuse all amiss for I have a poor chance to write. Your son, R. A. Pierson

⇒ ⇐

REUBEN ALLEN PIERSON TO JAMES F. PIERSON

Camp Moore, La.
July 3rd, 1861

[James F. Pierson]
[Mt. Lebanon, La.]
Dear Bro.

I received yours of the 1st Inst. this morning about day light making the second that I have received this week from you. I am still in good health and enjoy my new mode of life as well as any one could expect. Our regiment is now

24. Horace L. Rhodes, Company C, Ninth Louisiana Infantry, enlisted at Camp Moore on July 7, 1861, was captured at Rappahannock Station on November 7, 1863, and confined at Point Lookout, Maryland, until paroled on March 10, 1864. He was returned to Point Lookout after his second capture at Spotsylvania on May 12, 1864, and did not return to Mount Lebanon until the end of the war (*ibid.,* Vol. III, Pt. 2, p. 297).

25. Thomas J. Pitman of Bienville Parish joined Company C, Ninth Louisiana Infantry, at Camp Moore on July 7, 1861. He was elected first corporal on May 5, 1863, but was reduced to the ranks at his own request on August 31, 1864. Pitman surrendered with his regiment at Appomattox (*ibid.,* 154).

26. Thomas B. Tarkington of the Bienville Parish village of Salt Springs enlisted in Company C, Ninth Louisiana Infantry, at Camp Moore on July 7, 1861, and was elected third corporal in April, 1862. He was wounded in the shoulder at Sharpsburg, captured at Chancellorsville, and held captive at Fort Delaware until paroled and exchanged May 23, 1863. Sometime in 1864, he is said to have "deserted to the cavalry" (*ibid.,* 768).

27. Thomas J. Sanders enlisted in Company C, Ninth Louisiana Infantry, at Camp Moore on July 7, 1861, was captured at Rappahannock Station on November 7, 1863, and was confined at Point Lookout until paroled on March 10, 1864. He was wounded on May 12, 1864, at Spotsylvania and at Monocacy on July 9, 1864, but returned to his regiment in time to surrender at Appomattox (*ibid.,* 444).

28. Harris R. Johnson of Mount Lebanon enlisted in Company C, Ninth Louisiana Infantry, at Camp Moore on July 7, 1861, but transferred to the Second Georgia Infantry on October 1, 1861 (*ibid.,* Pt. 1, p. 449).

29. Julius D. Stall, a Mount Lebanon shoemaker, enlisted in Company C, Ninth Louisiana Infantry, at Camp Moore on July 7, 1861. He was killed in a skirmish near Winchester, Virginia, on June 4, 1863 (*ibid.,* Pt. 2, p. 677).

30. The Minden company was Company G, Eighth Louisiana Infantry, commonly known as the "Minden Blues" of Claiborne Parish (Bergeron, *Guide,* 90).

complete being the ninth from Louisiana. Our officers were elected yesterday evening and I think we have as good ones as the world could afford us. Dick Taylor[31] a son of Old Zach Taylor[32] is our colonel, Capt. Randolph[33] who fought through the Mexican War is Lieutenant Col. and Capt. Walker[34] of the Brush Valley Guards[35] is our Major and our officers entertain no doubt but that Dr. Egan will be our Surgeon. The following are the names of the companies which compose the 9th regiment and also the Parishes from which they came[:] 1st Bossier Volunteers, 2nd Bienville Blues, 3rd Moore Fensibles from Claiborne, 4th Jackson Grays, 5th Milican's [Milliken] Bend Guard[s] from Madi-

31. Richard Taylor, the son of President Zachary Taylor, was one of the few non-West Pointers to achieve high command in the Confederate army. Beginning the war as commander of the Ninth Louisiana Infantry, Taylor gained promotion to brigadier general on October 21, 1861, distinguished himself in the Shenandoah Valley campaign of 1862, and rose to major general on July 28, 1862. Transferred to the District of West Louisiana, Taylor achieved his greatest victory in the repulse of N. P. Banks's Red River campaign in April, 1864 (T. Michael Parrish, *Richard Taylor: Soldier Prince of Dixie* [Chapel Hill, 1992]).

32. As a major general in the U.S. Army during the war with Mexico, Zachary Taylor won national prominence as the victor of the battles of Palo Alto, Resaca de la Palma, Monterrey, and Buena Vista. On the strength of his military reputation, he was elected president of the United States in 1848 (K. Jack Bauer, *Zachary Taylor: Soldier, Planter, Statesman of the Old Southwest* [1985; rpr. Baton Rouge, 1993]).

33. Edward G. Randolph was born in Fairfield District, South Carolina, in 1829, and moved to Bossier Parish, Louisiana, in 1852. Educated in medicine and the law, he nevertheless became a prominent planter. During the Mexican War, he served as sergeant in Winfield Scott's army. With Louisiana's secession, he organized and was elected captain of the "Bossier Volunteers" (Company D, Ninth Louisiana Infantry) and then was elected lieutenant colonel on July 7, 1861, when the regiment was organized at Camp Moore. According to Henry E. Handerson of the Ninth, Randolph was "an excellent disciplinarian and drill-master, and to him the regiment owed all its knowledge of tactics and the greater part of its efficiency." Randolph was promoted to colonel on October 21, 1861, replacing Richard Taylor, but was not reelected when the regiment was reorganized and so resigned from the service on April 15, 1862. He was replaced in command by Leroy A. Stafford (Booth, comp., *Records*, Vol. III, Pt. 2, p. 245; Bergeron, *Guide*, 92; *Biographical and Historical Memoirs of Northwest Louisiana* (Nashville, 1890), 520–21; Henry E. Handerson, *Yankee in Gray: The Civil War Memoirs of Henry E. Handerson with a Selection of His Wartime Letters* [Cleveland, 1962], 30).

34. Neil J. Walker, "a fat, good-natured, short-winded and red-faced officer" of limited tactical ability, was elected captain of Company H, Ninth Louisiana Infantry, when the company was formed and then elected major on July 7, 1861, when the regiment was organized at Camp Moore. He was promoted to lieutenant colonel in August, 1861. When the regiment was reorganized he was not reelected and so resigned from the service on April 24, 1862 (Booth, comp., *Records*, Vol. III, Pt. 2, p. 967; Bergeron, *Guide*, 92; Handerson, *Yankee in Gray*, 30).

35. "Brush Valley Guards" was the popular name for Company H, Ninth Louisiana Infantry, recruited in Bienville Parish. W. F. Gray, its first captain, was not reelected in April, 1862; Grove Cook, its second captain, was killed in action at Chancellorsville; Cornelius Shivley was the company's third and final commander (Bergeron, *Guide*, 93).

son, 6th Desoto Rifles, 7th Stafford Guard from Rapides & Avoyles, 8th Brush Valley Guard[s], 9th Washington Rifles, and 10th Colyel[l] Guard from Livingston.[36] Where the companies have the name of their Parish I omit the Parish and also the Brush Valley Guard[s] as you know where they are from. We have not a single French or Irish company in our whole regiment. They are all whole souled country boys and will do as hard fighting as any regiment that ever left La. or any other State. The officers have already telegraphed to Davis[37] and reported that regiment as being ready at a moment[']s warning to march to any part of the Confederate States and we expect to be ordered soon either to Va. or Mo. We do not think that we will stay here more than a week longer at most. We are all very anxious to get off into active service that our twelve months may be counting off. Look over mistakes and pardon all amiss as it is beginning to rain and I am in the woods under a large beech tree. I will send this by Mr. J. D. Houston[38] who starts for home to night.

Your brother,
R. A. Pierson

[Harris R. Johnson, another member of Pierson's company at Camp Moore, wrote to his friends in Mount Lebanon at about the same time, by way of the mercantile firm of Rogers and Gibbs. His July 5, 1861, letter conveyed much the same news and sentiments. His letter was published in the Louisiana Baptist, *July 25, 1861, as follows:]*

Gents:

Thinking that you would like to hear from your old friend, and being too unwell to do anything else, I have determined to write you a few lines. Since our arrival here we have been kept quite busy drilling and performing other duties pertaining to camp life. We have formed a Regiment of North Louisiana men, composed of the following companies: Bienville Blues, Brush Valley Guards, Jackson Greys, Bossier Volunteers, DeSoto Blues, Washington Rifles, Moore Fencibles, from Claiborne Parish; Stafford Guards from Rapides; Co[l]yell Guards, from Livingston; Miliken Bend Guards, from Madison Parish. The following officers have been elected: Mr. Taylor, (son of old Zack Taylor,) Col., E. J. Randolph of Bossier Lieut. Col., Walker of Brush Valley

36. See *ibid.,* 92–93.

37. Confederate president Jefferson Davis.

38. J. D. Houston, A Sparta farmer, was mustered into Company C at Camp Moore on July 7 for three years but was discharged in 1861, perhaps because he was forty years old and married (Booth, comp., *Records,* Vol. III, Pt. 1, pp. 362–63).

Guards, Maj.; the other officers will be elected in a few days. We have not yet been transferred to the service of the Confederate States, but will be today or tomorrow.

The Right wing of our Regiment will start for Virginia the first of next week, our company will leave with it, as it is the Right Centre Company, and will carry the Regimental colors. Our boys are in fine spirits and relish the prospect of soon meeting the enemy and giving him battle, and I think that Bienville will be proud of our company for our men are determined to conquer or die.

Since our arrival there has been some talk in the camp of peace propositions being offered in the Federal Congress. I have no idea that any will be made that the South could in honor agree to, consequently we will be compeled as much as we regret this unnatural war, to fight to the death or force them to give us our rights.

The 4th was celebrated in camps by a Regimental parade. Capt. B. W. Pearce delivered the oration, which was enthusiastically received by a large concourse of citizens and soldiers.

We have some cases of sickness in camp, principally measles and diarrhea.[39] I am, myself, so sick with the diarrhea that I can scarcely walk, but hope to be well in a few days; being too sick to write longer I must close this letter. Present me kindly to Mrs. R——, Mrs. G——, Mrs. H——, and other friends and request them to remember me in their prayers. I will write to you immediately on our arrival in Virginia. I should like to hear from you but do not know where to direct you to send your letters. If you would write immediately upon receipt of this, and direct your letter to Richmond, Va., care of Capt. B. W. Pierce [Pearce], I would probably get it.

May the God who rules the destinies of nations preserve and protect you.

Your friend,
H. R. Johnson[40]

39. The most prevalent illness in all Civil War armies was diarrhea. "No matter what else a patient had," a surgeon noted, "he had diarrhea." Much of the sickness was a direct result of poor army rations, inadequately drained camp sites, ignorance of sanitation practices, and the natural carelessness associated with army life. For chronic diarrhea, physicians prescribed heavy doses of lead acetate, opium, aromatic sulfuric acid, tincture of opium, silver nitrate, belladonna, and ipecac, not infrequently all at the same time (H. H. Cunningham, *Doctors in Gray: The Confederate Medical Service* [1958; rpr. Baton Rouge, 1993], 158; Stewart Brooks, *Civil War Medicine* [Springfield, Ill., 1966], 117).

40. Harris R. Johnson, a native of Georgia and a resident of Mount Lebanon, was elected corporal of his company but transferred to the Second Georgia Infantry on October 1, 1861 (Booth, comp., *Records*, Vol. III, Pt. 1, p. 449).

➤ ◄

Reuben Allen Pierson to James F. Pierson

Camp Moore, La.
July 6th, 1861

[James F. Pierson]
[Mt. Lebanon, La.]
Dear Bro.

I received yours bearing the date 3rd Inst. yesterday morning not being quite forty eight hours on the road. I am in most excellent health and have been ever since I recovered from the diarrhea which I have had as soon as I landed here. There is considerable complaint among the boys and some of them have been quite sick. John Martin[41] has been very low now for two days; but appears to be mending. At this time he is not able to sit up a single moment. Our regiment is complete and we have received orders to go to Richmond, Va. We are expecting the officer every hour to muster us into the Confederate States service. We will probably be sworn in this evening. We expect to leave here some time next week but cannot tell for certain at what precise hour. All of the companies are well pleased with the field officers. Two companies arrived here yesterday from Claiborne [Parish] and one from Jackson [Parish] but they were both too late to get in the 9th regiment. President Davis has telegraphed to Gov. Moore that he will receive two more regiments from La. and there is now a chance for all the boys who desire to fight for their country. I had no idea how fast one would learn the military terms and the manuell [*i.e.,* manual] of arms till I come to try it myself. Mr. Houston leaves for home to night at eleven oclock accompanied by Mr. Shepherd who will bear this to you. I would send it by Mr. Houston but he intends going up through Miss. to see his daughter and will probably be hindered a day or two. This will likely [be] the last letter which I shall write you from this place but I will write as soon as I arrive in Va. if not on the way. I have gained a great reputation with all the boys who have been placed under my charge as guards. They all say that when they are guards they want me for their sergeant. It is raining and has rained constant for the last few days. From all accounts the southern corn crop will be double that of any preceeding year. Letters from all parts of the state are received here daily and all give accounts of overwhelming corn crops. Excuse all amiss and pardon blunders for I am in great haste.

I remain your Brother,
R. A. Pierson

41. John Martin, a farmer from Ringgold, Louisiana, died at Camp Moore before the regiment left for Virginia (*Ibid.,* 894).

➤ ⬅

REUBEN ALLEN PIERSON TO WILLIAM H. PIERSON
Camp Moore, La.
July 9th, 1861

Dear Father

I seat myself to write to you. I have just come in from guard duty having set up nearly all night. We are making preparations as fast as possible to leave for Virginia. I cannot tell precisely what day we will leave but feel sure that we will leave by next Sunday. As I have already written who are our officers, I have but little interesting news to write you. We are drilling four or five hours per day and becoming accustomed to hardships of marching very fast. I am in excellent health and as hardy as a buck negro. Several of our boys are quite sick though none dangerous[ly] except John Martin. He is quite low and without great care will not probably recover, though he may not be as dangerous as I think. He will not be able to stand the trip. There are 2 or three others who will have to go home and recruit their health before they can proceed to Va. We have but little war news. I will try and procure a paper this morning and send you. John Brown[42] leaves at ten. It is now half past nine. You will excuse this hastily written letter owing to the emergency of the occasion. By the time I next write you I shall be on the road to Va.

I remain your Son,
R. A. Pierson

➤ ⬅

REUBEN ALLEN PIERSON TO WILLIAM H. PIERSON
Grand Junction, Tenn.
July 12th, 1861

Dear Father

In haste I proceed to write to you. I am now in Tennessee and shall leave here for Chattanooga at 2 Oclock this evening and proceed from there to Richmond, Va. We left Camp Moore yesterday morning at 9 oclock and landed here at 8 this morning. We will get to Richmond Sunday or Monday when I expect we will not be very long in getting into a battle. We left five men at Camp

42. John C. Brown, a Sabine Parish farmer, joined Company C on March 8, 1862, at Mount Lebanon. He died at Richmond's Howard's Grove Hospital on February 4, 1863 (*ibid.*, II, 151).

Moore in charge of Dr. Egan too sick to travel. None were dangerous except John Martin and I think he is past all hope. We were saluted at every house by the Ladies. Some shouted, some waved their handkerchiefs, some shook banners at us, and in many places they ran out to the road with fruit and bouquets and threw them in the cars at the soldiers. I am in excellent health and so are most of our company. What country we have passed up to this time looks quite poor. The truth is I have not seen but one or two well cultivated farms since I left Jackson. As I am in great haste you will please excuse this hastily written and disconnected letter. I will write again when I arrive at Va. When you write address me at Richmond, Va. care of B. W. Pearce, Commander, Bienville Blues, 9th Regiment La. Volunteers. Give my love and respect to all enquiring friends, receiving the same yourself.

I remain your son,

R. A. Pierson

➤ ⟵

REUBEN ALLEN PIERSON TO WILLIAM H. PIERSON

Richmond, Va.
July 19th, 1861

Dear Father

I have arrived at my point of destination within one mile of the city of Richmond and am in excellent health. The excitement here is beyond the powers of language to fully describe. We can hear a thousand different stories here in one short day. At one time we hear that Scott[43] is going to advance upon Richmond, next that we will be sent to Manassas under Beauregard,[44] so we do not know where we will go or what we will do. We have been here two days and the last wing of our regiment landed about an hour ago. Our trip was one of great

43. Winfield Scott, the victor of Vera Cruz, Cerro Gordo, Molino del Rey, Contreras, and Chapultepec and the conqueror of Mexico City during the Mexican War, was general-in-chief of the U.S. Army from 1846 until 1862 and the principal strategic planner for the Union war effort during the first year of the Civil War. See *Memoirs of Lieut.-General Winfield Scott, LL.D.* (New York, 1864), and Charles Wilson Elliot, *Winfield Scott: The Soldier and the Man* (New York, 1937).

44. Pierre Gustave Toutant Beauregard, a Louisiana Creole, commanded Confederate troops at Fort Sumter and at the first battle of Manassas and was second in command under Albert Sidney Johnston at Shiloh. He temporarily commanded the Army of Tennessee and then was placed in charge of the defense of Charleston. In April, 1864, he returned to Virginia to assist in the defense of Petersburg. See Alfred Roman, *The Military Operations of General Beauregard in the War Between the States* (2 vols., 1884; rpr. New York, 1994); T. Harry Williams, *P. G. T. Beauregard: Napoleon in Gray* (Baton Rouge, 1955).

excitement from the very hour we left Camp Moore till we arrived here. We were applauded and cheered by Ladies at every station and from the windows and galleries of every house we passed. I have never seen such demonstrations of true love for southern rights nor ladies so zealous in any political affair as I witnessed on the road from Camp Moore to Richmond. If I were at home I would delight in relating many incidents which have occurred and many phenomena which I have witnessed since I left home. As for war news there is so much afloat and so little reliance to be placed in it that I have no idea what are the true positions of the two contending armies. Our fare is equally as good if not better than it was at Camp Moore. There are now about five thousand soldiers camped in this and the adjoining camps near Richmond and they are leaving here by regiments and filing in nearly every day. I saw Hon. Jefferson Davis yesterday evening. He rode all around the camp on horseback and often raised his hat to the soldiers as they applauded him with their shouts which resounded from one wall to the other of the encampment with such vehemence that the whole earth seemed to tremble at the sound. Our officers have all been a little sick since we have been here though they are all on the mend. Capt. Pearce is staying out in the city as he is a little unwell but I think he prefers conversing with Congressmen rather than endure the toil of drilling soldiers. There is considerable complaint with some of the boys against him. I rec[k]on that it will surprise you when I tell you that corn is just beginning to silk tassle here at this late date and in many parts of Tenn. they are busily engaged in ploughing their corn and harvesting their grain. Excuse mistakes and pardon all amiss while I remain your Son

R. A. Pierson

⇒ ⇐

REUBEN ALLEN PIERSON TO WILLIAM H. PIERSON
Manassas Junction, Va.
July 24th, 1861

Dear Father

I have arrived at length at the head quarters of Beauregard and Jeff Davis and have seen the latter. Some of the boys have had the pleasure of seeing both but I did not see Beauregard. We arrived here only about thirty-six hours after the great battle of which you have heard a thousand different stories ere this time.[45] I have taken great pains to enquire about it since I arrived here and scarcely find two men who agree or anything near agree with regard to the particulars. However one thing is sure. The Yankees got a most glorious whipping and thousands of them are yet left dying unburied on the field. I have been told by those that walked over the field a short time after the engagement that it was the greatest scene of destruction of human life ever known upon the American Continent. I have conversed with many of the soldiers who participated in the action and they all say that the bullets whistled like hailstone through the air but generally too high to do much damage. The Confederate boys lay upon their backs to load and fired from their knees as I have been told. I have seen many of the wounded and must confess that I had never formed any idea of the horrors attending a large battle. The Confederates took fifty two field pieces and among them was the great Rifled cannon upon which the north so much doted; it will throw a cannon ball a great distance. They also took about 13,000 stand of the best and latest improved small arms. The yankees retreated in confusion and were pursued by the cavalry of the south who destroyed many of them and took a great amount of plunder from them. All who have seen the field say that the yankees were much better equipped with knap sacks and other war implements than we are. We have a great deal of sickness in the regiment but it is mostly measels. Lieut. Ardis[46] is just taking them. Four of my mess mates are left behind viz[.] Fil [Phil] Collins, Tom Sanders, Tom Cawthon & Horace Rhodes, the first two with measels and the others with diarrhea. Three of them are left in Richmond and Cawthon is left at Gordonsville between this and Richmond. Collins was very sick but was mending when I left. I saw him comfortably situated in the St. Francis hospital[47] which is furnished with a large number of Lady nurses who call themselves the Sisters of Charity. We have now been here about 30 hours and will be in hourly expectation of orders to move on to Washington City as Beauregard is hastening the troops from here in that direction. It is believed that he will attack that place in a few days. I am well

45. The first battle of Manassas or Bull Run, fought on July 21, 1861, between the forces of Federal brigadier general Irvin McDowell and Confederate brigadier generals P. G. T. Beauregard and Joseph E. Johnston, resulted in a signal if strategically indecisive Rebel victory (William C. Davis, *Battle at Bull Run: A History of the First Major Campaign of the Civil War* [Garden City, N.Y., 1977], 112–31).

46. Casper N. Ardis, a Mount Lebanon farmer, was elected second lieutenant of Company C, Ninth Louisiana Infantry, when the regiment was organized at Camp Moore on July 7, 1861. In October, 1861, however, he resigned owing to ill health. He rejoined the company as a private on March 8, 1862, and served until the surrender at Appomattox (Booth, comp., *Records*, I, 73; *Biographical and Historical Memoirs of Northwest Louisiana*, 48–49).

47. Richmond's St. Francis De Sales Hospital was fortunate in having the skilled services of Catholic sisters and was one of the few hospitals in the Confederacy blessed with professionally trained nurses (Cunningham, *Doctors in Gray*, 73).

pleased with camp life. It is the very thing that suits me as you know that I have ever been fond of a roving and hardy life. All of the regiments from La. that took part in the battle fought bravely and won many laurels for themselves and for their native state. The Tiger Rifles[48] of which you heard so much talk when Paxton's[49] company returned from Camp Moore was in the battle and charged upon the New York Zouaves,[50] who had sent them word that they desired to shake hands with them on the battle field. The Tigers having no bayonets but being armed with large buoyie knives, rushed heedlessly upon the bayonets of the Zouaves and routed them with buoyie knives. They have the reputation here of being the worst daredevils on earth. There were many yankee pris[o]ners taken and some of them are still here. Others have been sent southward. They say they did not expect much fighting from the Southerners but thought they would soon whip out the whole country as they were told that the union men were nearly equal to the secessionists and would immediately take up arms to assist them. They all say that they have been duped and will not fight against us any longer. Excuse haste and mistakes. I send this by Jasper Nix[51] who returns tomorrow. Write soon and direct to 9th Regiment, La. Volunteers Va., care of B. W. Pearce, Capt. Bienville Blues. I remain your son

R. A. Pierson

48. This was Maj. Chatham R. Wheat's First Special Battalion, popularly known as the "Louisiana Tigers." The first Louisiana troops to see battle, at First Manassas, the battalion played a decisive role in holding the Union attack on the Confederate left until reinforcements arrived. The unit served well under Brig. Gen. Richard Taylor in Stonewall Jackson's Valley campaign and during the Seven Days' Battles. After the death of Major Wheat at the battle of Gaines' Mill, however, the colorful but often uncontrollable Tigers were disbanded and scattered among other units of the Louisiana Brigade. See Charles L. Dufour, *Gentle Tiger: The Gallant Life of Roberdeau Wheat* (Baton Rouge, 1957); Terry L. Jones, *Lee's Tigers: The Louisiana Infantry in the Army of Northern Virginia* (Baton Rouge, 1987).

49. John H. Paxton of St. Joseph enlisted in Company D, Sixth Louisiana Infantry, at Camp Moore on June 4, 1861. He was killed in action in Virginia on April 24, 1863 (Booth, comp., *Records,* Vol. III, Pt. 2, p. 87).

50. Organized and trained by Ephraim Elmer Ellsworth, the regiment known as "Ellsworth's Zouaves" also called the "First New York Fire Zouaves," and officially designated the Eleventh New York Infantry, was among the most colorful of Union military units. Even after discarding its flashy blue and scarlet uniforms, the regiment maintained its place in the public's attention with its rowdy behavior.

51. Jasper Nix, a member of Reuben Allen Pierson's company, was discharged in 1861 (*ibid.,* Pt. 1, p. 1286).

⇒ ⇐

REUBEN ALLEN PIERSON TO MARY CATHERINE PIERSON
Camp Bienville,[52] *Va.*
Aug. 5th, 1861

Miss M. C. Pierson

I again sit myself down to write you a short epistle. I have been in bad health for the past week but feel like I should soon be as well as ever; (that is in a few days) if I have no backset. This is the second day that I have missed my chill and feel much improved in strength; in every respect I am on the mend. We are now encamped on the precise ground which the enemy occupied previous to the great battle. We can see where they had their batteries planted and also where they formed a sort of breastwork by felling all the trees which stood near the edge of an old field. We are not encamped on the ground where the great battle was fought nor is any of our men on account of the miserable odor arising from the decaying of horses and other dead boddies. We have quite a pleasant place now and plenty of water (at about a half mile distant) as good as anyone could want. The health of the boys is improving and I think they will all be up in a few days, if they have proper attention paid them. We cannot form the slightest idea what move we will next make. There is as many different opinions on the subject as there are shades of color and more than nine tenths of them are wrong. Not even our colonel knows one iota about it. We are now in sight of the sixth and seventh La. regiments and the 8th will be on in a few days forming a La. briggade and it is rumored that Col. Taylor will be appointed briggadier general. Our boys are all willing that he should be promoted as he will not suffer them to have a single drop of whiskey, though he has been counseled to do so by Dr. Stone of New Orleans who thinks the introduction of it would be very advantagious to the health of the regiment. It is very difficult for us to procure shoes and we have to pay nearly three prices for them when we get them. For such shoes as Ben Stall makes we have to pay from six to eight dollars a pair. My shoes that I started with is still serving me, but they are beginning to give way and I know not where I will get the next. Tell Father to send me a pair of good strong water proof boots of Stall's make if he has an opportunity before winter. And you must knit and send me 2 good strong pair of wool socks and one or 2 pair of homespun jeans pants. I see in

52. After being encamped at Manassas Junction from July 22 through August, the Ninth Louisiana was, in the words of one of its soldiers, "more than decimated" by typhoid fever and dysentery. On the first of September, therefore, the Louisiana Brigade, under the command of Brigadier General W. H. T. Walker, was removed to a healthier location at Camp Bienville, near Centerville, Virginia, where it enjoyed better water and improved health (Handerson, *Yankee in Gray,* 33).

the banner[53] that the ladies are forming us societies to make and send us clothing for winter and Mr. Thurmond[54] I understand agrees to bring them to us. Nothing could afford more pleasure to the care worn volunteers of Bienville than to see these things coming about the last of September as we will have frost by that time and nothing would add more glory to a young ladies name and character than to be first and foremost in carrying this project into effect. We find many true patriots among the fair daughters of Virginia and long will the kind deeds of those lovely girls who nursed our sick boys, who were left on the road as we came on, be remembered with affectionate feelings of the tenderest kind. Phil Collins is still at Richmond but was able to walk around town a few days ago when I last heard from him. He told a young man that he was treated as well as he could have desired. I am looking for him on every day, but he will be apt to stay till he regains his strength which will take several weeks. Our officers are nearly all sick. Our Capt. has not drilled us three times since we left home and is now confined in his bed. Our 1st Lieut. [James C. Egan] has been appointed Surgeon and we have not elected any one to fill his place. Our 2nd Lieut. has not been able to drill us since we left Camp Moore and is now just getting up from the measels. We left him in the country about one mile from Manassas with one of our men to wait on him. He will not be able to take charge of the company in less time than one month. John Theus our 3rd Lieut. is the only officer we have fit to drill a company and he is complaining and not able to be out this morning so we are almost destitute of a leader. I have met with several of my old school mates since I arrived in Va. viz[.] Nat Allen, Meadors[55] and Professor Hambleton. I have also heard from Cooksie[56]

---

53. The *Southern Banner* was edited and published at Sparta by William Edwards Paxton from 1860 through 1861.

54. Catlet G. Thurmond was a Mount Lebanon postmaster, councilman, and merchant—the owner and proprietor of G. C. Thurmond and Company. On July 25, 1861, he wrote to the *Louisiana Baptist,* advising that "the ladies organize and form themselves into sewing societies" in order to make "drawers, shirts, socks, vests, pants, coats and blankets, line them well, pay particular attention to the stability of the material and the substantial manner in which they are made." Thurmond concluded by stating that he would "take pleasure in carrying them my self. . . . Let Claiborne and Bienville forget not their valiant sons, let *none* be forgotten."

55. This is perhaps J. C. Meadors, a private in Company I, Second Louisiana Infantry. Meadors enlisted at Camp Moore on August 6, 1861, was wounded and taken prisoner, but was exchanged and surrendered with his company at Appomattox (Booth, comp., *Records,* Vol. III, Pt. 1, pp. 932–33).

56. W. C. (Willie) Cooksey (also "C. W. C. Cooksey") was a private in Company I, Second Louisiana Infantry. This Claiborne Parish resident was once wounded but served until the end of the war (*ibid.,* II, 429).

and Mathews[57] who are both under Gen. McGruder.[58] Willie Workman[59] is also here and all who have been here long enough to become climatized are in very good health. My money holds out very well and will continue to do so for I have no chance to spend it as we are not allowed to leave the camp a mile under any circumstance, neither officers nor privates, and there is nothing for sale in that distance of the camp except a little corn meal, for which we can exchange flour, and we have an abundant supply of that and pork and bacon on hand at this time, for half of our mess is too puny to eat any meat except a little broiled on the coals.

I am writing about two hundred yards from the camp in a cool shady grove. The growth is mostly hickory but there are other kinds of timber and a variety of it around here, some fine poplar groves in the lowlands and plenty of shrubberry in many places. Viewing our location in all its bearings it is a very desirable and most exquisitively beautiful place for one to live, but as there are no happiness[es] attached to the life of a soldier even the place looks disgustful in the eyes of those who are disposed to find fault, and are nearly dead with the perplexing disease known as homesick[ness].

We[ll] Sister, Wesley Grice[60] is here in the Brush Valley Guards and enquires every day or so if I hear from home and how the health of the family is &c and yesterday he requested me to give his love and respects to you, all which I now do. He looks better than I ever saw him and is entirely well of the cough which troubled him in the winter, and without some accident he will return home a stout hearty man. I learned yesterday from Frank Long that Eloy Waters was married to a young man by the name of Strickland. Much happiness to them through life is my sincere wish. Write me all the news. Give my love to all young Ladies who enquire about my welfare and safety. Give my respects to all young men who mention my name in your presence. My warmest feelings of

57. Perry Mathews is perhaps the P. C. Matthews of Company C, Second Louisiana Infantry, who transferred to the Ninth Arkansas Infantry on February 2, 1862 (*ibid.*, 916).

58. John Bankhead Magruder was commissioned as brigadier general in the Confederate service and was quickly promoted to major general. Commanding the Rebel forces at Yorktown, Virginia, Magruder deceived George B. McClellan as to his strength and caused the Union commander weeks of needless delay. Lack of aggressiveness during the Seven Days' Battles cost him the favor of General Lee, however, and he was soon reassigned to the command of the District of Texas, New Mexico, and Arizona. His greatest success there was his recapture of Galveston on January 1, 1863. Paul D. Casdorph, *Prince John Magruder: His Life and Campaigns* (New York, 1996).

59. William Workman, a resident of Cheneyville, was a private in Company H, Eighth Louisiana Infantry. Despite Pierson's news of good health, Workman died of disease at Culpeper Courthouse on November 1, 1861 (*ibid.*, Vol. III, Pt. 2, p. 1163). Paul D. Casdorph, *Prince John Magruder: His Life and Campaigns* (New York, 1996).

60. Wesley Grice of Brush Valley was a private in Company H, Ninth Louisiana Infantry. He died at Camp Bienville on September 4, 1861 (*ibid.*, Pt. 1, p. 103).

friendship to all the family and relatives. Receive the wish of a brother, that you may be attended with success through life and after death take up your abode with the blest of heaven is my closing sentiment. Tell Jonathan[61] howdy. He must be a good boy and take care of mine and his hogs till I return. Excuse all amiss, look over foolishness &c. I remain your brother till death

R. A. Pierson

N.B. Direct your letter to Manassas Junction, Va., as that is the nearest office. We are encamped in 4 miles of the Junction and have a postmaster who goes every day for the letters.

> €

REUBEN ALLEN PIERSON TO JAMES F. PIERSON
Camp Bienville, Virginia
August 15th, 1861

Dear Jimmy

I hasten to reply to your neat and well dictated but not altogether satisfactory letter bearing date 21st Ult. sent by Mr. Robert Burnett.[62] I am just getting hearty after having a few chills which rendered me unfit for duty[;] with that exception I have had the best of health ever since I left home. Phillip Collins came up a few days ago and has gotten over the measels. It made him a little deaf in one ear and that is all the damage done to him. Most of our boys are on the mend now, but we have had more hard sickness in our regiment than I ever saw. 2 or 3 companies have lost as many as ten men by death. Our Co. has not been quite so unfortunate. We have lost only three including John Martin but still the boys have suffered almost incredibly from disease. We have had as many as 50 cases either on the sick roll or left behind on the road for more than a week in succession and so you will not be surprised when I tell you that we have only 16 or 18 men to drill after deducting those for guard service. Jimmy you speak of going to war next spring as though you were a stout hearty robust man and [I] dislike very much to say anything discouraging to you but as an honest brother, as a true friend I must say to you, if you are tired of life, if you prefer death, ah the most horrible of deaths—if this be your fancy, then I (though it be with reluctancy) say go on and join the army. But my dearest brother not that I would overrate your timidity

61. Jonathan Pierson, the seventh child of William H. and Mary Collins Pierson, was born on October 21, 1842. He was mentally retarded and lived with his family until his death in Natchitoches on October 24, 1890.

62. Robert H. Burnett, one of Pierson's uncles, was a Claiborne Parish planter. He was born in South Carolina, married a woman named Martha, and was the father of five children.

though speaking candidly I do not believe that you would any more stand the hardships of a campaign than fire would burn under water. To give you some idea let me enumerate the duties which we have to perform daily, and a few of the hardships which we have to undergo. Tattoo beats at ½ past 4 in the morning when every fellow must be in lines in the short space of 5 minutes to answer his name, then be trotted through the wet dewy grass for one hour. At 8 A.M. the drum again taps when all must be in their places instanter and drill two hours. At 4 P.M. the drum beats for battalion drill which lasts 1½ hours. Then you are given about 5 minutes to prepare for dress parade which keeps you standing in one position about half an hour. At 9 P.M. the drum taps for roll call again when every fellow is compelled to be awake and at his post or be put on extra duty. Besides this you are put on guard once at least every 2 weeks and have to be up all night and day and out in the weather rain or shine. You have your own cooking to do, your gun to keep as bright as silver and your quarters swept out perfectly clean. You have to sleep on the ground or some leaves or grass which you may pick up, and lastly if sick you have nothing except fat meat and bakers bread to eat unless you should meet with a very kind mess mate to care for you which is hard to find. Such is a true soldier[']s life—pause and think before you go farther. Frank Long died this week—A brother of Felix Bledsoe[']s [63] & Ben Howard's [64] half brother to Murry.[65] I heard from Perry Mathews day before yesterday. He has been given out by all the doctors. I expect he is dead. He was down at Yorktown in McGruders [Magruder's] division. If you hear from Dave write to me how he is getting along &c. Give my love and respects to all enquiring about me. My best wishes and regards to the family & tell Jonathan I will bring him a yankee trick when I return. Write soon to your brother

R. A. Pierson

P.S. Direct to Manassas Junction, Va.
N.B. I hear cannons firing in the direction of Alexandria, supposed to be a battle up there yesterday and today. No news has reached us except that 1500 Federalists had been taken pris[o]ners near the wire bridge on the Potomac river—by no means reliable.

63. Felix A. Bledsoe, a Fillemon farmer, was a private in Company D, Ninth Louisiana Infantry. He was wounded and captured at Rappahannock Station on November 7, 1863, and held at Point Lookout, Maryland, until exchanged on March 9, 1864 (*ibid.,* II, 10).

64. Benjamin E. Howard of Brush Valley was a sergeant in Company H, Ninth Louisiana Infantry. He died at Camp Bienville on August 12, 1861 (*ibid.,* Vol. III, Pt. 1, p. 364).

65. Murry B. Howard of Brush Valley was a private in Company H, Ninth Louisiana Infantry. He was killed at the battle of Sharpsburg on September 17, 1862 (*ibid.,* 365).

⇒ ⇐

DAVID PIERSON TO WILLIAM H. PIERSON

Camp Wilson Spring, August 15th 1861

Wm H. Pierson

Dear Father

Almost immediately after I wrote you from Camp Stephens,[66] Ark., we received orders to march into Mo. and since that time I have had no opportunity to write. We moved into Mo. until within about 17 miles of Springfield where our advance guard met that of the enemy. Then the main army halted and commenced arrangements for a battle. The enemy had pushed out about 5,000 men to engage us under Gen. Sigel,[67] but learning our true force, retired before us as we advanced into Springfield. So we moved up 7 miles out of the town without any general engagement. Had several skirmishes in which both sides claimed victory. We were stopping a day or two this near the place, I suppose to arrange a plan of attack, and had received orders to march at 9 Oclock of the night of the 9th. Had drawn in our pickets & would have started but for some rain & heavy clouds making the night too dark to march when the enemy saved us the trouble of marching by surprising and attacking us on four sides just at sunrise on the morning of the 10th. Gen. Lyons[68] had moved his entire command at sundown from Springfield and so well were his plans executed that the first we knew of their approach was the roar of their artillery from the hills which surrounded our camps. They had even contrived to plant one of their best

66. Camp Stephens, named in honor of Confederate vice-president Alexander Stephens, was located on the banks of Sugar Creek in northwest Arkansas (Willie H. Tunnard, *A Southern Record: The Story of the Third Regiment Louisiana Infantry* [1866; rpr. Dayton, Ohio, 1970], 42–43).

67. Franz Sigel, a native of Baden, Germany, became minister of war during the unsuccessful revolt against Prussian authority in 1848. Forced to flee the Continent, Sigel settled in St. Louis, where his liberal political philosophy and his great popularity with the Germans in Missouri drew the attention of Abraham Lincoln and won him a commission as a brigadier general. After service in the Trans-Mississippi, he was transferred to Virginia, where he was embarrassed in the Shenandoah Valley by Stonewall Jackson and, while commander of the Department of West Virginia, was routed by Maj. Gen. John C. Breckinridge at New Market on May 15, 1864.

68. Nathaniel Lyon, appointed commander of the St. Louis arsenal in February, 1861, used his position to ensure that Missouri remained in the Union by breaking up the pro-Confederate militia at Camp Jackson and forcing secessionist governor Claiborne F. Jackson from the capital. Promoted from captain to brigadier general on May 17, 1861, he was given command of the Federal forces in Missouri. He was defeated at the battle of Wilson's Creek or Oak Hills, where he was killed while personally leading an attack (Christopher Phillips, *Damned Yankee: The Life of Nathaniel Lyon* [Columbia, 1990]).

batteries[69] in our rear. Under all these disadvantages we commenced fighting and after a desperate struggle of five hours drove the enemy from the field, killing a thousand, taking many prisoners and six choice pieces of artillery. I can't give you a detail of the battle nor a precise description of the ground. It was a promiscuous fighting, up and down the creek & over hills for a distance of two miles. The first engagement of infantry was with our Reg[t] and about 2,000 of the enemy headed by Gen. Lyons in person. We had marched up a narrow hollow about a mile and a half when we discovered them posted behind a fence to our left. They commenced firing upon us when we were in columns, and but two of our Companies could return the fire. We quickly fell into line and fired and immediately charged, shouting to the top of our voices. Over the fence we went and drove the enemy from his position. We had gotten to within 20 yards of them by the time they commenced retreating, and you may know, poured death among them as they ran off. Whilst we were in the bushes forming our line, they sent their bullets among us thick as hail and would have killed half of our Reg[t] but we lay on our faces close to the ground and the balls passed just over us. Already every bush & tree was riddled above our heads. The first fire of the enemy brought down three of my Company in a few feet of where I was standing, one shot through the heart, the other two seriously wounded. Scarcely had we whipped the enemy at this point when orders came for the La. Reg[t] to go to the rear & take a battery of the enemy. We started off in quick time and in the face of shot & shell marched up to the mouths of the six cannon & drove the enemy from them & they are ours still. Gen. McCulloch was with us when we did this and declared the day was ours. The truth is, our Reg[t] was in the thickest of the fight the entire day, and it is conceded on all sides did the best fighting of any troops on the ground—in fact, saved the day on two occasions. The enemy was so completely routed that they never pretended to stop in Springfield where they were fortified, and our flag floats triumphantly over the place. Our Cavalry pursued them on the retreat and cut them to pieces—took prisoners, arms, ammunition, and wagons and trains.

Our loss in killed was about 400 with about 800 wounded. I have not seen Gen. McCulloch's report and can't give you the particulars. I would have writ-

69. The battle of Oak Hills, fought on August 10, 1861, between the forces of Union brigadier general Nathaniel Lyon and the Confederate forces of Ben McCulloch and the Missouri State Guard of Maj. Gen. Sterling Price, ended in a southern victory and the death of Lyon. The Third Louisiana routed a battalion of U.S. regular infantry and, under McCulloch's personal direction, carried a Federal battery with the bayonet. When Price later appropriated the battery as well as the credit for its capture to his own army, McCulloch became furious; this was a major cause for the deep rift between the two Rebel generals.

ten you earlier but have been sick ever since the day of the battle and am now so nervous & feeble that I hardly can write. I escaped without a hurt. Out of my company 1 killed, 1 supposed to be mortally wounded but yet alive, & two slightly wounded.

My Company fought bravely to the last and kept together & in line better than any other Company in the regt. The battle field as we passed over it was a horrible sight indeed. The ground was literally strewn with the wounded, dead, and dying: some with their heads shot off, some with bodies torn into with cannon balls, some with their legs shot off, and, in fact, wounds of every description could be seen. The groans of the wounded and cries for water from every side and all around was enough to sicken even the heartiest soldier. I was too much exhausted after the battle to walk over the battle field, but I saw enough in passing from one point to another whilst the battle lasted. After the fight was over the enemy sent in a white flag to bury their dead & take up their wounded which was allowed them, of course, but they did not half finish. We have buried a great many since for them, and the whole battle field stinks with their dead bodies yet. One thing I had forgotten to mention, viz., Gen. Lyons, the ablest & best officer the enemy had, was killed in the engagement whilst leading his men in the hottest of the fight. They sent in & got his body but did not bury it and it was buried by the Secessionists of Springfield. You will see full particulars of the battle in the papers before this will reach you and more correct than I can possibly give you, as I can only tell you what our Regt. did. And as soon as I get well and get a place to write, I will write you again. Excuse this badly written & put up letter.

Yours Truly,
D. Pierson

2

SCENES OF A SOLDIER'S LIFE

REUBEN ALLEN PIERSON TO WILLIAM H. PIERSON
Camp Bienville, Va.
August 17th, 1861

Dear Father

I again take up the pen to trouble you all. I sometimes think that I write too often, but when I remember how glad I am to hear from home I think that my writing so often will only be a source of gratification to you all. I am again in good health and intend in the future to take better care of myself than I have done before. I have already written to you to order me a pair of strong water proof boots and several other articles of dress. I want a good double breasted homespun jeans vest. It will be of more service to me than any other garment in this cold climate where the mornings look very much like it would frost in August. Be sure to have my boots made full large so that I can put them on either in wet or dry weather and also to wear course [*sic*] woolen socks with them. If you can procure them send me a large heavy pair of buckskin gloves. Send me two pair of coarse cotton drawers, a pair of Gumelastic leggin[g]s, if you can get them conveniently. I have a good waterproof coat which I bought at Grand Junction, Tenn.

I do not know how we will manage about moving with all our clothes in winter; we have been supplied with baggage waggons to move from Manassas up here, which is four miles. We did not even have to carry our knapsacks upon our backs. Our Colonel seems to have a great deal of sympathy for his men and will not suffer them imposed on in the least degree. True he is quite rigid in his discipline as all military commanders should be, but he is a gentleman in every sense according to my judgment. Our Captain is becoming very unpopular with the boys on account of his indolence and extreme[ly] timid health. He never has attempted to drill the company but once since we left home except once, and then only exposed his extreme ignorance about all military matters. He has been in bed the greater part of his time since we left Camp Moore. He sometimes comes out and talks to the company in a brief speech which would better become a congressman than the commander of a company. Much is said about him now, but little in his favor, and if we were forced into battle when his health was good it is my opinion that he would disgrace himself for life. This I write in confidence. Time will reveal the effects, which will follow. The health of our company is improving slowly; but still I never saw as many puny looking men in a band in all my life. We have 5 or 6 men now in camp who are very sick viz[.]: Lieut. [John] Theus, Charles Prothro,[1] Ed Stephens,[2] Robert Cason[3] & Mark Rogers.[4] The latter is from a cut with an adds [adz] while helping to repair the bridges burned down as our men retreated from toward Washington when they evacuated Alexandria some months ago. His leg is in a very bad condition having been cut on the knee joint and the swelling has almost gone up into the body which gives him great pain. Phil is in good health, and has entirely recovered from the effects of the measels. He learned while staying at Richmond that Ben Gardner[5] was there, and captain of a company. The man told him that Gardner made a speech in town the night before he left but as he was ready to start on for the company he had no time to go and see old Ben. He also heard that Tom Simpson, Jr., was in a company near Richmond. He did not see either of them but feels sure that it is true from what he was told.

There has been a report circulated extensively that a great many pris[o]ners had been taken by the Confederate forces up on the Potomac River a few days ago. We have not heard any thing certain up to this time. We heard the firing of cannon on the mornings of the 14 & 15 Inst. in a northern direction and sup-

1. Charles E. Prothro of Bienville Parish was a private in Company C, Ninth Louisiana Infantry. He was captured at Petersburg on March 25, 1864, and held at Point Lookout until the end of the war (Andrew B[radford] Booth, comp., *Records of Louisiana Confederate Soldiers and Louisiana Confederate Commands* [3 vols.; New Orleans, 1920], Vol. III, Pt. 2, p. 209).

2. Edward L. Stephens of Minden, Louisiana, was elected sergeant of Company C, Ninth Louisiana Infantry, when the regiment was organized at Camp Moore. He was reduced to the ranks, however, on August 1, 1863, and was mortally wounded on May 5, 1864, at the battle of the Wilderness (*ibid.*, 693).

3. Robert C. Cason of Buck Horn, Louisiana, was discharged from Company C on October 29, 1861 (*ibid.*, II, 285).

4. Mark D. Rogers a Mount Lebanon carpenter, died at Bristol, Virginia, sometime in 1862 (*ibid.*, Vol. III, Pt. 2, p. 375).

5. Ben Gardner of Company B, Fifteenth Louisiana Infantry, was captured at the battle of Williamsburg (*ibid.*, II, 970).

posed it to be fighting. Tell sister & Aunt to be careful and mark every thing they send me as disputes often arise about private marks on clothes, guns and everything else. Marke everything plain[ly] that you send me and I will be sure to get them. Excuse all amiss & write soon & often. I remain your affectionate Son till death

R. A. Pierson

P.S. I do not pay the postage on the letters I send, because it is believed that the Post Master at Manassas burns or destroys the letters and pockets the cash. So they go much safer and better without paying postage in advance. I have plenty of money to pay it but choose not to do so for the reason assigned above.

⇒ ⇐

REUBEN ALLEN PIERSON TO JAMES F. PIERSON
Camp Bienville, Va.
Aug. 22nd, 1861

Mr. James F. Pierson
Dear Bro.

I received yours bearing date 1st Inst. and was very glad to hear from home once more. You complain about my not writing oftener. I have written home more than once a week on an average since I left. I sent 2 letters home by Nix which has reached you long ere this time. I am not in good health but able to be on foot. I had a light fever yesterday but feel much better today. Our regiment still remains very sickly. We have about ten men in camps who are not able to leave their beds, besides several who are left behind or sent out in the country. Both of our Lieuts. are confined to their beds and are really very low. Ardis has not been able to drill us any since we left Camp Moore and is not able to sit up now. Theus has gone to a private house where Ardis has been staying ever [since] we got to Manassas. Theus looks very much like he had typhoid fever. It operates very slowly though he was a little better whe[n] he left than he had been for several days previous.

We hear news of a great battle fought near Springfield Mo. in which our men under old Ben McCulloch won a great and glorious victory and took a great quantity of spoils from them, killing some 800 and taking several hundred pris[o]ners. I see Dave's name is not in the list of killed and wounded officers which we received in yesterday's paper. We also heard it rumored that England has acknowledged the independence of the Southern Confederacy and will in a few days clear away the great blockade. Many of our best officers say they expect to dine at home by Christmas and be in a separate government from the federal

Union of which the Lincolnites have said so much and lauded with praises to the skies ever since they elected the Old Rail Splitter to the Presidential seat. If peace is made you may expect us home in a few days for you never saw such men want to see home as bad[ly] as some of our boys do. We do not expect to have any chance at the yankees now for two thirds of our regiment are unable to drill on account of sickness. The Bossier Company have already lost 13 or 14 of their company by death. The Brush Valley Guards have buried 11 [of] their comrades. It is enough to sicken the heart of one whose feelings are not as impenetrable as the adamantive rock to see and hear the agonies of those who are suffering the most intense pain from sickness, and lying on the damp ground without the slightest chance of giving them any aid for want of the materials to accomplish that end. We cannot procure the articles of food necessary for their nourishment on[e] half of the time and when we do we have to pay 3 prices, 3 bits a dozen for eggs, 40 cents a pound for butter and 35 cents a piece for chickens not larger than partridges. Many of the boys are out of money and have to do entirely without them.

Such are the miseries of camp life and many are the deaths which are recorded on that account. This may seem like a gloomy description of the horrors but language will not convey the true impression to the mind. Nothing but the experiencing of the sad and awful scenes could imprint vividly the impression of a soldier[']s hardships.

Excuse all amiss and pardon haste and write soon giving me all the dots. Little frivolous things are very entertaining to us who are far from home. My love to all enquiring friends, especially to the fair sex and my best regards to all the family. Howdy to all from Your Brother

R. A. Pierson

➣ ≪

REUBEN ALLEN PIERSON TO WILLIAM H. PIERSON
Camp Bienville [Va.]
Aug. 25th, 1861

My dear Father

I now have an opportunity of writing to you and of sending my letter by Mr. Boyd,[6] who leaves this place tomorrow for Louisiana. Send me by Mr.

6. David French Boyd was professor of ancient languages and English literature at the Louisiana State Seminary of Learning and Military Academy in 1861 when he enlisted in the Ninth Louisiana, rising to major in May, 1862. He was transferred to Louisiana in 1863, where he was reunited with Richard Taylor as chief of engineers on Taylor's staff. After the war, he returned to the state seminary as its superintendent and later as its president. See Germaine M. Reed, *David French Boyd: Founder of Louisiana*

C. G. Thurmond four boxes [of] Moffats pills, and one bottle of Phoenix Bitters.[7]

Our camps at this time are in a very bad condition, out of nine hundred men in the regiment only about 250 fit for duty. Several diseases are scattered among the different companies. Deaths are of frequent occurrence. So often indeed do they occur that they are hardly noticed by a passing remark. We have lost only four, Jasper Gough[8] died with typhoid fever night before last. There is only one case now in the company that is dangerous, a young man by the name of Wallace[9] but now he is considered to be mending. Price[10] & Wallace both have typhoid fever. Price is a good deal better. Some of the companies (Bossier and Brush Valley) have lost as many a piece as twelve men. In all the regiment has lost I suppose fifty men, but now all the companies are improving, turning out more men on dress parade now than for weeks and ere long I hope that I may write to you that disease will have entirely left our midst. As to myself, I have had fever for four days but succeeded in breaking it with quinine today. I feel considerably weakened by it but hope soon to resume various duties of camp life again.

Military affairs are at a standstill now, or rather if any important movements are taking place we are ignorant of them. It is said that the Washington Artillery[11] have moved on. I expect a big battle will take place before long. In fact I think now it is a calm before the storm. It looks like old Abe's want of common sense will cause devastation on both Governments. In fact it looks like he intends to "cut off his nose to spite his face." The general feeling I believe is

State University (Baton Rouge, 1977); David French Boyd, Reminiscences of the War in Virginia (1897; rpr. Baton Rouge, 1994).

7. Bitters is an alcoholic liquor distilled from a bitter herb, root, leaf, flower, or seed and used as a tonic or stimulant to the appetite or aid to digestion. Although the exact nature of these "remedies" is now a mystery, a fine discussion of patent medicines, medical treatment, and quackery on the old Southwest frontier may be found in William C. Davis, A Way Through the Wilderness: The Natchez Trace and the Civilizing of the Southern Frontier (New York, 1995), 97–103.

8. Jasper Gough, a carpenter from Sparta, died of typhoid fever at Camp Bienville on August 23, 1861 (Booth, comp., Records, Vol. III, Pt. 1, p. 67).

9. L. Jefferson Wallace of Shangston, Louisiana, recovered and served with the Ninth Louisiana through the war (ibid., Pt. 2, p. 976).

10. W. Oscar Price of Natchitoches, Louisiana, was killed in action at Sharpsburg on September 17, 1862 (ibid., 204).

11. Organized in 1838 by the Creole elite of New Orleans, the Washington Artillery was one of the Confederacy's finest artillery battalions. Four of its five companies served in the Army of Northern Virginia, originally under Col. James B. Walton. The fifth company served in the Army of Tennessee. See William Miller Owen, In Camp and Battle with the Washington Artillery (1885; rpr. Gaithersburg, Md., n.d.); Powell A. Casey, An Outline of the Civil War Campaigns and Engagements of the Washington Artillery of New Orleans (Baton Rouge, 1986).

that we want peace on honorable terms to the South. We desire once more to return to our homes but if peace is not made on those terms we will fight as long as health and strength is given us to fight the hated foes. My love to the family, regards to all enquiring friends. I remain your affectionate son

R. A. Pierson

P.S. Tell brother Henry to enquire of old Mr. Hueston if he ever sent me the money ($5.00) that I loaned him when he went to leave Camp Moore. If he did not, tell him to send it by Mr. C. G. Thurmond.

P.S. I suppose you will not recognize this as my handwrite. It is not but written by a friend as quinine has made me too nervous to write.

⋙ ⋘

REUBEN ALLEN PIERSON TO WILLIAM H. PIERSON
Camp Bienville, Va.
Sept. 18th, 1861

Dear Father

I have been confined to my bed for about four weeks with typhoid fever, so you may see why I have not written during all this long time. I am now just able to sit up to write. I now begin to learn what it is to be sick in a hospital so far from home that there is no chance to either go or receive any nourishment from there. I am mending very fast and shall hope to be able to walk out in a few more days if I take no backset which I intend to avoid with all my power and judgment. The war news is very exciting up here in Virginia at this time. All of our troops are moving on in the direction of Washington and it is supposed that Beauregard intends attacking the enemy when he gets all his troops arranged. Large numbers of troops pass over the road every day marching in the direction of the great Capital.

Sept. 19th, 1861. I again resume the task of writing today. I am still improving. I live principally on milk and bread. Tell Jim that if he could see the sick who are in the hospital here he would not feel so much like coming to war. There are about 600 men in our regiment not able for duty out of a little over 900. Phil Collins has been quite sick and is now in the hospital. He is able to walk out in the cool of the morning and evening though he is quite weak yet. The Doctor (Egan) says as soon as we are able to travel that he will send us to the general La. hospital which is being established at Richmond. If we are sent there we will remain there till we fully regain our strength which will take nearly a month. If you have an opportunity send me my overcoat as such an article will be quite comfortable in the hard cold climate of Va. Mark everything that you send with my name so that I will be sure to get my own things.

All the well ones of the regiment have moved about a mile in advance of the old camp but about 100 men were left sick at the hospital and I among the number. Mr. Shields[12] who joined us at Camp Moore died yesterday morning. I have known as many as three die in one day. Wesley Grice died about 3 weeks ago of the typhoid fever. Richard Cason[13] died some weeks ago. I could not give you a list of the sick of our own company unless I knew how many there are sick up at the camp. Over half of our men have been unfit for duty for about 2 months. Excuse all amiss. Give my love and respects to all the family and especially to all enquiring friends. Tell Miss Gahagan her compliments were very soothing to the ear of a poor sick soldier like angels['] visits. Such consoling words come but seldom to us.

Your affectionate Son
R. A. Pierson

⇒ ⇐

REUBEN ALLEN PIERSON TO MARY CATHERINE PIERSON
Culpepper Court House [Va.]
Oct. 8th, 1861

Miss M. C. Pierson

Dear Sister

After long delaying to write to you I am at a loss to know what apology to offer except it be the indolent habits into which I have fallen during the long spell that I have just recovered from. I am now able to walk around town nearly all day. The health of our regiment was fast improving when I left camps and I hope will continue to improve as the weather turns colder. We have had one light frost and I think will be more than likely to have another tomorrow morning. The wind is blowing quite cool from the north this evening. I find many kind friends here in Virginia but most of them are money friends, that is, friends for the pay they get out of the soldiers. There are a great many ladies attending to the sick and wounded soldiers, some from nearly every southern

12. Pvt. James Y. Shields died at Camp Bienville on September 18, 1861 (Booth, comp., *Records,* Vol. III, Pt. 2, p. 548).

13. Richard Cason of Buck Horn was a private in Company A, Ninth Louisiana Infantry. He died at Camp Moore on August 31, 1861 (*ibid.,* II, 285).

state. I see one very handsome young widow from La. She is beautiful enough to captivate any young man whose heart is susceptible of being won by the elega[n]ce & graces of Female delicacy. I have been very much mortified at hearing of the death of Henry Clay Key[14] and a young man by the name of Adear [Adeer][15] who died since we left the camp. They were both very sick when I saw them last which was the day before I left. I have not received my box of clothing, yet it was sent around to Fairfax by railroad while I was at Centerville, a little village on the direct rout[e] from Manassas to Fairfax. I think that I will return to my company next Sunday which will be the 13th Inst. As for war news I have but little. There has been no general engagement up to this time, but everybody is expecting to hear of a big fight daily, and there is a general rush made to the cars whenever they arrive at this depot which is on the rout[e] from Richmond to Manassas. Our briggade is now on the frontier and will be sure to have a hand in the next battle. The Louisianians have a great reputation for fighting at Bull Run. I have seen the graves of some of the heroes who sacrificed their lives on the battlefield for the sake of southern liberty. I have also seen where the cannon ball of the yankees passed through a tree 18 inches in diameter. I have seen a great many cannon balls which our boys found upon the field where they fought on Thursday. I have camped on the ground which was once occupied by General Scott and his barbarous hordes and this is some little of what my eyes have witnessed since I came to the Old Dominion. Will you be so kind as to tell Miss Belle[16] that I feel under many obligations to her for the comfort which she sent me and more than a thousand thanks for the little nice dainties she assisted in preparing and sent to me & Prentiss.[17] I can but wish her success in all her undertakings through life, that she may pass over the stormy sea of life in perfect peace and happiness without a single jargon or discord to mar the happiness of so amiable and lovely a being. May her guardian angel pilot her little barque over still waters and finally land her safely into the harbor of heaven where she may enjoy perfect bliss through endless ages to come. Give my love and respects to all who may think enough of me to enquire about my welfare, but especially to all my friends of the fair sex. Allow me to

14. Henry Clay Key, the son of T. A. Key and Harriet Key of Bienville Parish and a student at Mount Lebanon University, died at Camp Bienville on October 3, 1861 (*ibid.,* Vol. III, Pt. 2, p. 554).

15. James Adeer, a Mount Lebanon farmer, died of typhoid fever at Camp Bienville on October 2, 1861 (*ibid.,* I, 31).

16. Belle Randle was the daughter of John B. Randle, the steward of Mount Lebanon University with whom Reuben Pierson seems to have boarded for a time (Gerald Pollard, "The History of Mount Lebanon University, 1852–1912" [M.Ed. thesis, Louisiana State University, 1971], 43, 47).

17. Prentiss Jackson, a student from Mount Lebanon, died in a Richmond hospital sometime in 1862 (Booth, comp., *Records,* Vol. III, Pt. 1, p. 419).

present my warmest affections to all the family and relations and receive the same yourself while I remain your affectionate brother till death

R. A. Pierson

> ⟿ ⟾

DAVID PIERSON TO WILLIAM H. PIERSON

Camp Jackson, Ark., Oct 15th, 1861

Wm H. Pierson
  Mt. Lebanon
    La.

    Dear Father

Your letters sent by Mr. Sims[18] were delivered to day. I was glad to hear from you all as I always am, but more so now that I am almost alone—left behind sick. The Reg^t having gone back to Mo. I am very lonesome away from my company & you must know that a letter from home & the sight of a good old friend from Winnfield who can tell me all the news of my own parish gives me great pleasure. The Reg^t started to Mo. day before yesterday, but I could not go in consequence of weakness having just got up from the typhoid fever & a relapse from the same. I am at a good and comfortable private house in company with a Lieut. of our Reg^t and one of my men (Mr. Balton[19]) where I can receive every attention that I could desire. I am yet weak and feeble & gain strength slowly being affected with a dysentery that keeps me thrown back, but I [will] soon be able to go on & join my Company.

I have thought something about getting a furlough & going home for a while, but there has been so many applications that I have given it out. A few days before the troops left here, more than half the officers in our Reg^t applied to the Gen. for furloughs. Some were granted, others refused, & several even have resigned their commissions because they could not get them. The Gen.'s quarters swarmed with privates after discharges & furloughs, & he raved and cursed at being annoyed so much. So I concluded not to bother him. Besides, I don't think it right for officers to go home 3 or 4 months out of the service & doing the Government no good & receiving pay for the time and therefore I have concluded in case I do not get able to resume my duties in a month to resign & go home for good. If I do the Government no good, I will receive no pay. I know of

18. An L. P. Simms enlisted in Company H, Third Louisiana Infantry, on May 17, 1861, and was promoted to second corporal on May 15, 1862. He was captured at Vicksburg (*ibid.*, Pt. 2, p. 572).

19. D. Ballton of Winn Parish, a private in David Pierson's Company C, was paroled at Natchitoches on June 7, 1865. See Willie H. Tunnard, *A Southern Record: The Story of the Third Regiment Louisiana Infantry* (1866; rpr. Dayton, Ohio, 1970); Booth, comp., *Records,* I, 113.

instances where officers have lay sick for 3 or 4 months & gone home on long furloughs when they knew that their health would never permit their staying in Camps, just for the sake of the money. If I take a notion to resign, I have a horse that I can ride home & and will need no assistance from anybody.

Mr. Sims left the wagon & clothes about 85 miles from here & came on in order to get here before the Reg^t moved, but got here too late. He has gone on to overtake the boys. The wagon will get here day after tomorrow, and much will be the rejoicing among the Winn Rifles when they see the many little articles of comfort their friends have sent them from home. It is expected that the army will return to this place in about a month to go into winter quarters. Gen. McCulloch was heard to say so before he left. The several Regiments will be scattered about over the country so as to get forage and provisions. I am inclined to the opinion that the La. Reg^t. will be sent as far south as Fort Smith on account of the climate. Gen. McCulloch said the day before he marched that he expected a heavy fight up in Kansas, but I do not believe there will be any more fighting in this quarter this winter. Lane is reported as having a considerable force somewhere on the border, but I feel well assured that he will go into winter quarters on the approach of our army & will not dare to meet Old Ben & his boys. However, there is not much telling what may happen in war, & a fight may take place. A great many believe that the march is taken for the health of the soldiers & that the Gen. himself does not even so much as anticipate a fight. The Kansas Jayhawkers, as these bands of murderers are called, have committed many depredations in the joining counties of Mo., have overrun two of those counties, burning Houses & Towns, killing every southerner they could catch, and taking away all the horses and cattle & provisions. It may be that our army will adopt their mode of warfare & lay waste their Country in the same manner. If so, I hope that Louisianians will not be put at such bloody work.

The Missourians have recently gained a great victory over the Federalists taking 5,000 prisoners with their arms besides four pieces of artillery and three boat loads of provisions.[20] Gen. Price[21] is said to have an army of 30,000 men well armed & provided for. If they but do their duty now, Mo. can be soon be free from abolition tyranny.

20. Following the battle of Oak Hills, Sterling Price undertook a campaign to liberate Missouri. On September 20, 1861, the Missouri State Guard captured Lexington with its 2,500 prisoners, 3,000 rifles, 750 horses, and 7 cannon as well as $1 million the Federals had taken from the town bank (Albert Castel, *General Sterling Price and the Civil War in the West* [1968; rpr. Baton Rouge, 1993], 48–65).

21. Sterling Price, known to the adoring men of the Missouri State Guard as "Old Pap," was a tobacco planter and politician. During the war with Mexico, he served as military governor of New Mexico and earned a brevet to brigadier general. He later served in the U.S. House of Representatives and as governor of Missouri. Price commanded the Missouri State Guard at Oak Hills, at the battle of Lexington, and at Elkhorn Tavern. He was then transferred to Mississippi, where he took part in the fighting at Iuka

I had no such an idea as my letter, which I wrote you about the battle, being published. I expect it is a handsome piece of composition to go to press. I know it was hurriedly written & and at a time when I was busy tending to my wounded & and before I had time to gather any information in regard to the events [of the] battle, but it is all right. I have no particular objection but can't see what satisfaction it could be to anybody to see such a scribble as it must have been in print.

We have had a great deal of sickness in this camp. Many cases of Typhoid fever & a great many deaths. Out of my company since we left Fort Smith in July, 10 have died of sickness & one of killed in battle. Our Reg^t left 150 sick at the hospitle here when they left the other day. There are but few, however, dangerous. The State has done a noble part by our Reg^t in sending us blankets, shoes, & other clothing besides paying us for the time we were in the State service, & Gov. Moore[22] will never be forgotten by the volunteers of the 3^d Reg^t for his generous efforts in collecting & sending the goods in time to do us good. I have written you several letters lately which you may get before you do this.

The papers that you send me seldom come to hand. I have not got one in two months & cannot imagine what is the cause. Walker sends us the *Sentinel*[23] regularly, and, strange to say, but two packages have ever reached us. The wagon will get here in a few days & I will write you again. I have some Confederate notes to send you, & c. Excuse this long letter. I have nothing else to do but write now, & it affords me pass time to write & read all the time. I have a quiet place in the country & have to pass my time some way. Can't lay abed & am too feeble to walk much. My love to all & c.

Yours Affectionately,

D. Pierson

---

and Corinth. In 1864, he returned to the Trans-Mississippi and commanded a division at the battle of Jenkins' Ferry, Arkansas. Later that year, he led a spectacular raid through Missouri, only to be driven from the state again by Union forces. See Castel, *General Sterling Price;* Robert E. Shalhope, *Sterling Price, Portrait of a Southerner* (Columbia, S.C., 1971).

22. Thomas Overton Moore was one of Louisiana's largest antebellum landholders. Elected governor in 1859, he became an effective and resourceful organizer of men and materiel for the Confederate war effort. After the Federal invasion of Louisiana in 1862, Moore cooperated closely with Richard Taylor for the defense of the state and worked for the relief of citizens impoverished by the war. Despite this admirable record, he was defeated for reelection by Henry Watkins Allen in 1864 and retired to his Alexandria plantation (Joseph G. Dawson III, ed., *The Louisiana Governors: From Iberville to Edwards* [Baton Rouge, 1990], 138–42).

23. The *Southern Sentinel* was printed weekly at Winnfield from 1859 until 1883 by editor and publisher John L. Walker. The newspaper lasted through at least 1909 under other editors (Louisiana Historical Records Survey, *Louisiana Newspapers, 1794–1940* [Baton Rouge, 1941], 230).

⇒ ⇐

DAVID PIERSON TO WILLIAM H. PIERSON

Camp Jackson, Ark., Oct. 17ᵗʰ/61

Wᵐ H. Pierson
  Mt. Lebanon
    La.

Dear Father

The wagon has arrived, and we sick ones have had a slight peep into our immense & valuable stocks of goods & good things. The boxes & bales of clothing, blankets, & shoes & c. I would not open as I had them to store here not knowing that if would be safe to send them on to the Company now & preferring to have all together when the goods were given out. But my own little private box suffered from the blows of a hatchet as soon as it arrived. My surprise at finding so much as I proceeded to take out, my over joy at finding myself the owner of so much, and the thought of receiving them from home and other influences operating upon my mind all at once made me nervous for hours. I should not be surprised if I danced & cut up a great many capers over the contents of that little box. But I soon quieted down with a "Drink" in my throat & a segar in my mouth satisfied that a cold winter had no terrors for me. Tell Aunt Nan[24] that the "jeans pants" came in a good time as the last pair I had were well nigh worn out. The socks, too, were much appreciated as my toes were beginning to push through my old ones. I am now stepping about with a new pair of boots and socks also. As for shirts, I was pretty well supplied, but they will be no particular trouble to me[.] The overcoat you sent me I did not need as I accidentally made a purchase of one sometime ago & a very good one too. I sent yours back as I have but little chance of carrying it & the boys are all well supplied with clothing. Blankets, neck ties, & c. all thankfully received.

I send you by Mr. Sims three hundred & fifty dollars in Confederate notes—fifty of it for Henry—& could send you more but as I do not know what may happen to me I prefer to keep enough to meet any emergency.[25] I have had to loan Lieuts. Emanuel & Strother money & some to the Company. Strother has recently died & I won't get it in a year, & the Company has not been paid off. I will send you more the next pay I draw. Our parish & friends at home have done a noble part by us—have indeed sent us everything we needed and even more than we can use. The winter cannot hurt my men with their bountiful supply of blankets & good warm clothes. They have besides sending

24. Aunt Nan was Pierson's maternal aunt and stepmother, Nancy (Collins) Pierson, whom his father had married in 1848. She was born on January 25, 1810, in Edgefield District, South Carolina, the daughter of Dennis and Joyce Collins, and died in Natchitoches, Louisiana, on November 10, 1884.

25. This is David's eldest brother, Henry Lewis Pierson.

us clothing & c. sent the Company nearly five hundred dollars in cash to be used to alleviate the suffering of the sick.

Oct. 19th

Our friends leave for home today. My health is improving very fast. I almost feel as well as ever & shall go on to the Reg[t] in a week from now. Our army has increased very fast within the last few days—3 additional Regiments have come in besides two excellent "batteries." Hoping this may find you all well & c., I remain as ever,

Your Affectionate son
D. Pierson

⇒ ⇐

REUBEN ALLEN PIERSON TO JAMES F. PIERSON
Camp Bienville, Virginia
Oct. 20th, 1861

Mr. James F. Pierson
Dear Brother

I have just arrived back at camps this morning and consider myself able to undergo the hardships of the camp again. I have not been able for duty since about the 14th of Aug. being a little over two months. During this time I have received many letters, some from home and some from old friends. I have neglected answering [*illegible*] large [*illegible*] these [*illegible*]. Most of our company is now present & enjoying excellent health. In fact many of the boys look heartier than I ever saw them. Many who were boyish looking fellows begin to look like men. Notwithstanding the health has improved greatly. We still have some boys who are confined to their beds by disease. I left Tom Pitman yesterday evening at Culpepper [Court House]. He had been quite sick. He was first attacked with a severe ague, which was followed by a high fever and as that subsided he had an intense pain in the right eye which proved to be neuralgia. It passed to the left eye and that was easy [easing] when I left and he was mending when I left him. I also left Robert Cason at the same place. He was improving very fast but is still quite weak being affected with some old chronic complaint. I think that he will get a discharge in a few days. All the rest of our boys are on foot and fast getting well. I have never seen a livlier than our boys appear to be. They are as cheerful as a party of youths at a Christmas party. As for war news I have nothing but idle reports and speculations and these are so varied that our wisest counselors are at a loss to know what conclusion to draw. Our forces have retreated but the yankees are now pursuing them only in small scouting parties and these fly behind their fortifications at the sight of the Confederates. Much may be said but my opinion is that the next fight in Va. will be when our forces attack the Federals in their fortifications and not till then.

I found the little box of dainties marked to me yesterday evening when I arrived at Manassas and opened it thinking it might be my clothing, but when I saw what it was I nailed it up again and left it as I could not carry it four miles and walk. I am very thankful to Mrs. Randle for the fine bottle of wine she sent me. It was quite a treat to me, as such a thing cannot be bought at any price here. I have nearly entirely gained my strength and feel as well as I ever did excepting a slight cold. On arriving at camps this morning I found five letters for me, two from father, one from Henry, one from Leatherman[26] and the one from yourself. Tell Mr. Leatherman I beg that he will pardon me as I was not able to write when I received his first and have just received the other today to which I will respond as soon as circumstances will admit. Tell Henry that I beg his forgiveness for past neglect and will write him a long and full detail of a sick man[']s fare when in camp. Tell Sister nothing could have afforded me greater pleasure than to hear that she she had launched off her little bark to try the winds of life for self, and still more pleased at the occupation and boarding place which she has chosen. I am proud to hear of your progress in school. You will shurely soon graduate if you continue making such long strides, but be careful that you don[']t overdo the thing. Obtain all the information you can from Mr. Hay. He is very good in mathematics if you need help. You will find him a good counselor. Don[']t crowd yourself with too many studies but review once or twice all you try to master. Remember the old adage that what is worth doing is worth well doing. You will forget much, but then you have gone through a long course of hard study. Give my love and respects to all who may remember me and mention my name during my absence. Tell all my old school mates that I am experiencing the hardships of a soldier[']s lot—lying on the ground beneath a thin ausnaburg tent in this cold climate—but still I am fat[t]ening as fast as a possom in persimmon time. Excuse this scribbling epistle and I will try to improve by the time I write again. Write often [as] you have a good chance. I remain your affectionate Brother

R. A. Pierson

26. Frank M. Leatherman, a printer from Mount Lebanon, was at this time on detached duty as a guard for the division ordnance train. He was captured later in the war and paroled in May, 1865 (Booth, comp., *Records*, Vol. III, Pt. 1, p. 688).

⇒ ←

REUBEN ALLEN PIERSON TO MARY CATHERINE PIERSON
Camp Review [Va.]
Nov. 5th, 1861

Miss M. C. Pierson
Dear Sister

In accordance with a promise made when I left home I again seat myself upon our broomstraw floor to let you know how I am getting on in camps. I am enjoying excellent health, weigh 175 or 80 pounds and can stand more hardships than I ever could in life. We have just returned from a severe march over the muddiest road I ever saw. We were ordered out on the front for pickets on the morning of the 2nd Inst., which was the worst day I ever saw in my life, however, we cooked up our provision[s] in the rain and early on the morning were all ready to march. The sun rose clear and the wind blew quite cool from the north making it much better on us than a still day. We hurried on till after the sun had passed the meridian when we halted for a few moments to rest, and while we were seated on the wet ground resting our wearied limbs, we heard the sound of a horse's feet coming after us. Soon a courier arrives and gives us orders to march back to camp. Immediately we about face and trudge through the mud 8 long miles over the same ground we had marched that morning. We arrived in camps about sunset tired enough to sleep soundly without rocking. This a short description of my first march worth naming since I have been in camp. The health of our regiment is not as good as it was a few weeks ago. Most cases now are of pneumonia and the Dr. sends them back (as fast as they are taken) to the hospitals where they may be taken good care of and given little nourishments. All your acquaintances were mending when I last heard from them. I am expecting Tom Pittman and Phil Collins here daily. They were both doing well a few days ago. We have all received more clothing than would be necessary for a good supply [for] two winters. We have sent back a large supply to Manassas where they are guarded by men detailed for that purpose. I have am very proud to hear that you have taken up my profession and gone to teaching the youths of your country. Be careful for much of their future character depends on their training in the school room. Do what you conscientiously think to be right whether you please patrons or pupils, and in the end you will find this to be the best policy. Do not sit down upon the stool of ease but pursue your studies diligently and inform yourself while young for in age you may need your education. If not you will find it no disadvantage. Learning in the language of the fact is great.

When friends are gone and money is spent
Learning is most then excellent.

Give my best regards to Mr. Rabun & family[27] and to all my acquaintances
who may desire to know how I am getting on in the war. My special love to all
the family when you have the pleasure of visiting them. Receive a brother[']s
affectionate regards yourself. Excuse all amiss. I remain your brother till death

R. A. Pierson

P.S. Write as soon as you can after receiving this and write often as you can. I
will direct this to Lebanon and they can send it to you. Tell father that I do not
want any furlough as I am in excellent health.
P.S. 2nd. There is a slight probability of our being sent back to La. to winter; we
will know in a few days. Yours again

R. A. Pierson

> <

GEORGE WASHINGTON WILLIAMS TO JAMES F. PIERSON
Camp Moore La   Nov 6th 1861

Dear Jim
    I have before me yours dated Oct 31 which was rcs. yesterday. I was truly
glad to heare from you and to heare you enjoyed such good health. I have enjoyed very good health ever since I have bin in Camps until a few days back I
was taken with a very severe cold and I had a high fever for about 3 days but I
did not lay up for it. I think I will be all right side up in a few days. I feel very
dull this evening on account of setting up list knight. I was on Sentinel[']s post
last knight. Jim I havent any thing hardly worth writing. The health of our
Company is not good by any means though we havent any bad cases. We have
about 15 cases of measels which are getting along as well as could be expected to
the chance we have in Camps. However our Captain rented a house yesterday
and moved them into it wherare they will have a good chance to get up soon.
    Jim you seem to think that when a person becomes used to hard living that
they can enjoy it as well as those who live off the fat of the land but that is not

27. On September 24, 1860, William H. Pierson sold his Bienville Parish plantation to Hodge
Raburn (sometimes spelled "Raboun" or "Rabun"). A Sampson Raboun served as a tutor at Mount
Lebanon University (*Louisiana Baptist*, December 4, 1862).

the case with my self. I have thought that I knew something about hard times & hard living before I come in Camps but it was an entire mistake but still I dont find it any worse than I anticipated before I left home and speaking my honest sentiments I have not rued my bargain yet for I was bad dissatisfied before I left home from the fact that I felt like I was due my services to my Country and long to take a part in her behalf. I dont have any idea how long we will remain heare. We have bin expecting to leave ever since we come heare and we are still heare. We may not leave heare this winter. I cant say. A soldier cant tell one day what he will be doing the next. Sometimes Drilling sometimes on fatigue and sometimes on guard. Sometimes sick. I am begin[n]ing to think that I am a very good cook wheare theare is not a better.

You stated that you taken the letter that I wrote to Cousin Cassie out of the post office & conveyed [it] to her. You also stated that she said she intended to anser it. I have not received a line from her yet. I hope that I will soon. Theare is nothing that gives me more pleasure than to get a letter from my dear relatives & friends so please write to me. They must not waite for me to write first for my chance is bad. [*Illegible*] & Jacob Scoggin[28] are heare in our company. They are well. Jim I want you to tell me in your next how to direct a letter to Allen. I will close this letter. Give the best love of a nephew to Aunt Nan & Uncle William & all the rest.

Your Ever True Cousin
G W Williams[29]
Tangipaho[a] Pa[rish]

Please answer soon
Direct your letters to
Care Capt. W. T. Mabry,[30] 16 Regiment, La. Volunteers

28. Jacob S. Scoggin, a cousin of the Pierson brothers, was killed in action at the battle of New Hope Church, May 26, 1864 (Booth, comp., *Records,* Vol. III, Pt. 2, p. 490).

29. George Williams enlisted in the "Castor Guards" of Bienville Parish, which mustered into Confederate service as Company I, Sixteenth Louisiana Infantry, at Camp Moore on September 29, 1861. He was elected third lieutenant on September 1, 1862, and promoted to second lieutenant sometime thereafter. Early in 1864, he was detached to Company K and later was transferred to Company G, Twenty-fifth Louisiana, which he commanded at the war's end. Williams was the Pierson brothers' first cousin (*ibid.,* 1094).

30. William T. Mabry of Bienville Parish was elected captain of the Castor Guards on September 7, 1861. Mabry was not reelected when his regiment was reorganized on May 8, 1862, and on May 15, 1862, he died of wounds received at the battle of Farmington, Mississippi (Arthur W. Bergeron, Jr., *Guide to Louisiana Confederate Military Units, 1861–1865* [Baton Rouge, 1989], 112; Booth, comp., *Records,* Vol. III, Pt. 1, p. 827).

⇒ ∈

DAVID PIERSON TO WILLIAM H. PIERSON

Camp McCulloch
Nov. 8th, 1861

Wm H. Pierson
  Mt. Lebanon
    La.

Dear Father,

I wrote home two days ago by a discharged soldier going to Morehouse, but as Capt. Beard[31] leaves today for Shreveport I drop you a line by him. The prospect is getting good for a general engagement between the two armies in this section. The enemy is in or about Springfield with a large force. Gen. Price of Mo. is still falling back & we are lying here near the Ark. line, apparently waiting for an attack. Yesterday we had a general inspection of arms & ammunition which goes to prove more than any thing else that the Gen. himself expects a fight soon. The enemy is reported sixty thousand strong, but it is generally believed here that he has but thirty thousand. We have about that number should Price & McCulloch form a junction which report says they will do notwithstanding their extreme jealousy of each other.

There has been some bad management among our commanders, it seems to me, in allowing an enemy to march unmolested half through the State of Mo. & occupy even the ground upon which was fought the memorable Battle of Oak Hills. Springfield should have been held by the Missourians at all events, but instead of that they have retreated no less than two-hundred miles back completely on us to the Ark. line, & now it seems the next battle will be fought in Ark. The enemy may not come down upon us this winter; he may content himself to occupy Springfield again & have complete control of the State of Mo. The Mo. Legislature is in session at Pineville, Mo., & is said to have passed an ordinance of secession. I doubt whether they had a quorum at the time, & it is thought their action will have but little influence with the Government of the Confederate States. If we have a fight at all it will be over in a few days & if not we will soon be in winter quarters.

My health is fine—better than it has been since I have been in the service. Cold weather agrees with me admirably. The soldiers are generally healthy at this time. Lieut. Emanuel is quite sick just now, but I hope will be up in a few days. He was better yesterday.

31. This is probably James H. Beard, captain of Company D (the "Shreveport Greys") of the First Louisiana Battalion. He was later promoted to major of the Eleventh Battalion and to lieutenant colonel on August 3, 1863. As colonel of the Consolidated Crescent Regiment, he was killed in action at the battle of Mansfield on April 8, 1864 (Bergeron, *Guide,* 146, 148, 164).

We had an alarm in camps yesterday occasioned by the firing of several pieces of canon by a battery about 3 miles distant from here. Most of the boys thought the ball had opened again & that we were to have another Oak Hill arrangement of it. The excitement was soon over as we quickly found out the cause of the firing & everything quieted down as usual. We are expecting something to turn up hourly.

Yours Affectionately
D. Pierson

⇒ ⇐

PHILIP L. COLLINS TO WILLIAM H. PIERSON

Culpepper Courthouse Va
Nov the 9th 1861

Dear uncle and family

I take the present opportunity of writing you a few lines and I have an opportunity of sending it by R. C. Cason who has been discharged and is going to start from this place tomorrow. This leaves me not well though I am improving very fast at this time and hope I will soon be well again for I have not injoyed any health since I got to Virginia. Allen is in Camps. I heard from him yesterday. He was well and injoying him self very well. I see in the morning paper an account of a battle in Kentucky and our men completely routed the yankees and allso a battle near Savan[n]ah Georgia where we had to give up the fort.

I have nothing of interest to write. I remain

> yours til death
> Philip L. Collins

⇒ ⇐

REUBEN ALLEN PIERSON TO WILLIAM H. PIERSON

Camp Florida, Va.
Nov. 12th, 1861.

Mr. W. H. Pierson

Dear Father

I have an opportunity of sending you a letter by Mr. Clark who came on to bring some clothing for the "Bossier Volunteers,"[32] and I hasten to write I have been a little sick from cold for a few days passed but not enough to confine me for an hour to my bed. I received my bundle (sent by Mr. Candler) and find all

---

32. The "Bossier Volunteers" were officially Company D, Ninth Louisiana Infantry (*ibid.,* 93).

right side up with care. My clothes are the very thing for this climate and they come to hand in good time. We have not had any snow up here yet though it sleeted a little a few days back. We are now encamped in plain view of Beauregard[']s head quarters, and in sight of a large army. I can see 20 or 30 regiments from our quarters. Wood is quite scarce and in a few days there will not be a single oak tree in sight of camps; we will have to haul wood a mile or more. It is very pleasant on a still evening to listen to the music of some dozen or more excellent brass bands playing for dress parade all the same time, making the hills reverberate with sounds far sweeter than the approach of 20 yankee shows with all their fascinating songs and music. I have heard and as often read the famous stories of the Revolutionary days, the pleasures & the miseries of camp life depicted by the ablest pens of that day & the stories rehearsed by every mother to her prattling boy of the great deeds performed by his ancestors in the great struggle for independence. To all of these have I listened while my imagination was conjuring up a thousand horrid pictures of fields strewn with dead and groaning wounded—with blood standing upon the ground in puddles or trickling down the hillside in small streams. All these have I fancied to be the scenes of a soldier[']s life. But now I have experienced the true life of a soldier. I find them quite different from what I had always believed them to be. Go to the hospitals and there see every kind of disease that preys upon the human system, devouring men as fast as coffins can be made by a large factory or shrouds by a large clothing establishment, to inter them. See men with some contagious disease lying upon the cold wet ground an[d] in the rain till life cannot be their lot but a few short hours. I shall never, no never forget the scenes of 1861. You wrote to me about getting a furlough and coming home to recruit my health. The Col. refused to give a furlough to a Lieut. to go to see a brother who was at the point of death, the distance not being over 50 miles. I have never even so much as thought of asking for a furlough, and now I do not want a furlough. The health of our regiment is still bad. The mumps are taking a [pass] through in camp now. We have sent off the following cases viz[.]: Monroe Thomas, Wm. Scogin, Wm. Mims, Tom Cawthon and Smith Scogin [33] has them now in camp and will be sent away tomorrow. Tom Pittman & Richard

33. James Monroe Thomas of Sparta was a sergeant in Company C. He was sent to the rear, sick, from Camp Reserve in the fall of 1861, but returned to duty until deserting to the cavalry in 1864. William J. Scogin of Buck Horn returned from his sick leave in June, 1862. He was killed the following September at Sharpsburg. William D. Mims of Ringgold left the Ninth Louisiana sometime in early 1864, apparently transferring to a Confederate unit in the Trans-Mississippi Department. He was captured, exchanged, and finally paroled at Shreveport on June 13, 1865. James Smith Scogin of Buck Horn was captured at Rappahannock Station on November 7, 1863. After four months of captivity at Point Lookout, Maryland, he was exchanged but was recaptured at Winchester on April 19, 1864. He was not

Colbert[34] have not returned from the hospital yet though we are looking for them today. We heard from them a few days ago and they were both well. Collins was still puny when I heard from him. I do not think he will be back in camp soon though he is not much sick. I hope you have been more fortunate in receiving my letters. I write twice nearly every week. Excuse all amiss. Give my love to all the acquaintances and receive the affection of a distant Son yourself & family

R. A. Pierson

⇒ ⇐

REUBEN ALLEN PIERSON TO MARY CATHERINE PIERSON
Camp Florida, Virginia
Nov. 23rd, 1861

Miss M. C. Pierson

Dear Sister

I received yours bearing date 3rd Inst. and was much gratified to have the pleasure of reading a few lines from a loved Sister once more. I must congratulate you on your success [*illegible*] so fortunate as to fall into [*illegible*] where you are with many true [friends] and acquaintances, instead of being thrown out where you are an entire stranger. My health is now very good having entirely recovered from the severe spell which came so near [to taking] me beyond the gloomy shades of [earth]. I am due old Jack many kind [*illegible*] for his devotion to me in that of having sympathy enough to wish he had been present to administer to my wants while I was stretched upon a cot, in a detestable hospital far away from all the family and devoted old servant who has such feelings of true friendship for me. I also must confess that it seemed as if I would have given up all earthly possessions even to life [itself] to have been with a mother, a father, brothers, and [loving] sister, to have speaken a few cheerful [words in] my latest hours. I am proud to hear [of] Sallie's marriage. I wish her & Jim success [in all their] undertakings and a long life of undisturbed tranquility, while sailing over the raging billows of the sea of life. Tell all

exchanged again until February 14, 1865 (Booth, comp., *Records,* Vol. III, Pt. 2, pp. 809–10, 490, Pt. 1, p. 992).

34. Richard Colbert of Mount Lebanon was a corporal in Pierson's company. He was among those captured at Rappahannock Station on November 7, 1862, and was imprisoned at Point Lookout until exchanged on March 15, 1864. After the third battle of Winchester, September 19, 1864, he was reported missing in action. He was the brother of William B. Colbert and John A. Colbert, both also of Company C (*ibid.,* II, 375).

the negroes that I am still in the land of the living and hope to be spared till I return and shake hands with them again. Tell Miss Jane Thomas[35] that I am proud to receive such fine compliments from a young lady just entering the [prime of] womanhood. I have nothing interesting [to relate] of war news. We are encamped in the [midst of] a large army and surrounded by strong breast-works on which are stationed large batteries of cannon, and the artillery men are practicing daily upon these to render themselves useful [when] the neces-sity of the case demands their [services. It is a] very sublime scene to hear the roar of [the cannon] and the hissing of a bomb sailing through the air and then see the flame as it bursts in the air looking like a ball of fire bursting forth from nothing.

The general health of our regiment is not so good as it was a few weeks back, though we have nothing serious or dangerous at this time. I fear the pneumonia more than every thing else during [a spell of sickness]. [*Illegible name*] is well, you may tell his folks. [*Illegible first name*] Poole[36] is here. He has spent about a [month] with us and will leave for home tomorrow. [I send] this by him and hope you may receive it in a few days. There is a rumor in camp today that the La. brigade will be sent to Cumberland Gap on the Blue Ridge mountain[s].[37] I cannot vouch for its truth, but hope we may be so fortunate. I have received my bundle of clothing & box of extra [*illegible*] strongly reminded me of how [good it is] to have a good home with plenty [of loved ones] to supply the wants of nature. I saw thirty yankee pris[o]ners pass here a few days ago. They were well clothed and good looking men. The g[u]ard [marched] on each side of them with drawn [bayonets] while the roadside was crowded [with people] who hallowed at the top of their [voices] as they passed along. Excuse all amiss. Give my love to all enquiring friends and also to Mr. Rabun's family. Remember me to any young lady who enquired after my welfare. Write soon & often to your Brother in war.

R. A. Pierson

35. Amanda Jane Thomas, the daughter of David K. Thomas and Elizabeth Bryan Thomas, became the wife of James F. Pierson in November, 1865.

36. Two Poole brothers, both from Brush Valley, served in Company H of the Ninth Louisiana. William H. was killed in action at Gettysburg and John N., who enlisted on March 12, 1862, deserted in June, 1864 (*ibid.,* Vol. III, Pt. 2, pp. 171–72).

37. This rumor was false. The Louisiana brigade remained with Johnston's army until April 18, when as part of Richard S. Ewell's division, it left Gordonsville to join Stonewall Jackson in the Shenandoah Valley. Ewell did not catch up with the Army of the Valley, by then at New Market, until May 17, but he was soon to win glory in Jackson's famed Valley campaign (Terry L. Jones, *Lee's Tigers: The Louisiana In-fantry in the Army of Northern Virginia* [Baton Rouge, 1987], 63–68).

➣ ⬿

REUBEN ALLEN PIERSON TO WILLIAM H. PIERSON
Camp Florida, Va.
Novr. 26th, 1861

W. H. Pierson, Esqr.

Dear Father

It has been only a few days since I wrote James a letter and send it by Mr. Poole, but having another opportunity to send one by old A. P. King[38] who has been discharged from service on account of feeble health, I will write you a short letter. I am now enjoying excellent health—never felt heartier in all my life. The health of our company is only tolerable. Smith Scogin is the only bad case we have. He has pneumonia very bad; all the Lebanon boys are in good health. Collins is still in Culpepper hospital, and I suppose or at least have heard is taking the dropsy. I intend going to see him in a few days if I can get off. We expect to be sent into winter quarters in a few days. The weather is very cold. We had a light snow a few nights back which is still lying on the ground in some places. I have an abundance of clothes to last me till spring, and intend to take every precaution to make myself healthy.

We are now encamped in the midst of a large army where we can neither see or hear anything except the roar of the cannon or military preparations. We cannot buy anything at price so we live on the rations drawn from the com[m]issary which is very good, plenty of fat beef, and enough bacon for about 2 days in every week—we also draw a small ration of sugar & coffee enough for to make a cupful per day to each man. As for breadstuffs we have more than we use a portion of which is cornmeal. We marched out on review yesterday where I saw (for the first time) the whole La. brigade together. It was quite a brilliant scene. On every side as far as the eye coul[d] view might be seen the glistening bayonets of troops and the flying colors of each regimental flag as they marched some to and some from the grand review. But the most exquisite part of all was the commingled sound of about thirty excellent brass bands as they echoed from hilltop to hilltop. It seemed indeed as if it was a world of music. I saw General Smith[39] who looks as plain as some old farmer, but his keen eye and flashing

38. Sixty-one-year-old A. P. King of Salt Springs was appointed sergeant major of the Ninth Louisiana at Camp Moore but was discharged "for disability" at Centerville, Virginia, on November 15, 1861 (Booth, comp., *Records,* Vol. III, Pt. 1, p. 565).

39. Edmund Kirby Smith contributed materially to the South's success at the first battle of Manassas, where he was wounded. Following his recovery, he was assigned to duty in the West, where he led a small army to victory at the battle of Richmond, Kentucky, in August, 1862. In October, 1862, he was

countenance told of the sparkling intellect which lay hidden within. We received a telegraphic dispatch here this morning that Gen. Bragg[40] had succeeded in taking Fort Pickens.[41] I hope it may prove true and that many other victories of the same kind may follow till Old Abe and all his cabinet become convinced that a supreme being is sending a just punishment upon them for their wickedness in waging war upon an unoffending country who plead for justice and right. I am ever proud to receive the compliments of the young ladies and therefore must request that you give my best regards to all the ladies of our peaceful village, and especially to Miss Belle from whom I have received many tokens of true friendship. She is one of those who seldom forgets an old friend. Tell her Peter[42] is well and merry as a lark in spring. Give my respects to all old friends. Receive the same yourself and family. Give my love to Mr. & Mrs. Randle. Tell Mrs. R that nothing could have renewed in my mind the happy days spent while boarding with her so quick[ly] as the delicious bottle of wine which she sent me. It was indeed a treat. I must also return my thanks to a loved Father for the quart of old bourbon. It was the best spirits I have met with since I left home. Excuse all amiss and pardon any blunder and attribute it to haste.
I remain your affectionate Son
R. A. Pierson

---

promoted to lieutenant general and given command of the Trans-Mississippi Department. See Joseph Howard Parks, *General Edmund Kirby Smith, C.S.A.* (1954; rpr. Baton Rouge, 1992).

40. Braxton Bragg was assigned to the command of the region between Mobile and Pensacola, then to command of the Second Corps of Albert Sidney Johnston's Army of Tennessee and, in mid-1862, to command of the army. After the indecisive battles of Perryville and Murfreesboro, the costly and fruitless victory at Chickamauga, and the disastrous defeat at Chattanooga, Bragg was relieved of command. See Grady McWhiney, *Braxton Bragg and Confederate Defeat,* Vol. I (2 vols.; New York, 1969); Judith Lee Hallock, *Braxton Bragg and Confederate Defeat,* Vol. II (2 vols.; Tuscaloosa, 1991).

41. This, too, was a false report. When Florida seceded on January 10, 1861, the Federal garrison in and around Pensacola, Florida, withdrew to Fort Pickens in Pensacola Harbor, outside the range of Rebel guns. By mid-April 1861, Union reinforcements had made the fort invulnerable to Confederate attack, and blockading Federal warships rendered the port useless to the South. Accordingly, Bragg evacuated the city on May 9, 1862.

42. William H. Pierson purchased Peter, "a man of dark complexion, age about twenty years . . . sound of body and mind and a slave for life except in the infirmities of old age" from Hodge Raburn on September 24, 1860. See Deed Book F, Folio 563, Bienville Parish Records, copy in Pierson Family Papers, Cammie G. Henry Research Center, Eugene P. Watson Library, Northwestern State University of Louisiana.

➤ ⬅

REUBEN ALLEN PIERSON TO WILLIAM H. PIERSON

Camp Florida, Va.
Decr. 3rd, 1861

W. H. Pierson, Esqr.

Dear Father

I received your late favor sent by Dr. Egan last night and was exceedingly glad to hear from you and the family. My health is still good and I think with proper care I may come out through the remainder of our time without a single day[']s sickness. I am acting as orderly (our first sergeant being absent at Richmond sick). This excuses me from guard duty.

There is nothing of importance going on here now—now and then a little skirmish between the pickets. We have not been sent into winter quarters yet though we have been expecting an order to that effect for more than a month. We will go out on picket duty in a few days which will be my first trip. The Regt. has only been once and that was while I was sick. When I return I will give you the particulars of the tour. The weather is exceedingly cold to us up here—water freezes in a few moments after it is brought from the spring and the wind is blowing continually. You wrote to me to state in my next letter whether I had received my bundle of goods or not. I have received them all and also the $25.00 sent by Mr. Candler. I have as many clothing as could do me any service through winter. I have a splendid overcoat which cost me in a trading way ($5.75) five dollars and six bits. I have as much money as I want and will have more than I started with when we draw. The government will soon be indebted to us for four months, which will amount to over sixty dollars.

The general health of the regiment is still bad. Several have died in the last few weeks and others are now quite sick. Smith Scogin is at Manassas very low, and John Evans,[43] son of Hiram Evans was very sick at Richmond when I heard from there last. Collins is still at Culpepper Court House in bad health, but able to walk over town. I fear his health is permanently injured. The Key boys[44] are complaining with cold though nothing serious. George Whitley[45] is also a

43. John T. Evans of Sparta was sixteen when he joined the Ninth Louisiana on July 7, 1861. He was wounded at the second battle of Manassas, sent home on convalescent furlough, and was again slightly wounded at the battle of Spotsylvania (Booth, comp., *Records*, II, 792).

44. According to Booth, Henry Clay Key died at Camp Bienville on October 3, 1861. His brother, Joshua W. Key, was discharged on January 17, 1862. Both were Mount Lebanon residents (*ibid.,* Vol. III, Pt. 1, p. 554).

45. George W. Whitley was reported missing in action and presumably killed at Rappahannock Station on November 7, 1863 (*ibid.,* Pt. 2, p. 1072).

little unwell. Tom Pittman, Horace Rhodes, Lamar, Charles Prothro, Aaron Wells, Frank Harrison, the Colbert boys and Prentiss Jackson[46] are all as full of life and merriment as a drove of young mules. In fact all our company are in an improving way with but few exceptions. There is much rejoicing in camps on account of the return of our Surgeon. Most of the boys seem to think their lives are dependent on him. They flock around him as thick as bees flock to their king. Tell Jim I received his letter sent by Egan and will answer it in a few days. Tell Aunt Nan & Joe they must write to me in cahoots. I would like to hear from them. Give my love to all old friends especially Mr. Randle[']s family who seem like relatives when I think of the kind treatment shown me while boarding there. Excuse all amiss and attribute it to haste. I send this by Uncle Robert Burnett who leaves here this evening. Receive the warmest affections (yourself and all the family) of a dutiful Son.
R. A. Pierson

⇒ ⇐

REUBEN ALLEN PIERSON TO WILLIAM H. PIERSON
At Camp near Manassas, Va.
Decr. 22nd, 1861

Mr. W. H. Pierson
Dear Father
    I received yours dated the 11th Inst. in nine days and have neglected to write till now on account of my having written a letter to Jim the day I received yours. We are in our position for the winter and quite busily engaged in building huts to shield us from the severity of this climate. We have had a fine fall; the weather has been more favorable than any of us ever anticipated. It seems that the God who rules the seasons, as well as the destinies of nations has seen fit to smile upon us and protect us from the many diseases to which we are subject in exchanging our mild southern clime for the mountainous region of the Old Dominion. It is true that we have suffered considerable by colds contracted from ly-

46. John C. Lamar was a resident of El Dorado, Arkansas, at the time of his enlistment in Company C. He was wounded at Sharpsburg, captured at Rappahannock Station on November 7, 1863, and again at Fisher's Hill on September 22, 1864. Aaron B. Wells was mortally wounded at the battle of Chancellorsville, dying on June 19, 1863. Benjamin Franklin Harrison of Mount Lebanon was a private in Pierson's company until August 20, 1863, when he transferred to the regimental band. He was captured at Fisher's Hill on September 22, 1864, and exchanged after incarceration at Point Lookout on February 14, 1865. The brothers of Richard Colbert (n. 34, above), William B. and John R. Colbert, were residents of Mount Lebanon. John was discharged owing to ill health on August 23, 1861. William was promoted to second lieutenant on September 18, 1862. He was captured at Monocacy, Maryland on July 10, 1864, and remained imprisoned at Fort Delaware until the war's end (*ibid.,* Pt. 1, p. 627, Pt. 2, p. 1034, Pt. 1, pp. 205–206, Vol. I, 375).

ing upon the cold damp ground under a tent made of cloth, through which the piercing winds could easily pass. I am still in fine health. Whenever I feel the least symptoms of sickness I resort to the old remedy (Moffats Pills) which restores me to health and prevents disease. I have but little news to write. Frank Long died at Richmond a few days ago. The health of our company is still bad. There are 13 privates and two noncommissioned officers back at hospitals, and 12 privates reported sick in camp this morning with one noncommissioned officer, making the total sick in our company 28 while we only have 39 men for duty in camps. We have 7 men on extra or daily duty and two on detached service, also four noncommissioned officers in camp for duty making a total of 80 men not including [the] commissioned officers. Notwithstanding all this sick[ness, optimism] prevails, having lost three men in less than one month, still some say the health is tolerable good. I only make this statement that you and all others, who desire may know how things stand with us. Some of this number are staying back at hospitals to shirk out of duty, but very few in our company do this. There was a fight between the federals and our men above here one day this week. I have not learned the full particulars yet though our loss was severe. Times are very dull. Only three days till Christmas and no excitement. Our mess have eggs and sugar enough to make a nog, if we can only procure the spirits to mix with them & we have the promise of getting some. Some of our officers are of opinion that old Abe & his cabinet will have to knock under now as England has demanded Messrs Slidell and Mason,[47] on the passport of Lord Lyons,[48] so that she may obtain her rights and sustain her flag if it costs a war with the boasted fanatics who pretend to be contending for a great national union. Time can only unravel the hidden mysteries of the future and by waiting we will all see what is next. We received a letter from our Capt a few days since in which he said he would return in the spring or rather in January. He sent many compliments to the boys. Most of us are proud that he will return for we fare better when he is here on account of his influence with the other officers. Some few are down on him but still any man who commands a company will have enemies. I

47. On November 8, 1861, James M. Mason and John Slidell, Confederate diplomats en route from Havana to their posts in London and Paris, were removed from the R. M. S. *Trent* by officers and men of the U.S.S. *San Jacinto.* Only after Queen Victoria's government issued an ultimatum threatening war if the diplomats were not released did the Lincoln administration set Mason and Slidell at liberty. The so-called *Trent* Affair was the United States's closest brush with war with England and the Confederacy's best hope of involving a major foreign power on its behalf (Howard Jones, *Union in Peril: The Crisis over British Intervention in the Civil War* [Chapel Hill, 1993], 80–99).

48. Lord Richard Bickerton Pemmell Lyons, British minister at Washington, was in fact most conciliatory toward the Lincoln government and a warm friend of Secretary of State William Henry Seward. He agreed with his government's position that while it could not allow its flag to be insulted or its mails endangered, the United Kingdom did not believe that the United States intended any insult and was willing to believe that Wilkes had acted contrary to orders or on a misunderstanding of his orders (*ibid.,* 84–113).

cannot blame him for the turn he took to get his seat, that he might free himself from camp during the winter. A great many of our boys are nearly crazy to get furloughs to go home, but I think they will all fail. Both of the Lieuts are anxious to go but the Capt being absent ties them. You wrote to me in a very feeling manner upon the subject of our being separated and in all probability for life yet your earnest desire and prayer seemed to be that I should prepare myself to meet you once more if it was after death. I can only say that I am yet a wayward and reckless being out of the harbor of safety and nearing the verge of eternity. When I reflect upon these solemn and important thoughts my eyes overflow with tears and my heart aches with the burden of grief. I almost wish that I had perished while yet an infant or never had being. It is the earnest wish of my heart that we may all be spared till another summer when we may be allowed to assemble in a family group and there hold converse with one another. You spoke of hiring out my negroes[49] at the 1st of January. Do as you like with them, for I seldom think anything about what disposition would be best to make with them. They are mine and will be till this war panic shall cease. I owe a considerable sum in the stores at Lebanon & Sparta[50] and when I draw pay again I will send you 50 or 60 dollars which you can dispose of as you think proper. Tell my creditors to be easy. I shall not be absent always. The Confederacy is now in debt to us for four months['] service which will amount to some 60 dollars and I have that much owing to me in the company besides a little which I have kept for hard times. Excuse all amiss. Give my regards to all my old friends whom you may see, especially to any of the fair sex as no one esteems women more highly than I. She is the only jewel of earth worth man['s] attention, and she serves as a guiding star to him along the rough journey of life. I am becoming childish which never can please the fancy of a stern man like you. With my most sincere devotion to you and all the family I subscribe myself your affectionate Son though absent.
R. A. Pierson

49. Slave hiring was widespread in the antebellum South, with 6 percent of rural slaves and 32 percent of urban slaves on hire in 1860. The practice enabled masters having surplus hands to hire them out for odd jobs or seasonal work, while individuals with short-term labor needs could fill them relatively inexpensively. Slaves who were hired out were often subject to worse treatment than they would have received at home, because hirers had less direct financial incentive to take care of their laborers than did owners. The transaction did, however, provide slaves with new experiences, contacts, and knowledge (Peter Kolchin, *American Slavery, 1619–1877* [New York, 1993], 74, 109–10).

50. An 1860 traveler referred to Sparta, the seat of Bienville Parish, as "a serious little place" of about 225 or 250 citizens. Its prime attractions were a "small and, as yet, not very successful school, called the Sparta Masonic Female Institute," and a newspaper, the *Jeffersonian*, edited by James R. Head (Walter Prichard, ed., "A Tourist's Description of Louisiana in 1860," *Louisiana Historical Quarterly*, XXI [October, 1938], 1187).

3

WHO WOULD NOT BE A SOLDIER?

REUBEN ALLEN PIERSON TO DAVID PIERSON

Camp Carondelet, Va.
Jan. 10th, 1862

Capt David Pierson
Mt. Lebanon, La.
Dear brother

I received your second epistle from Mt. Lebanon yesterday and was glad to learn that you was enjoying yourself so well. I must confess that I was somewhat surprised to hear that you took a little too much of the overjoyful merely because you was given a party by Mrs. Paxton.[1] However that is more plain when I consider your troubles about the sudden disappearance of a young lady in search of Christmas. You give me quite a severe tongue lashing merely because I sent my regards to a young lady whom you well know that you avowed, you would not see for any sum if you could avoid it; when I last saw you. I assure you that I do not desire to tramp on your toes but if sending my respects to a young lady should press rather hard upon them I beg pardon and will not offer the same unpardon-

1. This is most likely Rebecca Wardlaw Paxton, the second wife of William Edwards Paxton. Paxton practiced law in Bienville Parish from 1854 until 1861, concurrently serving as editor of the Sparta *Jeffersonian* (1859) and the Sparta *Southern Banner* (1860–61), until he was elected captain of Company C, Nineteenth Louisiana Infantry. Leaving the company in 1862, he became assistant enrolling officer for Bienville Parish until the war's end, when he was ordained a Baptist preacher. From 1872 to 1874, he was president of Shreveport University. See W. E. Paxton, *A History of the Baptists of Louisiana from the Earliest Times to the Present* (St. Louis, 1888); *Dictionary of Louisiana Biography*, II, 636. For the memoir of the Paxtons' daughter, see Lucy Paxton Scarborough, "So It Was When Her Life Began: Reminiscences of a Louisiana Girlhood," *Louisiana Historical Quarterly*, XIII (July, 1930), 428–43.

able offense again. I spent a very dull Christmas though not as much so as I had anticipated previous to the day. My mess procured enough of the precious fluids to knock up a little nogg on Christmas eve night and on Christmas morning our kind Lieuts. gave a fine nogg to the whole camp. Some of the boys as you say, to reciprocate got a little tight, and you can easily imagine that we had a very merry time while the effects of King alcohol lasted—a general jabber was kept up for more than an hour, reminding me of a drove of puddle ducks about light of a fine spring morning. I have no war news to write. Everything is quiet. I have been in excellent health ever since I returned to camps and hope I may continue well the remainder of my time. Dr. Egan who was present when I received your last letter requested me to present his regards to you and ask you for him who was that which you spoke of to me, and about who[m] the respects I sent seemed to press upon your toes. You request me not to take my trials hard in performing the office of orderly. On the contrary, I enjoy myself better than I have at any time previous since I have been in camps. I am as well satisfied as I could be in such a rough life, am becoming used to all the hardships and privations of a soldier[']s life, and would sooner receive six feet of Confederate soil as my last inheritance of earth than yield one single iota of our rights. They have forced us to fight or yield obedience to their unjust and exaggerated notion of freedom and Liberty.

You speak in glowing language of Miss Belle—her patriotism and her sympathy for the valorous boys who have fled from all joys of a comfortable home, and come to the field of action, to offer their lives a sacrifice upon the altar of their loved country and who have said by their actions that they prefer an honorable death to a disgraceful subjugation. You must excuse this hastily written and unconnected letter. I am surrounded by noisy boys playing cards all around me and talking at the top of their voice[s]. Give my love to all acquaintances—to the family and especially to Miss C, if you chance to see here before you leave from home. Remember me as an old friend and well wisher to Miss Belle. I am your brother till death. R. A. Pierson

⇒ ⇐

REUBEN ALLEN PIERSON TO JAMES F. PIERSON
Camp Carondelet, Va.
Jan. 24th, 1862

Mr. James F. Pierson
Dear brother

I received your late favor bearing date the 3rd Inst. which was one day earlier than I had received any one previous. I am enjoying fine health which is very common of late days. You complain of a very dull Christmas which is truly somewhat surprising as Dave said he had such a great time. You say that the shirttailed gang had not brass enough to speak to [a girl]; much less gallant a young [lad] you have become[;] very modest all at once—have to get behind a tree or post to look at a woman. I am very glad to hear that your wiry edge is gradually wearing off. I suppose you have felt the bottom of a few slippers which makes you dread the thought of the girls. If the ladies do appreciate the gallantry of the brave boys, who have forsaken their homes, their relatives, their friends, and even denied themselves the pleasure of being present with those fair heroines whose images will be engraven upon the hearts of many brave boys when their locks shall be frosted with old age. Who would not be a soldier? The bright eyes of beauty sparkling with the lights of intelligence and love, speaks in tones sweet enough to buoy the feelings, almost[?] all, who possess the slightest principle of independence and manliness, and cause them to shoulder the instruments of destruction and offer their lives as a sacrifice upon the altar of the count[r]ies['] cause. I often think when alone what an awful scene it would be to see the inhuman fanatics of Lincolndom domineering over those fair creatures whose whole souls and prayers are given, freely in our behalf. The love, respect, and confidence of all true southern patriots should be with us for upon the actions and battles of the Army hangs the destiny [of our nation. I am] proud to hear that father has hired out Lettie[2] at such a good place and much better wages than I could have expected. Write in your next whether sister has taken a school down at old Zach[']s,[3] or not, and tell her not to forget to write. I have a very comfortable house and bed place. I send this by Capt. Capers[4] who leaves here before daylight tomorrow morning for Homer. Tell David I have written two letters to him since I learned he was at home. Well Jim I will give you a short history of our Christmas in camps. On the night before Christmas my mess had a nice little nogg and on the next our kind Lieut gave a nogg to the company which the boys appreciated highly indeed. Some of them got as funny as you please and the whole day was a scene of merriment seldom wit-

2. Lettie was a slave woman belonging to Reuben Allen Pierson.

3. Zachariah Thomas, a brother of David K. Thomas, was born on March 28, 1813, and became a pioneer settler of Bienville Parish and the first pastor of the New Providence Church, where William H. Pierson served as a deacon. He died on May 1, 1879 (Ida G. Tooke, "History of Ringgold and Lake Bistineau," Typescript in Tooke Family Papers, Cammie G. Henry Research Center, Eugene P. Watson Library, Northwestern State University of Louisiana, 3; John Ardis Cawthon, ed., *The Inevitable Guest: Life and Letters of Jemima Darby* [San Antonio, 1965], 88, n. 39).

4. Richard L. Capers was elected captain of Company A, Ninth Louisiana Infantry, when the company was organized at Camp Moore. He was not reelected when the regiment was reorganized in April, 1862, and presumably returned to his business as a merchant in Homer, Louisiana (Andrew B[radford] Booth, comp., *Records of Louisiana Confederate Soldiers and Louisiana Confederate Commands* [3 vols.; New Orleans, 1920], II, 247).

nessed in camps. Some of the Capts furnished a dinner to their boys, but more than half of them paid no attention to the day. Tell Miss Belle that her dolcie Prentiss together with Messrs Candler & Lamar[5] have just finished themselves a neat little shanty in which to spend their winter hours. Give my special regards to Misses Fannie Pittman & Belle Randle together with all others who ask about me. Extend my love to all the family and relatives. The general health of our company is now better than it has been since we arrived in Virginia, only 7 sick in camps. Everything quiet, no excitement about the advance of yankees. Tell David he must try & come down home about the 4th of July as I think we will all get home by that time. All the boys send their respects to you and say they are glad to see your letters and read them.

I am your absent brother

R. A. Pierson

⇒ ⇐

REUBEN ALLEN PIERSON TO MARY CATHERINE PIERSON

Camp Carondelet, Va.

Jany the 18th, 1862

Miss M. C. Pierson

Dear Sister

Having a chance to send you a letter by Josh. Key who is discharged from the company on account of bad health I hasten to perform what I believe to be my duty. Here I am sitting on a stool by a warm fire writing to my little Sis. again. All around is a jungled mass of camp furniture such as straw beds and boxes, knap sacks, haversacks, canteens, and cartridge boxes all thrown together in confusion for the want of some fancy fair belle to arrange them in suitable order. I never will be a bachelor; too much distaste has been formed for cooking and washing for me to condescend to settle alone out in this world, without

---

5. Three Candlers from Mount Lebanon served in Company C. Patrick H. Candler was the company's first sergeant. He apparently transferred to a cavalry command on September 1, 1864, and was captured at Paw Paw, West Virginia, in February, 1865. Francis M. Candler joined the company on March 8, 1862, was captured at Rappahannock Station, and was imprisoned at Point Lookout until exchanged on May 15, 1864. Thereafter, he served until the war's end, surrendering with his company at Appomattox. John William Candler also enlisted on March 8, 1862, and was also captured at Rappahannock Station. He was exchanged from Point Lookout on March 10, 1864, only to be recaptured at Spotsylvania and returned to Point Lookout on May 12, 1864. John C. Lamar of El Dorado, Arkansas, was wounded at Sharpsburg, captured at the battle of Rappahannock Station in 1863, and captured again at Fisher's Hill in 1864 (*ibid.,* 240, Vol. III, Pt. 1, p. 627).

one in whom I can confide all my secret meditations. I am willing to serve in defense of my southern home till every yankee who wages war against our institutions shall lie in gore upon the battle field, and then I will go in search; of what do you reckon? of honor, No, of riches, no, of some true and intelligent southern lady with whom to share the remaining portion of my days on this gloomy and uncertain sphere.

Enough of my conflab about future expectations. I may be laid beneath cold sod before I ever enjoy the priviledge of conversing with another young lady in old Louisiana. It is too serious a subject for meditation. I must write on something of a livlier turn. The boys all have a fine time telling stories about their old courting scrapes, how they cut out their rivals and also how they were slighted by one whom they dearly loved.

Well Cassie I don't know where you are practicing your profession this year, but reckon from what Jim wrote that you will hold forth near Old parson Zachariah's. If you do you must give my love to all my old friends. Tell them, though I am a soldier far away in old Virginia, memory sometimes wanders back to the dear hours of youth when I like a bird just lo[o]sed from a cage, roamed over the land and passed away hours as fleet as electricity conveys news from one point to another. I sometimes think when alone that if I was given whatever I desired on earth, I would be a youth just verging into manhood all the days of my life. Cassie as you have a much better opportunity to write than I can possibly have I do not think it unreasonable for me to ask that you will write as often as once every two weeks without failure. Remember this. Tell Miss Belle that I am well and in fine spirits. Prentiss is also in good health and as sober as a Judge. He makes an excellent soldier and always smiles pleasantly when asked anything about himself & Miss Belle. He likes to talk of the happy hours spent while attending school at the Mt. The boys are in tolerable health. Most of them are exceedingly merry. Excuse all amiss and attribute it to haste. It is growing late and I must close by saying Remember me kindly to all old friends & schoolmates, particularly the girls if you are teaching at Old Zach's. Give my love to all the family. Tell the old parson to remember me in his petitions to the divine being who reigns monarch over all the earth. Receive the affections of an absent friend and affectionate brother.
R. A. Pierson

P.S. I will try to send you a few little branches of Box Wood which will make the most beautiful bush in a yard that you ever saw. It will live from the limbs by inserting into the ground. I will go in search of them tomorrow before Josh leaves.
Yours R. A. P.

≫ ≪

REUBEN ALLEN PIERSON TO WILLIAM H. PIERSON
Camp Carondelet, Va.
Jan 31st, 1862

Mr. W. H. Pierson

Dear father

I have not received a single word from home in about one month, which is about the longest time since I left home. I am in excellent health and doing very well. You have received the letters which I sent by Joshua Key, and I hope the money has reached you safe[ly] (twenty five dollars) a Confederate twenty and La. five. I will send you as much or more by the next opportunity. The general health of our company is better now than it has ever been since we arrived in old Virginia, only five on the sick list and they are all on foot—all our boys are now in camp except three, McCoy,[6] John Pace[7] and a man by the name of Greer[8] who joined us at Camp Moore.

There is a report in camps that we will soon be ordered to Kentucky, but I have little or no faith in its truth. The weather has been very bad all through the present month—it has snowed three times and turned warm quite as often rendering the ground so muddy and slop[p]y till one could scarce get out without being halfleg deep in mud.

We are looking daily for our Capt and I expect he is now on his way to this place, the Legislature having adjourned on the twenty fourth Inst. and he had been refused an extension of furlough to go by home. We will look for him daily till he arrives. We have no excitement on account of an expected advance from our enemies. On the contrary the opinions of all our field officers concur in the belief that there will never be another general engagement at this point. All think that the western states will be the theatre of the next active operations.

We are in a very scarce land of provisions. Pork is worth from twenty to twenty five cents. Lard is not to be had only in very small quantities at three bits per pound. Butter is worth 50 & 60 cents, eggs 40 to 50 cents per dozen. Bacon cannot be had at any price. Notwithstanding these extraordinary high prices we are all faring very well. We draw plenty of flour, a little corn meal oc-

6. William Case McCoy, a farmer from Sparta, Louisiana, deserted the regiment in 1863 (*ibid.,* Vol. III, Pt. 1, p. 1160).

7. John W.H.H. Pace was discharged from Company C on April 18, 1862, "on a Surgeon's certificate" because of chronic illness (*ibid.,* Pt. 2, p. 56).

8. William A. Greer of Haynesville, a student when he enlisted in the Ninth Louisiana, was discharged because of chronic illness in 1862 (*ibid.,* Pt. 1, p. 98).

casionally, plenty of pickled beef and [a]bout one day[']s ration of bacon or pork every week. We get plenty of rice, a small quantity of coffee & sugar, enough soap to do our washing, one candle to about five men twice each week. This consists of our general bill of fare. As I wrote to Dave concerning his intention with regard to reenlisting after his present term of service ends, and whether he would like to go as a cavalryman the next tour, and having received no answer from him since that time, I would be glad to hear through you what his intentions are and whether he expects to remain in the field another campaign or not. I have determined to go again next fall or the spring following if the war goes on. I am but an individual, have no family or relatives that would suffer for bread should my life be sacrificed in the struggle.

The young men who have not ambition and moral courage to fight for the preservation of that rich legacy bequeathed to them—and purchased for them by the blood of their ancestors will be scoffed at and looked upon as base cowards unworthy [of] the name of southern man and unfit for the enjoyment of our glorious institution. The day is now dawning and will soon open bright and clear as a May morning, when we will be acknowledged as one of the best governments that holds a place in the catalogue of the nations of the earth. Let the unholy and base legions of Lincolndom pour forth their fury and rage in all its power—we will meet them [in the field and] we will defeat them or perish upon the soil of our loved and cherished southern republic. This is what southern men have vowed by their acts and not by words. Let us die a soldier[']s death or live a freeman[']s life.

I fear that I have already wor[r]ied your patience by indulging in such a train of thought; However I hope you will pardon the digression from my usual mode of writing. Excuse all amiss. Extend my love to all those who enquire about me, particularly the fair sex who appear to [be the] soldier[']s only consolation, yes his fancied angel [about] which he is ever dreaming. With my warm [wishes] to a father, mother, brothers & sister, I am your son as ever

R. A. Pierson

P.S. Write oftener or make Jim and Cassie write. I would like to hear from home once a week.
R. A. P.

⇒ ⇐

REUBEN ALLEN PIERSON TO JAMES F. PIERSON

Camp Carondelet, Va.
Feb. 2nd, 1862

Mr. James F. Pierson
Dear brother

I have another opportunity of sending a letter by George Brown,[9] who leaves camp tomorrow being discharged on account of "chronic diarrhea." He has suffered a great deal and is still in very low health. I received a letter from Green Hartsfield yesterday of the 21st Ult. being the only one I have got[ten] from Lebanon since the 1st of last month. You are certainly all very busily engaged in farming or some other occupation, which prevents you all from writing. The health of our company is very good, only six on the sick list and they are all on foot, nothing but cold ails them. As usual I am in fine health. All of our boys have returned from the hospitals except three viz[.]: Case McCoy, John Pace, and a man by the name of Greer who joined at Camp Moore. I am now as well satisfied as I could ever have anticipated before I commenced soldiering. I believe that I could enjoy as good health here in camp as I could at home. The boys are just getting climatized and [accustomed] to camp life and their time of service will soon expire and then their places will have to be filled by those who are as unfit for the service as the most ignorant pauper is to fill the President[']s chair. Notwithstanding the duties of camp are very irksome and takes men of the most energetic and ambitious stump to fill them. I believe that nearly all of the timid and histerical boys, who cannot scarcely live for the thoughts of mama, and home have been discharged or died and more than half of those who now constitute the "Blues" will not remain at home but a few days when they return.

The thoughts of the loved ones at home—of those dear rights which are precious enough to cause every true southerner to risk his all, even life itself, in their defense. I am at a loss to account for the actions of those young men who turn a deaf ear to the call of their bleeding country—who remain at home while it is plain to any sane being that duty, honor and every principle of humanity or love of country is beckoning them to assist in defending their homes from the depredations of our northern enemies. What respect can they expect to receive from a society which they vow they will not defend, by their acts? Even the ladies, like the heroin[e]s of Sparta, throw down the piano, the Melodian, the paint brush, and every article of refinement and use the needle, the distaff[?],

---

9. George W. Brown of Sailor, Louisiana, was discharged on February 2, 1862, on a surgeon's certificate of disability. He died soon after reaching his home (*ibid.,* II, 145).

the wheel, and the loom to aid in establishing our independence and crushing down the former dependence of trade between us and our inveterate enemies.

Our Capt arrived in camp this morning, looks exceedingly well, and has many agreeable stories to relate to the boys. He brings no letters or news from Bienville not having been home since Christmas. All the boys are extremely glad to see him and I would not be surprised if some of them come home in a few days on furlough. I have nothing of importance to write. Everything is distressingly quiet, not even flying rumor of any hostility between the two armies. Well Jim I dislike to be inquisitive and hope you will pardon me for asking how you are thriving in your religious faith. I am aware that it is a very serious subject & one which demands the foremost place in every mind. It is of more importance than all earthly considerations. My thoughts often wander over the immortality of the mind, and then back to my own depraved and sinful self till my eyes are flooded with tears and my heart burthened with grief. I am only a wayward sinful being and have no power to extricate myself from such a condition.

> This world's a fleeting shore for man[']s delusion given
> There is nothing sure no nothing, but heaven.

I leave this solemn theme as I always have whenever I meditated upon it, lost in the mysteries of deep thought. Excuse all errors, pardon the scattering manner of my expressions &c. Give my love to friends and relations whom you chance to meet while I remain your Brother
R. A. Pierson

P.S. I shall write two or three letters every week till you all get to writing oftener—tell sister I am sorry she is so pressed with duties, or her mind so engrossed with the beauty of some young lad, that she can seldom find time to write. I hope she will not forget an absent brother in so short a time. Yours
R. A. P.

⇒ ⇐

REUBEN ALLEN PIERSON TO JAMES F. PIERSON
Camp Carondelet, Va.
Feb. 4th 2 oclock 1862

Mr. James F. Pierson
Dear brother

I have just received yours of the 25th Ult. and as George Brown leaves in a few minutes I hasten to respond. Our Capt arrived in camp last Sunday morning. He is in fine health—all the boys are well and in fine spirits only th[re]e or four complaining and they are able to be out today. We had a heavy snow last Sunday which is now melting. It was about six inches deep on the ground. The ground is still covered, but melting fast today. I as usual am in fine health. All the Lebanon boys are getting very fat and look better than they ever did at home. I have no news of a war nature—everything quiet and still. We are quartered near Manassas about one mile and a half east. We have not drawn our pay for Nov. & Dec. yet but are expecting to be paid off in a few days. Tell sister not to be backward in taking her school. She will be much better satisfied while busily engaged than in idleness. If she needs any assistance in the summer I will try and act as a junior teacher for a few weeks. Monroe Thomas sends his love to the family. He is in fine health. Phillip Collins has recovered from his weaknes[s]. Yours in haste. Brown is leaving.

R. A. Pierson

⇒ ⇐

DAVID PIERSON TO WILLIAM H. PIERSON?

Boston Mountains, Ark.
Feby. 22, 1861 [1862]

I sit myself down on the ground, wet and cold, to write you. I should have written you oftener on my way up, but after I got [to] Little Rock I was in a very great hurry to reach the army, traveling almost night & day, having heard of a prospect of a fight ahead. When I got to the Regt. I found that it had left winter quarters & was on its retreat from a powerful Northern force, and camped at night in a narrow hollow without tents or any other baggage & without provisions. For six days since we have been retreating southward rapidly with the roughest, coldest weather I have ever seen. Almost every night we have been without our baggage, and the rain has fallen incessantly. Our winter quarters have been laid in ashes by our own hands, & much of our camp property was destroyed therewith. The beautiful town of Fayetteville shared the same fate three days ago, & as we marched away from it the smoke and flame of its burning houses rose like a cloud in the heavens. It was the most horrible sight I ever witnessed. Our whole retreat thus far has been one of continued horror & suffering. The retreat had commenced before I arrived and has continued ever since. About two weeks ago the enemy made a rapid movement upon Price at Springfield who commenced a retreat & running fight. Our forces joined him above our quarters and our whole force fell back & is still falling back. There has been some heavy skirmishing, but our Regt has not been engaged at all. Yesterday and today we have marched in the rear of the army, expecting an attack constantly, night and day. We are now near the top of Boston Mountain where it is believed a stand will be made, but this is not known except by the Gens. themselves. The enemy is reported from 40 to 50,000 strong. Gen. Price has about 5,000 & McCulloch has about 10,000 men. For want of transportation we burned large quantities of provisions & military stores in Fayetteville. Every mill that we have passed has been burned & all public buildings. I cannot portray the suffering nor divine the consequences of this retreat. For three days we have been without bread & have subsisted on boiled meat, raw turnips, and parched corn. Half the men here have lost all their clothes. My trunk & things are safe, but I have not seen them for several days, the trains being ahead. The first nights I stayed with the company I slept on the ground without even a blanket & and afterwards fasted for two days, marching all the while. You must excuse this letter. I mostly give you notes. It would require volumes to tell you all. This half sheet is all the paper I have, & it is borrowed. We will undoubtably have a desperate fight in a few days. Our men are chaffing for it, and the universal sentiment is, let them come, no matter how many. The troops have confidence in McCulloch and shout like wild men when he passes along our line. His reception by the boys a few days ago was most inspiring. Look out for a big fight soon & have no fears as to the result.

My health & that of my company is most excellent. Yours, & c.

D. Pierson

[LETTER FRAGMENT]

[March, 1862]

... they would have retreated on the night of the 8th or had we remained on the field two hours longer on the morning of the 8th they would have left. It is said Gen. Van Dorn[10] will assign as a cause of the defeat the cowardice of McCulloch's men after the Gen's death, but never did a little band (for few were engaged) fight more desperately than they. Gen. Raines of Mo. was put under arrest the next day after the battle for saying that nobody was whipped but Van Dorn.

10. Earl Van Dorn was first appointed commander of the District of Texas and then to command of the Trans-Mississippi Department. His first campaign ended in defeat at Pea Ridge, after which he was recalled to Mississippi to reinforce Albert Sidney Johnston's Army of Tennessee. He arrived too late to take part in the battle of Shiloh, and from June 27 until September 25, 1862, he was commander of the Vicksburg garrison. Van Dorn was severely criticized for his leadership in the disastrous Confederate defeat at Corinth and never again held army command. See Robert G. Hartje, *Van Dorn: The Life and Times of a Confederate General* (Nashville, 1967).

It is generally known that Gen. McCulloch totally dessented from the plans of Van Dorn in surrounding the enemy and that Price concurred. Our troops were in a bad condition to fight, having marched a long distance without rest or sleep & being half starved when the action commenced. This McCulloch saw and frequently spoke of to his officers. Gen. Van Dorn is very unpopular with the whole army. We all feel that our best friends & the champions of the West fell in the persons of McCulloch and McIntosh. There is talk of our being sent still farther south & evacuating this place, but I cannot believe it. The Northern army will be compelled very soon to advance or go back on account of subsistence which they cannot get where they are. I neglected to say that my company lost in the battle 2 killed & one taken prisoner—other companies suffered more. I escaped unhurt. I will write you again & perhaps say more. My health is good.

Yours & c
D. Pierson

⇒ ⇐

DAVID PIERSON TO WILLIAM H. PIERSON

Camp Near Little Rock, Ark.
Apr 17th, 1862

Wm H. Pierson
  Mt. Lebanon
    La.

Dear Pa,

Having a moment's idle time, I write you from this point. I wrote you several days ago, but have not had the opportunity to mail it till now, hence the two together. When we left Fort Smith it was contemplated that we would make our way the overland route to Desarc, but in consequence of heavy rains and the almost impassable condition of the roads this brigade under command of Col. Hébert has turned in the direction of Little Rock and is now within two miles of that place waiting for the cars to take us to Duvall's Bluff on White River.

For three days past & up to daylight this morning it has rained constantly, making the roads so bad that it has been with difficulty we could travel. A great many of our supply wagons have broken or bogged down so we have been deprived of tents or blankets at night. Such was the case with my company last night, and then fell the hardest rain I ever saw, perfectly flooding the ground with water. We stood up all night like a passel of geese and only got dry when the sun began to shine, about 10 o'clock in the forenoon. Our Regt. will perhaps take the cars tomorrow for White River where it is thought we will be placed on board steam boats & carried to Memphis, Tenn. It is known that a portion of Van Dorn's command has already gone to Memphis.

We are all very much elated with the prospect of getting into the big fight in the Miss. Valley. Our Regt. has pretty well plaid out. A great many of the officers have got sick leaves & gone off to recruit up. I am now the 2 in rank in the Regt. and today am in command in consequence of the absence of Capt. [John S.] Gardner.

When we get to White River I will let you hear from me again. My health is good—indeed better than it ever was at home. I lay on the wet ground with wet clothes on & yet have not taken the least cold.

Yours truly,
D. Pierson

[The following letter is from Thomas Augustus Tooke of Company C, Ninth Louisiana Infantry. "Gus" Tooke of Mount Lebanon was promoted to corporal of Company C on October 6, 1861, and then to sergeant. He was wounded at Gettysburg on July 2, 1863, and was hospitalized in Charlottesville and then furloughed home. Because of his injuries he never rejoined his unit. Although the salutation is "Dear Cousin," a handwritten note from Mildred Tooke Bell identifies it as being "from Papa to Mama in the war." "Mama" would have been Tooke's first wife, Sallie W. Price.[11]]

Camp—Virginia
April 26th, 1862

Dear Cousin

I will try & write you a few lines & I would have written long before this, but we have been marchen ever since we got to the Regt. I stayed in Richmon[d] just a week. I out traveled the company & wated untill they cout up. I had a fine time on the Road, & enjoyed the trip finely. But if we haven[']t cought it since we have been in camp, I would not say so. We got in to camp the night of the Sixteenth, & found the boy[s] without tents & or anything to cook in & but little to eat. We started to marchen in two day[s] after we got in, & Marched sixteen miles the first day & it Rained all day on us, & the next day we started by sun up or time for the sun to be up if it had not been raining, & we marched ten miles by twelve, & stopped untill the next morning & then came to Gordonsville ten miles farther & there resten 36 hours in the rain & mud all the time & and then left there and marched 9 miles out on the Stanton [Staunton?] Road, intenden to reenforce Jackson[12] but finden out that he did not nead us,

11. Booth, comp., *Records*, Vol. III, Pt. 2, p. 848; *Biographical and Historical Memoirs of Northwest Louisiana*, (Nashville, 1890), 205–06. The original letter is located in the Cammie G. Henry Research Center, Eugene P. Watson Memorial Library, Northwestern State University of Louisiana.

12. Thomas Jonathan Jackson, Robert E. Lee's most celebrated lieutenant, distinguished himself at the first battle of Manassas, where he won his famous sobriquet, "Stonewall." Jackson was promoted to

we come to a halt, & slept all night in a open feild without a tent & it a snowing all the time & it was the largest drops of snow that I ever saw & yesterday eavning we marched one mile & are now camped at this place. We have got fliers (or rather tents with both ends open[e]d) to sleep in, But we have but little to eat. I thought that I knowed something a bout Soldiering, but I find that I had never Soldiered it this way, marching from ten to sixteen miles threw the rain & having to toat [tote] all of my baggage is no good way but for all, I & Blake[13] have stood it finely. We both have got a bad cold from having to sleep on the weet ground, But I think that I can stand as much as eny other man, or at least I hope so, for I tell you we are agoing to catch it, such as hard marchen & hard living.

But for all that I would be purfectly sadisfied if we onely had some Officers to lead us. This you must not say enything about, for we have to make the best of a bad bargin that we can—

We had an election of company Officers the next day after we got to camp & in spite of all I could do the Recruits elected Al Pierson capten & and I know that he is as big a fool as there is in the company & when he was elected I had nothing to say in the election. John Theus & Jim Egan & Ardis come out like men & sayed that they would not have an office in the company. The boys then elected Sam Robason[14] 1 Leut & he is a plum clever fellow, but he is no drill officer.

Ed Arbuckle is 2nd.[15] Bill Colburt is third & I think that it will give him the big head, but you must not tell Mat so. Pat Candler is Orderlay Sergeant, Mon-

---

major general on October 7, 1861, and assigned to an independent command in the Shenandoah Valley. There, from early March through early June, 1862, he conducted his famed Valley campaign. Jackson then marched to Lee's assistance in time to participate in the Seven Days' Battles, Second Manassas, and Sharpsburg. When Lee reorganized the Army of Northern Virginia on October 10, Jackson was promoted to lieutenant general and given command of the II Corps, which he led at the battle of Fredericksburg the following December. Jackson's finest hour came on May 2, 1863, at the battle of Chancellorsville. There he marched his corps around Major General Joseph Hooker's right flank, delivering a smashing blow to the rear of the unsuspecting Union XI Corps. Reconnoitering in the gathering darkness, Jackson was accidentally shot by his own men and died eight days later. See James I. Robertson, Jr., *Stonewall Jackson: The Man, the Soldier, the Legend* (New York, 1997).

13. E. Blake Tooke, who enlisted as a private in Company C, was elected fifth sergeant when the army was reorganized in spring, 1862. He was killed in action at Winchester on June 14, 1863 (Booth, comp., *Records,* Vol. III, Pt. 2, p. 848; *Biographical and Historical Memoirs of Northwest Louisiana,* 205–206).

14. Samuel T. Robinson of Mount Lebanon was appointed second sergeant of Company C on December 21, 1861. Five months after his election as first lieutenant, he was killed in action at Sharpsburg on September 17, 1862 (Booth, comp., *Records,* Vol. III, Pt. 2, p. 358).

15. Edward Arbuckle was elected fourth sergeant of Company C when the Ninth Louisiana was organized at Camp Moore. After the death of Samuel T. Robinson at Sharpsburg, he was promoted to first lieutenant on September 18, 1862. He was captured at Strasburg, Virginia, on September 22, 1864 and held at Fort Delaware until exchanged. Although he overstayed his furlough, he was back with his regiment in time to be wounded at Spotsylvania (*ibid.,* I, 71).

row Thomas[16] 2nd, & I am 3rd & I cant see how come theyn to elect me, for I had nothing to say. Ed Steavens[17] is 4th and Blake is 5th. Tom Corthan[18] is first Corporal, John Graham[19] 2nd, Tom Tarkington 3rd, Ambrus Walker[20] 4th. And now dont you think that we have got a fine set of officers (over the left)—

April 28th, 1862

As we had to march befor[e] I could finish this letter I will now try & finish it this morning, as we have two hours befor we start to march again. We left the camp yesterday at sun up & marched all day, & have got (13) miles farther to March to day, befor[e] we reach Jackson's Army, who we are going to reenforce. We are now in the mountains, but cant say where we are. We have got so [*illegible*] green Regt to go in to a fight. Col. Randolph has quit us and Col. Walker has quit also & Roger Kavanaugh[21] & his company has been taken pris[o]ners on the way hear, & Capt. Stafford[22] is Col. & Capt. Peck[23] is Leut Col & Capt Williams[24] is Mager—

16. This is James Monroe Thomas of Sparta (see Chap. 2, n. 33).

17. This is Edward L. Stephens (see Chap. 2, n. 2).

18. This is Thomas J. Cawthon (see Chap. 1, n. 20).

19. John Graham of Ringgold enlisted on September 4, 1861, at Camp Bienville, Virginia. He was killed in action at Monocacy, Maryland, July 9, 1864 (Booth, comp., *Records,* Vol. III, Pt. 1, p. 75).

20. Ambrose N. Walker of Minden, Louisiana, was wounded at Sharpsburg, captured at Rappahannock Station, and imprisoned at Point Lookout until exchanged on March 10, 1864. Wounded in the hand at Spotsylvania, he was detailed to light duty in Georgia. In 1881, he was ordained as a Baptist minister (Booth, comp., *Records,* Vol. III, Pt. 2, p. 961; Paxton, *History of Louisiana Baptists,* 334).

21. James Roger Kavanaugh was elected captain of Company K, Ninth Louisiana Infantry, at Camp Moore and promoted to major on November 20, 1861. He was captured at Huntsville, Alabama, on April 11, 1862, and held at Camp Chase, Ohio, and Johnson's Island, Ohio, until paroled for exchange on August 27, 1862. He was dropped from the regiment's rolls on April 24, 1862 (Booth, comp., *Records,* Vol. III, Pt. 1, p. 501).

22. Leroy Augustus Stafford began his Civil War service as captain of Company B and was promoted to colonel of the Ninth Louisiana on April 24, 1862. He was wounded at Sharpsburg; captured at Chancellorsville on May 4, 1863; paroled two weeks later from the Old Capitol Prison in Washington; and promoted to brigadier general commanding the Second Louisiana Brigade on October 8, 1863. He was mortally wounded at the battle of the Wilderness, May 5, 1863, and died three days later. His adjutant, Capt. Henry E. Handerson, regarded Stafford as "a man of no special military ability and of no military education, fond of a glass of liquor, though very rarely drinking to excess, fond also of a friendly game of cards, affable and pleasant when unopposed, but violent and somewhat tyrannical when aroused by opposition" (Henry E. Handerson, *Yankee in Gray: The Civil War Memoirs of Henry E. Handerson with a Selection of His Wartime Letters* [Cleveland, 1962], 29).

23. William Raine Peck was elected captain of Company E, Ninth Louisiana Infantry, when the regiment was organized at Camp Moore. He was promoted to lieutenant colonel on April 24, 1862, to colonel on October 8, 1863, and to brigadier general on February 18, 1865.

24. Henry L. N. Williams, the first captain of Company F, was promoted to major of the Ninth Louisiana when the regiment was reorganized in April, 1862. Captured at Chancellorsville on May 4, 1863, he was exchanged in time to take part in the Gettysburg campaign, where he was mortally wounded, and died on July 5, 1863 (Booth, comp., *Records,* Vol. III, Pt. 2, pp. 1095–96).

Blake had a chill & fever night before last & was sent back to the Rear. I dont think that he will be sick much. I think he will be in camp in a few days. I am well, but mighty stiff from such hard marches. Bob & Ben Bell[25] are both a long in the march & are well & stand it finely. Tell Pa the first time you see him that all of our things was burnt & that we have sent all of the things that he brought back with us, back to the Rear, & I cant say whether we will ever see them again or not. All the clothes that I have along, I have on my [back.] Henry Tooke[26] got into camp day before yesterday & is well, and I am trewly thankful for the Goos quiles you sent me. I will have to close, for we will have to march in a short time. Write soon & direct your letters to Richmon[d] Va & they will be sent to the Regt. If you all dont hear from us you may know that I have not had a chance to write for I think of home & you all every day of my life. Give my love to all, & retain a good share of it for your self. I am

as ever T. A. Tooke

⇒ ⇐

REUBEN ALLEN PIERSON TO WILLIAM H. PIERSON
Near Stauntonville, Va.
Apr. 28th, 1862

W. H. Pierson

Dear Father

In great haste I seat myself on the ground to write you a short letter. We have not been still more than 24 hours at one time since we arrived at the Regiment. We are now within one day[']s march of Jackson[']s army and will leave at 9 Oclock this morning for to join him. We will be very apt to have some fighting to do in a few days. A great many of our boys are sick though none dangerous mostly from fatigue of marching. The election is over and I received 60 votes, Ardis 15, Theus 6 for Capt. Sam Robinson is elected 1st Lt, Ed Arbuckle 2nd and Wm Colbert 3rd. Theus & Egan have gone home, and will try to get ap-

25. A Robert Bell of St. Landry Parish enlisted in Company E, Tenth Louisiana Infantry, on July 22, 1861, and was captured near Chambersburg on July 26, 1863. He took the oath of allegiance to the United States and was thereafter listed as a deserter. Benjamin M. Bell, a Mount Lebanon resident, was a private in Company G, Eighth Louisiana Infantry. After serving from June 23, 1861, he was killed in action at the battle of Monocacy, Maryland, on June 9, 1864 (*ibid.,* I, 160, 158).

26. Henry T. Tooke of Ringgold enlisted in Company C, Ninth Louisiana Infantry but was transferred to the regimental band on June 1, 1863. He served throughout the war and surrendered with his regiment at Appomattox (*ibid.,* Vol. III, Pt. 2, p. 848; *Biographical and Historical Memoirs of Northwest Louisiana,* 205–206).

pointments in the militia. I have been in good health all the time notwithstanding the severity of the marches and the inclemency of the weather. Our recruits are learning to drill rapidly and if they could have one month[']s practice they would be well drilled soldiers. I have had no chance to procure a uniform as yet though I accident[al]ly got a sword from Capt Pearce who by the way is very kind to me. All the Thomas crowd[27] are well and doing well. We have an entire set of new field officers.[28] Col. Capt Stafford of Alexandria, Lt. Col Capt Peck of Madison Parish, Major Capt Williams of DeSoto Parish. I have no more time to write. Excuse haste and all amiss. Give my love to all enquiring friends receiving the same to yourself and all the family. I remain your Son

R. A. Pierson

P.S. When you write direct your letters to Richmond, Va.

⇒ ⇐

DAVID PIERSON TO WILLIAM H. PIERSON

[May, 1862]

[William H. Pierson,]

Our Regt. is much depressed at the Conscript Act yet, though we have reorganized & become regulars very few of our old officers were reelected in the reorganization. I had the good fortune to be chosen by my men to lead them again by a

27. Nine men named Thomas served in the Ninth Louisiana Infantry, three of whom were from Company C. G. M. Thomas was a Bienville Parish resident paroled at Shreveport at the war's end. James Bryan Thomas, born August 9, 1831, was declared missing and presumed killed at the battle of Sharpsburg on September 17, 1862. James Monroe Thomas of Sparta was promoted to sergeant at the same time that Pierson was elected captain. In August, 1864, he "deserted to the cavalry" (Booth, comp., *Records,* Vol. III, Pt. 2, pp. 806–11; Cawthon, ed., *Inevitable Guest,* 63, 88, n. 42).

28. With the waning of martial enthusiasm by the end of 1861 and the consequent decline in the number of volunteers, the Confederate government was forced, for the first time in American history, to resort to conscription to keep its armies manned. In April, 1862, the Confederate congress enacted the First Conscription Act, which declared all able-bodied, unmarried white males between the ages of eighteen and thirty-five liable for the draft. One-year volunteers already in the army were enjoined to serve for two additional years but were allowed to return home on a sixty-day furlough and to elect new field and company-grade officers. The furloughs greatly weakened the army just as the spring campaigns were getting under way, and many experienced officers were replaced with candidates who promised the men under their command a less rigorous disciplinary regimen. The Second Conscription Act, passed in September, 1862, and the Third Conscription Act, passed in February, 1864, extended the ages of liability from seventeen to fifty. See Albert Burton Moore, *Conscription and Conflict in the Confederacy* (New York, 1924).

decided majority though not without opposition. So I am now in for the war and have given up all notion of seeing home or attending to my private affairs for a long time. War & continued war is our portion. I should not have remained with my company had they not urged me to do so. I wanted to try some other branch of the service, but could not forsake my men when they wanted me to stay.[29]

Pa, I want you to hire me a stout young negro boy and send him by the first opportunity. Don't be particular about the price. I will send you some money by first opportunity. There will certainly be somebody passing by whom you can send if the Feds don't cut you off. I would prefer the boy was a good cook if such a one could be had, but that will make but little difference.

No battle today as was expected an hour ago—firing ceased—everything quiet now, weather fine, & c. I have had nothing from Henry since he left home. What has become of him? I saw George Williams a day or two ago. He is well. Don't fall out with me for failing to give you a description of the defenses here & of the looks of everything in general, for I assure you I know nothing at all & have seen nothing. Every fellow has to stay in his place here & attend to his own business, & hence I know less than some a hundred miles off. I have seen a few ditches & breastworks & big guns, but nothing to compare, I suppose, with what is really here.

We have plenty of provisions but suffer for vegetables. Coffee has played out at last, but we don't want that much in warm weather. An abundance of sugar is issued & we can make quiet as good a drink as coffee for a hot summer day. I shall go on duty tomorrow if I continue to get stouter. I believe I have written all that would interest you.

Yours Truly,
David Pierson

⇒ ⇐

DAVID PIERSON TO HENRY L. PIERSON

Camp Churchill, Near Corinth, Miss.
May 15th, 1862

H. L. Pierson, Esq.

Dear Brother,

Having an opportunity to send you a letter by hand to Monroe, I drop you a few lines. I have nothing to communicate that would interest you except that I

---

29. As James M. McPherson points out, the process of organizing new regiments, as authorized by the First Conscription Act, was certain to lead to disorganization in the army, "especially since many infantrymen decided to re-enlist in the more glamorous (and safer) cavalry or artillery" (James M. McPherson, *Battle Cry of Freedom* [New York, 1988], 430).

am well. We have been here some time—expecting a fight every day and still no great battle of Corinth. Our Regt. has been on picket 4 days since our arrival and most of that time was in sight or hearing of the enemy, and on the last day got into a heavy skirmish resulting in the wounding of 4 of our men. Heavy skirmishing is going on daily, and the roar of artillery does not astonish or alarm anyone at any moment. We have reorganized pursuant to the Conscript Act—field officers entirely new parties and most old company officers thrown out. I had the good or bad fortune to be reelected and shall stay with my men until the war ends or till Yankeedom puts an end to us. I can't give you any idea of the situation of things here as to the movements of our own or the enemies' forces. Everything is kept too secret & in fact is carried on on too large a scale. Much sickness prevails among the soldiers. I am confident that half of our grand division known as the Army of the West under Price & Van Dorn are unfit for duty. I wrote to Pa to hire & send to me by someone a young stout ne-gro boy at whatever cost it might require, and that I would send him money in a few weeks to defray the expense. I have the money & am merely waiting for some trusty person to go that way to send it home. If he does not get the letter, will you see him and attend to it for me? I suppose there will be persons passing from that part of the country to Corinth.

Nothing more. Write soon.

Yours Truly,

D. Pierson

➯ ⇚

REUBEN ALLEN PIERSON TO WILLIAM H. PIERSON
In Camp on the Shenandoah River
May 17th, 1862

W. H. Pierson

Dear Father

I write to you to let you know that I am in good health and getting on toler-able well. A great many of the boys are on the sick list. We have a small duty list, only about half the company yet, but few of these are to say dangerously ill and they have been sent back to hospitals so there is no dangerous sickness in camp now. There has been two deaths in the company since we arrived in Vir-ginia, viz[.] Perry Humphreys[30] and William Mathews. Humphreys died at a

---

30. Perry Humphries, a seventeen-year-old farmer from Mount Lebanon, died at Camp Bragg on Swift Run Gap, Virginia, on May 9, 1862 (Booth, comp., *Records,* Vol. III, Pt. 2, p. 389).

house near camp and Mathews died at Lynchburg Va. I have hired a negro boy from J. C. Lamar and therefore Hambleton has Peter to himself. He was left at Richmond sick as we came out and after I was elected to the Captaincy I was compelled to have a boy, and made my arrangement accordingly. I have got Joseph Williams[31] as a cook and keep him to look out in the country for provisions so I live very well and assist the boys all I can. I have not heard any news from Dave, only what you wrote by Pittman. We are expecting a fight in a few days. We are now in fifteen miles of the enemy and will advance this evening. I have not received my uniform yet but will in a few days. I sent to Richmond for it. John Williams[32] wrote to Uncle Abe that he would send him twenty Dollars but failed to get the change. He says he will send it by McGouldrick[33] who is coming on in a few days. I am in great haste and therefore hope you will excuse me for brevity. My love to all enquiring friends and the family.

Your Son

R. A. Pierson

Direct your letters to Richmond, Va.

⇒ ⇐

DAVID PIERSON TO WILLIAM H. PIERSON

Corinth, Miss., May 20ᵗʰ, 1862

Wm H. Pierson

   Mt. Lebanon

      La.

       Dear Pa,

Events which have transpired within the last few hours & an opportunity to send a letter by hand induce me to write you again. The army has been drawn out in line of battle for two days past, expecting, I suppose, an attack from the enemy. Yesterday we quit our lines and came into camps, everything being exceedingly quiet. Two hours after we arrived in camp, & before we had rested our tired limbs, we were started with another & far more important order than any

31. Joseph R. Williams went absent without leave on July 24, 1863, near Middletown, Virginia (*ibid.,* 1103).

32. John W. Williams of Bienville Parish was killed in action at the second battle of Manassas, on August 30, 1862. He was the son of Abraham Williams ("Uncle Abe") and a cousin of the Piersons (*ibid.*).

33. Richard H. McGoldrich of Ringgold was a farrier in the Ninth Louisiana. He was captured at Fisher's Hill, Virginia, on September 22, 1864, and imprisoned at Point Lookout until exchanged on February 14, 1865 (*ibid.,* Pt. 1, p. 1198).

one which we had previously received since we came here. It was about sundown last night when our Col. announced to us that we were to take up a line of march today with a view of attacking the enemy. Five days' rations are already prepared, and everything put in readiness this morning for the march. Among the rest, the examination of the sick forms no little item as there [are] always some disposed to get out of their duty & the order is peremptory that every man that is able to march must go into ranks. It is evident to my mind that Beauregard intends abandoning his entrenchments and marching boldly out to the attack of the enemy. What prompts him to this unexpected move, no one perhaps but himself & general officers understands. Some suppose it is a desperate move & the last resort, but I am inclined [to believe] that he does it with a full knowledge of some powerful advantage which is to be gained thereby or to prevent the enemy reinforcing in such numbers as to make his position dangerous.

We hear that Curtis[34] has been ordered to abandon Arks. and report with his whole command immediately to Halleck[35] at this place and that the forces at Nashville are also to be joined to them before this place & that place evacuated. We also hear that the enemy has suffered terribly from sickness, weakening almost to insufficiency their army, which if true accounts for their tardiness in advancing and the reinforcements which they ordered. It seems to be Beauregard's intention then to attack them before these reinforcements can arrive and if he is successful it will give us many advantages. We will start by 2 P.M. today, & no doubt by 10 A.M. tomorrow the action will commence. It may be a desperate struggle in which we will loose many of our bravest men, but all are anxious that the test should come and are tired of lying here in camps or out on the ground in line of battle in such awful suspense as we have been for weeks.

I am very well & will be at the head of my Company to witness & participate in the hardest struggle that has ever been & perhaps ever will be had for the Southern Cause.

Very Truly Yours,
David Pierson

34. Samuel Ryan Curtis was commissioned colonel of the Second Iowa Infantry and was promoted to brigadier general on May 17, 1861. For his victory at Pea Ridge, he was promoted to major general on March 21, 1862. Ironically, he saw no more active duty in the war, filling successively the commands of the Department of Missouri, the Department of Kansas, and the Department of the Northwest.

35. Henry Wager Halleck's early career was distinguished by the publication of several books on military subjects, giving rise to his nickname, "Old Brains." Although commissioned a major general in the regular U.S. Army at the beginning of the Civil War, his early promise came to nothing, prompting Lincoln to regard him as "little more than a first rate clerk." After experiencing failure at field command, he was called to Washington to serve as general-in-chief. When Grant was promoted to lieutenant general in March, 1864, Halleck was demoted to chief of staff. See Stephen E. Ambrose, *Halleck: Lincoln's Chief of Staff* (Baton Rouge, 1962).

[*To relieve the pressure on Confederate forces on the Peninsula, Thomas J. Jackson was ordered to the Shenandoah Valley, where he was to create a diversion by threatening Washington and thus pinning potential reinforcements to McClellan's army to the defense of the capital. On March 8–9, 1862, Jackson left his winter quarters at Winchester to attack the forces of James Shields at Kernstown, initiating the famed Shenandoah Valley campaign. Although commanding an army of only 4,500 men, Jackson seized the initiative on March 23 by boldly attacking the Kernstown garrison. Reinforced to 17,000 men, Jackson then attacked and defeated John C. Frémont's army at McDowell on May 8 and then turned on Nathaniel P. Banks, driving him from the Valley in a series of running battles from Front Royal on May 23 to Winchester on May 25.*

Deeply concerned by Jackson's successes, the Lincoln administration ordered Irvin McDowell and his 20,000-man army at Fredericksburg into the Valley, thus depriving McClellan of expected reinforcements, and instructed Frémont and Banks to trap the Confederates in the lower valley. Circled by three converging armies, Jackson raced south, narrowly evading the Union trap and earning his men the sobriquet "Jackson's Foot Cavalry." The campaign closed with Jackson's successful attack on Frémont's army at Cross Keys on June 8 and on McDowell's troops at Port Republic on June 9. Having neatly extricated his command, he rejoined Robert E. Lee's army east of Richmond in time to take part in the Seven Days' Battles.[36]]

⇒ ⇐

REUBEN ALLEN PIERSON TO WILLIAM H. PIERSON
In camp 20 miles north of Charlottesville [Va.]
June 11th, 1862

W. H. Pierson
Dear Father

I hasten to write as I have an opportunity of sending you a letter by Dr. Arbuckle who is going to return home. I have been through the hardships of a severe trip. Immediately after our organization we were transferred to Jackson[']s command and ordered to march from the Rhappahannock River to Gordonsville,[37] from there, after one day[']s rest we were ordered up to Liberty

36. Robert G. Tanner, *Stonewall in the Valley: Thomas J. "Stonewall" Jackson's Shenandoah Valley Campaign, Spring 1862* (New York, 1976).

37. Ewell's division marched from Brandy Station to the Shenandoah Valley, via Gordonsville, Stanardsville, and Swift Run Gap, arriving at Conrad's Store on April 30. After a frustrating delay, it joined Jackson's Army of the Valley at New Market on May 17, 1862 (Terry L. Jones, *Lee's Tigers: The Louisiana Infantry in the Army of Northern Virginia* [Baton Rouge, 1987], 68; Handerson, *Yankee in Gray*, 40–41).

Mills & from there to Stanardsville, then across the Blue Ridge through Swift Run Gap on the turnpike leading to Harrisonburg, then down the Shenandoah River to the Columbian bridge, then back up [*page torn*] road and across the Shenandoah then down the Sta[u]nton and Winchester pike to New Market then across to Luray then down to Front Royal where we had our first show at the yankees. We engaged them about 4 Oclock on the evening of the 23rd. Our Regt. did not get a shot as the yankees run immediately after they were attacked.[38] On the 24th we fought them at Middletown[39] but our Regt did not fire a single gun. None except the skirmishers were engaged in either of these battles, but on Sunday morning the 25th we had a general fight at Winchester,[40] completely routed them and took a vast amount of arms, medicines and commissary stores. We also took over three thousand pris[o]ners in the three days['] engagements. After two days['] rest we proceeded down to within a few miles of Harpers Ferry. Here news reached Gen Jackson that Gens Fremont, Millroy and Shields[41] were endeavoring to cut off our retreat. So [*page torn*] about and have succeeded in whipping them three times, taking some fifteen hundred more pris[o]ners, about ten pieces of artillery and a fine lot of their best guns. So in about three weeks we have whipped three of their ablest Gens, taken 5,000 pris[o]ners, many small arms, over a million worth of army stores &c. Notwithstanding this severe trip I have been in good health all the while for which I feel very thankful to the Divine Ruler of man[']s destiny. Our company has been very unfortunate in loosing men by sickness and extremely fortunate in the two hot fights where we were active participants, once charging and taking a fine

38. Henry Handerson of the Stafford Guards described the fight at Front Royal as "a hasty rush, a volley or two of musketry, and the battle was over, the fugitive enemy hastening away towards Winchester with our cavalry in hot pursuit" (Handerson, *Yankee in Gray,* 41).

39. On May 24, 1862, Jackson's Army of the Valley, marching north down the Valley from Front Royal to Winchester, fell on Nathaniel P. Banks's rearguard at Middletown. Ewell's division, in the Confederate vanguard, captured a number of supply wagons and sent their escorts into a panicked retreat. After clearing the road of wrecked wagons, Jackson continued the race for Winchester (Tanner, *Stonewall in the Valley,* 220–22).

40. The first battle of Winchester, fought on May 25, 1862, was the second Confederate victory of Jackson's Valley campaign. The charge of Taylor's Louisiana brigade was the decisive event of the battle, routing Banks's 20,000-man army and clearing the road to the Potomac (*ibid.,* 218–23).

41. John Charles Frémont, famed as "the Pathfinder" who had explored the way to California in the 1840s and as the Republican party's first presidential nominee, was named a major general by Abraham Lincoln at the outset of the war but proved a disappointment, first in Missouri and then in the Valley. Troops under Robert Huston Milroy, an Indiana lawyer and veteran of the Mexican War, were badly mauled during Jackson's Valley campaign in 1862 and even worse the following year by Ewell's corps at the second battle of Winchester. Thereafter, he never held a field command. James Shields, too, was a lawyer and volunteer officer in the Mexican War. A friend of Lincoln's, he secured a brigadier general's commission but was soundly defeated at Port Republic and never again held a command.

battery where the balls fell like hailstones in a hailstorm. We had two men wounded in the Winchester battle viz[.] Tom Cawthon and William Williams[42] and both slight. In the battle on the Shenandoah River about 4 miles below Port Republic 4 of my men were wounded viz[.] Alfred Carlton, William Mims, Jacob Boyet and William Blunt,[43] all slight. Not a single other company has been as fortunate as (C) still we were in the thickest of both battles. Eleven of the recruits which left Bienville with us as recruits have died, ten in the hospital and one in camp. The following is a list of the dead: Perry Humphreys, two young things, James Mitchael, John Swain, W. H. Britton, Tandy Brown, Jno Webb, Wm Worry, Wm Mathews, Ned Harper.[44] All of these have died in two months. Our company numbering one hundred and fifteen men rank and file has now only about sixty men in camp. I must [*paper torn*] my business is now claiming my attention. My respects to all friends especially the ladies. My love to all the family. I remain your Son till death

R. A. Pierson

42. This is apparently William B. Williams, a sergeant in Company A, Sixth Louisiana Infantry, who was wounded at Winchester and sent to the Fairview Hospital at Lexington (Booth, comp., *Records*, Vol. III, Pt. 2, pp. 1109–10).

43. Alfred Carlton was wounded at the battle of Port Republic, June 9, 1862. He was captured at Rappahannock Station, Virginia, on November 7, 1863, and confined to Point Lookout until exchanged on March 10, 1864. William D. Mims of Ringgold was granted a "sick furlough" in the fall of 1863, from which he did not return. He spent the remainder of the war in the Trans-Mississippi Department without leave and was paroled at Shreveport on June 13, 1865. Jacob B. Boyet of Buck Horn never recovered from his Port Republic wound, dying at White Sulphur Springs, Virginia, on December 4, 1862. William H. Blunt (or "Blount") of Buck Horn returned to his company after recovering from his Port Republic wound, was captured at Rappahannock, Virginia, on November 7, 1863, and confined to Point Lookout, where he contracted smallpox. He died on December 31, 1863 (*ibid.*, II, 256, Vol. III, Pt. 1, p. 992, II, 75, II, 16).

44. James Mitchell of Mount Lebanon died in the hospital at Charlottesville, Virginia, on May 11, 1862. John B. Swain died in the hospital at Charlottesville, Virginia, on May 10, 1862. W. H. Britton (sometimes listed as "Britain" or "Brittain"), a Ringgold farmer, died at Lynchburg on May 13, 1862. Tandy A. Brown of Sabine Parish died at Lynchburg, Virginia, on May 22, 1862. John S. Webb died at Lynchburg sometime in May, 1862. William Worry of Bienville Parish died in the hospital at Stanardsville, Virginia, in May, 1862. William G. Mathews of Mount Lebanon died at Lynchburg on May 8, 1862. Edward C. Harper from Buck Horn died at Charlottesville in May, 1862 (*ibid.*, Vol. III, Pt. 1, p. 999, Pt. 2, p. 750, II, 122, 155, Vol. III, Pt. 2, pp. 1017, 1164, Pt. 1, pp. 913, 194).

⇒ ⇐

DAVID PIERSON TO WILLIAM H. PIERSON
Camp Near Tupelo, Miss, June 22ⁿᵈ, 1862

Wm H. Pierson
   Mt. Lebanon,
     Louisiana

Dear Pa,

A member of the 3rd leaves tomorrow to run the blockade, & by him I take occasion to write you, though it would appear useless if it goes any distance in the mail, as it must, for I have not received a letter from you or any person west of the Miss. River in a time out of mind. I am very anxious to hear from home and will continue to write by every opportunity till I get an answer. I have nothing new or startling to communicate. Our camp is as quiet as a garrison in time of peace—each day & hour the routine of duty is performed, and at night the soldier sleeps as if no dangers encompassed him. The mornings are consumed in drill & fatigue duty and the evenings in cooking, eating, and lounging about reading newspapers if they can be had. The days pass & the week is gone without an incident to mark or do it. But "after a calm comes the storm," it [is] said, and I look for one soon here or hereabouts. The enemy is not following us, it is true, but they will turn up somewhere soon, no doubt in such a manner that will cause us to rush from our quiet & our weapons to glisten in the sunshine once more.

Matters of great importance are transpiring in other quarters if we only knew it. Beauregard has gone to Richmond, Price and Breckenridge have followed him, whilst Van Dorn has been ordered to Vicksburg and Bragg has been left here to do things up in his practical way as the Commander of the Western Army. Nobody knows the object of Beauregard's mission though it is whispered he will soon draw a large force from this army to reinforce Johns[t]on[45] to defend the Capital. We all want to go—anything for a change. Breck[inridge] has gone for his health & to talk politics perhaps, and Price has gone to be transferred to the Department of Ark., where he hopes, no doubt, to filch from the

---

45. Joseph Eggelston Johnston was rewarded with promotion to full general and command of what would become the Army of Northern Virginia after the Confederate victory at First Manassas. He conducted the affairs of the South's principal army until he was severely wounded at the battle of Seven Pines in June, 1862. See Joseph E. Johnston, *Narrative of Military Operations Directed During the Late War Between the States* (1874; rpr. Bloomington, 1959); Craig L. Symonds, *Joseph E. Johnston: A Civil War Biography* (New York, 1992).

brave Hindman[46] the laurels lately won by him in that state. Price has found out that talk and show won't hold him up here where brains & acts are standards by which men are judged; and is therefore anxious to get back to his old range where he can humbug & display to own advantage. By the way, Col. Louis Hébert has been made a Brigadier and is in Command of our Brigade (2nd). The boys of the 3rd gave a hearty *growl* on his arrival. Our own Col. is growing more & more popular every day. He is tight—a strict disciplinarian— but kind and obliging and always alive to the wants of his men. He is trying to get our Regt. transferred from Price's Division that we may be among troops from our own state.

Our Pickets report no Federals between this and Corinth, and today I have not the least idea where Halleck's powerful army is or in what direction. He may be lying in his entrenchments on the Tenn. River yet for better security lest Beauregard should fall upon him again in an unexpected moment.[47]

Every day or two we have rumors in camps about the prospects of peace, and just now some knowing ones are offering to bet largely that peace will be made in 30 days. I must confess that I am not half so sanguine and can't believe the greedy Yankee will stop till he ruins himself or us. The soldiers would like to have peace if it can be had on terms honorable. We are all sick & tired of this kind of life but are not willing to submit to such rulers as Pig [?] Butler[48] to have it. No. Rather had we live in camps our days out in rags & starvation and suffer over & over again the horrible things incident to war than submit to such terms. Home, peace, life is sweet, but dearer still is the privilege to live & act as freemen & die

46. Thomas Carmichael Hindman, after commanding a Rebel division at Shiloh, was promoted to major general and returned to Arkansas as commander of the Trans-Mississippi Department. His strict enforcement of conscription laws made him unpopular, and the War Department replaced him with Lt. Gen. Theophilus H. Holmes. Hindman continued in command of troops in northwest Arkansas but was defeated at the battle of Prairie Grove on December 7, 1862. Reassigned to the Army of Tennessee, Hindman commanded a division at the battles of Chickamauga and Kennesaw Mountain. See Diane Neal and Thomas W. Kremm, *Lion of the South: General Thomas C. Hindman* (Macon, Ga., 1993).

47. Following the battle of Shiloh, April 6–7, 1862, Gen. P.G.T. Beauregard's Army of Mississippi fell back on Corinth, Mississippi, to await the further movements of the combined U.S. armies of Ulysses S. Grant and Don Carlos Buell, now under the direct supervision of Maj. Gen. Henry Halleck. Halleck's otherwise unaccountable tardiness in following Beauregard's severely weakened army may be explained by the prevalence of disease in the Union army. By the time Halleck occupied Corinth in June, 1862, a third or more of his men had fallen ill. In July, 1862, more than half of his men and more than one-third of Beauregard's were on the sicklist. During the Corinth campaign, nearly half of the twenty-nine Union generals were stricken with malaria, dysentery, or some other ailment common to camp life (McPherson, *Battle Cry of Freedom*, 414–18).

48. Benjamin Franklin Butler commanded the forces that took possession of New Orleans in May, 1862, and was named military governor of Louisiana. His reputation as a corrupt administrator earned him the nickname "Spoons," and his notorious "woman order" threatening to treat the ladies of New

honorably. We hear now & then of a man in La., where the Feds have a foothold, going over to the enemy & giving up the struggle which mystifies us much, but they little know the metal [mettle] of this army if they think it will ever give up as long as there is a weapon to use or an arm to use it. The Feds may boast as much as they please about desertions from our ranks and revival of the Union sentiment when they occupy our soil, but they will find that there are plenty left to fight their cowardly hosts till doom's day if they want to hold out that long.

The health of the army is getting better daily. Our own Regt. is now in better condition than it has been for months past. Very few are sick in camps. My own health is quite good though recently I had the mumphs which made me quite sick for a day or two. I am over them now & on duty. Several members of our Regt. who were taken prisoners at Elk Horn have arrived in camps in the last few days having been exchanged for. They have many funny & strange things to tell about Yankeedom. They all say their treatment was very bad having been thrown into an old Penitentiary where there were cases of Small Pox & excluded almost from the light of day. Several died of that disease without medical attention & in a situation too horrible for human eyes to witness. It does seem to me that our authorities ought to retaliate for such brutal conduct or do something. Better hoist the black flag[49] than tolerate it.

I have not heard from Al or Henry, though I write them often. I hear that Milton Houston[50] has been elected Capt. of Mabry's Company & George Williams and Lieut. Mabry is dead. I don't have time to visit them & have not seen them since we left Corinth.

Write soon.

Your Affectionate Son,
D. Pierson

Orleans "as women of the street plying their avocation," won him the sobriquet "Beast" Butler. See Benjamin F. Butler, *Butler's Book* (Boston, 1892); Robert S. Holzman, *Stormy Ben Butler* (New York, 1954).

49. The black flag was an emblem specifying "no quarter" and was often associated with piracy. By spring, 1863, Capt. E. P. Petty of the Seventeenth Texas Infantry wrote to his wife that the Federal army in the Mississippi River valley was "carrying on a predatory was in its broadest and most barbarous sense." Yet, Petty wrote, he saw "no signs or prospects of our Commanders ordering the Black Flag to be raised." Because the Yankees were destroying crops and residences and "stealing negroes and every thing they can lay their infernal hands upon," Petty hoped that the black flag would be raised and that he could serve under it. "Whether it is raised or not I expect to make it my principal and act accordingly unless the booming of the cannon and the whistling of the minie balls shall sober and mollify me verry much" (Norman D. Brown, ed., *Journey to Pleasant Hill: The Civil War Letters of Captain Elijah P. Petty, Walker's Texas Division, C.S.A.* [San Antonio, 1982], 205–206).

50. James Milton Houston enlisted at Camp Moore, Louisiana, on September 29, 1861, and was elected first sergeant of Company I, Sixteenth Louisiana Infantry. On May 8, 1862, he was promoted to captain (Arthur W. Bergeron, Jr., *Guide to Louisiana Confederate Military Units, 1861–1865* [Baton Rouge, 1989], 112; Booth, comp., *Records*, Vol. III, Pt. 1, p. 363).

⇥ ⇤

DAVID PIERSON TO WILLIAM H. PIERSON

Camp Near Tupelo, Miss.
June 28th, 1862

Wm H. Pierson
    Mt. Lebanon
        La.

Dear Pa,

Your favor of the 10th June came to hand three days ago and having an opportunity to send a letter by hand to Monroe, I write you this though I have written so often that I am almost fearful you will get tired of paying postage on such worthless letters. As usual I have no news to write and can only say what the Telegraph tells us every day from Richmond: "All quiet along the line."[51] Positively, there has not been an item of news in relation to the movement of this army in ten days, neither has there been anything from the enemy. It seems both sides have come to a standstill as if by mutual consent, and I have some suspicions that an armistice and cessation of hostilities has been agreed to between the powers. Beauregard has not returned, Price is also absent still, and Van Dorn has been assigned to the Command of the Department at Vicksburg. What becomes of Lovell[52] I know not. Gen. Hébert (our old Col) is here in Command of the 2 brigades and issues a bushel of orders per day. He is much more efficient in issuing than executing orders. Our camps are very busy drilling, policing, and reciting lessons in Tactics, so that we have very few idle hours during the day. Our Regt. has been appointed as the sharpshooters of the Brigade, which is a position of honor and danger, and compels us to exercise much in the skirmish drill to become efficient for the post. The general health is good though some slow fevers are making their appearance in camps. The weather is dry and very warm. Water is getting scarce in the wells. We are preparing to discharge the non-conscripts just now to take effect the 16th July

---

51. "All quiet along the line" is undoubtedly an allusion to the vastly popular song, "All Quiet Along the Potomac Tonight." The title came from the news report—so common as to have become a cliché—that characterized the inactivity of the two armies in northern Virginia between the first battle of Manassas and the Peninsula campaign (Willard A. Heaps and Porter W. Heaps, *The Singing Sixties: The Spirit of Civil War Days Drawn from the Music of the Times* [Norman, Okla., 1960], 146–48).

52. Mansfield Lovell was promoted to major general on October 7, 1861, and assigned to command of the defenses of New Orleans. Despite the severe criticism heaped upon him when the city fell in April, 1862, Lovell was assigned to the command of a division under Earl Van Dorn. At the battle of Corinth, Lovell failed to act with any aggressiveness and was relieved of command by the end of the year.

1862 which will reduce our Regt. about one hundred men. Our Maj.[53] has gone home for recruits, but I suppose he will get but few as *Mr. Conscription* went before him with a stronger influence perhaps than the Maj. can exercise.

I have not yet heard a word from Al or Henry. I have written them often and it is strange I do not get a letter from Henry at least as letters are received here from Vicksburg every day. As to Al, if he is with Stonewall Jackson, as I suppose he is from what you wrote me of his being in Maryland, it is not at all strange as to him, for he must be too busy to write. My health is good and I am quite content. Nothing more.

Yours Truly,
David Pierson

> ≈ ⋐

DAVID PIERSON TO WILLIAM H. PIERSON

Camp Near Priceville, Miss.,
July 10th, 1862

Wm H. Pierson
  Mt. Lebanon,
    La.

Dear Pa,

Having another opportunity to send you a line by hand I do so, only to assure you of my continued good health & c. Nothing worthy of notice transpired in this Department since I wrote you last, but we are looking out for something to turn up daily. Several Divisions of the Army have been put in motion and some have gone north. It is Bragg's intention, perhaps, to strike for Middle Tenn. or Kentucky.

Today we have a fine rain, the first in a long while, and the air is once more cool and pleasant. I got a letter from Henry yesterday. He was well and apparently well satisfied. I also rec^d one from Al a day or two ago, in which he gives me the details of his tramps and campaigns in the Valley of Va. under Stonewall Jackson. He was safe and sound and his keen desire for a battle fully satisfied.

---

53. William F. Tunnard, the regiment's first major, was dropped from the rolls on May 8, 1862. Its second major, Samuel D. Russell, was promoted to lieutenant colonel on November 5, 1862, and to colonel on or about August 20, 1863, after commanding the regiment through the Vicksburg campaign (Bergeron, *Guide,* 77).

Our C^ol (F. C. Armstrong)[54] has been promoted Brigadier General of Cavalry, making two Brigadiers the old 3^d has turned out. When he receives his commission I will be promoted Major of the Regt., being the ranking Capt., if I can stand the examination before the board which I hope to do.[55]

I wrote you to send me a negro boy to cook for me, but of course do not expect you to do it now that the Blockade is established, & will make other arrangements.[56]

The news from Va. was received here with the wildest demonstrations of joy. Cannon were fired in the 3 Grand Divisions of the Army, and the shouts of the soldiers was deafening all along our lines.

Nothing more but rumor.

Yours Affectionately,

D. Pierson

54. Frank Crawford Armstrong was commissioned directly into the U.S. Army in 1855 and saw duty with the Second Cavalry on the Texas frontier. He remained with his regiment after the outbreak of the Civil War, serving in the Union army at the first battle of Manassas, but on August 13, 1861, Armstrong resigned his Federal commission to join the Confederacy. Armstrong was appointed McCulloch's adjutant and aide-de-camp. After the battle of Elkhorn Tavern, he was promoted to command of the Third Louisiana Infantry. He soon was transferred to cavalry service and was promoted to brigadier general on January 20, 1863. He commanded elements of the cavalry corps of Joseph Wheeler and Stephen D. Lee, and was with Nathan Bedford Forrest at the war's end.

55. In October, 1862, the Confederate States of America established military boards for examining the competence of its officers. Although the practice of electing officers continued, these boards did set a minimum standard of proficiency for company and field-grade officers and drove many incompetent men from command (McPherson, *Battle Cry of Freedom*, 327–28).

56. The Confederacy's waning military fortunes dimmed but did not destroy the region's confidence in the economic value of slave property. Although many southerners privately expressed pessimistic views regarding the future of the "peculiar institution" and were anxious to sell their bondsmen while they retained their market value, a brisk trade in slaves continued until the end of the war. Late in the war, many slaves were purchased with depreciated Confederate currency—with one male slave selling in Houston in 1864 for $4,500 in Confederate notes, for example—but others continued to be sold for specie or bartered for valuable property (Randolph B. Campbell, *An Empire for Slavery: The Peculiar Institution in Texas, 1821–1865* [Baton Rouge, 1989], 239–43; Randolph B. Campbell, "The End of Slavery in Texas: A Research Note," *Southwestern Historical Quarterly*, LXXXVIII [July, 1984], 171–80).

⇒ ⇐

REUBEN ALLEN PIERSON TO WILLIAM H. PIERSON

In Camp near Richmond, Va.
July 11th, 1862

W. H. Pierson, Esqr

Dear Father

I have somewhat better opportunities to write now than I have before. I have now become accustomed to the duties of a commanding officer and therefore my labors are not so severe. I have seen something of an active campaign. I have been through the whole Valley campaign with the Great Stonewall Jackson, have smelt gunpowder—listened to the whizzing of all kinds of balls, bombs and shot—have been at the charging of a battery—have helped to drive the enemies from their strong positions, and learned what the horrors of war are by being an eye witness to the most inhuman heart sickening and brutal slaying of men. I walked over the field early on the morning after the dreadful battle of Coal [Cold] Harbor[57] and the dead lay almost thick enough in some places to have walked on. The scene was one never to be forgotten. Where the battle raged the fiercest every twig was riddled and many trees not more than a foot in diameter had as many as forty balls in its trunk. The yankee wounded was still lying on the ground and begging for water and food of all who passed by. The dead wore as many different faces as the living. Many seemed to have expired laughing while others clinched their teeth and hands and seemed to have perished in awful agony. Some were still clinging to their guns as if they died fighting. Language would in no way express the true picture as it really was.

I am in good health having entirely recovered from the little fever which I suppose was brought on by fatigue and exposure during the fight before Richmond. Our Brigade is now encamped 4 miles from Richmond on the (Rail Road) road leading to Manassas. All the regiments are reduced to small battalions on account of the killed, wounded and absent sick, many of the latter class being worn out by fatigue. Every Captain except myself has failed on the march and resorted to riding on horseback or in ambulances, or applied for a sick furlough. The sickness in my company is decreasing for the last few weeks. I have not had a single death to report in more than a month. I see from a letter of H. T. Tooke written by his father, that a report has reached Bienville of Bryant Thomas[']s death. I will here state it to be false. He was left at Charlottesville

---

57. The first battle of Cold Harbor, also known as Gaines's Mill or the Chickahominy, was fought on June 27, 1862, when Confederate troops—notably John Bell Hood's Texas Brigade—pierced Fitz John Porter's line, forcing the Federals back beyond the Chickahominy River.

sick when we returned from the Valley. I have not heard from him in two weeks but did not consider him dangerous when he left. You will get more particulars concerning the battles before Richmond from the papers than I am able to give. Suffice it for me to say that none of the Bienville Blues was either killed or wounded though several of them had their clothing cut by balls.

I hear good news from Ark. this morning. It is reported that Gen. Hindman has captured Curtis with 6,000 other pris[o]ners. I hope the statement may prove true.[58] The Federals are meeting some reverses that will check their onward march in the South for at least this year. I am getting on finely with all the boys. They are satisfied and cheerful because I share the same privations with themselves. There is now sixty five present in all. Six have been wounded and are off at hospitals doing well. Some are coming almost daily who have been absent sick ever since we arrived in Va. Our fare is not as good as I would wish, nothing but bacon & flour. I sent to Rogers and Gibbs[59] two twenty dollar Confederate notes by J. C. Watts,[60] one for Mrs. Richard Reeve[61]; the other for Mrs. F. F. Rolison.[62] I also sent a letter directing them, Rogers & Gibbs, what disposition to make of it. I hope Watts has done all right about the matter. Please enquire concerning this and write me how it is.

Give my love to all who may enquire about my welfare. Especially remember me to the young ladies of my acquaintants. Tell Mrs. Randle I have enquired for the 4th Geo. [Georgia] but have not been able to find it yet though it is somewhere near Richmond I have been told. Extend my love to all the family. Receiving the love of a Son. When any of you all right direct your let-

58. This rumor was completely false. Thomas C. Hindman was at the time commander of the Trans-Mississippi Department and Samuel Ryan Curtis was commander of the Department of Missouri, but the two never met in battle.

59. Rogers and Gibbs was Mount Lebanon's leading mercantile establishment. Hiram Gibbs and George Washington Rogers were pioneer settlers of Bienville Parish. Rogers was the first secretary of the Mount Lebanon University board, and Gibbs later served as both secretary and treasurer (Gerald Pollard, "The History of Mount Lebanon University, 1852–1912" [M. Ed. thesis, Louisiana State University, 1971], 36–38).

60. James C. ("Cap") Watts, who spent most of his Civil War career on detached duty as a hospital orderly (including a period in which he was assigned to nurse the seriously ill Lt. Casper N. Ardis) was discharged from the army in the spring of 1862, since he was over thirty-five years of age (Booth, comp., *Records,* Vol. III, Pt. 2, p. 1011).

61. Richard Reeve enlisted in Company C at Mount Lebanon on March 8, 1862. He was captured at Chancellorsville and held at Fort Delaware until May 23, 1863. Again captured at Fisher's Hill on September 22, 1864, he was sent to Point Lookout until exchanged on February 20, 1865 (*ibid.,* 272).

62. Fred F. Rolinson (sometimes "Rollinson") of Minden enlisted in Company C, Ninth Louisiana Infantry, at Bienville on March 8, 1862. He was wounded at Gettysburg but returned to his company by August 11, 1863, "on pay day," and remained with the company until Appomattox (*ibid.,* 378, 379).

ter to Richmond 9th Regt. La. Vol. Co. C. Ewell[']s Division, Jackson[']s Army.[63]

I remain your Son till death

R. A. Pierson

P. S. Collins & John Williams are both well. All the boys from Lebanon are well. Yours

R. A. P.

≫ ≪

DAVID PIERSON TO WILLIAM H. PIERSON
Camp Near Tupelo, Miss.
July 17th, 1862

Wm H. Pierson

Dear Father,

Our non-conscripts are being discharged from the service now, and as I am satisfied they will run the *Blockade,* I take occasion to send you a letter by them. I discharge two from my Company which will reduce my command to thirty men. Other companies will be smaller than [*letter torn*] regt. almost broke up. What [*letter torn*] after being so much but [*letter torn*] much debated among [*letter torn*] are [*letter torn*] reg^t. will be disorganized and [*letter torn*] other commands, but I can hardly believe that our commanders will thus treat the old 3^d La., so long famous as being the oldest and best troops in the Western Army. It is agreed on all hands here that we are the best drilled & disciplined reg^t. in the army, and an officer just from Va. who saw us drilling the other day remarked to our C^{ol}. that he had seen no reg^t in the Army of the Potomac[64] that equalled ours in that respect. Under these circumstances, I cannot think that we

63. Richard Stoddert Ewell commanded a brigade at the first battle of Manassas. Rewarded with promotion to major general, he performed admirably as Stonewall Jackson's second-in-command during the Shenandoah Valley campaign, and following Jackson's death at Chancellorsville, he was appointed to command of II Corps and promoted to lieutenant general. See Samuel J. Martin, *The Road to Glory: Confederate General Richard S. Ewell* (Indianapolis, 1993).

64. The Confederate Army of the Potomac came into being on July 2, 1861, when P.G.T. Beauregard took command of the southern forces in northern Virginia. Under this designation it fought the first battle of Manassas and the battles of the Peninsula campaign under Joseph E. Johnston. On June 1, 1862, after Johnston was wounded at the battle of Seven Pines, Robert E. Lee took command of the South's most powerful army and officially renamed it the Army of Northern Virginia.

will have to give up our No. and Name to any reg[t], however large, but on the contrary that the *green* ones will be put into our ranks to be made efficient with ourselves. The non-conscripts are very glad to get off—not one refusing to be discharged that I know of. Many [men] would have remained if they had been granted a furlough of sixty days to visit their homes and take a little rest from the service, but the standing orders prohibit any from being given, and they all take the discharge. I am confident that a goodly number of them will return to their Companies or join some other command in less time than sixty days. Everything remains quiet here still, and now even a talk of leaving is not so much heard. Gen. Bragg is yet in command and is enforcing the most [*letter torn*] am told he had four soldiers shot [*letter torn*] have [*letter torn*] a tyrant but I am [*letter torn*] him put this army in a better fix [*letter torn*] than it had previously been. Today [*letter torn*] fine rains and there is no longer any want of water.[65] I wrote you before that I had prospect of being Maj. of the Reg[t]. by promotion, in consequence of the appointment of our Col. as Brigadier Genl. I will not be examined or promoted till he gets his commission which may be several weeks, but I feel confident that I will get the promotion sooner or later if nothing uncommon happens. I rec[d] a letter from Henry a few days ago. He was well & in camps. Nothing from Al since his campaign in the Valley of Va. under Jackson. My health is very good, and I am glad to state that none of my men are sick, being the first time that I could say so. I am detailed on a General Court Martial which convenes at Genl. Price's Head Quarters, and have an easy time, being excused from drill and all other camp duties. Besides, it agrees with my tastes more than the strict military, and I am glad to be thus situated for a while. Gen. [Price is a] familiar & clever old fellow—kind to [everybody] but I doubt these being the qualities [of character] of a good General. He is now [in] command of the Army of the West, Van Dorn's former Command. Our Lieut. Col. has to do the duties of Col. now, and fills the place very well. John Pearson[66] is going home and promises to see you for me. He can tell you all.

Write me as often as you can send a letter across the river.

Yours Affectionately,

D. Pierson

---

65. An unusually wet spring in north Mississippi was followed by a disastrously dry summer in 1862. Men and horses suffered for want of water. Henry W. Halleck's army was largely immobilized after Beauregard's evacuation of Corinth because of the falling level of the rivers and the consequent impossibility of transportation or supply by water (McPherson, *Battle Cry of Freedom*, 512).

66. John H. Pearson entered Confederate service as a private in Company C, Third Louisiana Infantry, on May 17, 1861. Overage, he was discharged at Priceville, Mississippi, on July 16, 1862, in accordance with the First Conscription Act. (Willie H. Tunnard, *A Southern Record: The Story of the Third Regiment Louisiana Infantry* [1866; rpr. Dayton, Ohio, 1970], 546; Booth, comp., *Records,* Vol. III, Pt. 2, p. 93).

⇒ ⇐

David Pierson to Mary Catherine Pierson
Camp Near Tupelo, Miss., July 19ᵗʰ, 1862

Miss M. C. Pierson
  Mt. Lebanon
    La.

Dear Sister,

Excuse me for not having written you before. I have wrote Pa so many letters void of interest that I was ashamed to tax you in the same way, besides, I have not had time and opportunity to write so many letters. But how is it with you, sister? Do you imagine I will be charitable enough to excuse you for your long neglect in not writing me? I know what your excuse will be, "Pa writes you and that is enough." But does Pa write your letters, and is it through him that I am to hear from you? Have you appointed him your private secretary in his old age, and does he perform the duties of his office so well that you do not even have to look at the matter yourself to see that he does it right? Shame on you sister. Now I propose to write you as many times as you write me—except when I am on the march. Don't get insulted at my soliciting your correspondence. It would afford me much pleasure to read a letter from you now & then whether it contained anything or not. But I know you can find things to write about, and things, too, that would be most interesting to me. I have but little to write now, but will try to do better next time. Think nothing of my jokes; it is mostly to fill up space that I have written thus. The weather is very hot and the drill very fatiguing. I will have a light time for some months if we stay here that long, being on an Army Court Martial and having nothing to do but sit in judgment on other men's sins. I finish this letter on Sunday, 20ᵗʰ July, just before the non-conscripts leave. Sunday is a sort of holiday among soldiers as well as "Negroes," and today of course I put on my Sunday clothes. I feel like I was *"dressed up,"* but if you could see me you would be surprised at what I call "dressed up." A shirt and pair of pants washed on half rations of soap and that had not felt a Smoothing Iron in months with shoes without blacking constitute the "dress part," for the coat has to be worn all the while. But clean clothes makes a soldier feel so gay that little is thought of ironing and polishing.

I had a great luxury for dinner today—green corn, the first this year. Our usual diet is beef, bread, and molasses. We get about enough bacon to use in the place of lard and but little rice or sugar. Necessity has learned us how to make light bread, and I do believe we have the best I ever saw. Here of late we get coffee enough to make a cup full apiece once a day. Our beef is often very poor, but yet we are such geniuses that we make it good by cooking. What we lack most is vegetables. I have had nothing in that line this summer except some Onions bought at [*illegible*] prices. The whole country hereabouts is entirely exhausted of everything of the kind. The Cavalry gets all such things—they having horses to ride and time to go around.[67] After all our inconveniences we get as a general thing enough to eat and are satisfied with what we get. I never was healthier or better contented at any place. I have become perfectly used to the life & enjoy myself about as well as I did at home. There is no demand for clothing now as there was last winter among the troops. We all have more than we can take care of. As for amusements, we have an abundance besides Gen[l]. Price's band plays so delightfully every morning and evening for us gratis.

Write soon.

Very Affectionately,
Your Bro.,
D. Pierson

⇒ ⇐

DAVID PIERSON TO WILLIAM H. PIERSON
Camp Near Tupelo, Miss., July 23ᵈ, 1862

Wm H. Pierson
Mt. Lebanon
La.

Dear Father,

An expressman leaves our Regt. today for Natchitoches, La, and by him I send you this letter. His name is Haynes. He will carry letters regularly from this Regt. to Natchitoches & from that point here or wherever we may be located. I have nothing new to write you & merely write to let you know that my health still continues good. I sometimes almost wish I could get a little sick so that I might get a furlough or sick leave of a few days to go to Mobile or some

67. Throughout the war a sometimes playful and sometimes bitter rivalry existed between the men of infantry and cavalry commands. William Andrew Fletcher, who had the distinction of seeing service in both Hood's Texas Brigade and Terry's Texas Rangers, remembered that infantry troops held their mounted comrades in vast contempt. Such remarks as "Mister, here's your mule!" "There goes the buttermilk cavalry!" "All those fellows do is find Yankees for us infantry to kill!" and "A hundred-dollar reward for just one dead cavalryman!" were met with such equally contemptuous retorts as "wagon dogs," "web feet," and "mud sloggers." Richard Taylor placed the feud in perspective. "Living on horseback, fearless and dashing," he observed of the Confederate horse soldiers, "the men of the South afforded the best possible material for cavalry. They had every quality but discipline, and resembled Prince Charming, whose manifold gifts, bestowed by her sisters, were rendered useless by the malignant fairy" (William Andrew Fletcher, *Rebel Private, Front and Rear* [1908; rpr. Austin, 1954], 82; Richard Taylor, *Destruction and Reconstruction* [1878; rpr. New York, 1994], 60).

other point & rest a few days from camp life. All my Lieutenants have been absent in this manner since we have been in this camp; not sick much, but just enough to get off whilst I am so extremely healthy that there is no chance for me. Here I must stay. Gen. Bragg was to have reviewed the Army of the West today, but did not come in consequence of a shower of rain this morning, and the review was made by "Old Pap" (Genl. Price) as we call him. It is an imposing sight to see fifteen or twenty thousand men marching in column, bayonets all fixed & bright, and a splendid brass band playing all the while. Genl. Bragg will review us before long I suppose. We are all anxious to see him. It is rumored that all the army at this point except two Divisions of the Army of the West will leave in a few days for Chattanooga. If it turns out to be true, our Reg^t. will remain here two months longer, perhaps. so far as I am concerned I am willing to stay, for I dread marching [in] this hot & dry weather and would rather be separated from so large a force.

Genl McGruder[68] will take command of the Army of the West in a few days & Price, who is now in command, will resume command of his Division. This shows what the War Department thinks of the "*Washington of the War.*" It is evident that Price has nearly played out, and I am of the opinion that the closing of the news papers on him has effected his downfall. Newspaper Generals did very well so long as their swarm of correspondents could follow them around and puff them abroad, but now that no such thing is allowed, men are judged alone by their acts & hence some of them have begun to flag. Look out for Jeff Thompson[69] to stumble.

Our Cmd'g Gen. Bragg handles things without gloves, and it is not so shaping his conduct & demeanor here as to secure both here after but so as to do the country some good. He will be an unpopular man, but no good soldier who does his duty as disinterested[ly] as a Genl should can be otherwise. Subordinate officers should be kind & generous to soldiers under their command, but a Genl Commanding a great Army has something else to do and think about be-

---

68. This report was false. John Bankhead Magruder successfully commanded the Rebel forces at Yorktown, Virginia, during the opening weeks of the Peninsula campaign, but lack of aggressiveness during the Seven Days' Battles cost him the favor of General Lee. He was reassigned to the command of the District of Texas, New Mexico, and Arizona. His greatest success there was his recapture of Galveston on January 1, 1863.

69. Merriwether Jeff Thompson, former mayor of St. Joseph, Missouri, raised and took command of a battalion of Confederate partisan rangers—the so-called Swamp Rats—in 1861 and began a four-year career as a raider in Missouri and Arkansas. In 1863, he became a member of Edmund Kirby Smith's staff, and in 1864 he took part in Sterling Price's Missouri raid at the head of a brigade. Although he referred to himself as a general, he held no official commission (Donald J. Stanton, Goodwin F. Berquist, and Paul C. Bowers, eds., *The Civil War Reminiscences of General M. Jeff Thompson* [Dayton, Ohio, 1988]; Bruce S. Allardice, *More Generals in Gray* [Baton Rouge, 1995], 219–20).

sides stopping to play the demagogue with every soldier he meets in order to secure his vote and applause. I believe Bragg told the truth when he told the people of Alabama in a speech "never to call upon an old soldier for a Speech or a politician to lead them into battle." I have not yet been examined for promotion to Maj., but will be soon as Col. Armstrong's appointment as a Brigadier is approved by the war department. Nothing from Al or Henry since my last.

All quiet hereabouts.

Your Affectionate
Dave

4

WE WILL BE RECOGNIZED
AS A NATION

REUBEN ALLEN PIERSON TO MARY CATHERINE PIERSON
In camp near Gordonsville, Va.
Aug 3rd, 1862

Mrs. M. A. C. Pierson[1]

Dear Sister

Owing to the extreme pressure of business on me since I arrived in Va. I have written home but seldom. Having now a short idle time I intend writing several letters to my old friends and will therefore drop you a few lines. First of all about Sparta. I have been in fine health all the while since I returned from furlough. This has not been the case with the rest of my company. When I think over the long list of names whose voices were united with ours as we shouted for joy when cheered by the ladies on our rout[e] to camp; seeing the names of many over whose lifeless bodies the soil of Va. now lies with nothing but the head boards to tell who lies beneath. Such thoughts sicken my heart when I reflect upon the grief [of] fathers & mothers, brothers and sisters, and oh the bereavement of widows and orphans. Sad, sad indeed must be the meeting of those bereaved when their friends and relatives return to give a full account of the sufferings of those whose lives have been sacrificed upon the altar of their country, a prey of the monster death. I sometimes think that I shall never desire to return home on account of the many bereaved whose sons, brothers, and husbands have fallen in this cruel war. I have seen the cannons flashing in battle at night till the light lit up the whole surrounding country. I have seen men fall in

---

1. This is Charity Pierson, the wife of Henry Pierson and Reuben Pierson's sister-in-law.

battle like trees before the hurricane. I have listened to the balls whistle like bees around a flower pot. I have walked over the dead bodies of men, and listened to the pitiful cries of the wounded after the battle was over. But all of these are but light and trivial affairs to that of meeting a fond father or mother; brother or sister; or bereaved widow and orphan; hearing their sad cries as they anxiously enquire what caused the death of the much loved one who is gone and, whether he had the proper care and attention while sick or not. These will be more trying than to face the battle's rage. Well Charity I will now tell you something about your relatives in the company. Bryant[2] has had the typhoid fever and is now getting well fast. I heard from him yesterday. Meldrick[3] is here in camp and a little sick, but nothing serious. He is able to walk about where he pleases. Zach Garrett[4] is at Lynchburg and mending fast. He has been sick a long time, but will be in camp in a few days. Monroe[5] was left sick in the Valley and I expect is taken pris[o]ner. Jimmy Nix[6] died of relapse from measels at a farmer's house near Stanardsville on the 20th day of May. McGouldrick hope[s] to bury him. The health of the company is now better than it has ever been since we organized. We have now over seventy men present and more than fifty of them are well and hearty and as jovial as school boys.

Our fare is quite rough now but we all eat it with sharp appetites. Beef and bread, and bread and beef constitute the variety of rations, with a small slice of bacon once a week. I would now add a few sentimental phrases to the young ladies of Bienville presuming that you could guess who they were for but on account of the many disasters that befall one in service in an active campaign. I must omit this; notwithstanding I reverence and adore the young ladies of my native old parish yet I would not endeavor to cultivate a feeling of love, when a few days might end my career on earth, and thus leave an affectionate young Miss in distress. In the language of a sentimental poet

> I would not that one thought of me
> Should give their bosoms pain

2. Isaac M. Bryant of Homer, Louisiana, recovered from his illness and served through the war without injury or capture (Andrew B[radford] Booth, comp., *Records of Louisiana Confederate Soldiers and Louisiana Confederate Commands* (3 vols.; New Orleans, 1920), II, 167).

3. Meldrick M. Hand of Ringgold was declared missing in action after the battle of Sharpsburg and presumed dead, since he never returned to his unit (*ibid.,* Vol. III, Pt. 1, p. 173).

4. Zach Garrett of Ringgold was absent, sick, from June of 1862 until October, 1863. Returning to his company, he was captured at the battle of Rappahannock Station on November 7, 1863, and was held at Point Lookout until March 9, 1864. He surrendered with his regiment at Appomattox (*ibid.,* II, 978).

5. For James Monroe Thomas, see Chap. 2, n. 33.

6. Jasper G. Nix is listed in Booth, but the entry contains no additional information (Booth, comp., *Records,* Vol. III, Pt. 1, p. 1286).

Give my love to all the young ladies generally. Tell them that for them the soldier grasps his musket, faces the enemy, and risks life with all its comforts for
their liberty and freedom. Who would not die in a cause which the ladies all
look upon as glorious[?] Who would not fight a giant when those he loved
cheered him on with their applause and admiration[?] I love the ladies yes I do.
Excuse all amiss &c. I remain your brother
R. A. Pierson

Direct your letters to Richmond, Va. 2nd Brigade Army of Va.

⇀ ↽

REUBEN ALLEN PIERSON TO WILLIAM H. PIERSON

Camp near Gordonsville, Va.
Aug. 5th, 1862

W. H. Pierson
Dear Father
     I have written so many letters without receiving any replies that I have al-
most despaired ever hearing from home again. I see a letter written by Squire
Thomas[7] to Monroe and Bryan, which was mailed at Mt. Lebanon on the 13th
July. This looks like letters pass [past]. I am in excellent health. Have never reported on the sick list since I returned. In fact my health is better generally than
it has been since I quit the farm. The general health of the company is now
good, however we have some sickness. We had very bad luck during the month
of May—thirteen of the company died in that month. Only three have died
since. There are now 70 men present in my company and over fifty of them for
duty. We have four absent who were wounded in the battles of Winchester and
Port Republic.[8] I will give you the names of those who have died in the company numbering 16 in all: W. H. Britton, T. W. Humphreys, W. G. Mathews,

     7. "Squire" Thomas is David K. Thomas, the father of James Monroe Thomas, James Bryan
Thomas, and Amanda Jane Thomas, who was to marry James F. Pierson in November, 1865 (*ibid.*, Pt. 2,
pp. 807, 809).
     8. The twin battles of Cross Keys (June 8) and Port Republic (June 9) successfully extricated
Stonewall Jackson's Army of the Valley from a trap set by John C. Frémont, marching from the west, and
James Shields, marching from the east. The Louisiana Brigade's assault on the Union left at Port Repub-
lic captured a Union battery and forced Shields from the field, allowing Jackson to exit the Valley and
join Lee against McClellan on the peninsula (Robert G. Tanner, *Stonewall in the Valley: Thomas J.
"Stonewall" Jackson's Shenandoah Valley Campaign, Spring 1862* [New York, 1976], 278–81; Robert K.
Krick, *Conquering the Valley: Stonewall Jackson at Port Republic* [New York, 1995]).

Jas. Mitchell, J. B. Swain, E. C. Harper, John Webb, Wm. Worry, J. D. King,[9] W. A. King,[10] T. A. Brown, J. G. Whitley,[11] J. G. Nix, J. T. Watts,[12] John L. Morgan,[13] James Reeve.[14] This is a complete list of all the deaths up to this date. Most of them died from pneumonia, or relapse of measels. We were very much exposed when we first came out and this caused the death of many good soldiers. We have been transferred from our old brigade to a new one. We are now in a brigade with the 1st, 2nd, 10th, & 15th La. regiments, and we are now in A. P. Hill[']s division.[15] It is currently reported in camp that we will be sent to La. in the fall. Gen. Taylor has been promoted to Maj. Gen. (so says rumor) and will be given a command in La. As we are his old regiment we think he will carry us with him; but this is all speculation and amounts to nothing. I fear if we come back to La. that we will all have another tour of sickness which is worse than the slaughter of many battles.

We have all seen some of the horrors of war and they are terrible indeed. I have seen the dead and wounded lying in piles, the ground literally covered with blood. I have heard the groans of the dying, pittifully crying for help in the last agony of death. I have seen the fire blazing forth from the enemies['] battery and heard the balls whiz around from their lines. Everything is very different from what I had imagined it to be; a man can rush heedlessly on through battle over the dead and dying with as little remorse of conscience as he could shoot a wild beast. The excitement it is true is great and nothing can picture it so well to one[']s mind as the witnessing [of] it with one[']s own eyes. We are now encamped near Gordonsville and are expecting a battle in a few days, though we may not have one in a long time. If you get this continue to write often and I will get some of your letters. I received a letter from Henry as

9. James D. King, a farmer from Buck Horn, died at Gordonsville on May 17, 1862 (Booth, comp., *Records*, Vol. III, Pt. 1, p. 568).

10. William A. King, a farmer from Buck Horn, died on May 20, 1862 (*ibid.*, 571).

11. Joshua G. Whitley died on May 25, 1862, at Lynchburg, Virginia (*ibid.*, Pt. 2, p. 1072).

12. Joseph T. Watts died on July 4, 1862, at Lynchburg, Virginia (*ibid.*, 1012).

13. John L. Morgan joined Company C at Mount Lebanon on March 8, 1862, but was absent from the company, sick, through May and June. He died at Lynchburg on July 20 of an unspecified disease (Booth, comp., *Records*, Vol. III, Pt. 1, p. 1050).

14. James Reeve (or "Reeves") joined Company C in Bienville on March 8, 1862, but was absent from the company, sick, through May and June and was reported to have died in the hospital (*ibid.*, Pt. 2, p. 273).

15. Ambrose Powell Hill led a brigade in the Peninsula campaign and the famed "Light Division" from the Seven Days' Battles through Chancellorsville. With the reorganization of the army after Jackson's death, Hill was promoted to lieutenant general and given command of the newly constituted III Corps. Unfortunately for the southern cause, Hill's performance as a corps commander never measured up to his promise as a division commander. See James I. Robertson, Jr., *A. P. Hill: The Story of a Confederate Warrior* (New York, 1987).

late as the 17th July by which I hear you are all well. I have but little news. Everybody is looking to England and France for mediation or at least recognition. I have but little faith in mediation but think that the clamor of the people will demand recognition and by this means we will be recognized as a nation separated from the vile Fanatics of the North. I am getting along very well with the affairs of my company and think all are well satisfied. You must excuse me for writing so seldom. I have but few opportunities to write; seldom ever stationed for more than 2 or three days and then as busy as I can be all the time attending to my company affairs. Tell Mrs. Randle I have enquired for Walter and the 4th Geo. Regiment[16] but have not been able to find either as yet; if I should hear anything of him I will write immediately to her. Give my best regards to all enquiring friends. Remember me specially to all my lady friends. Extend my regards to all the family. Receive the best wishes of a dutiful son. Yours till death
R. A. Pierson

Direct all your letters to Richmond, Va. 2nd Brigade, A. P. Hill[']s division.

⇒ ⇐

DAVID PIERSON TO WILLIAM H. PIERSON

Camp Near Saltillo, Miss.
August 5th*, 1862*

Wm H. Pierson
   Mt. Lebanon
      La.

Dear Pa,

   Your favor from Caldwell Parish by Dr. Morse came duly to hand relieving me of much anxiety about the fate of Al from whom I had not heard a word since the battle of Richmond till your letter came. It is strange that Capt. Gunnels[17] should have kept my money so long without turning it over into the hands of Wm Walker[18] or yourself. He promised most faithfully to attend to it

16   The Fourth Georgia Infantry served in A. R. Wright's brigade during the Peninsula campaign and later in the brigades of Roswell Sabine Ripley, George Doles, and Philip Cook, who was the regiment's first colonel (Joseph H. Crute, Jr., *Units of the Confederate Army* [Midlothian, Va., 1987], 86).

17. W. L. Gunnels was mustered into Confederate service on May 17, 1861, as captain of Company I, Third Louisiana Infantry, but when he was not reelected at Corinth on May 8, 1862, he resigned and returned home (Willie H. Tunnard, *A Southern Record: The Story of the Third Regiment Louisiana Infantry* [1866; rpr. Dayton, Ohio, 1970], 522; Booth, *Records*, Vol. III, Pt. 1, p. 137).

18. William and Jack Walker were among the pioneer settlers of Mount Lebanon (Bienville Parish Historical Society, *History of Bienville Parish* [N.p., 1964], 97).

as soon as he got home. I hope you found no trouble in getting it and that you will make whatever use of it you may think proper. It was a fortunate thing for me that I sent it home at the time I did, for a little while afterwards I had my pocketbook stolen containing all I had—about three-hundred dollars including fifty dollars in gold (the same you let me have when I was at home) besides several valuable papers. It was taken from my pocket at night whilst I was asleep in my tent, and I have failed thus far to get any clue to the thief and really have no hopes of recovering it. I did not care for any but the gold which I was keeping rather as a curiosity and miss very much. As it so happened, I had several small amounts owing to me by members of the Regiment and have collected enough to answer my purposes. The Government is owing me about four-hundred dollars now, which I will draw in a few weeks and then I will have plenty again. You will perceive by the heading of this that we have changed station since I wrote you last. This place is situated about 12 miles above Tupelo on the Mobile & Ohio Railroad. We left the latter place very precipitately on the 29 ultimo, only ten minutes being given to prepare for marching, and it was generally understood at the time that there was trouble up this way and I have since learned that the Gen[l] himself was alarmed about some Federal Cavalry said to be approaching, but it all turned out to be a false alarm and two Brigades (the 1st and 2[d]) had to march 12 miles in the heat of the day without rest and be separated from all baggage for over two days all for nothing. These false alarms do more injury in an army than anything I know of. They not only dispirit the troops but almost invariably result in the loss of much valuable property such as arms, camp equipment, & c. besides cause soldiers and subordinates to lose confidence in the man who is responsible for them. We are now in about three miles of our lines and have heavy picket duty to do, all the roads in the neighborhood running northward being constantly guarded. We are apt to have considerable work to do as all the army except two Divisions of the Army of the West have left & gone to Chattanooga. Price is now in Command here, but it is thought even by his friends that McGruder or some other Gen[l] will be placed over the department. It is known as the Department of the Tennessee[19] and embraces North Miss. and a portion of North Ala. Gen[l]. Price has just issued a flaming order promising to drive the enemy across the banks of the Ohio. It is thought by some that we will move northward simultaneously with Bragg's forces from Chattanooga and by others that our small force is left here merely as

19. The Confederate Department of Tennessee entailed all of Tennessee as well as northwest Georgia and part of northeast Alabama. The department's first commander, Braxton Bragg, was superseded in November, 1863, by Joseph E. Johnston. In July, 1864, Johnston was in turn replaced by John Bell Hood. On August 15, 1864, the department was dissolved and replaced by the Department of Tennessee and Georgia.

a guard upon the R.R. & protection of the valley from raids by the enemies' Cavalry. Our gallant Colonel F. C. Armstrong who recently left here with a small force of Cavalry as acting Brigadier Gen[l]. has turned up at Courtland, Ala., with a brilliant success. The news is that he defeated the enemy at that place, taking 133 prisoners including several officers besides capturing large quantities of provisions and other military stores & destroying the Rail Road (Memphis & Charleston) at that place. I believe that he is not inferior to Forest[20] or Morgan[21] and only wants an opportunity to show his skill as a Cavalry officer. His appointment will no doubt be confirmed by the President. Look out for a storm at Chattanooga soon. There have gone a host of fighting Rebels there. Nothing from Al yet nor from Henry in a long time. My health is good—health also good in camps. We hear that communication has been opened at Vicksburg between the East and West by the withdrawal of the Fed fleet. If so we ought to get letters from home now. I send this by Mr. Cottingham,[22] our suttler, who starts to Caldwell Parish tomorrow morning.

Nothing [*letter torn*].
Yours Affectionately
D. Pierson

20. Nathan Bedford Forrest was regarded by Ulysses S. Grant as "the ablest cavalry general in the South." Although deprived of a formal education, Forrest was a natural leader and a brilliant cavalry officer. As a raider, he contributed mightily to the Confederate cause, disrupting enemy supply and communication networks in Tennessee and capturing prisoners far in excess of his own numbers. As a tactician, he conducted a number of small but classic set-piece battles, including the flawless performance at Brice's Cross Roads, Mississippi, on June 10, 1864. See Brian Steele Wills, *A Battle from the Start: The Life of Nathan Bedford Forrest* (New York, 1992); Jack Hurst, *Nathan Bedford Forrest: A Biography* (New York, 1993).

21. John Hunt Morgan was elected to command of a company of Kentucky infantry and was soon promoted to colonel of the Second Kentucky Cavalry and then to brigadier general. Operating under the command of Maj. Gen. Joseph Wheeler, Morgan and his men made a spectacular reputation as raiders, slashing deep into Tennessee and Kentucky in the summer and fall of 1862 and into Indiana and Ohio in the summer of 1863. His Ohio raid was the longest cavalry raid of the war. Morgan was captured at New Lisbon, Ohio, but escaped, only to be killed in a cavalry skirmish at Greenville, Tennessee. See James A. Ramage, *Rebel Raider: The Life of General John Hunt Morgan* (Lexington, Ky., 1986).

22. This is perhaps Moses L. Cottingham of Winn Parish (U.S. Census, 1860, Winn Parish, Louisiana, 969).

⇒ ⇐

REUBEN ALLEN PIERSON TO WILLIAM H. PIERSON

Charlottesville, Va.
Aug. 17th, 1862

W. H. Pierson, Esqr.

Dear Father

I am now absent from my company for the first time since I have been elected. I took the fever about ten or twelve days ago, but thought that I would stay with the company as we were expecting a battle hourly.[23] I contrived to keep up by riding in the ambulance till the battle came off when I went with the company through the whole affair. I lay out on the cold ground in line of battle through the whole night, having fever all the while. My company came out unhurt excepting one man who was knocked down with a piece of a bombshell. He was able for duty the next day. I am now staying at a Hotel in the beautiful little village of Charlottesville. I fare as well as I could wish—have plenty of vegetables and fruit which is something rare with me. I have a light chill every day, but not enough to confine me to bed more than an hour each day.

We have been transferred from our old brigade and placed in one composed of the 1st, 2nd, 9th, 10, & 15th La. Regts. and we have been transferred to Stonewall Jackson's division.[24] I have been absent from the company only four days and think I shall return in a few more days. I shall endeavor to break up the chills as soon as possible. I will send you as much as two hundred dollars by the first good opportunity. I have three months['] wages due me the first of September which will amount to three hundred and ninety dollars. I have been through some as close places as I ever expect to be in; and have but little fear of the consequences. The destruction of human life has been enormous in all the battles before Rich-

23. On July 13, 1862, Robert E. Lee dispatched Jackson to Gordonsville, Virginia, to "restrain, as far as possible, the atrocities" which Federal major general John Pope "threatened to perpetrate on upon our defenseless citizens." Jackson reached Gordonsville on July 19, but for two weeks no action occurred. Then, on August 9, Jackson's command clashed with the II Corps of Pope's Army of Virginia, led by Jackson's old antagonist, Nathaniel P. Banks. In a day of heavy fighting, Jackson repulsed Banks's assault and counterattacked, driving the Federals from the field. The battle of Cedar Mountain was a prelude to the second battle of Manassas (Robert K. Krick, *Stonewall Jackson at Cedar Mountain* [Chapel Hill, 1990], 7).

24. With the end of the Seven Days' Battles, the Army of Northern Virginia was reorganized, with Richard Taylor promoted to major general and transferred to the Trans-Mississippi Department. The old Louisiana Brigade was given to Brig. Gen. Harry Thompson Hays, the former colonel of the Seventh Louisiana, and the Second Louisiana Brigade was formed of the First, Second, Ninth, Tenth, and the new Fifteenth Louisiana. This brigade was to be commanded by William E. Starke, formerly the colonel of a Virginia regiment and for that reason resented by the Louisianians. It became a component of Jackson's former division, now commanded by William Taliaferro (Terry L. Jones, *Lee's Tigers: The Louisiana Infantry in the Army of Northern Virginia* [Baton Rouge, 1987], 111–12).

mond; some places the dead lay in piles altogether, Yankees and Confederates lying side by side. I hear from home but seldom. Have had but one letter from home since Tom Pittman arrived in camps. That was written by Jimmy in May. I hear from Bienville occasionally by the letters of others. I saw a letter written by D. K. Thomas mailed at Mt. Lebanon on the 13th of July. I receive a letter occasionally from Dave and have received one letter from Henry. I have written home often and have received no response. I fear that you fail to get my letters. You must excuse me for complaining of not getting letters. I see others are receiving letters constantly. We are expecting a heavy battle near Culpepper Court House today or tomorrow. The yankees are about 100,000 strong and our men are advancing with about an equal force. Our forces are commanded by Gens. Lee, Jackson, Johnson & Longstreet. The yankees are led by Pope, Burnside & others.[25] I shall continue to write once a week till I entirely recover my health. Give my best love and respects to all enquiring friends, especially the young ladies. Remember me kindly to all the family relations. Receive the love and best wishes of an absent son

R. A. Pierson

P.S. Direct your letters to Richmond, Va. 7th La. Brigade, Jackson[']s Division.

⇒ ⇐

DAVID PIERSON TO WILLIAM H. PIERSON
Camp Near Saltillo, Miss., Aug. 24th, 1862

Wm H. Pierson
  Mt. Lebanon
    La.

Dear Pa,

Your favor of the 3rd came to hand on the 12th Inst. I would have replied earlier but have been looking for you here by every train since I received your let-

25. John Pope's successes at New Madrid, Missouri, and Island Number Ten led to his promotion as major general and appointment to command of the Army of Virginia on March 22, 1862. Lee and Jackson soundly defeated Pope at the second battle of Manassas on August 29–30, 1862. Thereafter, he held a succession of commands on the Indian frontier (Warren G. Hassler, *Commanders of the Army of the Potomac* [Baton Rouge, 1962], 56–76).

Ambrose E. Burnside achieved some success on the coast of North Carolina, for which he was rewarded with promotion to major general and command of a corps in the Army of the Potomac. Appointed to command of the army on November 7, 1862, Burnside led it to a disastrous defeat at Fredericksburg on December 13, 1862, and thereafter was given command of the Department of Ohio, a relative backwater. He partly redeemed his reputation at the defense of Knoxville during the fall of 1863 and was returned to command of his old corps in Virginia. See William Marvel, *Burnside* (Chapel Hill, 1991).

ter. I have given you out now and hope you will not incur the danger of being captured by the Federals on my account. If you can hire a boy for me, do so and wait for an opportunity to send him by someone coming this way. I have nothing new to write you—no change of any importance has taken place in this quarter since my last. An army of twenty-five thousand men is lying here idle under Gen. Price whilst the enemy is permitted to plunder and destroy in sight of our lines. I can't understand it. Price's friends say he is tied down by orders from Bragg not to move or engage the enemy till he tells him. Whilst others are inclined to the opinion that the Old Chieftain is afraid to hazard his fame by active operations. I thought I never would get tired with ease and quiet, but the reports we receive here from the citizens in regard to the depredations of the enemy in the country north of us and so near to our lines is enough to enrage anyone and really, if I had my way I would at least make an effort to punish them. It is known that the enemy is engaged in cutting down green corn, burning fences & farm houses, shooting and stealing stock, and decoying away all the Negroes in the country. It is a shame that the soil of Miss. should thus be overrun and her people, who have so nobly sustained our cause, be driven from their homes or perish at the hands of her enemies when relief is so near at hand. Belden[26] says that Van Dorn has called on Price for reinforcements in view of an expected attack by land on Vicksburg and that Price has refused to furnish any—further that the former has applied to Bragg to compel the latter to comply. We of the 3rd La. are in hopes it is true as we want to get down into La. or go anywhere to get out of a Missouri clique. Every officer in this Reg[t] except two signed a petition a few days ago to be transferred to Van Dorn's Dept. Nobody but a Missourian stands any chance here and we naturally want to get away.

Very little is heard of Bragg and his command though it is evident he is steadily moving northward and pressing the enemy hard. I believe he will drive them out of Tenn. in less than two months. We were all surprised to hear of the Federal Gunboats back at Vicksburg again and mortified at their success on the La. side. If the 3rd La. could have been where the 31st[27] was, they would not

26. Twenty-six-year-old H. C. Belden joined Company C as a private on May 17, 1861, but was elected second lieutenant with the reorganization of May 8, 1862. For much of his period of service he was confined to the hospital and resigned on January 8, 1863 (Tunnard, *A Southern Record,* 498; Booth, comp., *Records,* I, 157).

27. The Thirty-first Louisiana Infantry, commanded by Col. Charles H. Morrison, was organized at Monroe, Louisiana, on June 11, 1862, and ordered to Milliken's Bend opposite Vicksburg. There, on August 18, a Federal gunboat captured the transport *Fair Play* and its cargo of arms, which the Thirty-first was unloading. A small landing party then drove the regiment away from Milliken's Bend and pursued it to Tallulah, Louisiana. The Thirty-first to some degree redeemed its reputation by performing admirably during the siege of Vicksburg but was of little service after its parole (Frank E. Vandiver, *Plowshares into Swords: Josiah Gorgas and Confederate Ordnance* [Austin, 1952], 139; Arthur W. Bergeron, Jr., *Guide to Louisiana Confederate Military Units, 1861–1865* [Baton Rouge, 1989], 143–44).

have had such an easy time in burning the Depot and destroying public property. We think so, of course.

The weather is getting some cooler—the nights are especially cool & pleasant. All things considered, we are passing a pleasant time. The cars come up daily bringing Mobile papers only two days old, thereby furnishing us with all the late news from all quarters except home. The citizens are very kind and bring us peaches and apples at ten cents per dozen and now and then a few water melons at a dollar a piece. I have had only one melon this season, and the peaches are small and indifferent. I got a letter from Al two days ago dated 5th Aug. He was in fine spirits. Nothing from Henry lately. Excuse this letter—I write hurriedly as the young man by whom I send this across the river is about to be off.

Yours Affectionately,
D. Pierson

P. S. I just have heard that the Feds have evacuated Baton Rouge.[28]

D. P.

➤ ◄

REUBEN ALLEN PIERSON TO JAMES F. PIERSON

Frederick, Md.
Sept. 7th, 1862

James F. Pierson
Dear brother

I have an opportunity of sending a letter by a Mr. Corbett,[29] a member of the Brush Valley Guards. I have been marching and fighting nearly the whole time since I arrived at my regiment upon returning from furlough. The Bienville Blues were ordered to take up the line of march immediately after their reorganization and have never been still as long as two weeks at any time since. We have marched nearly all over the state of Va. and are now in the state of

28. In an attempt to secure Vicksburg's southern flank, Maj. Gen. John C. Breckinridge attacked Brig. Gen. Thomas Williams' garrison at Baton Rouge on August 5, 1862. Williams was killed in the assault and his troops driven back to the Mississippi River, but there the Federals took shelter under the guns of the Union gunboats and were safe from continued Confederate assaults. The Confederate ram *Arkansas,* which was to have cooperated with Breckinridge, suffered engine troubles and never reached the scene of the fighting, thus largely canceling the Confederate victory. The battle of Baton Rouge did, however, buy enough time for the Confederates to occupy and begin to fortify Port Hudson, twenty-five miles up the river. On August 21, the Federals evacuated Baton Rouge (John D. Winters, *The Civil War in Louisiana* [1963; rpr. Baton Rouge, 1991], 113–24; Tom Z. Parrish, *The Saga of the Confederate Ram Arkansas: The Mississippi Valley Campaign, 1862* [Hillsboro, Tex., 1987], 191–200).

29. Leonardus D. Corbett (or "Corbitt") of Sabine, Louisiana, was discharged "for disability" on August 26, 1862 (Booth, comp., *Records,* II, 439).

Maryland as you will see by the heading of this letter. We commenced an advance upon Pope[']s grand army about the 16th of Aug. Our Gens. endeavored to cut off their retreat by moving around their left flank, but Pope discovered this move and retreated before we succeeded in reaching his rear. He crossed the Rhappahannock River and planted heavy batteries to prevent our crossing in pursuit. This only served to aid Jackson in his strategy. He soon discovered a ford near Warrenton Springs where he could cross unobserved by the enemy, and with three divisions he hastened around to Manassas where he surprised the guard and captured all the com[m]issaries and a train of cars loaded with all the paraphernalia of an army. He also took several hundred pris[o]ners and over two hundred slaves who had gone over to the yanks from the surrounding counties. Jackson had now succeeded in accomplishing what he had long desired. He had got in the rear of Pope and cut off his communication from the city of Washington. We remained in a few miles of this place four days fighting all the while—holding the enemy at bay till Longstreet could bring up reenforcements to overpower him and capture his whole force. But owing to some mismanagement, most of Pope[']s forces made their escape. We took a few thousand pris[o]ners, many arms and a large lot of field artillery of the finest make. I have no idea as to the number killed and wounded on either side, but from what I saw I am certain that the enemies['] loss was four times that of ours. In the two last days['] fights our little Brigade killed and wounded their full number or over with the loss of only 150 men in all killed and wounded. In one place where the yankees charged us behind the embankment of an old railroad the ground was literally covered with their dead and wounded. Our regiment suffered considerable but not so much as some others. My company lost in all the fighting of the four days one killed and three wounded.[30] Cousin John Williams who has been nearly always [ready] for duty and participated in every battle was killed by a grape or canister striking him in the head and tearing out his brains. After the enemy had fled and the firing ceased, he lived to see them run and rejoiced at our success. He was a gallant soldier, a good companion—beliked by all the company and died in the faithful discharge of his duty. His loss is deeply mourned by all the members of Co. C. and many of them offer up their warmest sympathies to his weeping mother and sad hearted father. Many will be the tears of his loving brothers and sisters when the doleful news reaches their ears. But it was God[']s will to remove him from this world of

---

30. The second battle of Manassas or Bull Run, fought on August 29–30, 1862, was, as Pierson reports, a major Confederate victory, leaving John Pope's Army of Virginia disorganized and demoralized and paving the way for Robert E. Lee's first invasion of the North. The most colorful event of the battle was probably the Second Louisiana Brigade's repulse of one of Pope's assaults by hurling stones at the enemy after its ammunition supply was exhausted. See John J. Hennessy, *Return to Bull Run: The Campaign and Battle of Second Manassas* (New York, 1993).

trouble and pain and I sincerely hope he is happy in eternity where he may meet all his kindred and friends after they shall have paid the debt which all all must pay. The three wounded were John T. Evans severely in the head but is now fast recovering as I have learned from one of the boys who has just come up tonight from behind; Wm. Scogin in the thigh very slight; and James Sledge[31] in the shoulder very slight. Both are up and waiting on those who are badly wounded. Our company has been much more fortunate than any other in the regiment and we should all be thankful to him who rules all things according to his own good will and pleasure, for our preservation through so many dangers. I have often thought of the prayers and petitions rendered up in our behalf by fond and loving Christian friends at home. I would as one of the wandering and misguided sinners of the absent soldiers ask a continuation of the prayers of all true devoted Christians in my native country and around my loved and ever cherished home. This may seem as strange notions for a soldier to be indulging in surrounded by wickedness on every side, but yet the heart that can remain unmoved and stubborn after passing through as many dangers & making so many miraculous escapes must truly be made of adamantine. When others fall around on the right and left and are momentarily hurried into eternity the question naturally arises what protects me from a similar fate, the only answer being one Who gives life and Who alone can take it away.

Give my love and regards to all enquiring friends, accepting the same yourself. The health of the company is only tolerable, something over 50 present being the largest company in the regiment. I must close. Corbet is leaving.
Your brother till death
R. A. Pierson

⇒ ⇐

REUBEN ALLEN PIERSON TO WILLIAM H. PIERSON
[FRAGMENT, CA. SEPTEMBER, 1862]

After the surrender of Harpers Ferry[32] the troops rested until about 12 oclock at night and were then marched for Shepherdstown where they crossed the

31. James S. Sledge of Vernon, Louisiana, was detailed as a nurse in the spring of 1862 and was captured at Winchester. Exchanged on August 5, 1862, he was promoted to fifth sergeant on August 1, 1864. At some point, he transferred from Company C to Company K, and was with his unit when it surrendered at Appomattox (Booth, comp., *Records,* Vol. III, Pt. 2, p. 592).

32. On September 15, 1862, the 12,000-man garrison of Harpers Ferry surrendered to three Confederate divisions under Stonewall Jackson after a two-day siege. Although the capitulation eliminated an immediate threat to Lee's rear as he marched into Maryland, Jackson's troops were so delayed that the Rebel army, already seriously outnumbered, was left without many of its veterans—including the two Louisiana brigades—at the subsequent battle of Sharpsburg (Jones, *Lee's Tigers,* 128).

Potomac the next morning about sunrise, and advanced upon the enemy who were camped near Sharpsburg,[33] a little village about two miles distant from the river. Here they lay in line all that day and night exposed to a heavy can[n]onading, and early the next morning they charged upon the enemy and drove them from their position, but owing to our brigade's having no support on the left the yankees came in on their flank and came near cutting them off, compelling them to fall back in some confusion. But they soon rallied and drove the enemy back again. They fought nearly the whole day and were twice repulsed but at night held the whole ground and the next day brought off their wounded & dead and buried the dead, removed the wounded over the river and sent them to Winchester. Some of those who were too severely wounded to bear removing were left and fell into the hands of the enemy when we fell back across the river. In this engagement my company suffered severely. Five were killed dead on the field and one mortally wounded who has since died, 1st Lt. S. T. Robinson,[34] Privates W. O. Price,[35] W. J. Scogin, H. M. Jeffress,[36] and E. Legget[tes] [37] were killed on the field. Jesse Woodward[38] was mortally wounded and died 2 days after. Some fifteen were wounded who are all doing well. H. P. Theus,[39] J. C. Lamar,[40] A. N. Walker

33. Robert E. Lee led his Army of Northern Virginia north of the Potomac River for the first time on September 4, 1862. George B. McClellan attacked Lee's army at Sharpsburg, Maryland, on Antietam Creek on September 17. A day of uncoordinated and piecemeal assaults failed to rupture Lee's wafer-thin line, but the greatly weakened and dangerously outnumbered southern army withdrew across the Potomac that night, ending the Confederacy's best hope for a successful military conclusion to the war. See Stephen W. Sears, *Landscape Turned Red: The Battle of Antietam* (New Haven, 1983).

34. Samuel T. Robinson of Mount Lebanon was appointed second sergeant of Company C on December 28, 1861, and was killed in action at Sharpsburg on September 17, 1862. No record of his promotion to first lieutenant can now be located (Booth, comp., *Records*, Vol. III, Pt. 2, p. 358).

35. W. Oscar Price of Natchitoches, Louisiana, was killed in action at Sharpsburg on September 17, 1862 (*ibid.*, 204).

36. H. M. Jeffress of Union, Louisiana, was killed in action at Sharpsburg on September 17, 1862 (*ibid.*, 434).

37. Eli B. Leggettes of Vernon, Louisiana, was killed in action at Sharpsburg on September 17, 1862 (*ibid.*, 715).

38. Jesse Woodward is not listed in Booth, comp., *Records*.

39. Hezekiah P. Theus of Ringgold was furloughed home after receiving a wound at Sharpsburg. He returned to his unit in February, 1863, and apparently served until the war's end (Booth, comp., *Records*, Vol. III, Pt. 2, p. 799).

40. John C. Lamar, a student from El Dorado, Arkansas, was wounded in action at Sharpsburg on September 17, 1862; returned to his unit; was captured at Rappahannock Station on November 7, 1863; was incarcerated at Point Lookout until March 15, 1864; was again captured at Fisher's Hill, September 22, 1864; was returned to Point Lookout until February 15, 1865; was exchanged; and surrendered with his company at Appomattox (*ibid.*, Pt. 1, p. 627).

& W. J. Heflin[41] are the worst. I heard from them yesterday and infer from what they wrote that they are out of danger. I suppose some of them will get leave[s] of abscence. Corp. Tarkinton[42] and Jas. Morgan[43] were both wounded and may also get furloughs. Three men of the company who went in were not found either dead or wounded and we have heard nothing from them since. I hope they were only taken pris[o]ners and we will soon hear from them. The following are their names: W. T. Loftin,[44] Jas. B. Thomas & M. M. Hand. Prof. Lindon[45] and Daniel Carter[46] have been taken pris[o]ners and paroled. They will probably get furloughs home till ex-changed.

My health is bad. I have been having chills for more than three week[s] but am able to be on foot. I am with the company but not on duty. I was absent both at the surrender of Harpers Ferry and the battle of Sharpsburg, Md. I was then sick at Martinsburg, Va. My respects to the home folks and vicinity.
I remain your Son
R. A. Pierson

41. W. J. Heflin of Buck Horn joined Company C at Camp Bienville on September 4, 1861. He was captured on July 26, 1862, but exchanged on August 2 in time to participate in the Sharpsburg campaign, where he was wounded. He was again wounded at the second battle of Winchester, on June 14, 1863, there losing a leg. He spent several months in various hospitals in Virginia, Georgia, and Mississippi and was then assigned to light duty in Georgia (*ibid.*, 255–56).

42. Thomas B. Tarkinton of Salt Springs, Louisiana, was wounded in the shoulder at Sharpsburg but returned to duty, to be captured at Chancellorsville on May 3, 1863. After his exchange from Fort Delaware only twenty days later, he "deserted to the cavalry" and surrendered at Natchitoches, Louisiana, at the end of the war (*ibid.*, Pt. 2, p. 768).

43. James Morgan of Ringgold was wounded at Sharpsburg but rejoined to his company until the fall of 1863, when he failed to return from a sick furlough. Thereafter he was listed as a deserter (*ibid.*, Pt. 1, p. 1049).

44. William T. Loftin (sometimes "Loften") of Minden, Louisiana, was captured at Sharpsburg and held at Fort Delaware until exchanged on October 2, 1862. He was wounded at Chancellorsville and again at Monocacy. After August 31, 1864, he was in Louisiana without leave (*ibid.*, 779).

45. F. H. Lindon (sometimes "Linden"), a Prussian-born instructor of instrumental and vocal music and French at the Mount Lebanon Female College, enlisted in the Ninth Louisiana on March 8, 1862, and joined Company C in Virginia. He was captured at Second Manassas and paroled to his home until exchanged. Thereafter he returned to his unit, serving from November, 1862 until August 31, 1864, after which he seems to have returned to Louisiana without leave (*ibid.*, 763; *Louisiana Baptist,* June 11, 1861).

46. Daniel A. Carter of Sparta enlisted in the Ninth Louisiana on March 15, 1862, was captured during the retreat from Sharpsburg, and was quickly exchanged. He was again captured at Rappahannock Station, on November 7, 1863, and held at Point Lookout until March 10, 1864. Thereafter he served with Company C until Appomattox, receiving a slight wound at the battle of Spotsylvania (Booth, comp., *Records,* II, 273).

⇒ ⇐

W. F. HOWELL TO WILLIAM H. PIERSON

Camp Baldwin Mississippi
September 24th, 1862

W. H. Pierson, Esq.,

Dear Friend,

It is with sorrow that I announce to you sad nuse [news] of the fate of your son, Capt. D. Pierson. On the 19th inst. at the battle of Iuka, while at the head of his company and just as the command "Charge" was give, he received a shot which took effect in the right side of his forehead and, following skul[l] bone round, came out near the back part of the head but did not brake the bone. He instantly fell to the ground and exclaimed to the company, "Go ahead boys!" He was taken off the field by the infirmary chore [*i.e.*, corps] and carried to the hospital.[47] A nurse was detailed from the company and left to wate on him. The Surgeon of the regt. was also lef[t] to wate [on the] wounded. Some of the boys say they saw him the next morning and he was doing well, was in his right mind. All was taken prisoners in the hospital together. The Dokter says if he lives three days he will be well in a week. I was in ten miles of Iuka at the time and would have been with him, but the federals had piquets on the road which cut me of[f] from the army. I have written you a letter by mail in which have given all the particulars.

Yours Truly,
W. F. Howell[48]

[Of the battle of Iuka, Second Lt. P. Lesten Prudhomme of Company G, Third Louisiana Infantry, wrote from Saltillo, Mississippi, to his father, Lesten Prudhomme, in Natchitoches, Louisiana, on September 25, 1862.][49]

---

47. In 1862 the Confederate army instituted an ambulance corps. Authorized to wear a distinctive uniform and imbued with an especially high morale, these "medics" evacuated the wounded from the battlefields, often under fire. Lacking men, medicines, and ambulances, the "infirmary corps" nevertheless did wonders with the resources at hand (H. H. Cunningham, *Doctors in Gray: The Confederate Medical Service* [1958; rpr. Baton Rouge, 1993], 114–16; Courtney R. Hall, "Confederate Medicine," *Medical Life*, XLII [1935], 473). For an excellent account of the battle of Iuka, see Peter Cozzens, *The Darkest Days of the War: The Battles of Iuka and Corinth* (Chapel Hill, 1997).

48. W. F. Howell was a sergeant in Company B, Third Louisiana Infantry. He was killed in action at the siege of Vicksburg, June 11, 1863 (Booth, comp., *Records*, Vol. III, Pt. 1, p. 368; Tunnard, *A Southern Record*, 528).

49. P. L. Prudhomme to Lesten Prudhomme, September 25, 1862, Saltillo, Mississippi, Prudhomme Family Papers, Louisiana Collection, Louisiana State University Archives. Others of Prudhomme's letters may be found in the Carmen Breazeale Collection and the Robert DeBlieux Collection, both in the Cammie G. Henry Research Center, Eugene P. Watson Memorial Library, Northwestern University of Louisiana.

Dear Father

For the last four days we have been in a state of feverish excitement about a thousand rumors concerning a fight at Iuka between Price's forces and Rosancrantz, and last night getting a correct version of it by some of our wounded, I hasten to transmit them to you. Paul and Fulbert are safe.

Price went to Iuka and took possession of the place the enemy having been driven off the day previous by Armstrong's cavalry. Commissary stores and 40 bales of blankets were captured, all of which I understand has been safely brought off. On the 19th the enemy came down in force and preparations were made to attack them. A flag of truce was sent in by Rosancrantz asking surrender of our force to prevent bloodshed stating Lee and Jackson had been whipped in Maryland and our cause was lost. Price answered he did not believe in the defeat of our Generals and that were it so, it was a greater inducment for us to fight so much the more obstinately.—About 4 in the evening our Brigade came in contact with a large force of the enemy well posted on a hill and immediately a most murderous fight commenced and lasted till after dark. Reenforcements came to us and we remained in possession of the field. Early next morning we commenced to retreat towards Baldwyn there being danger of our communication being cut off and we arrived at Baldwyn on the 23rd. The loss on our side is estimated in killed, wounded and missing at 4 or 500. The enemy's supposed great. A battery of 9 pieces was charged and captured by our forces but the horses being nearly all killed only three were taken the balance spiked.—

I here record the death of Joseph M. Tauzin[50] son of Marcelin. He was shot through the head and died without a struggle. I regret him for I considered him a friend and he was a most excellent young man and liked by all the boys. What a terrible blow for poor Marcelin. But such are the chances of war and we must humbly submit to the will of our Maker.

It is estimated that 250 of our Regmt was in the fight and 108 are killed, wounded and missing. In the darkness of the night our flag was captured, which is much regret[t]ed by the boys. Our brave regiment already much reduced is now almost down to nothing. I do hope it will be recruited and not disbanded and thrown into some other to fill it. It has won itself a name even among the enmy and so I think the Government should let it exist.

I am still as you perceive from the heading of this, at the hospital, and waiting for an opportunity to meet the command. I am very well. The place is so dull I hardly know what to do with myself.—

50. Joseph M. Tauzin enlisted in Company G as a private on May 17, 1861, and was elected sergeant at Corinth on May 15, 1862 (Booth, comp., *Records*, Vol. III, Pt. 2, p. 773).

I give you a list of the casualties in our company which suffered much and all the boys had their clothes more or less perforated with bullet holes. Paul wrote me it was the hottest fight he had yet experienced.—

Pel[ican]. R[ifles] No. 1

Killed. Sergeant J. T. Tauzin.
Severely wounded. Jean Guinchamp, Escoveda. Slightly wounded Corporal F. Sanchez, Privates R. Allaman, W. A. Charleville, J. B. P. Hyams, Eugene Guinchamp, Guiton and E. C. Murphy. The three latter so slightly that they keep with the command. Charleville and Hyams in thigh flesh wound. Sanchez wrist, Allaman elbow, both flesh wounds.

Company Pelicans No 2.

Lieut. Gervais Trichel wounded right arm (flesh wound). Privates wounded.—O. Laplante, W. W. Ivy, T. H. McKasky severely. Slightly wounded Joseph Charleville flesh wound in right arm, Benson Davis.—Lt. Col. Guilmore right arm broken (shot) horse disabled. Major Russell['s] horse killed under him. Adjutant J. H. Brigham wounded in hand, horse killed under him. Captain Pierson, Winn Rifles, pretty severely wounded in head, but not considered dangerous. In fight two commissioned officers were killed and fifteen wounded in our Regmt. Lt. Col. Guilmore and Major Russell acted most gallantly throughout the engagement. Genl. Little[51] commanding Division being killed, Maj. Gen. Hebert took command and by his bravery and gallantry on the field received the applause of the troops. This is not the only time he has deserved credit in Acct. for at Oak Hill and Elk horn he deserved praise.—With this I send you a paper, the latest date I have. The news on our side continue favorable. May God grant a continuance of it and peace to our suffering and bleeding country.

My kind regards to Phanor, Ben, Narcisse and the Neighbors. Kiss Ma, my sisters, nephews and nieces for me and believe me your ever affectionate and devoted son

P. L. Prudhomme

51. Lewis Henry Little was appointed adjutant of the Missouri State Guard, and his star rose with that of his friend Sterling Price. As a colonel in the Confederate army, he commanded the First Missouri Brigade at Pea Ridge, winning promotion to brigadier general. When Price assumed command of the Army of the West, Little took over his old division, consisting mostly of Missouri troops. Despite misgivings about the wisdom of the campaign as well as ill health, Little was in the vanguard of his division at Iuka, Mississippi, on September 19, 1862, when he was killed instantly by a bullet that had passed under Price's arm (Albert Castel, ed., "The Diary of General Henry Little, C.S.A.," *Civil War Times Illustrated,* XI [October, 1972], 4–11, 41–47).

P.S. Tell mother not to send my boots nor hand trunk for I have no use for them. Shoes are preferable for marching, and as for the trunk there is no transportation. I have a pair of saddle bags that answer the purpose but she might send me a carpet bag if she has any.

The boys tell me it is a miracle that they were not all killed so hot and close was the fire. I forgot to mention that from our company J. M. Morran, Bearman and Hartman were missing. No one knows whether they were killed or taken prisoners.[52] I hope it is the latter.

⇒ ⇐

REUBEN ALLEN PIERSON TO WILLIAM H. PIERSON
In camp 12 miles from Winchester [Va.]
Oct. 1st, 1862

W. H. Pierson
Mt. Lebanon, La.
Dear Father

Again I sit down to write home without having received a line from home. I have written as many as seven letters home since I received a letter from any of you all while others are receiving letters daily from Lebanon. Why is it that I receive none? The only answer that [I] can imagine to the question is you are all to busy to write. We have all been stationed in camps around Winchester ever since the battle of Sharpsburg. We marched down on the Potomac once and remained five days, during which time we tore up the track of the Baltimore and Ohio R.R. for more than twenty miles, burned the ties and ruined the iron by bending it across the fires. The enemy seems but little disposed to advance upon us; we are now within a day[']s march of Harpers Ferry where the enemy have been stationed for several weeks. They remain within their fortifications not thinking it prudent to attack us. Everything is quiet in camp. Rumors are frequently circulated around that we have been recognized by Belgium but no one believes a word of them.

The health of the troops is generally good so far as my knowledge extends. My company with 68 present has nine on the sick list but none of those is confined to bed, mostly complaining from colds. There is still much talk of our

52. James M. Morran apparently returned to his company shortly after the battle of Iuka, for he was later reported wounded and captured at Vicksburg. S. W. Behrman was captured at Iuka, paroled, and eventually exchanged but never rejoined his company. M. S. Hartman was reported missing in action after the battle and never was heard of again (Booth, comp., *Records,* Vol. III, Pt. 1, p. 1056, I, 156, Vol. III, Pt. 1, p. 215).

being sent back to La. I have but little faith in it myself. But a few weeks will develop what course will be taken in the matter. When I hear I will write home. I have not been paid off since May and the Government is now due me six hundred and fifty ($650) dollars. I expect to receive pay in a few days & will send home a part of the money the first opportunity. If I have a chance I will send you 100 pounds of fine tobacco. Tell Jimmy I think by his coming to my company I can get him a position either in the commissary or quartermaster['s] department where he will have a horse to ride. Tell sister if she can spare time to write to me at least once every two weeks.

The account given of the daring deeds performed by Capt. John Hodges[53] & myself in the La. Baptist,[54] by someone who had just returned is utterly false and the author was certainly not there. In the first place Capt. H was absent sick during the whole trip till we crossed into Maryland. 2nd the 9th Regt. nor Col. Stafford never refused to charge at any time or place. The author of that story cannot be one of the wounded Blues, but must be someone who generally gets sick about the time the cannons begin to roar. We have two commissioned officers present only. Lt. Colbert had a severe attack of pneumonia a few days since and was sent to the hospital at Winchester. He was improving when he left but I have not heard from him since his brother went with him. I have not have not heard any late news from the absent sick at Lynchburg, Charlottesville or Gordonsville. I have not heard from those who were missing at the battle of Sharpsburg though I hope they are only pris[o]ners. With my best regards to both friends and relatives I remain your affectionate Son till death
R. A. Pierson

53. John J. Hodges, a Bossier Parish law student at the time of the outbreak of the war, was the original captain of Company D. He was promoted to major of the Ninth Louisiana on July 4, 1863—Henry L. N. Williams having been killed at Gettysburg—and then to lieutenant colonel on October 8, 1863. He was wounded and taken prisoner at the battle of Monocacy on July 9, 1864, and held at Fort Delaware and Point Lookout until exchanged on November 15, 1864 (*ibid.,* Vol. III, Pt. 1, pp. 323–24).

54. The *Louisiana Baptist* was founded at Mount Lebanon in 1855 by the Reverend Hanson Lee. When Lee died in 1863, the paper was continued by W. F. Wells. In about 1869, the paper merged with the *Memphis Baptist.* Only three wartime issues of the paper—two at Louisiana State University and one at Northwestern State University of Louisiana—are now extant (W. E. Paxton, *A History of the Baptists of Louisiana from the Earliest Times to the Present* [St. Louis, 1888], 489).

⇒ ⇐

REUBEN ALLEN PIERSON TO JAMES F. PIERSON

In camp near Bunker's Hill, Va.
Oct. 8th, 1862

James F. Pierson
Mt. Lebanon, La.

Dear brother

I received your letter some time ago but have been detained from writing on account of other pressing business. I have troubled with chills and fever some this fall; but am now in fine health. The company are generally well that [*illegible*] those who are present in camps. There are 62 now present and 39 absent. I have heard from several of those who were the worst off lately, not more than one week ago. They are all improving. Horace Rhodes,[55] Thomas Page[56] & William Norrid[57] who are in Lynchburg and have been quite low are all able to walk around town but still look bad. Frank Colbert[58] is at the same place & was improving fast when his brother John left him a few days since. The wounded have all been sent off to Staunton and were doing well a few days ago. Everything is very quiet here now and has been ever since the noted battle of Sharpsburg Md. The yankees were too badly cut up to pursue us and we were completely worn out from hard marching and continual fighting. We have fallen back to within 12 miles of Winchester and have been resting and recruiting for some two weeks. All the Virginia regiments have been recruited by conscripts and are now drilling and organizing them for the service. Gov. Moore refuses to send any more troops to Va. and all our officers are using their influence to get us transferred back to La. We will know in a few days what will be done about the matter. You wrote to me asking my advice with regard to coming and joining my company. I should be glad to have you here with me that I might give you all the assistance I could, but if you will wait till I can as-

55. Horace L. Rhodes, a student at Mount Lebanon Academy at the beginning of the war, recovered from this illness only to be captured, first at Rappahannock Station on November 7, 1863, and then at the battle of Spotsylvania on May 12, 1864. His first captivity was spent at Point Lookout, the second at Elmira, New York (Booth, comp., *Records,* Vol. III, Pt. 2, p. 297).

56. Thomas L. Page of Ringgold was a corporal in Company C. He was sent home on a sick furlough but returned to his command in time to be captured at Strausburg, Virginia on September 22, 1864. He was confined to Point Lookout until February 15, 1865 (*ibid.,* 59).

57. William S. Norrid, who joined Pierson's company on March 8, 1862, died in the hospital at Lynchburg on February 15, 1863 (*ibid.,* Pt. 1, p. 1297).

58. Benjamin Franklin Colbert of Mount Lebanon joined the Ninth Louisiana on March 8, 1862, probably in response to the threat of conscription, and soon succumbed to disease. He was furloughed home to recover in February, 1863, never returned to his unit, and was listed as a deserter (*ibid.,* II, 376).

certain whether we will be transferred back or not I will write you immediately and if I can get you any position on horseback I will do so. You would do well to join a cavalry company unless you can get in as a courier or orderly. If I come back I will write as soon as I arrive at Vicksburg. I have sent a complete list of the killed, wounded & missing, also of the absent sick, to Mr. Wells[59] for publication, which I hope will relieve the anxious enquiring of the citizens in Bienville concerning their friends and relatives. Our living now is very hard, nothing but beef and flour and nothing to cook that with. Lt. Ed Arbuckle is still at Charlottesville sick but was able to walk around in the room when I heard from him last. Give my love & respects to all enquiring friends &c. Your brother

R. A. Pierson

P.S. Jasper Hilburn[60] has just arrived in camp and is well. This is the first time that he has been in camp since we left Winchester last spring. Yours

R. A. P.

⇒ ⇐

REUBEN ALLEN PIERSON TO WILLIAM H. PIERSON
In camp 12 miles from Winchester, Va.
Oct. 26th, 1862

W. H. Pierson
Dear Father
    As I do not receive any news from home I will endeavor to write the oftener so as to avoid keeping you all in the same [suspense] that [I am] forced to endure. Since my last nothing of interest has occurred except our transfer from the 2nd La. Brigade back to our old Brigade. This change throws us into Ewell's Division[61] again which I believe is generally agreeable. We have just returned from

---

59. See n. 54.

60. Jasper W. Hilburn was left sick at Winchester in the spring of 1862 and was captured when Federal troops overran his hospital on June 22. He was exchanged on August 5, 1862, to be wounded at Rappahannock Station on November 7, 1863. After a convalescent furlough in Alabama, he returned to his company to serve until the surrender at Appomattox (Booth, comp., *Records,* Vol. III, Pt. 1, p. 305).

61. On October 5, 1862, the Ninth Louisiana was transferred back to Harry Thompson Hays's First Louisiana Brigade, in exchange for the Fourteenth Louisiana Infantry, and remained with that brigade for the remainder of the war (Bergeron, *Guide,* 94).

a trip down on the Potomac during which time we tore up about 20 miles of the Baltimore and Ohio Railroad track, burned the cross ties across the iron and ruined the whole. When the yankees discovered our advance they hurried across the river to the other side and planted their batteries at every ford along the river to prevent our pursuing them. After we had accomplished our design we returned back to camp. McClellan lives in dread of us. By day and night he never hears of our advancing but that he falls back immediately to his fortifications.

Our troops have been stationed in camp about five weeks resting and recruiting. They are now as jovial as a set of college students and are in remarkable good health. Out of 70 who are present in my company only about five are complaining & the worst case among that number is one who has a bad boil; some of the boys have come from the hospital scarcely able to walk & are now getting stout and hearty. Our fare is very rough, nothing but beef and flour with about 2 table spo[o]nsful of salt to 5 men per day. I am in fine health having recovered from the spell of chills which I was troubled with when I last wrote. Most of our absent sick are at Lynchburg and I have not heard from them in some two weeks. They were all able to walk around town at last accounts. There is much talk of our being transferred back to La. and the lastest rumor is that we will start as soon as the weather is too cold and wet for the enemy to advance in this country. I hope that we may return and spend the winter at least in La. I heard today that John Evans had arrived at home. I hope he may soon recover for he is as brave a little hero as ever fired a musket, and he made his mark before he was wounded. I have received but one letter from home since Jas. Morgan came. I am getting along finely with the company; other commanders seem to envy me on account of my smooth disposition and the obedience which I receive from my men; all of them seem proud that they belong to Co. C.

We have several letters from home dated as late as the 5th Inst. I have not heard from David since the 15th of Aug. nor from Henry since some time in that month. The weather continues mild. Occasionally a heavy frost falls but all the fall not a single wet day has come. The earth is very dry and the dust troublesome on a march. Give my best regards to all enquiring friends. Receive the love of a son yourself and all the family. Tell Sister and Jimmy to write oftener as they have much better opportunities than I have. I hope by the time I write again to be nearer home. Tell Jim not to start to the war till after Christmas. I will write to him again by that time. I will send this by a man who leaves for Shreveport tomorrow. Your son till death

R. A. Pierson

⇒ ⇐

REUBEN ALLEN PIERSON TO MARY CATHERINE PIERSON
In Camp near Rockbridge, 12 miles east of Winchester [Va.]
Novr. 8th, 1862

Miss M. C. Pierson

Dear Sister

I received your hastily written letter and Father[']s piece of a letter sent by Prof. Lindon the 1st of this month. He arrived in camp the night of the 31st Ult. bringing us letters and much late news from home. I was very thankful for the nice woolen socks you sent by him as I was out and could not purchase any from the country. I am in fine health as usual and getting along well enough. I should have sent some money home before now but have not been able to collect up what was due me by the government. It is now due me 600 Dollars and I understand we will all be paid off next week when I will send a few hundred home. We are not well supplied with blankets and clothing yet. Some of the boys have not a single blanket and are very much in need of one as we had a fine snow yesterday. A few of the boys are stark barefooted and many others will be in the same condition in a short time if we do not get a supply of shoes. I heard this morning that a large lot of tents, blankets, clothing & shoes were on the road between here and Staunton, intended to supply the wants of Jackson[']s corps of the army; if this be true we will soon be supplied with all the necessities of a winter's campaign. The general health of the company is very good, over seventy men present & not a single one but what is able to eat his rations. I have not heard from Lieut. Colbert in several days though he was mending when I last heard.

Mr. B. F. Harrison & Jasper Hays[62] have returned to camp from Richmond where they have been guarding pris[o]ners since the 1st of July. They are both in good health. They bring me news that W. T. Loftin who was one of the missing at the battle of Sharpsburg is in Richmond a paroled pris[o]ner, so he is safe. Pa seems to think in his letter that the yankees got the best of the fight at Sharpsburg but when he finds that they have never attempted to advance upon us or offer us battle from that day to this he must conclude that they were content to let us alone. They fear Jackson and his men as the little quadrupeds of the forest does the Lion. They avoid a conflict with him as long as the necessities of their government will permit them to remain still. Well Cassie I have been in camps so long till I have forgotten how to appear in the presence of a lady. I was at a

---

62. The Company C roll of July 31, 1862, shows Jasper Hays of Mount Lebanon detached for guard duty at a Richmond prison. He returned to his unit in August and served until the final days of the war, when he was captured at the fall of Richmond on April 3, 1865 (Booth, comp., *Records*, Vol. III, Pt. 1, p. 235).

house the other day where there was a neat young Lady and must confess that I felt as much out of place as a sheep in a Lion[']s cage. My whole time and attention has been occupied in attending to the welfare of my company.

I hope Dave has had the good fortune to get home by this time and has recovered from his injuries in the battle and will have a happy time while at home. Tell him he must write to me. I often think that I will quit writing to you as you have only written me two letters since I left in the spring. Still, though I know that I should prove negligent because you are so. The talk of our being transferred to La. is still quite current. Tell Jimmy not to be too impatient if he wants to join Co. C. & be with me. I will give him a chance yet before Christmas. I would be glad to have him with me. Tell Mrs. Randle I have never been able to find Walter though I have often enquired for him. I have never been able to find the 4th Geo. Regt. I have not received a line from brother Henry in a long time. I received a letter from Cousin Frances a few days ago. She writes me all the news from that section. The letters sent by Lieut. Upshaw[63] has never come to hand or been heard of; he is still absent. Tell Joseph I will answer his letter in a few days. Give my love to Aunt Nan, Pa & Jonathan. Tell him I will send him a yankee trick before long; tell him he must not forget me. Give my love to all enquiring friends &c. I remain your brother till Death

R. A. Pierson

P.S. Please write as often as convenient giving all the little interesting items that occur in the country, also who is left, who has hired substitutes &c. Yours

R. A. P.

⇒ ⇐

REUBEN ALLEN PIERSON TO JOSEPH PIERSON
In Camp, Novr. 20th, 1862

Mr. Joseph Pierson[64]
Dear Brother
    I have delayed writing to you a few days on account of getting some news to interest you, but I am still without any. Since the battle of Sharpsburg we have

---

63. Thomas A. Upshaw of Brush Valley was elected second lieutenant of Company H, Ninth Louisiana Infantry—the "Brush Valley Guards"—on April 15, 1862. He was subsequently promoted to first lieutenant and transferred to Company I as company commander (*ibid.*, Pt. 2, p. 898).

64. Joseph Pierson, the son of William H. and Nancy Pierson, was the half-brother of David, Reuben, James, and Henry Pierson. He was born in Bienville Parish on August 28, 1849, and died in Red River Parish on March 5, 1887.

been in camp most of the time. [We] have only taken three trips except when [we] were moving camps and then was out but [a] few days being employed at destroying railroad track. We are still encamped near Front Royal on the Shenandoah River. The yankees are reported to be in considerable force only about twenty miles distant from us but as they never come out only in small squads, and run back when they perceive any signs of our advance I am of [the] opinion that their forces are quite limited in this section. I was very proud to receive your juvenile letter. It was so full of humor and also showed that you had not forgotten your absent brother. Well Joseph I had a nice duck for dinner today and plenty of milk yesterday so you may guess that I fare very well if I am a soldier. I hear that Mr. Wells is coming to bring us all some shoes & I am very glad for several of the boys are now barefooted and it is nearly an impossibility to get them at any price here. I gave eleven dollars per pair for course brogans and could have sold them for fifteen since. Such are the extortionary rates now asked & every day they grow worse. Fresh pork is selling at from twenty to fifty cents per pound and salt cannot be bought at any price. I saw some selling about a month ago at one dollar per pint. It is very scarce. Butter brings any price asked; bacon cannot be had. The weather is cloudy but pleasant. We have had but little rain and only one light snow up to the present date. The weather has been unusually mild and favorable for this climate this fall. The pris[o]ners who were taken during our trip by Manassas into Maryland have all been exchanged and are now in camp on duty. The health of the company is excellent, 76 men present and none sick enough to require medical attention. Horace Rhodes is still at the hospital but has been given a recommendation for furlough & I hope may succeed in obtaining one. If so he will succeed in spend the winter at home. Prof. Lindon is well and in fine spirits. I will send you all some tobacco by Mr. Wells if comes out. Give my love to all old friends. Receive the same yourself & extend it to the family.
I remain your brother
R. A. Pierson

P. S. Write me if you have heard from James since he went off to Texas and let me know how he likes his new business. Tell Dave he must write me as he is at home & doing well I hope. Write how Henry was getting along when you last heard from him. I hear from you all very seldom. Send me a nice dressed buck skin by the first opportunity and I will send you a five dollar Confederate bill. Tell Jonathan I hope he is well and doing fine. I suppose you are going to school. If so you must study hard and strive to outstrip all your classmates in all your studies. Your brother
R. A. Pierson

⇒ ⇐

REUBEN ALLEN PIERSON TO WILLIAM H. PIERSON

In camp near Fredericksburg, Va.
Decr. 9th, 1862

W. H. Pierson
Mt. Lebanon, La.
Dear Father

I avail myself of the present opportunity of writing a short letter. My health has been quite bad for several days. I came near having a spell of pneumonia and have scarcely recovered from it yet. We have all been removed from the Valley & are now encamped along the Rhappahannock River in front of Fredericksburg. The enemy are said to be in large force on the other side of the river. The picket lines are in full view of each other, the river only between them; still they are not allowed to fire upon each other and everything goes on quiet. I do not believe that there will be another engagement here before next spring & I hope that something may turn up to put an end to this war in a very short time. The weather is very cold here now. The ground is covered with snow and the sun melts it but little during the day though the weather is quite clear. Some of the boys are still without shoes and consequently have to keep themselves about the fire. Most of them have good clothes and none of them are without a good blanket. We have been looking for Wells to bring us on a lot of shoes for some time but he has not arrived up to this time. A lot of shoes would be quite a treat to us now.

The general health of the company is excellent considering the exposure to which they are daily subject. Our fare is very bad; nothing but beef and flour and no chance to buy anything in the country. We have not heard anything of Bryant Thomas or Meldrick Hand yet & I fear that they are among the slain. Young Loftin has returned. He was taken pris[o]ner but heard nothing of the other two boys. I received a letter from Dave a few days since which I answered immediately. We had the hardest march when leaving the Valley that we have ever taken since we have been in the service. We averaged over twenty miles every day for more than a week. Many of the boys gave out on the road but most of them have come up lately. The latest dates received from Mt. Lebanon was the 17th Ult. If you find anyone who desires to come on and join this company tell them to come on and they will be received. The company now only numbers ninety nine privates & noncommissioned officers. I should be glad to receive about thirty recruits next spring which would fill the company to the maximum number again. Excuse all amiss &c. Give my love to all enquiring friends. Receive the same yourself and extend to the family. I remain your affectionate Son

R. A. Pierson

P.S. Direct your letters to Richmond, 1st La. Brigade, Ewell[']s Div.

R. A. P.

⇒ ⇐

N. M. MIDDLEBROOKS TO DAVID PIERSON
Camp near Troy, Miss., Dec. 16th, 1862

Capt. David Pierson
Mt. Lebanon, Louisiana
Dear Friend,

This leaves myself and the Company in good health with the exception of Billy Carrson.[65] He has been complaining two or three days with cold, but I hope nothing serious. No news of interest at this point, 8 or 10 miles below Grenada. It is supposed this morning that they are advancing on us again. Whether we will fight them at this place I cannot tell. I don't think our forces strong enough unless we get reinforcements to fight them, for they will again flank us.

Belden came up to see us a day or two ago, staid two days and returned back to the Hospital. I told him for my sake and the Company's to resign so we could put somebody in office that would help to do the duties & c. He told me he would, but I fear he will not, for he is getting well paid and no duty to do. Van Thompson[66] has been back once since you left, staid three or four days, and fell back to Jackson again, just as we were leaving the Brigade. Henry Muirhead[67] is still absent.

Belden told me you wanted to know what the boys most needed. Well, I think they most need Blankets, Socks, and yarn Pants, Shoes, & c. If you can, get me two pair of stout woolen pants and a couple of overshirts.

65. William J. Carson of Winn Parish enlisted as a private in Company C, Third Louisiana Infantry, on May 17, 1861. Wounded on June 11, 1863, during the siege of Vicksburg, Carson was captured with the rest of the garrison on July 4 and was subsequently paroled in March, 1864. For the remainder of the war he awaited exchange at Natchitoches, Louisiana, in Brig. Gen. Thomas Allen's brigade. He was paroled on June 6, 1865 (Tunnard, *A Southern Record*, 506; Booth, comp., *Records*, Vol. III, Pt. 2, p. 824).

66. Van B. Thompson enlisted as a private in Company C, Third Louisiana Infantry, on May 17, 1861. After the regiment's capture at Vicksburg, he was paroled to Natchitoches for exchange (Tunnard, *A Southern Record*, 559).

67. Henry Muirhead, who joined Company C as a private on May 17, 1861, was hospitalized in September, 1862, and never returned to active duty (Tunnard, *A Southern Record*, 543; Booth, *Records,* Vol. III, Pt. 1, p. 1081).

Tell Ace[68] if he is well to come to the Company as soon as he can. The boys are anxiously awaiting his return to elect him Lieut., and I am anxious myself for I had rather for him to have it. I shall wait for him as long as I can before I get an order for an election.

But I am very anxious for the second relief to come around, for if there is any chance this winter for a furlough, I want one, and if there is no other officer present I of course will fail.

If I could see you I could tell you a heap since you left, all sorts of ups and downs, and more downs than ups.

Love and respect to all inquiring friends.
I remain as ever, your devoted and sincere friend,
N. M. Middlebrooks[69]

P.S. Direct to Grenada, Miss.

⇒ ⇐

REUBEN ALLEN PIERSON TO DAVID PIERSON

In Camp near Fredericksburg, Va.
Dec. 17th, 1862

Capt. D. Pierson
Mt. Lebanon, La.
Dear Brother

I received your letter of the 11th Ult. a few days ago and was very proud to hear that you have made so miraculous an escape from the wound received at Iuka. I hope you will recover without any material injury either mentally or physically and that your fine appearance (which every soldier is struck with who sees you) may not in the least be disfigured. I further hope you may be quite successful in any advances that you may make to the angelic being (in the form of a woman) of which you speak so eloquently. In the conclusion of your letter she is doubtless a model of perfection as I have no disposition to question your fancy. I am in rather bad health at present. I came near having pneumonia a few days since. Only lively caution saved me from it. All of the [*two words illegible*]. In front of Fredericksburg along the bank of the Rappahannock River the en-

---

68. "Ace" is Asa Emanuel.

69. N. M. Middlebrooks was elected first sergeant of Company C when the Third Louisiana was organized on May 17, 1861. He was wounded at Wilson's Creek on August 10, 1861, and promoted to second lieutenant on October 14 of that year. When the regiment reorganized at Corinth in May, 1862, he was elected first lieutenant and promoted to captain, when David Pierson became the regiment's major on February 10, 1863. Middlebrooks was wounded during the siege of Vicksburg, and after the garrison's surrender, he was paroled to Natchitoches (Tunnard, *A Southern Record,* 541; Booth, comp., *Records,* Vol. III, Pt. 1, p. 966).

emy are said to be in heavy forces. Just across the river no firing has occurred up to this time.

The general health of the company is good. [*Illegible*] seventy present and none confined to bed. The [hills] are covered with snow and melting very little on the sunny sides. It is clear today but water freezes in a few minutes after it is brought up. Some of the boys are still barefooted and others have no good clothes but I hope we will soon be supplied as we are camped near the railroad and only a few hours['] run from the [*illegible*]. I have not seen a paper in weeks and know but little about what is going. Rumors are plentiful about mediation and intervention but this is [*two words illegible*] marched to the Valley [*illegible*] here was a very trying one; we averaged more than twenty miles per day for over a week. This you know was very heavy marching. We crossed the Blue Ridge where there was a distillery and all hands both officers and men got on a general binder and merry yes very merry was the times. Our fare is very bad, nothing but beef and flour and the poorest country to forage on I ever saw. I have a man who does nothing but forage and work for me and he has quite a hard task at that.

I [*illegible*] not tell you how I am getting along with the company but [*two words illegible*] you to those who have been furloughed after receiving wounds [*two words illegible*].
I remain your brother
R. A. Pierson

⇒ ⇐

REUBEN ALLEN PIERSON TO MARY CATHERINE PIERSON
In camp near Port Royal, Va.
Decr. 23rd, 1862

Miss M. C. Pierson
Mt. Lebanon, La.
Dear Sister

As I have an opportunity of sending a letter to Vicksburg by Mr. Ferguson[70] I avail myself of this chance. It is but two days till Christmas and we are all still soldiering in Va. There is much talk of our being sent back to La., but I place very little confidence in any rumor for I have long since learned that it would not do.

---

70. James Ferguson of Company E, Ninth Louisiana Infantry, died at Lynchburg in July, 1862 (Booth, comp., *Records*, II, 832; see also *Biographical and Historical Memoirs of Northwest Louisiana* [Nashville, 1890], 420).

We have not received the goods sent by Mr. Wells yet though we are looking for them constant[ly]. Mr. Ardis went after them three days ago. Wells made quite a short stay with us only one day & a piece. He was in good health. We have just got rested since the great battle of Fredericksburg.[71] We received marching orders on Wednesday evening the 10th Inst. but did not leave camp till near night the 11th. We marched till after midnight that night & struck camp, built up good fires & lay down to rest our wearied limbs with orders to leave at daylight the next morning. We did not leave camp till after sunrise the morning of the 12th & after marching a mile or two we could plainly hear the roar of cannon in front. We soon arrived in full view of the battlefield, which was naturally a very picturesque looking scene. A beautiful valley surrounded by a chain of hills, the former in cultivation and the latter woodland, principally second growth of thick pine saplings. Our troops occupied this latter position which was of great advantage in concealing our force. Our brigade (the 1st La.) was at first posted on the road behind this chain of hills but in the evening we were ordered forward about a q[u]arter of a mile to support a regt. of artillery; soon after we were posted the enemy began to advance & Gen. Jackson ordered the batteries not to open fire till they got within grape shot range. This they soon [had] done when about 50 cannon opened fire upon them at once. At the same time a brigade charged them on our left. The fire of our artillery soon called forth a hot response from the enemies['] batteries. Both continued for about an hour, which brought on night & the yanks withdrew their artillery. We was moved over to the left the next morning where occasional shots were exchanged by the skirmishers till about 3 P.M. when the enemy sent forward a flag of truce to ask leave to bury their dead. The 3rd day they employed in bur[y]ing their dead and under cover of darkness that night they fell back across the river. All has been quiet here since that time. Only two of Co. C. were wounded (both slight) in this fight. Our artillery slew the enemy in piles. Their whole loss is estimated at 20,000, ours not exceeding two thousand.

I have not been in good health for several weeks but am on the mend at present. The Co. is generally well, over seventy present & none confined to bed. The wagon has been sent after our boxes to the depot today & I suppose they will come tonight. The weather has been most excellent this fall only two light snows & but little rain. It seems that Providence has specially favored the Confederate army by sending such fine weather. The small pox has at last made its appearance

71. The battle of Fredericksburg on December 13, 1862, was a disaster for the Army of the Potomac under Maj. Gen. Ambrose E. Burnside. In a day-long series of frontal attacks against Lee's position on Marye's Heights above Fredericksburg, the Union army suffered 12,653 casualties to the Army of Northern Virginia's 5,309. The two Louisiana brigades were held in reserve during the battle but did lose a total of 91 men to the heavy Union artillery fire (Gary W. Gallagher, ed., *The Fredericksburg Campaign: Decision on the Rappahannock* [Chapel Hill, 1995]; Jones, *Lee's Tigers*, 143–44).

in our brigade & I hear that two cases have been sent from the 9th Regt. It will spread very slow[ly] as all the men have been well vaccinated and prepared for the disease. I have no fears of the disease myself. I had fever for three days when I was vaccinated and my arm was sore for one month. I hope you will excuse all amiss in this lengthy letter. I am in good [health] excepting a cold at present. Remember me kindly to all enquiring friends. Give my best regards to [the] ladies, for if it were not for them patriotism would be a humbug & speculation would undermine and destroy our newly organized Confederacy. They are the ones who implore the aid of man in behalf of the poor soldiers who are fighting to substantiate the rights of the most valuable property of our land. Woman is man[']s Guardian angel on earth & always clings to what is right let the excitement be what it may. Extend my love to all the family while I remain as ever your affectionate brother

R. A. Pierson

P.S. I sent you four papers of needles by Mr. Wells which I hope will be of service to you.

R. A. P.

> €

DAVID PIERSON TO WILLIAM H. PIERSON
Jackson, Miss., Dec. 24ᵗʰ/62

Wᵐ H. Pierson
  Mᵗ. Lebanon
    La.

Dear Pa,

We arrived here this morning at daylight and I have reported at Head Quarters and learned that I am exchanged. No difficulty about the few days that I had stayed over my time. We had a pleasant trip from home to Vicksburg—stayed over at the latter place and day & night taking quarters with the 27ᵗʰ La.[72] which was quartered in the city as police guard. Was well accommodated and enjoyed ourselves excellently. I wrote you a note from Monroe by Henry and sent you fifty dollars—twenty-eight of which was paid me by those Gentlemen that I engaged with for Henry to take to Mt. Lebanon.

We got to Monroe too late on Sunday night to buy the thread you sent for, and the cars left before daylight the next morning, so I had no opportunity to get it at all. We were frightened out of our wits about Small Pox the night we got to Monroe, and camped out in an open field near the Depot, spending a dis-

72. Henry Lewis Pierson, the oldest of the Pierson children, was a second lieutenant in the Twenty-seventh Louisiana.

agreeable and sleepless night. We are all well and calculate to take the cars for Granada tomorrow. I would start today but for a friend who is going to the Reg^t and wants to stay till tomorrow to see some Christmas. I have heard nothing of interest from the Command about Grenada except that they are daily expecting an engagement and have sent all baggage to the rear. The men are only allowed to keep one blanket and half their cooking utensils by which I should judge they are seeing some hardships just now. The army is represented to be in excellent health and spirits. The men are all eager for a fight and murmur considerable about retreating so much. Jeff Davis was in Vicksburg while we were there, but I did not get to see him. He was out yesterday inspecting the works on the Yazoo. When I left there last night a fight was reported to be progressing somewhere up the river. I did not learn where or between what forces. I saw large and brilliant light north of town, and it was thought that the enemy had landed and were engaged in burning houses. The President is looked for here today and will visit our army at Grenada immediately.[73] His appearance is creating quite a sensation wherever he goes, and his timely visit will do much good, no doubt, in the way of encouraging & inspiriting the troops. All the prisoners belonging to the 3rd La. were exchanged last week and went to the command on Friday last. Our Col. & Major are still absent but looked for daily.

I left Henry well. At present no more, but remain.

Affectionately Yours,
D. Pierson

⇒ ⇐

JAMES F. PIERSON TO WILLIAM H. PIERSON
Grenada, Miss., Dec., 27th, 1862

W. H. Pierson

Dear Father,

We arrived at this place yesterday evening and found everything quiet. But this morning an order came for two days' rations to be cooked and preparations

---

73. During the winter of 1862–63, the armies and the people of the trans-Appalachian Confederacy were voicing great discontent with the leadership being provided by Braxton Bragg and John C. Pemberton. Jefferson Davis concluded that he must personally visit the theater "with the hope," he wrote to Robert E. Lee, "that something may be done to bring out men not heretofore in service and to arouse all classes to united and desperate resistance." On December 10, 1862, the president left Richmond for Bragg's army at Murfreesboro. After reviewing the Army of Tennessee and consulting with its commander on December 13, Davis proceeded to Mississippi, where he met with Pemberton and inspected his forces along the Yazoo River. The president's presence, according to his most recent biographer, "created something of a sensation that some soldiers thought encouraged the troops, who otherwise felt themselves forgotten by Richmond" (William C. Davis, *Jefferson Davis: The Man and His Hour* [New York, 1991], 481–85).

to be made to march to the depot and take the cars for the 1st station this side of Canton, Miss. The supposition is that the Yankees are going to try to cut off the communication between this army and that at Vicksburg. Dave had not reported for duty yet and will not until tomorrow. The Yankees are landed at the mouth of the Yazoo in strong force and marching in the direction of the Rail Road.

I have not attached myself to the army yet, but will before long. I have enjoyed the trip excellent and [am] well pleased so far. I will take the cars for Canton this evening or tomorrow morning. The people are in high spirits about this place, but expect to be surrendered to the Yankees in a few weeks. There is no report of any enemy above this place. The general opinion is that they have gone to the Yazoo and are trying to flank our army at this place. We met Kirby Smith's whole command on Christmas night at Jackson going to Vicksburg, numbering about 26 Reg. of infantry and all the Artillery and Cavalry besides, in all about 25,000.

We are all well. Write soon.

Your Son till Death,
Jas F. Pierson

David Pierson
Courtesy C. Pierson Marshall,
New Orleans, Louisiana

William H. Pierson, father of David,
Reuben Allen, and James F. Pierson
Courtesy C. Pierson Marshall,
New Orleans, Louisiana

Ben McCulloch, commander
of the Army of the West
Thomas W. Cutrer Collection

The battle of Wilson's Creek, August 10, 1861, by Louis Kurtz
Thomas W. Cutrer Collection

Earl Van Dorn,
second commander of the
Army of the West
*Courtesy Mississippi Department
of Archives and History*

The battle of Pea Ridge, March 7–8, 1862, by Louis Kurtz
Thomas W. Cutrer Collection

Richard S. Ewell
*Courtesy Cook Collection, Valentine
Museum, Richmond, Va.*

Jubal Early
*Courtesy Museum of the
Confederacy, Richmond, Va.*

Richard Taylor,
commander of the
Louisiana Brigade of the
Army of Northern Virginia
T. Michael Parrish Collection

Sterling Price, tintype portrait
Courtesy Archives Division, Texas State Library

Sidney Amanda Pipes Pierson, wife of David Pierson
Courtesy C. Pierson Marshall,
New Orleans, Louisiana

David Pierson as Louisiana district judge
Courtesy C. Pierson Marshall,
New Orleans, Louisiana

5

WHEN THE HOUR OF BATTLE COMES

⇒ ⇐

JAMES F. PIERSON TO MARY CATHERINE PIERSON

Snyder's Mill, Miss.,[1] *Jan. 18ᵗʰ, 1863*

Miss Cassie Pierson

Dear Sister,

I have been in camps about 4 weeks and must confess that I am not very much displeased with my new profession, although it is one of a great deal of hardship and exposure, but I find it by no means worse than I anticipated. I enjoy myself very well with the boys of the 3ʳᵈ who are very much familiar and kind to me. There are a great many French boys in the Reg. and I amuse myself a great deal when I idle listening at them talk. They gather together in large crowds and all talk at once which makes me laugh a great deal, and they in their turn laugh back at me for becoming so amused. But I am sometimes almost ashamed to accept of their kindness which they offer to me on all occasions. We first overtook the Reg. at Vau[gh]n's Station[2] on the Rail Road between Canton

---

1. Snyder's Mill, at Snyder's Bluff, was located on the Yazoo River some ten miles above Vicksburg. The bluff was the keystone of the left wing of the city's outer defenses, stretching along the Yazoo from the Mississippi River to Hayne's Bluff. On December 29, in the battle of Chickasaw Bluffs, Pemberton's Confederates repulsed William T. Sherman's attempt to storm the position and capture Vicksburg from the north. In the day's fighting, Sherman suffered a total of 1,779 casualties to the defenders' 187. On January 2, 1863, Hébert's brigade occupied the line and Hébert took command of this "front door" to Vicksburg (*The War of the Rebellion: A Compilation of the Official Records of the Union and Confederate Armies* [130 parts in 70 vols.; Washington, D.C., 1880–1901], Ser. I, Vol. XXIV, Pt. 2, p. 365, hereinafter cited as *OR;* Samuel Carter III, *The Final Fortress: The Campaign for Vicksburg, 1862–1863* [New York, 1980], 99–103).

2. Vaughn's was a station on the Mississippi Central railroad on the upper reaches of the Big Black River some thirty-five miles north of Jackson. In 1900, Vaughn became the site of the nation's most celebrated railroad accident when John Luther "Casey" Jones wrecked a locomotive there.

and Grenada. Two days afterwards we took up the line of march 22 mi. Next day marched 4 mi. into town where we were transferred to a steam boat and then landed in four miles of this place about 9 o'clock the following night which was Thursday. Next morning at four o'clock orders came for us to march out to fight at day light. After arriving in the breastworks we could plainly see the gunboats about 3 miles distant. They remained there until about 10 A.M. and then advanced within 1¾ miles of us where they came in contact with our batteries on the river below and were fired into. They returned the fire for about two hours and then rallied down the river again and have never made their appearance since. We are encamped in the hilliest country that I ever saw and the muddiest place in the Confederacy. Last Thursday night I luckily got a pass to go into the country and stay until I got well, for I had been a little sick for a day or two, so I started and went 3 miles into the country and came to where an old free negro lived, so I put up with him and was treated very well. I stayed with him until this morning and returned to camps. When I got here Dave had gone into the country sick, but is mending and says that he will come to camps tonight, but I do not believe he will come now for it is nearly night and he will likely come tomorrow. We are in a mess with A. W. Currie,[3] and he is off at Vicksburg sick, so I am left to keep tent by myself with Peter to cook for me. Dave had a very severe attack of the Cholera Morbus and he is not yet over it. We are not more than 12 miles from Vicksburg and I hear every day from Henry for there is traveling backward and forward daily. I have nothing more at present.

I Remain
Your Brother till Death,
J^{as} F. Pierson

---

3. A. W. Currie was elected sergeant of Company H, Third Louisiana Infantry, on May 17, 1861, and in the reorganization at Corinth was promoted to second lieutenant. He was captured with the rest of his regiment at Vicksburg, and after receiving his parole at Natchitoches in March, 1864, he was promoted to captain (Willie H. Tunnard, *A Southern Record: The Story of the Third Regiment Louisiana Infantry* [1866; rpr. Dayton, Ohio, 1970], 511; Andrew B[radford] Booth, comp., *Records of Louisiana Confederate Soldiers and Louisiana Confederate Commands* [3 vols.; New Orleans, 1920], II, 509).

⇒ ⇐

DAVID PIERSON TO WILLIAM H. PIERSON

Camp Snyder's Mill, Miss.,[4] *Jany. 20th/63*

Wm H. Pierson
  Mt. Lebanon,
    Louisiana

Dear Pa,

I have at last received my promotion. The order came yesterday by which I was promoted to the rank of major to take effect from the fifth day of November 1862, and I have forwarded my letter of acceptance. Nothing has transpired of any moment since I last wrote you which was about a week ago.

We are still encamped on the Yazoo River about 14 miles from Vicksburg and decidedly in the muddiest place I ever lived in. We have some few tents, but the majority of the Regiment are living as best they can under trees, board shelters, or in the ground. Some ingenious Frenchmen have erected houses out of long cane which is to [be] found in great abundance all over the country. You would be amused as well as astonished to see them. The weather has been very bad— only one fair day in the week, and it so cold as to freeze one away from the fire. Three days ago we had a severe snow-storm which, if it had lay on the ground, would have been fully six inches in depth. Jim and I have a tent (not a good one by any means) with a plank floor in which, by the assistance of some cane tops and fodder (the latter of which I filched from my horse) and a blanket a piece, we manage to keep tolerably comfortable. The mud has been so bad that we have been compelled to agree to a harsh law about it, to wit: That no one shall go inside the tent with his shoes on. So we just stop at the door and pull off before entering so as to keep the floor and our blankets dry & clean. We will not suffer the same inconvenience long, for the Genl., after long persuasion, has permitted us to send men after our baggage which is on the Rail Road below Grenada. When we get it we will have tents and blankets and clothes enough to keep comfortable. As to eating, we fare sumptuously just now but have fears about its giving out. We get pork, potatoes, butter, and chickens from the farmers in the country at reasonable *prices.* The neighborhood, which is a wealthy one, is bountifully supplied with everything in the way of substantial eatables,

4. Pierson's was one of five regiments constituting Brig. Gen. Louis Hébert's brigade of Maj. Gen. Dabney H. Maury's division of the Army of the West. In Maury's absence, Hébert commanded the division and the post at Snyder's Bluff. The tactical command of his brigade temporarily devolved upon his senior colonel, William W. Witherspoon of the Thirty-sixth Mississippi Infantry. When Maury was transferred to the Department of East Tennessee on April 15, 1863, Maj. Gen. John Horace Forney replaced him in command of the division and Hébert returned to his brigade. By March 31, 1863, Hébert's brigade had been augmented by two regiments and four battalions of Mississippi infantry (*OR,* Ser. I, Vol. II, Pt. 2, p. 326, Ser. I, Vol. XXIV, Pt. 3, p. 704).

but will no doubt in a very short time be drained by the soldiers. Jim was a little unwell a few days ago and went into the country where he soon recovered & is now in camps quite well. I just returned to camps yesterday from a visit into the country where I enjoyed the hospitalities of a planter a day and night who refused to be paid a cent for it. I was quite unwell, but now am fully recovered. I have been in command of the Reg^t ever since my arrival & find it no light job. Lt Col. Russle will be here in a few days when I will have some leisure.

Yours Affect'ly,
D. Pierson

⇒ ⇐

JAMES F. PIERSON TO WILLIAM H. PIERSON
Camp Snyder's Mill, Jan. 23rd, 1863

Mr. W. H. Pierson

Dear Father,

I am still in camps and in good health. I have been in very good health since I have been in camps. I think that I will be able to stand the campaign as well as any of the men. We are looking for a battle here every day. The bombardment has been going on at Vicksburg for two days, but they have [*line illegible*] but they can run up to us in two or three hours. We are in a very muddy camp for it rains about every three days and is now raining, but I am in a good tent and I can keep tolerably dry, but some of the boys are without any tent yet, and they fare pretty badly. The first rain that fell in camps we were all without a tent and had to stay wet all night in the hardest rain that I ever saw fall, but I had the croup a little and the Dr. sent me to the hospt. where I got dry and slept well all the next day and have been as hearty as a buck ever since. I have been on guard once and did not mind it at all. I have been around here a great deal hunting pork, butter, eggs, lard, & c. I will give you a few items of the cost of such articles. Pork, $.50; lard, .75; butter, 1.00; and eggs from 1.00 to $1.25 pr. dozen. We have a few lbs. of lard which we take a great deal of care of. I went into the country about 9 miles. Had a very nice dinner, and the lady gave myself and Dr. Whitehead[5] as much little dainties as we could tote on our horses, namely lard, about 5 lbs.; spare ribs; back bones; & sausage meat, about 3 lbs.; one dozen onions, and then two young ladies presented us with a large pound cake which we brought to camps with us. Dave

---

5. P. F. Whitehead was a twenty-three-year-old native of Kentucky who was residing in Missouri at the outbreak of the war. Thereupon he was appointed surgeon of the first regiment of Sterling Price's Missouri State Guard but was transferred to the Third Louisiana shortly before the reorganization of May 8, 1862. After serving with the regiment through the siege of Vicksburg, through which, wrote Tunnard, "he was untiring, unceasingly occupied," Whitehead was promoted to senior surgeon of Col. Thomas Moore Scott's Louisiana Brigade of the Army of Tennessee. At the onset of the Atlanta campaign he was transferred to Maj. Gen. William Wing Loring's division, in which he served until the surrender at Greensboro, North Carolina, on April 26, 1865. He then returned to private practice in Vicksburg.

has bought two horses, and we can ride when we want to go far off. He bought one mare, about 9 yrs. old, very poor, at 65 dollars, with the bridle and saddle, which was worth $50. The other one cost him $2.50 without any bridle or saddle, but he is a good young horse about 5 years old. I am expecting to send this across the river by some men who are detailed to go home and bring up deserters. I have nothing more at present. Peter and Dave are both well. Give my love to all the family. Tell Cas to write to me soon.

Write soon.

Your Son till Death,
J^{as} F. Pierson

Dave has been promoted to Maj. Direct your letters to Vicksburg, Miss., Hébert's Brigade.

⇒ ⇐

REUBEN ALLEN PIERSON TO WILLIAM H. PIERSON

Camp near Port Royal, Va.
Monday night 12 oclock Feb. 2nd, 1863

W. H. Pierson, Esqr.
Mount Lebanon, La.
Dearest Father

Everything is quiet around. The soldiers are nearly all snoring, wrapped in their comfortable blankets, while here I sit all alone writing home. This is the second letter which I have written this week to you, but as Dr. Egan has been transferred to Monroe La. and leaves here early in the morning I thought you would excuse me for writing so often. I send this letter by the Doctor and also two hundred ($200) Dollars in Money. Corp. Walker and James Morgan has [*sic*] both arrived in camp. They bring news from home to the 4th January. I did not receive a letter by them though I was expecting one. I received the present sent me by John Evans a twenty [dollar] Gold piece. I am very thankful and must confess that I was somewhat surprised at the receipt of it. I will

---

Of Whitehead, Sgt. Willie H. Tunnard wrote, he "was most thoroughly skilled in every branch of his profession. He soon endeared himself to the men by his untiring efforts to relieve their sufferings, and his unvarying politeness of manner and genial affability. Of fine personal appearance, refined and polished manners, it is not surprising that the men learned both to admire and respect him. No higher compliment can be paid to his skill as a surgeon—no statement attest to the confidence placed in that skill— than the mention of the fact that, at Vicksburg, every member of the regiment requiring the amputation of a limb, or some delicate surgical operation, would allow no other physician to operate on them than Dr. P. F. Whitehead" (Tunnard, *A Southern Record,* 167, 297, 564; Booth, comp., *Records,* Vol. III, Pt. 2, p. 1070).

keep it as a momento of home. Thomas Page received a furlough at Lynchburg on the 17th Jan. and I guess is at home now. If you can get Stall to make me a pair of good boots before he leaves. Send them to me for it is almost impossible to get such an article. Three of the boys have been granted furloughs and will start for home in a few days. W. H. Blount,[6] J. A. Williamson[7] and R. H. McGouldrick are the favored ones. The company is in excellent health as you will see by a report which Dr. Egan brings with him. I am only tolerable well, have a cold but do not stop duty. We have a case of small pox in the company which showed itself today. John Norrid[8] is the patient. He will be sent off tomorrow. I fear it will spread though all of us have been well vaccinated during the fall and winter.

Everything is quiet along our lines. Brigadier Gen. Early[9] has been promoted to Maj. Gen. and now commands our (Ewell[']s old) Division. The news is very cheering for the last few days and from all the signs I think peace will soon be made. Tell sister I send her a copy of the Southern Illustrated News[,] a literary paper published at Richmond Va.[10] It has some fine stories about the war. I am sleepy and will close.

Your affectionate Son

R. A. Pierson

6. William H. Blunt of Buck Horn had been wounded at the battle of Port Republic on June 9, 1862, and was to be captured at Rappahannock Station on November 7, 1863. Imprisoned at Point Lookout, he contracted smallpox and died on December 31, 1863 (Booth, comp., *Records,* II, 16).

7. James Andy Williamson, a resident of Bienville Parish, spent a great deal of his term in service on special details—guarding baggage at Manassas, as a striker for the regimental blacksmith, and as a wagoneer. Perhaps because of these detached duties, he was never wounded or captured but deserted from his company in 1863 (*ibid.,* Vol. III, Pt. 2, p. 1113).

8. John A. Norrid was sent to the army hospital at Guinea Station, Virginia, where he recovered from smallpox. He then rejoined his unit, served until the surrender at Appomattox, and returned to his home in Bienville Parish (*ibid.,* Pt. 1, p. 1297).

9. Jubal Anderson Early commanded a brigade from the first battle of Manassas through Fredericksburg. Promoted to major general, he commanded a division of II Corps at Chancellorsville, Gettysburg, and the Wilderness. This service earned him a promotion to lieutenant general and temporary assignment to the command of II Corps. Robert E. Lee detached Early's corps to the Shenandoah Valley in 1864, to relieve pressure on the Army of Northern Virginia by threatening Washington. There, after initial success, his command was virtually destroyed by Philip H. Sheridan's army. See Jubal A. Early, *War Memoirs: Autobiographical Sketch and Narrative of the War Between the States* (1912; rpr. Bloomington, 1960); Charles C. Osborne, *Jubal: The Life and Times of General Jubal Early, CSA* (Chapel Hill, 1992).

10. The *Southern Illustrated News,* founded in September, 1862, to fill the void created by the loss of northern literary magazines, was edited by John Reuben Thompson and published the poems and short fiction of such notables as John Esten Cooke, Paul Hamilton Hayne, James R. Randall, Henry Timrod, and William Gilmore Simms (Richard N. Current, ed., *Encyclopedia of the Confederacy* [4 vols.; New York, 1993], III, 985–86; Louis D. Rubin, Jr., *et al.,* eds., *The History of Southern Literature* [Baton Rouge, 1990], 182).

⇒ ⇐

DAVID PIERSON TO WILLIAM H. PIERSON

Vicksburg, Miss., Febry, 5th, 1863

Mr. Wm H. Pierson

Dear Pa,

We arrived at this place yesterday after a very fatiguing and horrible trip on the stage the night previous. We were very fortunate in making the connection with the cars at Monroe, saving ourselves scarcely one minute's time. We remain here till this afternoon waiting for our company after which we will take the earliest boat up the river. I am glad to state that we have information of a rise in the Arks. River and that boats are already going up as high as Little Rock. The weather is still cloudy with some rain last night. River at this point muddy & covered in drift wood. Say to Mr. B. Prothro that his business with the *Whig* office is attended to, & to Mr. Gibbs that I have left the letter he gave me for the *Sun* office at the Post Office, there being no person at the office of the *Sun* to leave it with. The town is muddy & disagreeable, but business active on the river.

Yours & c.,

D. Pierson

⇒ ⇐

DAVID PIERSON TO WILLIAM H. PIERSON

Camp Snyder's Mill
Feby. 18th, 1863

Wm H. Pierson

Mt. Lebanon,

La.

Dear Pa,

The return of a gentleman from Winn who has been here for several days on a visit to his son affords me an opportunity of sending you a letter. I wrote you a few days ago in answer to a late letter from you, but as I sent that by mail, which is very uncertain, I take the liberty to trouble you again. The weather continues rainy and bad—very disagreeable. We are still stuck in the mud at our same old camp on the Yazoo, the most detestable spot on the face of the Globe. If it were not for Vicksburg and the country around, I would be perfectly willing to abandon this spot, at least, to the Yankees. They seem to like such places from the length of time they remain in the swamp and mud opposite Vicksburg. They may have all such for me. A portion of our baggage left behind when we came here came up yesterday and the remainder will be here tonight. One of my trunks, the only one yet arrived, had been broken open and everything worth having taken from it. I lost at least 250 dollars worth of clothing at present prices from it. It was broken open somewhere upon the route. I have no clue to the wrong-doer, nor do I expect to ever hear from anything in it again. My other trunk & some blankets have not come up. I am in hopes to get them safe, though there is scarcely room to hope from the way our other baggage was treated. I am still in Command of the Reg^t. and from present indications am like to remain so for awhile. The Col. & Lieut. Col. don't seem to think it their duty to be here.

There is nothing near at this point. We have heard so much cannonading and have had so many false alarms that no occurrence, however seemingly startling, is calculated to excite us into the belief that a battle is inevitable. Our authorities are very watchful and careful to prevent surprise. It seems from the measures taken that they must expect some great and unheard of stratagem on the part of the enemy. A Reg^t. is required to stay in the ditches every night, no matter how cold or how hard it rains. Tonight is our turn, and I dread it no little. It is so cold and damp, and no fires can be had. Jim and I had a comfortable place in the ground, but a few nights ago it caved in, and we have preferred to pitch our tent on level ground hereafter. Two nights ago a man in Comp. "H" was killed instantly by the falling in of a mud house constructed of heavy logs and dirt.[11] All hands are shy of houses now. My health is good, Jim's tolerable well. I have detailed him as my orderly and he has nothing to do. We mess with the Adjt. who has a good cook, but our living is a little hard, the eatables having given out for miles around the country. We get some pork and potatoes from the Commissary Department. I have not heard from Henry for several days. Got a letter from Al not long ago. He is the best contented human on earth. Excuse bad penmanship. I am hurried to death about everything and take everything easy too, but still I am in a hurry. Pete has acquired much proficiency in his department.

Yours Affectionately,
D. Pierson

⇒ ⇐

DAVID PIERSON TO MARY CATHERINE PIERSON
Camp Snyder's Mill, Miss., Feb 18th/63

Miss M. C. Pierson
Dear Sister,

As I have a good opportunity of sending a letter across the river, I hasten to write it. I am glad to be able to say that I am in the best of health and getting

---

11. This unfortunate was C. S. Jeeter (or "Jeter"), who died on February 15, 1863 (Tunnard, *A Southern Record,* 375, 530; Booth, *Records,* Vol. III, Pt. 2, p. 440).

along finely. We are expecting orders every day to go up the Yazoo River to Yazoo City. I am glad that there is a prospect of our leaving this place, for the country is completely eaten out of everything, and up there, there has been no soldiers stationed and probably we will find something to eat. It is about 70 miles by water and about 40 by land. I presume that we will go by water. As we came down, we were well treated by the ladies of the city and also presented with a beautiful flag. I long for the order to come for us to go back up there. We have had one of the worst spells of weather that I most ever saw. It has been cloudy for over a week, so much that the sun has not been seen in that length of time, and for the last forty-eight hours it has rained incessantly. This morning it has slacked raining for the first time in two days, but it has slacked to put in with renewed vigor, I fear. I have become so inured to camp life that nothing seems to affect me. I am, as I have said before I left home, able to stand anything that anybody else can stand. One of the Reg. was killed night before last by a log of wood which was put in the top of a dirt house. He was killed about 11 o'clock in the night, supposed to be asleep. It had been raining about 8 hours as hard as ever I saw it fall when his house caved in, the log coming down upon him and mashed him to death. Dave and myself had us a tent set up in a hole dug out of the side of the hill and about the same time our house caved in on us, but we were not quite as unfortunate as the soldier that was killed, but we had to get up and move in the Adjutant's tent which was close by, and slept very well till morning. We have received but one letter since we left home. I had begun to think that you all had certainly forgotten us and did not write, but we got Father's letter which relieved my anxiety a great deal. I now think that if I can only know that you all are well and doing well that I would be perfectly contented. I have no particular anxiety to go back home. I only want to know that you all are getting along easily. As for my part, I can get along anywhere that anybody else can. Dave and Peter are well. Peter wants to go home, but not as hard as he did at first.

I received a letter from Al since I came to this place. He said that the boys were all in good health, but few of them sick, none of them from about Mt. Lebanon. Since the above was written the baggage arrived and Dave has received both his trunks broken open and the last bit of clothing taken out. I lost all my clothes. I have not a shifting suit. One pr. of pants that I never have had on, 1 pr. shoes that I left in the trunk, so I am left without anything. I have but one blanket, and that I brought with me from home. The shoes that I have are not worth anything for they are nearly worn out, but I will get a pair made by the regimental shoemaker in a few days. As for my clothes, I do not know what to do.

When we went to leave Vau[gh]n's Station on the R. R. we were ordered to put everything in the wagon but 1 blanket to be carried to the Q.M. Department where everything we had was stolen. I have been waiting patiently for the baggage to come up that I might shift the muddy and dingy clothes that I have on, and now imagine my displeasure at not receiving anything for all the good new suit that I left when we marched from Vau[gh]n's Station to Yazoo City. But it is no use to care for anything in this place. But if you see any opportunity to send me a couple of shirts, I would be glad to get them. You may meet with an opportunity to send them to Henry at Vicksburg and then he can send them to me.

There is no such a thing in the stores over here to be had, and if the Government don't furnish it to me, I shall be compelled to go ill-clad. If there is any chance for us to send Peter across, we will send him and let him get us some things. I have an opportunity of sending this across the river by Mr. Bonnet who has come to see his son, one of the Winn Rifles.[12] I have lately been detailed as an orderly for the Reg. and do not have to go on fatigue duty. The reg. has all gone out in the breast work on picket duty tonight. I do not have to lie out there with them. There was a call for vols. in our Reg. today to go aboard of a boat to go up the Yazoo River and into Yazoo Pass and take a gunboat which is said to be cruising around up there. The whole Reg. wanted to go, but only 50 men were allowed to go, 4 of which went from our company. I do not think that we will be likely to leave here soon, for they have already called and received men enough to defend the Yazoo River above here, and all the men that we can spare to defend this post. The Yankees are in heavy force above the city, and the firing is kept up nearly every day down there. We can hear the firing pretty distinctly being only 12 miles distant.

We have not been disturbed yet by them, but I do not know how soon we will have to go out and lie in the muddy trenches, but I hope that they will hold off a few weeks longer and then spring will open and we will have warm weather!

We have been living better for the last week than we were previously. We now draw ½ lb. of pork to the man pr. week and potatoes and peas also once a week. I will now stand a very good chance to come home again next spring, I think, but if I do not, I will not feel disappointed for it is a very uncertain thing. I would like to get home again about next summer if I get a good chance, but I do not want to quit the army yet. I am still in the notion to stay here until this trouble is ended, and then I can be satisfied at home and feel like that I was not doing wrong. You must write to me soon. Write all the news about the old stamping ground.

12. James R. Bonnet was elected fourth sergeant of Company C in the reorganization of May 8, 1862. His brother D. R. Bonnet, also of Pierson's company, was mortally wounded at the battle of Wilson's Creek and died in Springfield, Missouri, on August 18, 1861 (Tunnard, *A Southern Record*, 362, 500; Booth, comp., *Records*, II, 36).

Give my love to all the family. Enclosed I send Father a scab of Vaccine matter which may be of service to him or to Dr. Egan.

Yrs. & c.

J. F. Pierson

⇒ ⇐

REUBEN ALLEN PIERSON TO WILLIAM H. PIERSON
Camp Near Guinea Station, Va.
Feb. 19th, 1863

W. H. Pierson
Mount Lebanon, La.

Dear Father

I received yours of the 30th Ult. yesterday and was very much astonished as I have been thinking that communication was entirely cut off from home. I was very sorry to hear that Wells had lost his pocket book containing all the money sent by different members of this and other companies of this regiment. As for what I lost myself it matters but little; but to think of the poor boys who only get eleven dollars per month and who have stinted themselves to send home a portion of their hard earned gains and then for it to be lost. Such seems quite hard, but nevertheless it is done and there is but little use of grieving over spilt milk. I am in tolerable good health. I have had chills this month but have entirely missed them and recovered from the effects. The general health of the company never was better. Seventy six present in camp and some sixty four for duty. We have had one case of small pox in the company as I wrote you in a previous letter. John Norrid was the person. I heard from him the other day. He was getting well very fast. It has not spread any yet though three weeks have elapsed since he was sent off. Not even his messmates have taken it though they slept in the same tent with him till after he had broke[n] out. I was in the tent and saw him after he had broken out. The splotches are much larger than measels but look very similar. The whole of our company have been well vaccinated and I think are now almost proof against the disease. I regret very much to have the painful task of announcing the death of John C. Brown.[13] He died at Howard['']s Grove Hosp[ital][14] Richmond Va. on the 1st day of Feb. of small

13. John C. Brown of Sabine Parish enlisted in Company C on March 8, 1862, at Mount Lebanon. He died at Howard's Grove on February 4, 1863 (Booth, comp., *Records,* II, 151).

14. Howard's Grove Hospital, one of the six major military hospitals operating in Richmond, was especially designated as the care-giving institution for smallpox patients (Current, ed., *Encyclopedia of the Confederacy,* II, 796; Emory M. Thomas, *The Confederate State of Richmond: A Biography of the Capital* [Austin, 1971], 114; H. H. Cunningham, *Doctors in Gray: The Confederate Medical Service* [1958; rpr. Baton Rouge, 1993], 53, 64–65).

pox. He was beloved by all the company and had won the universal esteem of every fellow soldier. He was an exception among young men. His moral habits were worthy of being followed by all young men. He was a faithful Christian and good soldier. We deeply mourn the loss of such a good man and tender our heartfelt sympathies to his bereaved relatives and friends at home. I hope we may all conduct ourselves so during this life that we may meet him after death, where pain and parting will be known no more. I sent you a letter and two hundred ($200) Dollars by Dr. Egan which I hope you will get. Everything is quiet here now. The yankees are withdrawing their forces from in front of us on the Rhappahannock and doubtless intend concentrating their forces around Charleston & Savannah. I have written home weekly all this year till the 1st of this month when I heard that the mail communication was cut. Since then I have not written. You must continue to write occasionally and if I only get a few of the letters I shall be amply repaid for all my trouble of writing if I write three times per week. Tell Uncle Abraham Williams I have had no opportunity of collecting John[']s pay but will attend to it the 1st time I go to Richmond. I shall send in the final accounts of all the deceased members of my company in a few days and then their accounts can be audited and settled immediately. The weather has been very bad for the last five weeks; it has either been snowing or raining over half of the time. The ground is too rotten for wagons to travel any-where, only on roads causewayed and then near[ly] halfleg deep in mud. I have never seen as much bad weather in so short a time. I receive a letter from Dave, Henry, or James occasionally and thus get news from home. They are all at Vicksburg. I am glad to hear that Jim is so well satisfied with camp life. I hope he may continue to be healthy and do well; he says his prospect is very good to get a position in the company. I wish him much success. Give my best regards to all enquirers. Extend all the love of an absent member to the family while I remain your Son

R. A. Pierson

P.S. Direct all your letters to Richmond Va. as they will come direct[ly] to me in any part of the State. Yours affectionately

R. A. P.

⇒ ⇐

DAVID PIERSON TO WILLIAM H. PIERSON

Camp Snyder's Mill, Miss.
Feby. 25ᵗʰ, 1863

Wᵐ H. Pierson
  Mt. Lebanon,
    La.

Dear Pa,

   Time still wears away without an occurrence to dispel the monotony that has settled down upon the camps at this post. The same old routine—drilling, inspections, guard mountings, musters, & c. with heavy firing at Vicksburg almost daily is enacted now as it was one month ago and not a single item takes place to mark the change from day to day. The enemy is making desperate efforts to get up something new & exciting, but there he has been foiled in every attempt. Failing to open the *Canal* as early as he had supposed, an attempt was made last week to get their boats through Yazoo Pass into the Yazoo River above this point, but our Genˡ being *wide awake,* had taken steps to prevent such a thing, and the enemy, as usual, was disappointed. It is believed by our Divisional Commander that the enemy is maturing a plan to attack this point which is known to be the key to Vicksburg. Not a gunboat has been to see us in nearly a month and no demonstrations whatever made in this direction in that time, while other points have been threatened almost daily. It is supposed from these signs that this will be the next point of attack, and we have been patiently awaiting for the expected storm for several weeks. The enemy has evidently found Vicksburg a harder nut to crack than he had first supposed and if every soldier here will do his duty the combined hosts of Lincoln cannot take it. That we will have a desperate struggle here in the course of this spring and summer is apparent to everyone, unless indeed a cessation of hostilities should be declared before the Feds are ready to commence the assault, but in that I have no confidence. Our Army is large and well proportioned, in the best of spirits and health, and if I am not badly mistaken, will give a good account of itself when the hour of battle comes. The horror hitherto had by our troops of gunboats is about laid aside and now no more importance is attached to them than any floating vessel. A few days ago when it was rumored that such a craft was in the pass, the Genˡ called upon this Regᵗ. for volunteers to man a transport for the purpose of boarding the Yankee vessel and capturing her. The boys all wanted to go, and it was with difficulty that I could decide as to their merits. The [*illegible*] gone but, since [*illegible*] I learn that the enemy have abandoned their project and left the pass.

Our baggage came up the other day minus everything valuable. Both my trunks had been broken open and every article of any use taken from them. All my blankets to the number of eight went the same mysterious way. I have procured some however, and we are tolerably comfortable. As to eatables, we have fared pretty well so far but the prices are such that I fear our money will give out before we draw again, and then it will be hard indeed with us. The Commissary Dept. furnishes nothing but the poorest beef and coursest corn meal. If we are reduced to it, I suppose we will relish it with a good appetite. Jim is as hearty as I ever saw any boy, and can boast of destroying more rations than anyone in the mess. I have him detailed as orderly which releases him from all duty with his Company and makes his duty very light. I think about a year in camps will improve his health and make a man of him. I am still in Command of the Reg^t. with but little prospect of being relieved. C^{ol} Gilmore [15] will never be fit for duty again, and it is doubtful whether C^{ol} Russel will come back till summer.

Although within 14 miles of Henry, I have not seen him but once and had as well be 100 miles from him so far as seeing and being in his camps any is concerned. Al writes me constantly and always cheerfully. It was rumored yesterday that Gov. Moore had made a requisition on the President for five La. Reg^t., among them the Third Infantry, also that Gen. Price was going to Ark. with his Mo. troops. For myself, I had rather stay here than to go down on the coast in La., but a large majority of the Reg^t. is in favor of going home to fight. I send this letter by one Mr. Springer who leaves here today for Alexandria. I am very busy now—have hardly time to write at all & this must be my excuse for a belated letter.

Yours Affectionately,
D. Pierson

15. Jerome Bonaparte Gilmore was the second lieutenant colonel of the Third Louisiana Infantry. He was promoted to colonel, the regiment's third, on November 5, 1862, but after being wounded at Iuka and captured at Vicksburg resigned his commission on August 20, 1863 (Arthur W. Bergeron, Jr., *Guide to Louisiana Confederate Military Units, 1861–1865* [Baton Rouge, 1989], 76–77; Booth, comp., *Records,* Vol. III, Pt. 1, p. 27).

⇒ ⇐

REUBEN ALLEN PIERSON TO WILLIAM H. PIERSON

Camp Near Fredericksburg, Va.
March 8th, 1863

W. H. Pierson
Mount Lebanon
Dear Father

In the abscence of any news from home I again forward you the latest intelligence from the B.B.'s. We are now encamped near the battlefield of the great Fredericksburg fight. We have the pleasure of reviewing the ground on which we lay when the whole elements seemed to be alive with the fiery missiles of war. Things wear a different appearance now than it did then. The graves of those who perished in the action are scattered around in all the little groves. Many of the yankees were left on the field and our troops were so worn down with fatigue from the three days['] fight, that they took but little pains in burying them. They are still exposed to view in many places, some with their hands and arms sticking out, while others['] heads are projecting and present the most hideous pictures, their teeth glistening as though grinning at the passers by. Many of them were slain here.

The last letter that I received from you was dated the 30th January and conveyed the news of Mr. Wells' sad misfortune in loosing [losing] his pocket book containing all the money sent by various individuals of this company & regiment. I have written to him informing him what are the general impressions of those interested in this matter. Many of them had received the news from their parents & friends before I received his letter and were disposed to suspect that all was not right. I have shown his letter to nearly all concerned but it avails but little. So far as I am individually concerned I feel confident that he lost the money and do not think that the man should be turned out of doors on account of this sad misfortune. If he was legally bound for the money I do not think that anyone could be so heartless as to demand it and thus bring his family to suffering. Now if Wells has acted unfaithful[ly] and appropriated this money to his own use he justly deserves death.

The general health of the company is excellent at present, eighty men present in camp and a very few complaining. Joseph Poulan was sent off sick to the hospital this morning. He was quite feeble but mending. Elias Carlton[16] arrived

---

16. Elias Carlton, a resident of Buck Horn, enlisted in the Ninth Louisiana on February 8, 1863. He was listed as missing and presumed dead on July 2, 1863, at the battle of Gettysburg (Booth, comp., *Records*, II, 256).

here a few days since and joined Co. C.; he was sworn into the service at Pol[l]ard Ala. and received transportation from that point to here. I have received two recruits in the last two weeks. The other was Robert A. Koonce[17] who come off with young Mobley[18] last fall. I would be proud to receive about twenty five more. That number would fill out the company to the maximum number. The late conscript act passed by the federal congress calling out all able bodied men between the ages of twenty and fifty years will throw the largest army into the field ever marshalled by any nation provided that law can be enforced in all the free States.[19] The western States may rebel against this monarchy, and if such a course is resorted to by them the whole continent of America will be merged in blood for a time. The struggle will be for Liberty or anarchy; and will decide the destiny of this government in all time to come.

I am in fine health as usual and have quite an easy time lying up in camp doing nothing. The weather has been very unfavorable for military operations since the 1st of January.[20] The rain and snow has kept the ground thoroughly saturated all the while so that it has been a very difficult matter to procure supplies for the army, and at times the Quarter Masters have been compelled to carry provisions on pack horses on account of the impossibility of traveling the

17. Robert A. Koonce of Sparta served as a first lieutenant in Company I, Sixteenth Louisiana Infantry, from September 29, 1861, until his resignation in July, 1862. On February 28, 1863, he enlisted in Pierson's company at Camp Ewell, Virginia. He was wounded in the hand at Chancellorsville, captured at Strasburg on September 22, 1864, and held at Point Lookout until February 10, 1865. He was with his unit when it surrendered at Appomattox (*ibid.,* Vol. III, Pt. 1, p. 593).

18. Allen J. Mobley was a private in Company I, Sixteenth Louisiana Infantry, discharged because of illness in July, 1863. William J. Mobley was an eighteen-year-old student at the Mount Lebanon Academy when he enlisted in Pierson's Company C on March 8, 1862. He was wounded at Sharpsburg, promoted to sergeant, and surrendered with his company at Appomattox (*ibid.,* 1004).

19. The United States passed its first conscription act on March 3, 1863, with the first draftees being called in July of that year. The government was forced to this expedient measure by a shortage of volunteers, but compulsory military service embittered the public, both north and south. The draft, therefore, was resisted in various ways, including the massive New York Draft Riot of July 11–13, 1863. Although conscription did not topple the Lincoln administration as Pierson predicted, only about six percent of the men whose names were selected for induction into the army actually served.

20. Following his ill-starred attack on Lee's position at Fredericksburg, Ambrose Burnside ordered an ill-conceived march up the Rappahannock River to turn the Confederate left flank. On the day the Army of the Potomac moved out, however, a torrential rain began to fall, accompanied by high winds. After two days of such weather, Burnside abandoned his so-called Mud March and returned to Falmouth, opposite Fredericksburg. A second storm on January 27–29 deposited at least six inches of snow, further debilitating the northern Virginia roads (A. Wilson Greene, "Morale, Maneuver, and Mud: The Army of the Potomac, December 16, 1862–January 26, 1863," in Gary W. Gallagher, ed., *Fredericksburg Campaign: Decision on the Rappahannock* [Chapel Hill, 1995], 195–205).

roads. I have just learned that John Holland[21] is dead. The news came in a letter to J. A. Colbert[22] brought by Lt. Wren[23] of the 8th La. Regt. I am very sorry to hear of his death. The troops are generally well clad & shod and in fine spirits. The rations are very light but the men seem to enjoy them. They have learned to be quite shifty and will get along with less than half than they could have done when we first came out.

I have received two letters from Jimmy since he has been out. He is fine health and is now acting orderly of the regt. We do not anticipate any active operations before May as the roads are impassable and will be for some time to come. We are in plain view of the yankees, and can see them maneuvering on the opposite side of the river. You must continue to write regularly and I will receive a few of them; tell Sister to write as often as convenient. Give my regards to all old friends. Especially my lady friends. I am proud to hear that Mr. & Mrs. C——has concluded to give me or Dave Miss A——. I accept that as quite a compliment. I heard that a young lady of Mt. L[ebanon] drank a toast to the B[ienville] B[lue]s at a party given at Mr. Thurmond[']s. Such compliments are very cheering to us while here in the army. With my love to all the family and relatives.

I remain your affectionate Son
R. A. P.

>∈

JAMES F. PIERSON TO MARY CATHERINE PIERSON
Camp Snyder's Mill, Miss., March 15th, 1863

Miss M. C. Pierson
    Mt. Lebanon, La.

Dear Sister,

Having heard nothing from home in 2 months, I begin to get anxious to receive some news from some of you. Dave has rec'd one letter from Father about a month ago, and that is all that we have gotten from any of you. I see that

21. John Holland, who enlisted at his hometown of Mount Lebanon on March 8, 1862, was absent, sick, on every roll of his army career. He was furloughed home in January or February of 1863, and there he died on an unknown date (Booth, comp., *Records*, Vol. III, Pt. 1, pp. 334–35).

22. John A. Colbert of Mount Lebanon was wounded at the battle of Chancellorsville on May 4, 1863, and was discharged later that same year because of his wound (*ibid.*, II, 376).

23. George L. P. Wren, second lieutenant of Company G, Eighth Louisiana Infantry, was a teacher from Minden. He was captured at Port Republic, wounded at Sharpsburg and at Chancellorsville, captured again at the Wilderness, and held at Fort Delaware until the end of the war (*ibid.*, Vol. III, Pt. 2, p. 1166).

some letters still come through by mail. Ed Brantley[24] received one from his sister yesterday evening which came through by mail in short time. I have received no news from Allen lately. He was in good health the last time I heard from him. I have enjoyed better health since I have been in the army than I ever have in my life. I have not been sick a moment since I have been in the army. I have grown a great deal since I have been here, and in two years longer I will make as large a man as Dave if I keep my health. Peter does not stand it so well. He has been down with the chill and fever for four or five days past, but has missed his chill and is up again. Every person in the whole army are excited a great deal about the fate of Vicksburg. Some think the Yankees will get it; others think differently, but all agree that the enemy intend to make one desperate effort before many days. They came up the Yazoo River yesterday within four miles of this place and shelled the woods, and finally the transports (three) anchored out in the river while the gunboats went back down into the Miss. River, it is thought, to bring up more transports and try to establish a camp on the Chickasaw Bayou. The transports are still to be seen anchored there, but the gunboats have not returned. A portion of the division has been sent up the Yazoo River to Yazoo City. The enemy have got within 12 miles of our works and it is thought that they will get into the river above here and tare up our gunboat which we are constructing in the river a mile below Yazoo City. The last report they fighting [sic], but with nothing decisive about it. Moore's Brigade[25] passed by here night before last to reinforce our troops. I listen with eager ears to the result of a battle in which I am sure that the fate of Vicksburg stands or falls, but we have an enemy army along the banks of the Yazoo and Big Black. I reckon that in all the troops in the vicinity we have nearly 100,000 effective men. I have a pass to go to Vicksburg tomorrow, and I will get to see the fleet above the city. I was there about one month ago and saw the whole fleet when it had collected to its largest number, and it was a sight that is seldom witnessed. The fleet has about half of it disappeared and moved off up the river from some cause unknown by our side. It is said to reinforce their fleet in the Yazoo Pass which connects the Yazoo with the Miss. River, but nothing certain is known. Our troops are fed very scanty here now. I think that we are fixing for a siege here. It is said that the Yankees have us flanked if they gain the Yazoo River above here, for then they will march to Jackson, some 25 miles, and then on to

24. Edward C. Brantly was a private in Company C. He was captured at Vicksburg and reported for exchange prior to April 1, 1864 (*ibid.*, II, 94).

25. John Creed Moore commanded the Second Texas Infantry at the battle of Shiloh and a brigade at Corinth, Vicksburg, and Chattanooga. He was then reassigned to the defense of Mobile but resigned his commission on February 3, 1864.

the river below Vicksburg, cutting off the communications on all sides. The country is entirely destitute of anything in the shape of food or clothing. I lost nearly all my clothing when we left Vau[gh]n's Station, but I have got a pretty good supply again. Dave sent to Mobile by our suttler and got a full supply for us next summer. I will send this across the river by hand, so you will likely get it sooner than by mail. Write to me as soon as you have a chance to send a letter across the river, and if not, mail it and it will get here after a while. Give my respects to old friends and relations. My love to all the family.

I remain,
Your Brother till Death,
James F. Pierson

➤ ❴

DAVID PIERSON TO MARY CATHERINE PIERSON

Camp Snyder's Mills, Miss., March 16th, 1863

Miss M. C. Pierson
  Mount Lebanon,
    La.

My Dear Sister,

Having an opportunity to send a letter across the river by hand tomorrow, I take occasion to write you though I have not the pleasure of acknowledging receipt of a letter from you since I left home. We have not heard from home in quite a long while. I have only received one letter, and that has been so long that I have almost forgotten it. I sometime think it strange that I don't get letters oftener. Others are continually getting them by mail from the west side of the river. Why couldn't I? Jim has gone to Vicksburg to see Henry and the sights and will not return before tomorrow. He seems well pleased so far with his new occupation—soldiering. It has been in my power so far to exempt him from the hardest duty, and he has had but little to do since he was mustered in. His health has improved wonderfully, and I believe camp life will agree with him. I was in the City a few days ago—saw Henry, Tom McGraw, and Hendrick—all were well, but *desperately homesick.* Even Henderick has lost his usual cheerfulness and seems quite sad. Al writes me often, and to judge from the tone of his letters was never better satisfied. I believe he was made to be a soldier—it suits him so well. As for myself, I cannot say that I like it as a profession but have learned to adapt myself to circumstances and am quite easy satisfied.

We are at the same camp we landed at on the 2d January last. I could not have believed that we would remain here so long without a fight, and today the prospect for one is more distant than at first. We have often expected it, and as often been disappointed. A few days ago the enemy came up to within three miles of us, shelling the woods from their boats and threatening to land a force to give us battle, but the storm has blown over and we are still quietly encamped around our fortifications. A large force is now threatening to flank us by way of Talahatchie River, a small tributary of the Yazoo, but there is no telling or guessing how it may turn out, and after all, it may be a mere feint to draw us out from our works so they can give us battle on fair ground. I learned from the Genl Commanding this morning that the gunboat *Essex* had passed Port Hudson[26] and started on a cruise up the river. If so, our boats will have another opportunity to fight with a monster. I have been deceived so often about a battle here that I am not inclined to venture a prediction any more. I have actually become careless about it. A rumor of the approach of the enemy gives me no alarm or uneasiness and often fails to excite the least feeling on the subject. There is still much talk of peace. Some offer to bet high on its being made by the 1st of July, others that it will be made earlier and still others that it will not be made in less than three years. There are almost as many opinions about it as there are minds. It is all speculation at last, and is not within the knowledge of our wisest to see the end of this struggle. Speaking of peace, I learn that the folks at home have already made it and are preparing to have a grand jubilee when the soldiers come home. Let them hope on. It will do no harm, but I fear their expectations will not be realized in the year 1863. The weather is quite warm and pleasant, and spring time is fast approaching. Even the soldiers' camp looks pleasant and cheerful on such days as we are beginning to have. Provisions are very scarce and some days the men get nothing to eat but bread. They are very cheerful, however, and willing to endure privation in the hope of seeing a better day. Jim & I have managed so far to keep tolerably plentiful by paying an enormous price. If I had a few cows and a dozen hens, I would not desire a handsomer fortune. Butter is worth 2 dol. a pound, & eggs, 2 dol. pr. dozen. What do you think of it? Money is plenty and goes free as water. I have just got me a fine uniform from Mobile. I wish you could see it. I think it very pretty.
  Write soon.

Affectionately Yours,
D. Pierson

26. Port Hudson, Louisiana, some 110 miles below Vicksburg, was, by spring, 1863, one of the two remaining Confederate strongholds on the Mississippi River. See Lawrence Lee Hewitt, *Port Hudson: Confederate Bastion on the Mississippi* (1987; rpr. Baton Rouge, 1994).

➤ ❦

DAVID PIERSON TO WILLIAM H. PIERSON
Camp Snyder's Mills, Miss., March 21ˢᵗ, 1863

Mr. Wᵐ H. Pierson
  Mt. Lebanon,
    La.

Dear Pa,

    As Mr. Stoval[27] from Winn and Lieut. Allums,[28] who has resigned, leave to-morrow for Louisiana, I take occasion to write you. My letter will be brought to you by Allums if it can reach him in time and by Mr. Stovall if it does not. We are all excitement here this morning. Snyder's Mill or Hayne's Bluff, which is one and same place, is likely to become the scene of important and stirring events within a short time. The enemy are in Big Deer Creek about fifteen miles north of us with a fleet of gunboats and transports and early this morning heavy cannonading could be distinctly heard in that direction which was supposed an argument between them and Genˡ Featherston[29] who left here three days ago with an expedition to check their progress and prevent them from stealing everything in that country. From where the enemies' fleet now lies, it can easily reach the Yazoo River above us—between here and Yazoo City—in case they succeed in driving back Featherston's Command. Accordingly, Genˡ Hébert, Commanding at this point, has made and is now making preparations to receive them above the raft. We are ordered to hold ourselves in readiness to take positions at a moment's notice. Artillery has been flying about all the morning and altogether everything looks like war again. If the enemy should succeed in getting into the Yazoo above us, I hardly think they will attempt to land in force as in that case their communications could be easily cut off and the whole party captured. I rather believe it is their purpose to plunder and annoy us with their Gunboats. They never can navigate the Yazoo till they take

    27. Either of two Louisiana soldiers named Stovall may be the one to whom Pierson refers. Josiah L. Stovall was first sergeant and later junior second lieutenant of Company A, Thirty-first Louisiana Infantry; W. B. Stovall was first lieutenant of Company F, Twenty-seventh Louisiana Infantry. Both were captured at Vicksburg (Booth, comp., *Records,* Vol. III, Pt. 2, p. 718).

    28. B. S. Alums served as third lieutenant or junior second lieutenant of Company E, Twenty-seventh Louisiana Infantry. He enlisted at Camp Moore on April 30, 1862, but was on sick leave in August, 1862 (*ibid.,* I, 52).

    29. Winfield Scott Featherston was the first colonel of the Seventeenth Mississippi Infantry in the Army of Northern Virginia. Promoted to brigadier general, he served at Second Manassas and Fredericksburg before being transferred to the Army of Mississippi in 1863. After the fall of Vicksburg—when he and his brigade escaped capture because they were on detached duty—he fought in all of the remaining battles of the Army of Tennessee.

this point, and that, I humbly imagine, will be too big a task for them. The raft—which has been constructed across the river at this point—is so strong that a quarter of a mile of driftwood is now pressing against it without effecting it in the least. We then have quite a number of heavy guns commanding the river below and above and unless they should land a force above strong enough to whip our whole army and flank this point and Vicksburg, they never can succeed in capturing either. Our Reg^t has a prospect of being recruited considerably before long. I hear from our Recruiting Officers in Natchitoches and Madison parishes that they have nearly a hundred men. My old Company (C) received 14 yesterday, and among them my old friend Asa Emanuel whom the boys have elected 1st Lieut. I am very glad he came back, and feel more like I was at home, he is so much company to me. If we should get as many as 200 recruits I shall have no fears of the bursting up of the Reg^t on account of small numbers. Jim is quite well satisfied and is really looking better than I ever saw him. He got a letter from Al dated 7 March a few days since. He was well and everything quiet in his Command. Our Col. and Lt. Col. have neither of them made their appearance here as yet, and I am left alone to do the duties of my own and their offices. I am kept very busy, but am perhaps better satisfied than if idle. I am getting the name of being very strict and tight and have been compelled to do things which would be very unpleasant under other circumstances. We get pork rations now that the beef has given out, and we are much better situated as to comfort than in six months before. We get a new uniform in a week for the whole Reg^t.

Yours & c.,

D. Pierson

⇒ ∈

JAMES F. PIERSON TO NANCY COLLINS PIERSON
Camp Snyder's Mill, Miss., April 1st, 1863

Mrs. Nancy Pierson

    Mt. Lebanon, Louisiana

Dear Aunt Nan,

    We received your kind favor a few days ago and was extremely glad to hear from you all to hear that you were all well. Dave is not well. He has a very bad cold which he took from exposure while we were up on Deer Creek. The water is all over the country up there. Consequently we had to travel about in little skiffs in which we always wet our feet and some times stay wet for two or three days. The enemy have fallen back up there, and we have come back to our same old camp. I was out on Picket while up there. I fared very well, but had no shifting suit, so I had to sleep in wet clothes and in muddy ground, but it all has no effect on me, only makes me the healthier. As for something to eat, I get about enough to eat to keep me from eating enough to make me sick, so I continue in good health. And as for being satisfied, I am as well satisfied here as I could be anywhere. I care more for you all at home than I do for myself. If you all keep well, I can stay satisfied until the war is over, which, I think, will not be more than two years longer. Peter, I fear, will not stand it well. He has had the pneumonia pretty badly, but is mending a little. I think he will be up again in three or four days. We have had some pretty cold weather for the last three or four days, but not cold enough to kill the fruit. I hope that the fruit will not be killed this year, as I am wanting fruit this year worse than I ever wanted it in my life. I am very sorry that the community has such a limited opinion of Broth. Geren.[30] I think that he ought to be excused to preach to them all. This part of the army is sending out recruiting officers every month, and if he don't look sharp, some of them will get him. There are some that won't listen to his preaching but will tie him to a horse's tail, and then he'll find himself in some company. I think the young ladies very patriotic who gave him the exalted position of one of the crinoline guards. I would like to see Mr. Geren attempt to preach to this Regt. They would take him into camps, as they call it. Our Regt. has been recruited a little. Our company have 13 new recruits, which helps it out pretty considerably. The whole Regt. have about one-hundred and fifty, so now we have about five-hundred in all. Since the above was written we have rec^d Father's letter of the 8th March. Tell Cassie that I want her to keep well and not be always sick. Tell Joe that he must be a smart boy and study hard while he has a chance. Tell Father that we would like to have some of those nice hams of his, but I can't see any way of getting them. I would like to take him a load of flour in the place of his nice hams. Flour is selling here in the Commissary at 8 cts. pr. lb., but bacon has gone up here to 75 cts. pr. lb. and lard at a dollar; butter, $2.50; eggs, $1.50. We have a letter from Allen of the 18th of March. He was well and all the company. Tell Cassie if she can spare a little of her valued time to write to me or I will put her on the Geren list. Tell Joe to write soon. Give my respects and regards to all old friends. I remain

Yours Affectionately,

J. F. Pierson

---

30. John Laird Geren, a Baptist preacher, was the son of Jasper N. Geren and Margaret Laird Geren of Webster Parish (*Biographical and Historical Memoirs of Northwest Louisiana* [Nashville, 1890], 683–84).

⇒ ⇐

DAVID PIERSON TO WILLIAM H. PIERSON

Camp Snyder's Mills, Miss.
April 3rd, 1863

Wm H. Pierson
   Mt. Lebanon
      Louisiana

Dear Pa,

We have received two letters from you within the last week, the latest of which bore date of 15th March, also one from Aunt Nan. The contents of all were eagerly devoured and gave us much pleasure. I must confess that the latter was the most interesting for which you will excuse me, of course, as there [was] something from the young ladies in it. I very much regret having wrote you anything about our losses as perhaps it has induced you to believe that our suffering has really been more than what it has. It is true I missed my fine blankets and fine clothes, & c. at first, but have so far supplied their place now as almost to forget it. As for Jim, of course he writes home the darkest side of the case to make you appreciate the fact that he is soldiering, but the truth is, he has had plenty of clothes and been very comfortably situated as well as myself, with one or two exceptional times and places. He has just drawn from the Government a full soldier's outfit consisting of a uniform suit, shirt, shoes, socks, and cap, and by some cunning of his own had nearly supplied himself before. I have had but little time to write you within the past two weeks owing to an expedition in which we were concerned up Deer Creek last week. The enemy had endeavored to get into the Yazoo above the raft by opening the bayous and lakes in the overflow above and were met and repulsed by Genl Featherston on the Sunflower. They next commenced operations on lower Deer Creek which is a very small stream emptying into the Yazoo about eight miles above this point, thinking that by cutting their way through the overflow down that stream they would be able to send their Gunboats into the Yazoo above the raft and destroy our steamers and perhaps land a force and flank our position here and at Vicksburg. To meet, and if possible capture, this force, an expedition was gotten up by Genl Lee[31] composed of the best troops in the whole army, being five picked

31. Stephen Dill Lee served as a member of P.G.T. Beauregard's staff during the bombardment of Fort Sumter, distinguished himself at Second Manassas and Sharpsburg, and was reassigned as chief of artillery of the Army of Mississippi. After Vicksburg, he was assigned to command of a cavalry division operating in Alabama and Mississippi. In May, 1864, he was appointed to command of the Department of Alabama, Mississippi, and East Louisiana. Only two months later, he was promoted to lieutenant general and given command of a corps of the Army of Tennessee. His corps took part in John Bell Hood's disastrous Tennessee campaign, and Lee was wounded at the battle of Nashville. See Herman Hattaway, *General Stephen Dill Lee* (Jackson, Miss., 1976).

regiments and among them the 3rd La. We left camps on the 23rd ul^t and went up the creek in advance of the rest of the troops accompanied by Genl Lee. A small steamer took us up the stream about 10 miles from its mouth[;] when we landed when we took to flatboats, canoes, dugouts, & c., the whole country being overflowed. In this manner we worked our way up to within a few miles of where the enemy had some pickets on dry land, and halted in a narrow strip of land on the banks of the creek. Here we waited for the balance of the command, intending to proceed as soon as they arrived and attack the enemy. Three days passed by, which we spent in constructing a log fort, fishing, bathing, & c. The last regiment came one evening at dark, and I had orders to move forward early the next morning and drive in the enemies' pickets, and had actually commenced preparations when the Genl received a dispatch that the enemy was retreating. They had heard of our approach by means of some runaways and flew precipitately. So we were all disappointed in not having a fight with Gunboats and returned the same way we went. Altogether it was a novel trip and offered us much amusement and relief from the monotony of camps. Genl Lee paid the old 3rd Reg^t a very high compliment in selecting it from among so many troops for such service, and while with him he made the boys a little speech in which he expressed himself as being entirely satisfied that they would prove themselves as gallant as he had heard of them and if he should require their services.

Yesterday was a lively day with us again, and it was at one time thought we would have a brush in spite of ourselves. About 10 o'clock A.M., while setting in my tent reading, I received an order to get the Reg^t in readiness for action with as little delay as possible. We were under arms in five minutes and off for the trenches, and had not proceeded far before we were more fully satisfied that something was up from the smoke and boom from heavy artillery from the enemies' Gunboats not over a mile from us. I received orders to halt behind a hill which afforded us protection from the shells and rode up to see what was going on. On reaching the top of a high hill I saw four Gunboats lying broadside in the river *talking* with their batteries. The Genl was under the impression that several transports was just behind, coming up with troops to storm our works and kept us out till 12 o'clock today waiting for them. The Gunboats, after shelling a while without hurting anything except a poor sheep that was grazing with his flock in the field next to the river, left, since which we have heard nothing from them. Last night we lay upon the river bank deployed for a mile as skirmishers to prevent the enemy from making a landing if he should try us it the night. The balance of the forces were a mile in our rear, lying in the trenches on the hills.

I believe I have I given you all the news, and, I fear, have been tedious. I forgot to say that Jim lost his gun on the Deer Creek expedition by accident. He came very near going wild when we got into canoes and somehow or other let the gun drop into the water. His Capt. investigated the matter to see whether he should pay for it or not, and decided that it was by accident. I have been suffering with a cold ever since our trip till today—was actually on the sick list yesterday till the excitement; got up and got better amazingly fast. Pete is just recovering from a severe illness. Jim continues in fine health. My old friend Asa Emanuel has come back to his Company. He brought several recruits with him, among the rest your man Howell[32] who would not be mustered in at first but went to Vicksburg to get position from the authorities and while spunging [sponging] around was picked up by the Commandant of Conscripts. I do not know what will become of him next. We get plenty to eat just now. Our Commissary got a lot of flour a few days ago which he sells at the low rate of seven cents pr. pound. I have just bought a piece of venison and occasionally get a nice ham. We have no beef now, but get full pork rations and the consequence is we have more sickness than before. There is a small lake near us which I am told is the best fishing ground in the state. We are catching some now. The woods, or I might rather say the canebrakes, abound with wild turkey, and now and then the boys waste a cartridge in killing one—which is strictly forbidden. I hear tonight that Lt. Col. Russell is on his way to join the Reg^t, & I am heartily glad of it.

Excuse my penmanship & c.

Yours Affectionately,
D. Pierson

> ⋲

DAVID PIERSON TO NANCY COLLINS PIERSON

[April 3, 1863]

My Dear Mother,

As I am writing Pa, I will take the liberty of inclosing a line in the same envelope to you to thank you for your kind letter which came to hand in due time. You were certainly very considerate in writing at the time you did and knew, of course, that you could not give me more pleasure than to do so when the young ladies were all present that I might hear from them also. As you was the medium through which the girls sent their requests and regards to me, you will not close your official duties till you give me a showing. Therefore will you please say to Miss Belle that I must cheerfully accede to her request in that of undertaking the task of choosing her a soldier. At the same time you can inform her of my entire confidence in my ability to make the selection and that I take

---

32. A Pvt. J. R. Howell, Company G, Third Louisiana Infantry was captured at Vicksburg (Booth, comp., *Records*, Vol. III, Pt. I, p. 368).

great pleasure in recommending to her good graces a certain Infantry Major whose name cannot be conveniently spelled without a P. Thanks to the other young ladies whose regards I received through you. And assure them that they will never be forgotten by a grateful soldier. Tell Sister that I have not forgotten her while engaged in the game of choosing—that I have selected for her a gallant Lieut. whom I will bring home with me at the close of the war and perhaps before. I have nothing additional to what I have written Pa except that I have just received a letter from Al who is well and in high hopes of a speedy close of the war. I must tell you that I saw and made the acquaintance of a brother of Mrs. Lincoln's[33] the other day who is an officer in the army at this place—his name is Todd. He is an enthusiast in the cause of the South. Many believe that the war will end this summer when we will all go home, and then what a gay time we will have.

Affectionately Yours,
D. Pierson

⇒ ⇐

REUBEN ALLEN PIERSON TO MARY CATHERINE PIERSON
Camp near Hamilton's Crossing, Va.
April 5th, 1863

Miss M. C. Pierson
Mount Lebanon, La.
Dear Sister

In the abscence of any letter from you I again write to inform you that I am yet in the land of the living. As usual I am enjoying the best of health, have an appetite as keen as a hungry wolf but thanks to Mas Jeff Davis I get plenty of bacon and biscuit with an occasional mess of rice and now and then some sugar & molasses. We can purchase but few articles of food extra of what we draw.

33. Mary Todd Lincoln was the daughter of a wealthy and influential Kentucky slave-holding family. Her brother, Dr. George Rogers Clark Todd, was for a time commandant of a prison camp in Richmond and served for the duration of the war as a Confederate surgeon. Her half-brothers—Samuel, David, and Alexander—also joined the Confederate army. Samuel Todd, a private in Company I, Louisiana's Crescent Regiment, was killed at Shiloh in April, 1862. David H. Todd, referred to here by Pierson, was captain of Company A, Twenty-second Louisiana Infantry. He was so severely wounded in the defense of Vicksburg that he was at first reported dead, and he lived as an invalid for the remainder of his life. Alexander Todd, a captain on Brig. Gen. Benjamin Hardin Helm's staff, was killed in action in a skirmish near Baton Rouge on August 4, 1863. Helm, Mrs. Lincoln's brother-in-law and a great favorite of President Lincoln, was killed at the battle of Chickamauga (William C. Davis, *Breckinridge: Statesman, Soldier, Symbol* [1974; rpr. Baton Rouge, 1992], 320; William C. Davis, *The Orphan Brigade: The Kentucky Confederates Who Couldn't Go Home* [1980; rpr. Baton Rouge, 1983], 116–17; Justin G. Turner, *Mary Todd Lincoln: Her Life and Letters* [New York, 1972], 155).

Our Sutlers[34] have a few beans & peas which we buy and have a feast of liquor about once a week. We can procure Oysters here at from five to ten Dollars per gallon of which we are all passionately fond (the best and healthiest diet for a soldier in the world). Everything is quiet along our lines today. We were on Piquet last Wednesday and Thursday but had special orders not to have any communication with them but our boys would sauce them whenever they hallooed across the river at us. They seemed very anxious to argue the question of "What is the best mode of stopping the war?" They all seem to be quite tired of the long continuance of a war which appears to be waged merely for the freedom of the slaves in the Southern States. They have but little interest in this matter anyway. The weather continues very unfavorable for military operations. The earth is now covered with snow and the wind has been quite cutting from the North all day; the ground is very wet and miry thus rendering the maneuvering of artillery quite difficult if not impossible. I think that it will be May before we begin active operations against the yanks; while they show no disposition to advance upon us. My opinion is that they are waiting to organize a considerable army of their conscripts as reenforcements before undertaking so hazardous an enterprise. Robert Smith[35] has arrived in camp and brought us a fine lot of letters; which by the way is quite a treat to all of us. The general health of all the troops in this portion is reported by the Surgeons as being excellent. "Co. C." is not altogether as well as it has been. Two men are so unwell as to be confined to their tents, P. L. Collins & James Morgan. Colds are the principal that ails them. I think neither is by any means dangerous. I see from late numbers of the La. Baptist that the 28th Regt.[36] has been in a considerable skirmish with the yankees in the swamp and are lauding themselves with praises for their extreme courage & bravery. When they have seen the service that we did last summer then their ambition will be satisfied at the laurels which they now have won without saying much about it.

I wrote an April fool home a few days since. Write me an answer if you have heard anything from it. I write the young ladies name in the inside of the envelope of this letter to whom it was directed. We drill twice each day whenever

---

34. Sutlers were officially appointed civilian merchants who accompanied the armies, north and south, vending such necessities and luxuries as were not furnished by the government. Stationery, tobacco, newspapers, and alcohol as well as food were among the items stocked by the entrepreneurs. See Francis A. Lord, *Civil War Sutlers and Their Wares* (New York, 1969).

35. Robert A. Smith of Mount Lebanon was promoted to sergeant of Company G, Eighth Louisiana Infantry, on April 24, 1862. He was wounded at Bristow Station, August 27, 1862, and furloughed home to recuperate. Again wounded at Gettysburg, he was taken prisoner when Lee's army retreated toward the Potomac on July 4, 1863. He was assigned to De Camp General Hospital, David's Island, New York, until exchanged on September 16, 1863. Permanently disabled, he was detailed back to Louisiana (Booth, comp., *Records,* Vol. III, Pt. 2, p. 628).

36. This issue of the *Louisiana Baptist* is no longer extant.

the weather is pretty and clear and have Brigade drill about once a week. Our regiment is said to be the best drilled and disciplined of any in the Brig. We have over four hundred men for duty in the Regt. "Co. C." has about seventy. We frequently amuse ourselves at leisure times by a game of ball. This is quite a show sometimes. As many as one hundred are engaged at once.

I intend visiting the ruins of Fredericksburg in a few days. The city I am told is literally riddled from the effects of the bombardment in December last. But few homes are left untouched and the ste[e]ple of one church has three cannon ball holes through it. I have nothing more of interest to write and must beg you to pardon this short skeleton of a letter.

I saw Willie Cooksie about two weeks ago. He was in excellent health and spirits. He staid one night with us. You must be sure to tell this [to] Miss Belle. A. L. Bynum[37] is encamped within a few hundred yards of us. He belongs to the Donaldsonville artillery.[38] Tell the Misses Keys[39] he is as lively as ever and a soldierly looking little man. Give my love to all the family and also to my lady friends. Extend my regards to all interrogators and remember me as an Absent Brother.
R. A. Pierson

37. A. L. Bynum, a New Orleans resident, was captured at Frederick, Maryland, on September 12, 1862, exchanged from Fort Delaware on November 10, 1862, and transferred to the Washington Light Artillery (Capt. James F. Hart's South Carolina Battery) in April, 1864. He was still with the army at the time of Lee's surrender (Booth, comp., *Records,* II, 209).

38. The Donaldsonville Artillery Company, commanded by Caps. Victor Maurin and R. Prosper Landry, served with the Army of Northern Virginia in every major battle from Williamsburg through the siege of Petersburg. After the Peninsula campaign, it was assigned to Richardson Anderson's division of Longstreet's corps, and after Chancellorsville, it was reassigned to A. P. Hill's corps (Bergeron, *Guide,* 29–30).

39. These were the daughters of Tandy A. and Harriet Key of Mount Lebanon: Virginia, age twenty-four; Harriet, eighteen; and Arabella, sixteen. The Keys owned a plantation valued at three thousand dollars. Two of their sons, Henry Clay Key and Joshua W. Key, were in the Ninth Louisiana; a third, John W. Key, was one of Mount Lebanon's three storekeepers and an officer in the Louisiana Baptist Convention (*Louisiana Baptist,* July 25, 1861; "Some Large Landholders of Bienville Parish, 1850," *Louisiana History,* XXIV [Summer, 1983], 288; Walter Prichard, ed., "A Tourist's Description of Louisiana in 1860," *Louisiana Historical Quarterly,* XXI [October, 1938], 1188).

⇒ ⇐

REUBEN ALLEN PIERSON TO WILLIAM H. PIERSON
Camp near Hamilton's Crossing, Va.
April 8th, 1863

W. H. Pierson, Esqr.

Mount Lebanon, La.

Dear Father

I have just received a letter from sister bearing the date the 8th of March but as I received a letter from Joseph sent by Robert Smith of the 17th the other day sister[']s letter contained very little news that I had not already heard. It is a great source of satisfaction to even receive old letters from home. I had written to Cassie only two days before the receipt of hers and consequently I will address this to you. I am in excellent health; in fact all of the troops in this department of the southern army are in most excellent condition every way, well armed—well clad—in high spirits—very sanguine of victory whenever the hour comes to meet our enemies; and under much better discipline than they have ever been at any time previous. All of our Brig. Gens. are striving to have the best drilled and disciplined Brigades, hence the improvement has been very great this winter. Everything continues quiet along our lines although we have reports daily that the yankees are advancing. These reports grow out from the fact that they are making demonstrations on the opposite side of the river. Their maneuvers are made merely for ostentation and show. Whenever they attempt a forward movement they will strive to their utmost to conceal it and to take us by surprise but Gen. Lee who is always as vigilant as the Eagle will be sure to find them out in time to be ready to repulse any advance which they may attempt. The weather continues quite unfavorable for military operations; we had a considerable snow here on the 5th Inst.; the last of which melted off this morning, and the roads are quite mud[d]y and so much cut up by the army wagons as to be almost impassable.

Today looks very much like spring was coming; the birds were singing quite merry this morning, and the clouds were gathered up in beautiful banks which very much indicate the approach of another summer. I received a letter and Surg[e]on's certificate from Thos. Page today; the certificate states that he will not be able for duty in forty days, probably longer. I guess he will come out before this reaches you—hope I shall get a fine package of letters by him. I have received a second letter from Mr. Wells concerning the loss of the money sent by him. I am somewhat surprised at the loss of the trunk containing the letters; while he was very successful in getting one trunk home with various little articles for sale. I see published in the Baptist an Obituary of Jacob Boyet[40] (if I do not mistake) which I wrote and dropped in among the letters that Mr. Wells carried off. How this was carried through & the letters lost is quite a mystery to me. He speaks of his being very reluctant in taking the money but I remember well that he did not refuse anyone who applied to him. He states that he is not responsible for the money legally as though he expected every soldier to enter suit against him immediately. We have the war to fight out before we can ever see Mr. Wells much less bring an accusation against him. If he really lost both the money and the trunk of letters, and succeeded in getting another trunk through, he surely manifested a disposition to neglect the letters for the sake of his own interest. We are soldiers in the Southern army it is true and our letters may be of minor importance to Mr. Wells but I thank God that such is not the feelings of a majority of the people in Bienville. I must leave this perplexing subject, hoping all may come out right in the end.

I only drop you the hints concerning Mr. Wells that you may know something of what is going on here; there is a general dissatisfaction. Please keep this to yourself. We have only two men sick in camp and they are both up today (Collins & Morgan). Tell Mrs. Lindon the Proff. is well. I will try and write once a week this year and hope you may be so fortunate as to receive most of my letters.

Give my respects to all acquaintances &c. Tell sister I will write to her again soon. I remain your affectionate Son.

R. A. Pierson

Direct all your letters to Richmond, Va. "Co. C." 9th Regt. La. Vols.

⇒ ⇐

REUBEN ALLEN PIERSON TO MARY CATHERINE PIERSON
Camp near Fredericksburg, Va.
April 13th, 1863

Miss. M. C. Pierson
Mount Lebanon, La.
Dear Sister
As I have just received a letter from father and having written to him only a few days since I will direct this to you. I send you by mail this morning a paper, Joseph a little song book, and Pa & Aunt a tract which Gen. Jackson sent

40. This issue of the *Louisiana Baptist* is no longer extant.

around with the request that every soldier in his corps should read before commencing the spring campaign. It is called "Our Dangers & Our Duty,"[41] and I think is one of the best things that I have seen written upon this war. We all prize it very highly on account of the source from which it emenates. Anything sent to the soldiers by Gen. Stonewall Jackson is of course in itself very great. The general health of all the troops in this department of the southern army is excellent. I have seventy seven men present this morning and only three on the Dr. list. They are all well enough to walk around camp. Winter is just passing away here now and the trees beginning to bud and the flowers to open. This I know will sound strange to you but I should not be the least surprised to see another snow during this month. It sleeted last spring as late as the 24th of May, so you see that we do not expect warm weather before the 1st of next month under any circumstances. I visited the ruins of Fredericksburg last Friday. The place is a very old one having been founded over one hundred years ago. Some of the houses were totally destroyed during the bombardment of the 12 & 13 of Dec. last, while others are very slightly damaged. The town is now occupied by Gen. Barksdale's Miss. brigade.[42] There is still a number of the citizens living there. Many ladies may be seen promenading the streets and I learned that there was a ball nearly every night in some part of the city given by the soldiers. This will sound very harsh on your ears when I tell you that the yankee batteries command the city and could set it on fire at any moment. This reminds me of the story told of "Nero's fiddling while Rome was burning." Everything continues quiet in front of our lines; it is rumored that the federals are leaving the opposite side of the river and moving off their forces to some other points. I guess they are changing their base of operations and trying to turn up somewhere that

41. *Our Danger and Our Duty*, by the Reverend James Henley Thornwell, a prominent South Carolina Presbyterian known as "the Calhoun of the Church," went through five known editions from 1862 through 1864. Fearing a lack of moral fervor among the southern people, in this, his last publication, Thornwell painted a horrific portrait of the South defeated by Union arms and suffering under Union domination. In order to avoid a bitter and brutal reconstruction, he urged, the Confederacy must rise to the present military crisis and make "every pass a Thermopylae, every strait a Salamis, and every plain a Marathon" (James Oscar Farmer, *The Metaphysical Confederacy: James Henley Thornwell and the Synthesis of Southern Values* [Macon, Ga., 1986]; T. Michael Parrish and Robert M. Willingham, *Confederate Imprints: A Bibliography of Southern Publications from Secession to Surrender* [Austin, Tex. (1987), 752–53]).

42. William Barksdale, first colonel of the Thirteenth Mississippi Infantry, rose to command of the Mississippi brigade of the Army of Northern Virginia. The brigade, which Longstreet referred to as "Confederate hornets," rendered its most notable service in the defense of the crossing of the Rappahannock River at Fredericksburg on December 11, 1862, where it delayed for hours the completion of Federal pontoon bridges and inflicted severe casualties on Burnside's engineers. Barksdale was mortally wounded in an assault on Little Round Top on July 2, 1863, dying the next day in enemy hands. Among his regimental commanders was William C. Falkner, grandfather of the Nobel Prize–winning novelist William Faulkner and the prototype for Col. John Sartoris in such novels as *Sartoris* and *The Unvanquished*.

Lee will not expect. I should not be surprised if we were ordered off from our quarters in a very few days. We cannot expect to lie up in idleness many days longer. The time for active work has come & if the yanks advance on Lee he will be more than apt to flank them and force them to leave their present strongly fortified position. I receive letters tolerably regular from Vicksburg. The last was from Henry. All were then well. I see from various letters which have been received here that considerable speculation is indulged in by the people at home concerning the ability of the Southern States to feed the army now in the field. This is only a Ghost created by the imagination. Virginia alone can support the army now stationed within her borders and this is at least one third of the whole army. If the only hope of our enemies is founded on the supposition that we will soon be starving they would do well to go home for that I believe to be one of the moral impossibilities. The great fleet at Charleston attacked our forts and batteries a few days since but met with a sad reverse.[43] Our prospects are much brighter now than they were about one year ago. The winter has passed without affording any advantage to our enemies while in Jan., Feb. & March of 1862 Fort Donelson[44] fell, Fort Henry, New Orleans[45] and several other important places were surrendered. It seemed that they would overrun our country in a very short time, but as the battle is not always to the strong we turned the tune early in the spring and victory has continued to be ours from that time to the present. We all receive the Baptist here occasionally and it is read with great interest; the controversy between J. L. Geren and Dr. Courtney is really amusing.[46] I must confess that Mr. Geren is quite presumptuous to at-

43. On April 7, 1863, Rear Adm. Samuel F. DuPont led seven monitors and two ironclad battleships, *Keokuk* and *New Ironsides,* into Charleston Harbor in an attempt to close this vital Confederate port. Rebel mines and obstructions slowed DuPont's flotilla, and seventy-seven pieces of heavy artillery mounted in Fort Sumter and Fort Moultrie shot it to pieces, scoring four hundred hits, sinking *Keokuk,* and heavily damaging all of the monitors. See Stephen R. Wise, *Gate of Hell: Campaign for Charleston Harbor, 1863* (Columbia, S.C., 1995); T. Harry Williams, *P. G. T. Beauregard: Napoleon in Gray* (1955; rpr. Baton Rouge, 1995), 175–79.

44. Maj. Gen. Ulysses S. Grant, operating on the Tennessee and Cumberland Rivers, captured Forts Henry and Donelson on February 6 and 16, 1862, respectively. The strategic importance of these capitulations was considerable, forcing the Confederates to abandon a large portion of Tennessee and setting the stage for the splitting of the Confederacy (Benjamin Franklin Cooling, *Forts Henry and Donelson: The Key to the Confederate Heartland* [Knoxville, 1987], 268–69).

45. On April 24, 1862, the ships of Rear Adm. David G. Farragut's West Gulf Blockading Squadron ran past Confederate forts Jackson and St. Philip, twelve miles above the mouth of the Mississippi River. The following day, the squadron steamed the remaining seventy miles upstream to now-defenseless New Orleans, accepting the surrender of the South's wealthiest and most populous city and largest port on April 25. See Chester G. Hearn, *The Capture of New Orleans, 1862* (Baton Rouge, 1995).

46. Franklin Courtney was born in Kings and Queens County, Virginia, on June 4, 1812. He received a medical degree from the University of Pennsylvania in 1833 and in 1850 emigrated to Mount

tempt to sustain himself in such a plain case, against one whose experience and general knowledge is so extensive as that of the Dr. Tell Mrs. Lindon that the Proff. is all right side up with care. I have no casualties to report since the death of Wm. S. Norrid. I hope to have no more in a long while. The boys are all well acclimated and will enjoy better health here in camp than they did at home. Give my best regards to all enquirers. Receive and extend the same to all relatives. Write me in your next if you ever hear from Sister Miranda[47] and how she is getting along. Give me all the news of the country whenever you write and be sure to write often.

Excuse all amiss.

Your Brother till death

R. A. P.

Direct all your letters to Richmond, Va.

Lebanon, where he advertised himself as a "physician, surgeon and accoucher." In 1855, he claimed that his twenty-five years of practice in the South "justifies the belief that he understands the pathology and treatment of the diseases of this latitude." He was also a Baptist preacher and president of the board of trustees and professor of theology at Mount Lebanon University. He was also a frequent contributor to and, for a time, editor and part owner of the *Louisiana Baptist.* For John Laird Geren, see n. 30 above. Unfortunately, this issue of the *Baptist* no longer exists (*Biographical and Historical Memoirs of Northwest Louisiana,* 683–84; *Louisiana Baptist,* June 11, 1861; W. E. Paxton, *A History of the Baptists of Louisiana from the Earliest Times to the Present* [St. Louis, 1888], 525–27).

47. Martha A. Miranda Pierson, the oldest of William H. Pierson's daughters, was born in Stewart County, Georgia, on June 20, 1833. She married a first cousin and was thereafter largely ostracized by the family. During the war, she lived in Jackson Parish, Louisiana, but afterward moved to Arkansas, where she died on December 12, 1896.

⟫6⟪

THE DEMON LOUISIANANS

⟫ ⟪

DAVID PIERSON TO WILLIAM H. PIERSON

Camp Snyder's Mills, Miss.
April 20th, 1863

Wm H. Pierson
  Mt. Lebanon
    La.

Dear Pa,

We are still at the same old camp and very quiet. I am only induced to write now for fear that my last, which was written a week ago, has not reached you, not that I have anything new to communicate. The Yankees have returned in greatly increased numbers, and, it would seem, have commenced the siege of Vicksburg in earnest. As yet they have accomplished nothing except to run several boats past our batteries at Vicksburg.[1] It is reported that they have a large force at New Carthage, which is a small town below the city on the La. side, and that they intend crossing the river at that point and attack it from the south side. How well they will succeed or what preparations have been made to meet them I am not able to say. That they will attack us at some point very shortly is beyond a doubt, and the sooner they do so the better for us as they now have the Red River blockaded through which we have received the greater portion of

---

1. Pierson seriously underestimated the importance of this event. On the night of April 16, Rear Adm. David Dixon Porter ran eight gunboats and three transports past the powerful Vicksburg batteries, encouraging him to try again on the night of April 22, this time sending down a large supply flotilla. On April 30, the Union vessels below Vicksburg ferried two of Grant's corps to the east side of the Mississippi River, opening the route by which the Federals marched to besiege the city on May 22. See Samuel Carter III, *The Final Fortress: The Campaign for Vicksburg, 1862–1863* (New York, 1980), 154–57.

our supplies. The loss of the New Iberia salt mines is regarded as a great calamity to us.[2] We have news of the defeat of our army under Gen[ls] Taylor and Sibley[3] in La. and the possession of the whole coast country by the enemy up to the mouth of the Red River. All we have heard as yet is from Federal sources, but such particulars are given as show at least that our army has fallen back towards Alexandria, whether defeated or not.

The most successful raid by the enemy in this war was made three days ago in this state. A strong force of Cavalry was landed on the Tennessee River near Iuka and suddenly penetrated the country to within sixty miles of Jackson, Miss., where they burned a Depot on the Southern Rail Road and tore up the track for a considerable distance, thereby cutting off this army for the time being from Richmond and all the East.[4] If they had been strong enough to hold the position we would have been in a bad fix, but plunder was their object, and right well did they accomplish it, for it is stated that the whole country through which they passed was literally laid in ashes. All kinds of stock and provisions were either taken away or destroyed. I believe they have gone back, to the disgrace of our authorities who failed to capture them. The enemy has abandoned his efforts to get into the rear of Vicksburg by way of the Yazoo and its tributaries, so we, who are twelve miles from the city guarding a raft on that stream, are likely to have a quiet time till the day of a general engagement.

Al has not written me in some time, by which I suppose he is in an active campaign. I see from the papers that a struggle is soon to commence in Va. for

2. In May, 1862, a mine of pure rock salt was discovered at Avery Island, Louisiana, some ten miles south of New Iberia. During the following year, the mine produced 22 million pounds of salt for the Confederacy. On April 17, 1863, Union colonel William King Kimball captured the mine, burned its buildings, and destroyed its steam engines (Ella Lonn, *Salt as a Factor in the Confederacy* [New York, 1933], 32–33, 208; John D. Winters, *The Civil War in Louisiana* [1963; rpr. Baton Rouge, 1991], 231–32).

3. Henry Hopkins Sibley was given command of the Confederate invasion of New Mexico Territory. His intemperate use of alcohol seriously diminished his capacity for command, and after losing its supply train at the battle of Glorieta Pass, Sibley's brigade retired to San Antonio, where it was reassigned to Edmund Kirby Smith's Trans-Mississippi Department. Thereafter, Sibley played no significant role in the war but was court-martialed for his failures at the battles of Irish Bend and Fort Bisland, Louisiana, on April 13–14, 1863. By March, 1865, he was without a command and no longer assigned to active duty. See Jerry Don Thompson, *Henry Hopkins Sibley: Confederate General of the West* (Natchitoches, La., 1987).

4. On April 17, Col. Benjamin H. Grierson led 1,700 Federal cavalry south out of La Grange, Tennessee, into northeast Mississippi. Hard pressed by pursuing Confederates, near West Point on April 21 Grierson detached one-third of his command under Col. Edward Hatch to mount a diversionary raid to destroy the Mobile and Ohio Railroad between La Grange and Columbus, Mississippi. The diversion was successful, and as Pierson suggests, the weight of the Confederate pursuit fell upon Hatch's command, while the remainder of the Federal cavalry rode on through central Mississippi, finally entering the Union lines at Baton Rouge on May 2. Hatch returned to La Grange. See D. Alexander Brown, *Grierson's Raid* (Urbana, 1954).

the possession of Richmond again. I had hoped that the war was ended in that section, but it seems the enemy is commencing to tighten the coil around us again and threatens us, at least, from every point. A battle will soon be fought in Tenn., and if it results in a general engagement between the two armies, it will have more to do with the future of the war than any battle that has yet been fought. If our army is beaten, the Confederacy is cut in two; if successful, we regain the state and a position on the Miss. River above Memphis.

How this letter will reach you, I am unable to say. I will write oftener that some may get home. I learn that some measures have been adopted to transmit mails across the river by expressmen. We have not heard from home in a long while, and can hardly hope to hear by letter soon from there. Jim is looking better than I ever saw him. Henry was in good health two days ago. Peter has at last gotten able to do something—has only been up a week in about two months. My own health was never better. Rations good & plenty, weather fine, camps cheerful, and fishing excellent.

Affectionately Yours, & c.,

D. Pierson

> <

REUBEN ALLEN PIERSON TO NANCY COLLINS PIERSON

Camp near Fredericksburg, Va.
April 24th, 1863

Mrs. Nancy Pierson
Mount Lebanon, La.
Dear Aunt

I seize upon the present favorable opportunity of writing to you. The company is in excellent health and fine spirits—scarcely any complaining in the whole regt. The Surgeons have quite an easy time of it now not exceeding one hour[']s work per day and that is generally spent in examination of the convalescence. I received a letter yesterday from Peyton Maddox[5] (a brother of Wm Maddox) who belongs to this company and is very sick at Petersburg with

5. Peyton P. Maddox of Homer, Louisiana, was elected sergeant in Company C. He was absent, sick, from January through April, 1863, but rejoined his unit in time to be captured at Rappahannock Station on November 7, 1863. He was exchanged from Point Lookout on March 15, 1864, and was with his regiment until at least October of that year. The end of the war found him at Jackson, Mississippi, however, where he surrendered to Federal authorities on May 19, 1865 (Andrew B[radford] Booth, comp., *Records of Louisiana Confederate Soldiers and Louisiana Confederate Commands* [3 vols.; New Orleans, 1920], Vol. III, Pt. 1, p. 835).

pneumonia; the gentleman who wrote the letter for him stated in conclusion that he was quite low. Peyton is a good soldier and I hope will soon recover his health. Everything is very quiet in front of our lines. The yankees show no signs of an intention to advance while I believe the strict policy of Gen. Lee is to remain on the defensive for some time yet. The weather continues very unfavorable for military maneuvers. It has been raining for the last two days and the whole country is deluged in a sheet of water. After this spell it will be ten days or more before the roads will dry off sufficiently to make much speed in either advancing or retreating. It seems as if the divine Ruler of the Universe was procrastinating the great battle which appears to be so imminent between the forces of Gen. Hooker[6] & those of Gen. Lee. These too [sic] great and powerful armies which was fighting nearly all the time last year, has been lying in plain view of and striking distance of each other for near five months as quiet and apparently with as little concern about the war as if the scepter of Peace had again been restored throughout the land. We have preaching close to camp every Sunday by a man on Gen. Jackson[']s Staff.[7] We have had two sermons in our regiment lately by a young Dr. of the 5th La. I had the pleasure of hearing the last one which was last Sunday. The text was: "How shall we escape if we neglect so great salvation." The sermon was quite interesting and instructive. I think he is a man of pure motives and desirous of doing all the service he can for the welfare of his fellowmen.

I am in very good health as usual. Our fare is only tolerable good. We have ¼ pound of bacon and one pound of flour per day to each man. This by economy and good cooking keeps us all in fine order & many of the boys are quite fleshy. Most of the boys make light bread with their flour and there is quite a spirit of rivalry among them as to who shall excel in the art. They frequently compare each other[']s baking to see which is the nicest and in justice to them I must say that many of them beak [bake] as nice bread as I ever saw anywhere.

6. Joseph Hooker was appointed a brigadier general on May 17, 1861, and assigned to the defense of Washington. Leading a division during the Peninsula campaign, Hooker won the sobriquet "Fighting Joe," as well as command of I Corps of the Army of the Potomac, which he led at Sharpsburg and Fredericksburg. Promoted to the command of the army on January 26, 1863, Hooker advanced on Lee's army beyond the Rappahannock River. Hooker forfeited an excellent battle plan and an initial tactical advantage at Chancellorsville to Lee's bold and aggressive counterattack and, after four days of fighting, on May 1–4, 1863, fell back defeated and demoralized. During the opening week of the Gettysburg campaign, Hooker sought and was granted relief from the command of the army but returned to command of I Corps on June 28, 1863 (Warren G. Hassler, *Commanders of the Army of the Potomac* [Baton Rouge, 1962], 126–58).

7. This is most likely Robert Lewis Dabney, a Presbyterian minister and Jackson's adjutant. His *Life and Campaigns of Lt.-Gen. Thomas J. Jackson* (New York, 1866) was one of the first biographies of the Confederate hero.

We draw peas, rice & sugar occasionally but by no means regularly. About once a month we draw a mess of beef[,] sometimes fresh & at others pickled. Our fare is very scant of course but [one] could not tell it from our looks for a more healthy, robust crowd could not be started in the Souther[n] army. I had a fine mess of white shad this morning but they are very dear & consequently we cannot afford them very often. I send sister two papers every week. The Magnolia & Southern Illustrated News.[8] They are both very good papers and show the great improvement made upon our literature during the war.

Well Aunt Nan I should be much pleased to visit home & see you all but my duty to my country & my company demand my constant attention and so long as my health remains good I shall continue to stick to my duty. I have many fears as to whether this letter will ever reach you as the Mississippi river is full of yankee crafts at this time and I expect all communication is cut off. The latest letters received here by mail from Bienville are to the 1st Inst. I have no men but what are able to eat their rations present in camp. Give my respects to all enquiring friends. Tell Mrs. Randle that Walter is encamped about six miles from us. J. C. Lamar & T. J. Cawthon was there last Wednesday and say he is in fine health. He belongs to the 4th Geo. Regt. I remain your affectionate Son R. A. Pierson

I want you all to continue to write & direct your letters to Richmond, Va. 1st La. Brig. Early's Division, Jackson[']s Corps

⇒ ⇐

JAMES F. PIERSON TO WILLIAM H. PIERSON
Camp Snyder's Mill, Miss.
April 28ᵗʰ, 1863

Wᵐ H. Pierson

Dear Pa,

As Mr. Rabun[9] leaves here this evening to go home, I seek this opportunity to write to you, though I know of nothing that could interest you. I am in very

---

8. The *Magnolia*, originally the *Southern Ladies' Book*, was first edited by Philip C. Pendleton and later by William Gilmore Simms. Among its finest contributions was Augustus Baldwin Longstreet's series "Georgia Scenes" (Louis D. Rubin, Jr., *et al.*, eds., *The History of Southern Literature* [1985; rpr. Baton Rouge, 1990], 138, 157–59, 161–62).

9. This is Hodge Raburn (or "Rabun"), who purchased the Pierson plantation in Bienville Parish in 1860. Three Rabuns from Union Parish—C. P., Thomas J., and Sgt. John Mc.—served in Company I of the Thirty-first Louisiana Infantry. All were captured at Vicksburg (Booth, comp., *Records*, Vol. III, Pt. 2, p. 231).

good health and am doing very well. Pete has again got able to do our cooking and washing. We are all very dull here as we have nothing to do but to lie here in camp and do nothing. I am glad to hear that you are all getting along smoothly. I hope that I will have a chance to come back in the summer and eat Peaches and Watermelons & c. But if I cannot, I can stay here and be satisfied anywhere. I do not want to get out of the service, for I am very well contented here, and I would not be so at home. Mr. Rabun is in a great hurry and is going back to Vicksburg tonight and that only gives us but about 5 or 6 hours to chat [with] him, so I do not like for him to leave so soon.

Our boys are all in the best of health. I think that I will be able to tough it through the war with the start that I have got now. I feel like that I was pretty well initiated by this time. We are expecting a fight here every week, but it is very uncertain when it will take place, if ever. We have another raft nearly completed here again, and a better one than we had before. Dave has gone to V[icks]b[urg] today, being summoned there on a court martial. It has been raining here a great deal in the last 3 days. Crops look flourishing here now. The mail route is about closed now and I have nearly despaired of hearing any more from home, but you all must write every time you get an opportunity of sending it across the river. We will write as often as we get the chance. We see more chances to send them across than you do, but you must not let a chance pass. I am a little suspecting something of Hodge as he is in such a stew. If he doesn't mind that, they will get him at V'burg in the Conscript Act, but I expect that he left home for the draft to cool down to keep out of it. You must let me know the strai[gh]t of it the first time that you write. I have no more time to write. You must take of all your bacon as it is very scarce here and almost every where. Give my love to all the family and my respects to Mrs. Randle & c.

I am your respectful son,

J^{as} Pierson

⇒ ⇐

REUBEN ALLEN PIERSON TO WILLIAM H. PIERSON
Camp near Fredericksburg, Va.
May 8th, 1863

W. H. Pierson
Mt. Lebanon, La.
Dear Father

I received your late & more than welcome letter sent by Thos. Page yesterday. We have just gone through another hard battle which lasted six days commencing on the 29th of April & ending on the morning of the 5th Inst. This great battle has resulted in the complete defeat of the much lauded Joe Hooker and his chivalrous disciples.[10] During this hard struggle our brigade was in many skirmishes and one desperate charge. Our loss was very heavy some regiments losing half their number in killed, wounded & missing. The 9th Regt[']s total will not reach ninety. Our Col. and Maj. were both captured while falling back after we had driven the yankees more than a mile. I do not think either of them were wounded as both were seen after we started back.[11]

Two Capts. were killed in the engagement viz[.] Capt. Grove Cook[12] & Capt. Cummings.[13] Two Lieuts. were wounded namely Lt. Ross[14] of Co. F. & Lt. Magee[15] of Co. I. Neither of them considered dangerous but Lt. Ross's is quite painful while Magee's is only slight. The following are the casualties of my company. Killed on the field[:] Joel Foster.[16] Mortally wounded[:] Corp. T. J. Cawthon who died that night. Wounded[:] John E. Stewart[17] (leg broken),

10. The battle of Chancellorsville, fought on May 1–4, 1863, was Robert E. Lee's masterpiece. There he and Jackson defeated Joseph Hooker's Army of the Potomac, a force outnumbering the Army of Northern Virginia by about two to one. Ironically, however, on the day that Pierson wrote this letter, Stonewall Jackson died of wounds sustained on the evening of May 2, when he was accidentally fired on by his own pickets. At Chancellorsville, the Ninth Louisiana held the line on Marye's Heights overlooking Fredericksburg, buying time for Lee and Jackson to dispatch Hooker before Maj. Gen. John Sedgwick could bring help from that direction. For two days, Early's division held the attenuated line at Fredericksburg before being beaten back by Sedgwick's wing. Early turned on the enemy at Salem Church, however, and with the aid of Lafayette McLaws' and Richard Anderson's divisions, pushed Sedgwick back across the Rappahannock (Ernest B. Furgurson, *Chancellorsville, 1863: The Souls of the Brave* [New York, 1992]; Terry L. Jones, *Lee's Tigers: The Louisiana Infantry in the Army of Northern Virginia* [Baton Rouge, 1987], 145–57).

11. Although Hays's brigade lost 63 killed, 306 wounded, and some 300 captured in its two-day fight with Sedgwick's wing of the Union army, the Ninth did not, as Pierson believed, lose its colonel and major (Jones, *Lee's Tigers,* 155).

12. Grove Cook of Brush Valley became captain of Company H when W. F. Gray was dropped from the company's rolls on April 24, 1862. He was mortally wounded at Chancellorsville on May 3, 1863, and was succeeded by Cornelius Shivley (Booth, comp., *Records,* II, 424; Arthur W. Bergeron, Jr., *Guide to Louisiana Confederate Military Units, 1861–1865* [Baton Rouge, 1989], 93).

13. W. T. Cummings took command of Company B when Leroy A. Stafford was elected colonel of the Ninth Louisiana on April 24, 1862. He was severely wounded at Second Manassas and killed in action at Chancellorsville on May 4, 1863. He was succeeded by A. C. Bringhurst (Booth, comp., *Records,* II, 501; Bergeron, *Guide,* 93).

14. Jesse G. Ross was promoted to second lieutenant on April 24, 1862. He was mortally wounded at Chancellorsville, dying on May 9, 1863 (Booth, comp., *Records,* Vol. III, Pt. 2, p. 391).

15. William Magee of Franklinton returned to his company after recovering from his Chancellorsville wound but failed to report for duty at the expiration of a furlough in February, 1864 (*ibid.,* Pt. 1, p. 838).

16. Joel (sometimes "Joseph") Foster of Salt Springs joined Company C at Bienville on March 14, 1862. He was killed in action on Marye's Heights on May 4, 1863 (*ibid.,* II, 905).

17. John E. Stewart of Sparta enlisted in Company C at Bienville on March 15, 1862. After being wounded at Chancellorsville, he was sent to the Louisiana Hospital in Richmond and then furloughed to Alabama as permanently disabled (*ibid.,* Vol. III, Pt. 2, p. 704).

John A. Colbert[18] (arm broken), A. B. Wells[19] (in hip, severe but not danger-ous), J. H. Cox[20] (flesh wound in leg), R. A. Koonce (in hand), W. T. Loftis (stuck on hip with piece of shell, slight) & W. H. Rabun[21] (on leg quite slight). Missing[:] Corp. T. B. Tarkinton, Richard Reeve & P. A. Thompson.[22] These are the total of our losses during the battle and believe that part of the loss was occa-sioned by our own men firing into us. A North Carolina brigade came up in our rear and fired while a Georgia brigade on our right which was also charging fired upon our right flank. The yankees could not stand the La. yell but broke before we got within long range distance of them. They were posted in a very strong position, having a long chain of hills in their rear, and a road which formed an excellent breast work besides several fences which would have afforded sufficient shelter to have protected them from our fire; all these they ran off and left in the most shameful and confused style. They ran before we got in sight of them. Even the yell of the demon Louisianans as they call us was more than they could bear; all the pris[o]ners who were captured said they knew that we were the La. boys as soon as we screamed. They said they had rather fight a whole Division of Vir-ginians than one of the La. brigades. The yankees have all crossed back over the river and now occupy their old position. From all that I have heard I suppose we have captured over ten thousand pris[o]ners and more than twenty pieces of ar-tillery; summing the whole matter up in a few words the victory is a great one & will I hope lead to some great results.

The army here is scattering out and going into camp for the purpose of rest-ing. Most of the men are entirely broken down having been under arms for eight days in succession and having neither rested nor slept but little during the whole time. Many men fainted by the wayside and had to be borne off the field by the litter bearers. This has been one of the most trying times I have ever wit-nessed since I have been out. The fortitude and endurance of the men have been taxed to the utmost extent. Still they bear it all almost without a murmur. With such soldiers and our present leaders our enemies can never accomplish the unwholy design which they have formed for our subjugation. If we are only

18. John A. Colbert of Mount Lebanon was discharged in 1863, perhaps because of his Chancel-lorsville wound (*ibid.,* II, 376).

19. Aaron B. Wells was mortally wounded at Chancellorsville, dying on June 19, 1863 (*ibid.,* Vol. III, Pt. 2, p. 1034).

20. James Henry Cox, a Shelby County, Tennessee, resident, enlisted in Company C on March 8, 1862, at Bienville. In May and June, 1862, he was detached as a ward master at the Dehom Hospital in Charlottesville, Virginia. He was paroled at Natchitoches on June 7, 1865 (*ibid.,* II, 465).

21. Willis Hamilton Rabun (or "Rabon") enlisted in Company C at Bienville on March 15, 1862. He was killed in action at Gettysburg on July 2, 1863 (*ibid.,* Vol. III, Pt. 2, p. 231).

22. Priam ("Prince") Albert Thompson enlisted in Company C at Bienville on March 8, 1862. He was declared missing in action at Chancellorsville and was presumed killed (*ibid.,* 823).

true to ourselves and God be for us the time will surely soon come when we shall be redeemed from the miseries of this horrid war and restored to our homes in peace and our enemies will then return to their idols and continue to worship their almighty dollar as has been their former customs. The health of the company is now much better than could be expected considering the exposure to which the men have of late been subjected; all the boys are on foot but many of them are so hoarse as to be almost deprived of the power of speech. All have very bad colds but none are confined to bed. We were all remarkably glad to see Tom Page and hear from home as soon as we came out of the battle.

I have stood the trip finely, have been through the whole engagement and still feel tolerable well. I am much hardier than most men—must have an iron constitution or I would surely fail some time. The boys kept up and done their duty as become[s] noble and gallant soldiers and they are entitled to all the glory of our brilliant charge. I am quite sorry to say that a few behaved unbecoming whose names and characters will have to pay dearly for their conduct. I must not give names as others will be sure to perform this part of the sad task. Give my regards to Dr. Egan—show him this letter and tell him Dr. Love[23] is our Surgeon—he will know that all is well in that respect.
Regards to all enquiring friends
Your affectionate Son
R. A. Pierson

Excuse this. I will write again in a few days when I get better rested and become more composed.

⇒ ⇐

REUBEN ALLEN PIERSON TO MARY CATHERINE PIERSON
Camp near Fredericksburg, Va. May 9th, 1863

Miss M. C. Pierson
Mount Lebanon, La.
Dear Sister
I received yours of the 11th Ult. day before yesterday. I had just returned from the battle ground where we had been for 8 days. As usual the victory is ours. The much lauded chieftan of the yankees (Joe Hooker) has been forced to

23. William S. Love, a Louisiana physician, was appointed assistant surgeon of the First Special Battalion, Louisiana Infantry—the notorious "Tiger Rifles"—on October 1, 1861. On July 1, 1862, he was promoted to surgeon, and the following September he was transferred to the Fifteenth Louisiana Infantry. Then, on April 20, 1863, he was assigned to duty with the Ninth Louisiana. He was captured with the fall of Richmond on April 3, 1865, and paroled on May 1 (*ibid.*, Pt. 1, p. 800).

retire to the north bank of the river with the loss of over ten thousand pris[o]ners besides enormous losses in killed & wounded. We thought that we had endured as much as the human race was capable of bearing but all of our former hardships are but sport compared with what we have undergone in the last ten days. We have been constantly changing positions from place to place[,] at times marching 8 or ten miles at as quick time as we could travel. Some men fainted by the way and had to call the surgeons to their relief. We went three days and nights almost without closing our eyes for sleep, occupying the front line nearly the whole time. With all these trials our men appeared perfectly cheerful. Few were heard to murmur in any way but all were eager to have a chance at the yanks and on Monday our brigade charged them and drove them for a mile from their breastworks; they fled like a flock of scared sheep but our men in their eagerness to capture the whole party rushed on till nearly every man was exhausted and then coming up with a fresh line of the enemy we were forced to fall back and in the retreat some of our men who were the worst broken down fell into the hands of the enemy. The loss in "Co. C" is as follows. Killed[:] Corp. Tom Cawthon and Private Joel Foster. Wounded[:] John A. Colbert right arm broken, J. H. Cox in leg very slight, W. T. Loftin, on hip slight, W. H. Rabun on thigh, John E. Stewart leg broken, R. A. Koonce in hand, A. B. Wells in thigh severe but not considered dangerous. Missing and supposed to be prisoners[:] Corp. Tarkinton, Privts. Richard Reeve & Albert Thompson. Total in killed, wounded, and missing[:] twelve. Our Col. & Maj. were both captured and are now in the hands of the enemy. Their whole army has fallen back across the river and now occupies the same position which they formerly held. They had three men to our one. From their own statements we learn that they had seven army corps while we had only Jackson[']s little corps and two divisions of Longstreets viz[.] D. H. Hills[24] and McLaws.[25]

Well Cassie by the aid of Him who rules the earth, the seas, and the heavens, I have passed through another desperate battle and come out unhurt. My guardian angel has shielded me from the death-like missiles of our enemies and

24. Here Pierson is in error. Daniel Harvey Hill, who had commanded a division in Longstreet's corps since the Peninsula campaign, had been appointed commander of the Department of North Carolina and was there with his command during the battle of Chancellorsville. The second division of Longstreet's corps present was that of Richard H. Anderson. See Leonard Hal Bridges, *Lee's Maverick General: Daniel Harvey Hill* (New York, 1961).

25. Lafayette McLaws entered Confederate service as colonel of the Tenth Georgia Infantry. Promoted to major general after the Peninsula campaign, McLaws led his division of I Corps through the early campaigns of the Army of Northern Virginia until the siege of Knoxville, when he and Longstreet suffered a major disagreement. McLaws was thereafter assigned to Joseph E. Johnston's command and ended the war in North Carolina.

brought me through untouched and language cannot portray my feelings of obligations toward my maker. I ought surely to live a better life & set an example
worthy of one who holds the position that I do. My own individual actions
have great weight in influencing the members of the company to conduct
themselves as become not only soldiers of Southern rights but also Soldiers of
the cross. I have determined hereafter to use all my efforts to suppress all im-
moral practices and to impress the idea of the all important work of preparing
for death while our lives are yet spared. I make no profession of Christianity
myself but I do hope that I may be the recipient of God[']s special mercy and
be changed from the love of worldly things to the admiration of all that is lovely
and beautiful in the path of a Christian[']s life.

The health of the company at present is much better than one would expect
after the great exposure to which they have been subjected for the last ten days.
Many of them are troubled with colds but none sick enough to be confined to
bed. We are all now lying up in comfortable quarters resting ourselves for another trial. If our enemies may see fit to bring on another engagement the army
here fears no odds. The confidence in our leaders and soldiers remains un-
shaken and a battle here signifies a victory. Tell Mrs. Lindon that Proff. is all
right side up with care and sends his compliments to you all. Thomas Page arrived here after the battle. He is looking very well. Capt. Grove Cook of the
Brush Valley Guards was killed in the engagement, also Capt. Cummings of the
Stafford Guards from Rapides Parish.

We are getting tolerable plenty of rations now and I hear that the Commissary General intends increasing our rations when we take up the line of march.
Ask Mrs. Lindon what the inscription on the door of my room was that at-
tracted her attention and caused her to compliment me. Give my regards to all
who may enquire after my welfare &c.
Your affectionate Brother
R. A. Pierson

I have received my boots and socks all right sent by T. L. Page and am under a
thousand obligations to my kind folks at home for the gift.

⇒ ⇐

DAVID PIERSON TO WILLIAM H. PIERSON

Camp Snyder's Mills
May 10th, 1863

Wm H. Pierson
    Mt. Lebanon
        La.

Dear Pa,

I have delayed writing you several weeks in hope of having an opportunity to send a letter by hand across the river, and at last have found one. We have had stirring times at this place since my last. Some two weeks ago (I forget the date now) the enemy came up the Yazoo in what was thought at the time to be a formidable force, being about fifteen transports and five Gunboats. Our forces had been weakened considerably by the withdrawal of troops to our line below Vicksburg, and it was seriously apprehended that we would see trouble. But the expedition proved to be a feint to cover more important movements below. We did not escape entirely, however, for the boats, after coming up within range of our heavy batteries opened and continued an incessant cannonade the best part of two days. The firing was the heaviest I have ever heard. When the boats came up, our Regt was on the river bank, deployed as skirmishers behind a levy, and we had our full share of the shelling. We were almost between our own and that of the enemies' guns, and the shells were screaming over our heads by hundreds, and rather too close to be pleasant. We were not altogether idle, for when a blue coat would make his appearance on the upper decks, our boys would take a pop at him, and several times with success. During the fight the enemy effected a landing of a considerable body of troops a mile below our position where the transports had stopped and sent a party up towards us, who were engaged by the left of our line and driven back. They had first driven in a small squad of our men that were placed below the boats as vidett[e]s, wounded and captured the Lieut. in command. No other infantry were engaged but our Regt, and we have received the lion's share of praise in the Jackson papers. Our Artillerymen did noble work. The ground about their guns and the parapets in front of them were literally ploughed up by huge shells & solid shot, but they stood to their guns in the thickest of the storm and replied shot for shot. Our whole loss was three men and the Lt. in our Regt. That of the enemy is not known, but some of them fell, it is sure. The boats were struck repeatedly, but with what effect we could not determine. One boat dropped down the river in the midst of the fight, and it is supposed was disabled. Shells from a mortar fell all around in the hills and hollows—in camps and wagon yards. Two bursted close to my tent, scaring Peter out of his wits, who was then alone and under positive orders to hold his position. Jim was in ranks and stood to his post like a Trojan, but giving signs of great wonder and astonishment at the scene. Fighting Gunboats was a new thing, not only to him but to us all, and our experience has been such that I dare say there is but a little anxiety for a repetition. They are a terrible machine, and have every advantage on their own side, especially against infantry. They could rake the levy we were behind with grape, close their portholes, and be out of danger from our minie balls. During the fight a deserter came across the open field in full view of both armies at full speed, cheering for old Kentucky, and gave himself up to our men. He was fired at by his men when leaving their lines, and returned the fire with his pistol. The affair created a great excitement among our soldiers who hovered around him in great crowds congratulating him as warmly as if he had been a kinsman. He was an intelligent fellow and gave us much information about the enemy. Lt. Col. Gilmore has arrived from La.—is still suffering from his wound—has refused to accept his promotion to the rank of Col. and tendered his resignation as Lt. Col. of the Reg^t. It will doubtless be accepted by the Dept., and I will stand a chance of being promoted to Lt. Col. We are not permitted to participate in the campaign below the city, being left at this post in the great battle that is now imminent between Grant and Pemberton.[26] We have glorious news today from every quarter. Reinforcements have arrived at Vicksburg from Charleston. "T. G." Hooker is badly drubbed in Va. For[r]est has captured sixteen-hundred of the enemy in Ga.[27] Kirby Smith has whipped Banks in La. (so report says).[28] Wirt Adams has made a dash into Grant's lines below town and captured a Reg^t at Port Gibson.[29] Parties here are offering to bet high on peace being made by the 4th July next, but I must confess I am not so sanguine. I have no news from Al

26. With the Federal navy below Vicksburg, Grant was able to cross to the Mississippi side of the river below Vicksburg. His troops then initiated a broad encirclement of the city from the south, fighting Lt. Gen. John C. Pemberton's Army of Vicksburg at Port Gibson, Raymond, Jackson, Champion's Hill, and Big Black River before the investment was completed on May 22. See Earl S. Miers, *The Web of Victory: Grant at Vicksburg* (New York, 1955); Carter, *The Final Fortress;* Michael B. Ballard, *Pemberton: A Biography* (Jackson, Miss., 1991).

27. On April 11, 1863, Col. Abel D. Streight led a raiding party of two thousand mule-mounted Union infantry out of Nashville. With orders to threaten Confederate rail communications in northwest Georgia in order to draw Brig. Gen. Nathan Bedford Forrest into a showdown battle, Streight moved into northern Alabama. There Forrest, with only six hundred troopers, ran him to ground and, with an elaborate ruse, forced him to surrender his entire command on May 3, 1863, at Cedar Bluff, Alabama (Brian Steele Wills, *A Battle from the Start: The Life of Nathan Bedford Forrest* [New York, 1992], 103–19; Jack Hurst, *Nathan Bedford Forrest: A Biography* [New York, 1993], 117–24).

28. This "report" was untrue.

29. William Wirt Adams, after commanding the First Mississippi Cavalry at Shiloh, Corinth, and Vicksburg, was promoted to brigadier general on September 28, 1863, and, for the remainder of the war, commanded a brigade of Nathan Bedford Forrest's corps.

since the fight in Va.—he was well at last accounts—about 20th April. Our provisions still hold out—rations being very good. Today we drew flour at 20 cts. pr. lb. We get plenty of milch & butter from the country by paying war prices, also vegetables, and are living in style. Henry was well a few days ago; his Regᵗ is still at Vicksburg, guarding the city. The health of the army was never better, and the best of spirits prevail among the troops. There is no despondency now; everybody has settled down into the belief that we have got the Yankees to whip and that its no child's play, and hence the stern determination among all grades to fight it out as soon as possible. We have not received a letter from home in a long while, but suppose it is in consequence of the mail facilities being cut off. Excuse this epistle. I am writing by candlelight & much hurried.

Yours Affectionately,

D. Pierson

[With Grant's passage of the Vicksburg batteries on April 16 and his subsequent victories at Port Gibson (May 1), Raymond (May 13), Champion's Hill (May 16), and Big Black River (May 17), the Confederate position along the Yazoo River became untenable. On May 17, therefore, Pemberton ordered Louis Hébert, the commander of the portion of the line along the Yazoo River, to fall back into the trenches of Vicksburg. There his brigade took position astride the Jackson Road, with Reuben Pierson's regiment occupying the so-called Third Louisiana Redan. This fortification became the focal point of Grant's assaults on the city and the key to the Confederate defense. It withstood daily artillery bombardment and small arms fire and, on May 19 and 22, repulsed heavy Federal assaults.

At about 5:00 P.M. on June 25, 1863, the Federal troops besieging Vicksburg exploded a mine beneath the Third Louisiana Redan, ripping a hole in the regiment's line. In the explosion and the melee that followed, twenty-eight of the defenders were killed or wounded. David Pierson was among the latter, many of whom were struck by fragments from homemade hand grenades.[30] A second Union mine was detonated on July 1, completely destroying the redan, but the explosion was not followed by an infantry attack. The breach in the Confederate line was quickly mended.

On July 2, Hébert reported to Forney his field officers' assessment that "their men could not fight and march 10 miles in one day. . . . This inability on the part of the soldiers does not arise from want of spirit, or courage, or willingness to fight, but from real physical disability, occasioned by the men having been so long shut up and

---

30. Willie H. Tunnard, *A Southern Record: The Story of the Third Regiment Louisiana Infantry* (1866; rpr. Dayton, Ohio, 1970), 259; Carter, *The Final Fortress,* 277–84; *The War of the Rebellion: A Compilation of the Official Records of the Union and Confederate Armies* (130 parts in 70 vols.; Washington, D.C., 1880–1901), Ser. I, Vol. II, Pt. 2, pp. 372–73, hereinafter cited as *OR.*

crampt up in pits, ditches, &c., in the trenches; many are also in ill-health, who still are able to remain in the works. . . . The spirit of my men to fight is unbroken, but their bodies are worn out."[31]

On July 7, Pierson and the other officers and men of the Third Louisiana signed a parole pledging not to *"take up arms again against the United States, nor serve in any military, police, or constabulary force in any Fort, Garrison or field work, held by the Confederate States of America, against the United States of America, or as a guard of prisons, depots or stores, nor discharge any duties usually performed by officers or soldiers against the United States of America until duly exchanged by proper authorities."*[32]

"The siege of Vicksburg," wrote Pierson's division commander, *"was a contest which tried more the endurance and resolution of the men and their company and regimental commanders than the skill of their generals."* General Forney reported that during the siege, the men of his division *"did their duty and their whole duty to the entire satisfaction of their general, and I trust of their country."* The patience with which they *"submitted to the many privations and hardships to which they were subjected, and the unabated courage and cheerfulness which they sustained throughout,"* he wrote, *"are worthy of all praise, and merited a better fortune."*[33]*]

⇒ ⇐

REUBEN ALLEN PIERSON TO WILLIAM H. PIERSON
Camp near Hamilton's Crossing, Va.
Sunday evening, May 17th, 1863

W. H. Pierson
Mt. Lebanon, La.
Dear Father

As I have an opportunity of sending a letter across the Mississippi by Major Boyd I will send you a letter. He starts in the morning. Everything has been remarkably quiet here since the late battle, but if the weather continues favorable a few days I shall look for stir[r]ing times. We had a very hard time during the late engagement and sustained considerable loss. We were on the front line nearly the whole time; our (Early's) division were left to guard the entrenchments around Fredericksburg and the yankees brought the whole of Sedgwick[']s corps to operate against us. We should have held the position against all

31. *OR,* Ser. I, Vol. XXIV, Pt. 2, p. 374.

32. Charles A. Bruslé Papers, Louisiana and Lower Mississippi Valley Collections, LSU Libraries, Louisiana State University.

33. *OR,* Ser. I, Vol. XXIV, Pt. 2, p. 369.

the odds but on Sunday the 3rd Inst. they flanked us on the right and we were forced to fall back and give up Marye's Heights. The enemy did not hold this position but a short time. On Monday morning early two of our brigades charged and took the Heights with very little loss; on the evening of the same day we closed in on every side of the yankees['] position, leaving them no way of escape except to recross the river which they did in great haste leaving their piquets on post in many places; which we captured on Tuesday morning. Our brigade (the 1st La.) was in a desperate charge on Monday evening the 4th Inst. and sustained a heavy loss. I will again send you the casualties of my company for fear you may fail to get my first. Killed[:] Corp. Thos. J. Cawthon and Privt. Joel Foster; wounded[:] John A. Colbert, John E. Stewart and A. B. Wells seriously. R. A. Koonce, W. H. Rabun and J. H. Cox slightly, also W. T. Loftin slight. Missing[:] Corp. T. B. Tarkinton, Privates Richard Reeve and Prince Albert Thompson. The last named are all supposed to have fallen into the hands of the enemy. The general health of the company has not been so good since the battle. As before many of the boys are suffering from severe colds contracted during the engagement; others have been troubled with a disorder of the bowels. None of these I am proud to say are by any means dangerous nor are they confined to bed. All are able to stir around camp. I have attended two sermons today and this somewhat revives my drooping spirits. The 1st sermon was preached at the former Head Quarters of Lt. Gen. Thos. Jonathan Jackson. The sermon was a funeral sermon of the departed hero and was preached by an intimate friend of the Gen's one Dr. Lacy.[34] His text was 2nd Timothy, 4th Chapt. 6, 7, & 8 verses & reads "I have fought the good fight. I have kept the faith. I am ready to be offered up. I go to wear the crown prepared for me by my heavenly father." I know I have not quoted the text correctly as I quote from memory. You can look it out.[35] Suffice it that I add the sermon was appropriate and caused many veteran soldiers to shed a tear. This army is wrapped in mourning and sad are the countenances of everyone at the mention of the great hero's name. I believe that this corps will fight with much greater desperation in [the] next battle on account of the death of their idolized leader. I am in fine health, stood the late trip far beyond my own expectations—come out without a scratch and thank Almighty God for blessing me with such good fortune. I now say to you as a father be not alarmed about my welfare for I have have determined to seek that Christ who died for sinners. I can do better and I will amend in future. I am not a profane or wicked man yet one thing I yet lack. This I will seek until I obtain rest. Excuse me for thus speaking and commit

34. The Reverend Doctor Drury Lacy also officiated at the wedding of Thomas J. and Anna Morrison Jackson, July 16, 1857 (Frank Vandiver, *Mighty Stonewall* [New York, 1957], 115).

35. Pierson's memory was, in fact, perfect.

this to the flame. It is my sentiment. P. L. Collins, Z. Garrett, J. M. Thomas, in fact all your acquaintances are well except Ezra Denson.[36] He has the diarrhea but is improving. Give my regards to all enquiring friends, receive and extend to the family the same. Write often and request sister to do the same.

In haste I remain Your affectionate Son
R. A. Pierson

I close in haste so as to send the letter by Maj. Boyd who leaves tomorrow morning.

Yours
R. A. P.

⇒ ⇐

REUBEN ALLEN PIERSON TO WILLIAM H. PIERSON
Camp near Fredericksburg, Va.
May 18th, 1863

W. H. Pierson
Mt. Lebanon, La.
Dear Father
    Enclosed you will find an obituary of Thos. J. Cawthon which you will please have inserted in the Baptist[37] and pay the charges. I am in fine health and at all times ready to do my duty. I have as little fear of disease in the army now as I ever did at home. The health of our Co. is only tolerable. Most of the boys have been a little unwell since the battle but nearly everyone has regained their former health. I will add a short obituary of Joel Foster who was killed on the same day with Cawthon. Everything is quiet here this evening. The yanks show no disposition to advance.
Excuse brevity

Your son as ever
R. A. Pierson

---

36. Ezra W. Denson, a Minden printer, served as Richard Taylor's orderly before being elected sergeant. He was captured at Rappahannock Station and exchanged from Point Lookout. He was killed in action at Monocacy (Booth, comp., *Records,* II, 604).

37. This issue of the *Louisiana Baptist* no longer exists.

⇒ ⇐

REUBEN ALLEN PIERSON TO WILLIAM H. PIERSON
Camp near Hamilton's Crossing, Va.
June 1st, 1863

W. H. Pierson
Mt. Lebanon, La.
Dear Father

As I have an opportunity of sending a letter by hand I will drop you a short letter. Since the great battles around Fredericksburg we have been lying idly in our old winter camps. Everything has been & still is remarkably quiet in front of our lines. The yankees show no disposition to advance and our Gens. appear to be waiting for them to bring on the attack. I sent you a list of the casualties of my company and several of the boys sent lists of the entire regiment. All of those who were marked missing and were captured have been exchanged and are now in camp. Albert Thompson I fear was killed as none of those who have returned can give any account of him and one of Co. D. describes a man who was lying dead on the field that suits his description. I feel for his dear old father for I know his heart will bleed at the reception of the sad and mournful tidings. Tell his father I have very little doubt but that he fell and has sacrificed his life for his country's cause; he was a true and faithful soldier and leaves many friends to mourn his untimely loss. The wounded are all doing well. I have heard from them in the last few days and am proud to say that none of them appears now to be in any danger of loosing [*sic*] a limb or life. All of the wounded except three have returned to duty and are as well as ever. Our loss (I mean Co. "C's") has been lighter than the loss of any other Co. in the regiment and we have been in every battle and have a reputation for being in the thickest of every battle. The secret of our good fortune I attribute to t[w]o causes. 1st Our men are all accustomed to the use of fire arms and do not shoot each other, while other companies (at least some of them) have foreigners mixed up with them, who are as awkward with a gun as a ten year old boy and consequently are greater to be feared than our enemies. 2nd I feel that the petitions of our pious old fathers and mothers, brothers and sisters are often heard in heaven and blessings are showered upon our heads for the sake of those Christian friends who so often plead our cause before a throne of Grace. I do think that we should endeavor to conduct ourselves as is becoming of intelligent and moral beings. I feel and think much more on this subject than I am able to express. The general health of the boys is remarkably good, in fact better than I ever knew the same number of men to enjoy at home or anywhere else. It is a very rare thing to see a man confined in bed here in camp—sure there are some on the sick list but most of them are of naturally weak constitutions. Several of our boys have gone home on furlough this spring and I hope will return to bring us letters from there, as there has not a single line been received in the company from La. for the past two weeks. The lates[t] date was up to the 2nd of May. The news from the city of Vicksburg is very unsatisfactory yet it is cheerful. Several dispatches have been received stating that the city was in no danger of being taken but still it is very strange indeed that no official dispatches have been received from Gen. Joe Johnston, or have been suppressed by the government if received. This creates a suspicion among the troops here that all is not well. I have not heard a word from Dave, Henry or Jim since the commencement of the fight and of cours[e] suffer considerable uneasiness about them. However I hope they may all come out safe and that by the united efforts of Pemberton's and Johns[t]on's army that Grant[']s boasted forces may be completely demolished. It is true that I am separated far away from home and kindred but do not imagine that I or any of the brave and noble boys whom I have the honor of leading are lowspirited or desponding. Such I assure you is not the case. A more cheerful and animated band cannot be produced in the Southern army than we are. It would reli[e]ve the anxious hearts of many sad mothers and fathers if they could visit our camp and see how well contented and how brotherly we all get along. Seldom a cross or even harsh feeling arises between the boys.

Well Papa as the communication is cut off between here and home and I have an opportunity of sending this by Lieut. Natton[Nattin] [38] of Bossier Parish who starts for home tomorrow morning. I desire to say to you that I hope you will suffer no uneasiness on my account for I am reconciled in the discharge of my duty and if I fall (which I fear but little) and my life is sacrificed upon the altar of liberty I hope I shall die happy, for no one could die in a holier or more noble cause. My greatest aspiration is to have a clear conscience (that I have done my duty) in my dying moments. This I feel confident I shall possess and if it is the will of God I hope to die a Christian as all the wealth of earth is not worth one moment[']s time in heaven. I hope you will excuse my passionate style of writing on the subject of death, a subject that will naturally arouse the deepest feelings of the human soul and one which we should all ponder well while yet our lives are spared. I shall endeavor to send you a letter by every opportunity and hope you will do the same. Collins is in good health. He sends a letter to his mother by the same hand that I send this. Tell Mrs. Holland, Uncle Abe Williams & Mrs. Boyet if you should see them

38. John H. Nattin of Collinsburg enlisted as a private in Company D, Ninth Louisiana Infantry, at the beginning of the war and was elected second lieutenant in April, 1862. In 1864, he returned to Louisiana as captain of a cavalry company (Booth, comp., *Records*, Vol. III, Pt. 1, p. 1255).

that I would have settled up their deceased friends['] accounts long ago but have no opportunity of sending the money to them and the pay is sure at some day. Give my regards to all enquiring friends. Tell sister that I have stopped sending her the papers as I deem it useless. I have paid over to Abe Evans[39] twenty five ($25.00) which he says his father will pay to you as for what Pat Candler and Tom Pittman has got from me. That will be all right at any time. It is dark and I must close. With much regards to all the family &c.

I remain your affectionate Son
R. A. Pierson

> <

REUBEN ALLEN PIERSON TO WILLIAM H. PIERSON
[FRAGMENT]

[ca. July 15, 1863]

I have been under arrest for near two weeks and am not in command of the company. My Col. arrested me because one of the men crossed over the fence into the field with his gun to get around a mudhole. After having me under arrest for two days he sent me word that I could take charge of my company again but I applied for a trial and honorable acquital which I hope to obtain soon. I went into the late battle with my gun and acted my part as a soldier in the ranks.[40] God saw fit to spare me and I am still here. Our army has fallen back to Hagerstown Md. six miles from the Potomac and we are now resting from the fatigue of our long trip. The men are generally in fine spirits and would give the yankees a hearty welcome with bloody hands[41] if they were to

39. Abraham J. Evans, a farmer from Ringgold, Louisiana, served through the war with Company C without a wound, a serious illness, or a promotion (*ibid.,* II, 790).

40. Robert E. Lee's second invasion of the North began on June 3, 1863, when the Army of Northern Virginia slipped out of its lines below Fredericksburg, sidestepped the Army of the Potomac, and raced into Pennsylvania. Maj. Gen. George Gordon Meade, now in command of the Union army, kept his force between Lee and the Federal capital and sought to bring the southerners to bay. Somewhat inadvertently, advance elements of the two armies stumbled into each other at the crossroads town of Gettysburg, where for three days, on July 1–3, 1863, they fought the most decisive battle of the Civil War. The Army of Northern Virginia struck the left, right, and center of Meade's army but failed to break the Union line. On July 4, Lee led his men back toward Virginia, crossing the Potomac on July 14. See Harry W. Pfanz, *Gettysburg: Culp's Hill and Cemetery Hill* (Chapel Hill, 1994); Harry W. Pfanz, *Gettysburg: The Second Day* (Chapel Hill, 1987).

41. This is an allusion to Ohio Whig senator Thomas Corwin's condemnation of the United States's war with Mexico. In February, 1847, he invited the Mexican army to greet America's soldiers "with bloody hands" and to welcome them "to hospitable graves" (Robert W. Johannsen, *To the Halls of the Montezumas: The Mexican War in the American Imagination* [New York, 1985], 276).

attempt to drive us from our present position. We brought off several hundred head of beef cattle, a large lot of bacon, over one thousand horses and other necessaries with us from Pennsylvania including a large lot of medicines. During our whole trip we have captured over twenty thousand pris[o]ners, several pieces of artillery and an immense amount of small arms and ammunition. It is true we have lost many noble and gallant men but we should have lost equally as many in a battle of Virginia and besides we would not have procured a single lot of supplies. What will be the next move I am unable to say. Our Generals are wide awake and will do all for the cause they can. With such men as Lee, Ewell, Hill[42] & Longstreet[43] I am willing to tie my future destiny in this war. They have already proven themselves worthy of the confidence of their men and now they have the whole matter in their own hands. I have not heard from Henry, Dave or Jimmy since the siege of Vicksburg. I fear they have not come out safe if at all. I long to hear from them and hope they may yet be all right. All of the boys are out safe with the exception of those already mentioned. Robert Smith of the Minden Blues was severely wounded and left in the hands of the enemy. None of our Co. were left. They are all safe across the Potomac by this time. I will close as I am tired.

I remain your affectionate Son

R. A. Pierson

N. B. Direct as usual.

> <

REUBEN ALLEN PIERSON TO WILLIAM H. PIERSON

Camp 9th La. Regt.
near Bunkershill, Va.
July 19th, 1863

W. H. Pierson, Esqr.
Mount Lebanon, La.

Dear Father

I received your late favor of the 20th June yesterday evening and you may imagine with what joy I scanned over the contents of the more than welcome

---

42. This reference is to Lt. Gen. Ambrose Powell Hill, commander of III Corps.

43. James Longstreet, Robert E. Lee's "Old War Horse," was the commander of I Corps and senior lieutenant general of the Army of Northern Virginia. See James Longstreet, *From Manassas to Appomattox* (1896; rpr. Bloomington, 1960); William Garrett Piston, *Lee's Tarnished Lieutenant: James Longstreet and His Place in Southern History* (Athens, Ga., 1987); Jeffry D. Wert, *General James Longstreet: The Confederacy's Most Controversial Soldier* (New York, 1993).

sheet. I had nearly despaired of hearing from home as we had already received the news of the fall of the Queen City Vicksburg. The fall of this place is quite a sad misfortune to our infant government, and will only tend to prolong this cruel and fratricidal war. Before receiving the news of the sad misfortune I began to imagine that the dawn of peace had already commenced arising but now a dark pall is thrown over the scene and the lowering clouds of new troubles seem to be enveloping the bright rays of a few short weeks ago. Our hopes must rest on the God of battles who hath assured us that the race is not to the swift nor the battle to the strong.[44] I have but little fear of the final result. Adverse fortune may for awhile darken our prospects but in the end we will come out conquerors. Many of our best men have already sacrificed their lives on the altar of Freedom and many more may be called upon to share their unhappy fate but a determined and united people never was and never will be enslaved by such a fanatical and brutal race as our enemies are. Some few may grow faint hearted and fall by the wayside but most of the men of the South will die in preference to being subjugated by the merciless hordes of King Abraham. We have just returned from an extensive tour into Pennsylvania. The country through which we passed was one of the best improved, and most systematic farming countries I have ever seen. They sow their grain with a patented machine covering it at the same time. They reap, pile in bundles, thrash and fan the grain all with different machines. In Maryland & Penn. the crops were remarkably fine. I have never seen such heavy grain crops anywhere as in those states. While on the trip we captured several thousand pris[o]ners, a few thousand beef cattle, a large lot of horses, some three or four hundred wagons beside[s] about 20 pieces of nice artillery. All these were brought off safely on our retreat. We fought a desperate battle at Gettysburg on the 1st, 2nd and 3rd Inst. We drove the enemy from all his outer works but failed to carry the heights on which his main batteries were planted. The loss was very heavy on both sides but I am inclined to the opinion that their loss was much the heaviest. Their papers estimate the loss on their own part at from 30 to 50 thousand. Our loss will fall much short of these figures. The whole army is now safely encamped on the Virginia shore resting and recruiting up. Our army is still in fine health and spirits and if the yankees advance upon us we will give them a dread of the hardy boys of Gen. Lee's command. The loss in our regiment was as follows. Maj. Williams killed. Adj. Crawford[45] killed & about 75 killed wounded & missing. In Co. "C"

44. "I returned, and saw under the sun, that the race is not to the swift, nor the battle to the strong, neither yet bread to the wise, nor yet riches to men of understanding, nor yet favor to men of skill; but time and chance happeneth to them all" (*Eccles.* 9:11).

45. Richard T. Crawford, second lieutenant of Company D, was promoted to adjutant of the Ninth Louisiana on March 4, 1862. He was killed in action at Gettysburg on July 2, 1863 (Booth, comp., *Records,* II, 478).

Chas. Palmore[46] was killed and W. H. Rabun was killed, both shot through the head. Wounded[:] Sergt. T. A. Tooke, Privts. C. K. Chesnutt[47] and F. F. Rolinson severely; Sergt. P. H. Candler, J. D. Spears [Speers],[48] J. S. Sledge[49] & J. R. Williams[50] slightly. I hope none of the wounds may prove fatal. Heflin who was wounded at the battle of Winchester[51] and had a leg amputated is getting well very fast. Aaron Wells died at the La. Hosp. on the 19th of June from a wound received at the battle of Fredericksburg.[52] He was a brave and noble soldier, feared nothing and his loss will be felt heavily by the members of Co. "C." Gradually our best boys are being taken away and we will soon be reduced to a small band. Our list of casualties are growing very fast and soon over half of those who first came out in April 1862 will be numbered with those who were. No more will their presence charm our eyes but they will be indelibly stamped upon the tablets of memory. This is a mournful theme to me yet its truth forces it upon my mind by day and by night.

I am in good health and should be very thankful for my good fortune in having been so often spared amid dangers and perils almost beyond number. I have been in three severe battles this spring and have come out unhurt in every instance. The God that holds the destiny of nations and individuals in his hand has seen fit to spare me for other scenes and other times. When my time comes

46. Charles Palmore of Sparta enlisted in Company C, Ninth Louisiana Infantry, on March 15, 1862. He was killed in action at Gettysburg on July 2, 1863 (*ibid.*, Vol. III, Pt. 2, p. 63).

47. Charles K. Chesnutt of Sparta enlisted in Company C at Bienville on March 8, 1862. He was wounded at Gettysburg on July 2, 1863, returned to duty, and was paroled at Charlottesville on May 19, 1865 (*ibid.*, II, 324).

48. James B. Speers of Mount Lebanon enlisted at his home town on March 8, 1862. Although wounded at Gettysburg on July 2, 1863, he rejoined his company in September. He was captured at Spotsylvania on May 12, 1864, and held at Point Lookout and Elmira until November 15, 1864. His service record notes that at the end of the war he was in the Trans-Mississippi Department "without leave" (*ibid.*, Vol. III, Pt. 2, p. 658).

49. James S. Sledge of Vernon, Louisiana, was captured at Winchester in June, 1862, while on detached duty as a hospital steward. Exchanged on August 5, 1862, he was promoted to fifth sergeant on August 1, 1864. At some time he was transferred from Company C to Company K, Ninth Louisiana. His service record fails to mention his Gettysburg wound (*ibid.*, 592).

50. Joseph R. Williams, after an otherwise-unremarkable career with Company C, deserted on July 25, 1864, while on the march near Middletown, Virginia (*ibid.*, 1103).

51. In the second battle of Winchester, fought on June 14–15, 1863, Richard S. Ewell cleared the lower Shenandoah Valley of Federal troops and made clear the path for Lee's invasion of Pennsylvania. The Confederate victory over Maj. Gen. Robert H. Milroy was nearly total, as II Corps surrounded the Union garrison, capturing nearly 4,000 prisoners, 23 cannon, 300 wagons, and 300 horses. Rebel losses amounted to fewer than 50 killed and 219 missing (Edwin B. Coddington, *The Gettysburg Campaign: A Study in Command* [New York, 1968], 86–88; Jones, *Lee's Tigers*, 78–81).

52. During the battle of Chancellorsville, Hays's Louisiana Brigade was posted to Marye's Heights above Fredericksburg. The fighting there is often referred to as the second battle of Fredericksburg, not to be confused with the battle fought in December, 1862.

I hope to be ready to meet the summons with perfect resignation. I hope to be able to get off home next fall or winter on furlough if my life is spared till then. Excuse the bungling way in which this letter is written. I must close though I could write much more. Give my love to all enquiring friends and particularly to the family relations. Your affectionate Son
R. A. Pierson

⇒ ⇐

REUBEN ALLEN PIERSON TO MARY CATHERINE PIERSON
Camp near Rapidan River, Va.
August 11th, 1863

M. C. Pierson
Mount Lebanon, La.
Dearest Sister

As I have an opportunity of sending you a letter across the Mississippi by hand I shall of course avail myself of the opportunity. My health has been remarkably good since I last wrote to you. I have been again one of the favored. I have been in 2 severe fights since I left Fredericksburg but in both of them I had the good fortune to escape unhurt. I have never shunned danger but have been one of the favored few. God has seen fit to shield me from all harm and I am now resolved to strive with all my power to be prepared to meet death whenever I am called to go. The fight at Gettysburg was the worst battle that I ever witnessed. Each party seemed to hazard all upon the issue and we should have gained the day but for a want of cannon ammunition. The battle lasted three days commencing on the 1st of July; we whipped the enemy too badly for him to attempt to follow us up. We fell back slowly offering battle for several days near Hagarstown before we crossed the river. The yankees dread to hazard an engagment with the army under Gen. Lee on anything like fair ground; they know we are superior in valor to their men and therefore they always seek some advantages of position. Everything is quiet here. We are drilling daily to become as efficient in military maneuvers as possible. I hear a great many rumors about the despondency of our army in the west but pay little attention to any rumor for but little reliance is to be placed in any news these times. The following is a list of casualties in my company both at Winchester and Gettysburg. At Winchester killed Sergt. E. Blake Tooke & Private Julius D. Stall. Wounded W. J. Heflin leg amputated above the knee, E. N. Hartwell[53] & R. L. Price both very

53. Edward N. Hartwell of Mount Lebanon enlisted in Company C on March 8, 1862. He was taken ill and subsequently captured at Winchester when the Confederate hospital there was overrun on July 26, 1862. Exchanged on August 5, he was wounded and captured at Frederick, Maryland, on July 10,

slight. At Gettysburg killed Charles Palmore & W. H. Rabun. Wounded Sergt.
Pat Candler slight (now well), Sergt. T. A. Tooke severe in the shoulder (doing
well), C. K. Chesnutt severe in shoulder (not heard of in some time), John Palmore slight, F. F. Rolinson sever[e] in hip (doing very well), J. D. Spears slight
(in foot), J. S. Sledge in arm slight. Missing John Moore & Elias Carlton. These
are all the casualties in my company since the battle of Fredericksburg. A. B.
Wells died of his wound received at Fredericksburg. Many of our best men are
being killed off but we must fight it through be the cost what it may.

Well Cassie I have not heard a word from Henry, Dave & Jimmy since the
siege of Vicksburg. I suppose they were captured or killed. I hope soon to receive some intelligence from them—trust they are all safe and pray we may all
be permitted again to meet. Dear Sister we have rumors here in camp that
many of the most prominent men of our state have given up our cause in dis-
pair and are now advocating reconstruction. I hope such is not the case for it
would pain my heart beyond description to think for one moment that all the
gallant heroes who have fought, bled and died for this boon of freedom have
sacrificed their lives upon the altar of Liberty. Aye! have shed their precious,
their noble blood only to drag down and disgrace their families into eternal
servitude. I for one would welcome death a thousand times rather than live to
behold the day of reunion with such a hateful, with such a band of rob[b]ers,
murderers & unhumane creatures as we are now fighting. The wourld [sic] cannot find a parallel for their beastliness. I almost imagine that the keeper of
Hades would refuse such beings admittance into the infernal regions. (Excuse
harsh language on that subject.) The weather is quite warm though clear &
beautiful; we have occasional summer showers which is very refreshing to the
growing crops. These are generally very promising in the Old Dominion State.
If I have a good opportunity I intend trying to get a furlough this winter and if
the way is open I will come home but if not I will visit Georgia and spend a few
weeks with some of my relatives in that State. I would not run any risk of my
safety to get through at Vicksburg believing as I do that another year must end
this war. I shall be cut off from all my correspondents if the mail is stopped
from crossing the Mississippi. I have not been in command of the company
since the 28th of June having been arrested on that day by a fractious Col. who
offered to release me after keeping me in suspense for about 36 hours, but I refused & demanded a trial which will come off in a few days now. I have no fears
of the result and besides I am supported by all the Officers of the regiment for
my course of conduct. I have not sent you the paper in a long time as mail
communication was too uncertain. If I have an opportunity I will send you the

---

1864, but was exchanged on February 20, 1865, after more than seven months in various Federal hospitals
(Booth, comp., *Records*, Vol. III, Pt. 1, pp. 215–16).

Life of Stonewall Jackson[54] as soon as I can get it. Give my kindest regards to all &c. Remember me particularly to my lady friends around the Mount. My love to all the family after receiving the same yourself. Write as often as you have an opportunity. To fail will be cruel. Your brother as ever

R. A. Pierson

I shall send this by Lt. Stark Jackson[55] a cousin of Prentiss's.

⇒ ⇐

REUBEN ALLEN PIERSON TO WILLIAM H. PIERSON
Camp near Orange Court House, Va.
Aug. 22nd, 1863

W. H. Pierson, Esqr.
Mt. Lebanon, La.
My dear Father

As W. H. Blount (a member of my company) has received a furlough for 30 days to visit Miss. and as I have some hopes that he may see an opportunity of sending this beyond the river I seize the only method of writing to you. I have been blessed with excellent health all this summer, have been in two hard battles since that at Chancellorsville, and have escaped thus far unhurt, while many of my brave little band composing Co. "C" have either fallen dead on the field or been wounded in battle. Blake Tooke & Julius Stall were both killed at Winchester, Charles Palmore & Hamilton Rabun at Gettysburg making four killed dead on the field. W. J. Heflin was wounded and had leg amputated at W. and Gus. Tooke & Chas. Chesnut were seriously wounded at G. beside Elias Carlton and John Moore [who] were missing at Gettysburg[,] making 8 in all who have been disabled this trip into Pennsylvania.

54. This is *The Life of Stonewall Jackson from Official Papers, Contemporary Narratives, and Personal Acquaintance,* by John Esten Cooke, a famed novelist and a captain on Jeb Stuart's staff. It was published in Richmond in 1863 by the firm of Ayres and Wade. This first of all Confederate biographies, according to Douglas Southall Freeman, "cannot be regarded as a distinguished work" but does provide many of the now-familiar details of Jackson's life (John O. Beaty, *John Esten Cooke, Virginian* [New York, 1922], 80; Douglas Southall Freeman, *The South to Posterity* [New York, 1951], 14–15).

55. R. Stark Jackson of Cheneyville was a sixteen-year-old student when he enlisted in Company I, Eighth Louisiana Infantry, on June 19, 1861. He was elected first sergeant when his company was organized, promoted to second lieutenant on August 14, 1861, and to first lieutenant on February 26, 1863. He was severely wounded at the battle of Bristow Station, August 27, 1862 and, after failing to recover, resigned from the army on August 22, 1863 (Booth, comp., *Records,* Vol. III, Pt. 1, pp. 419–20).

We have been encamped for three weeks near the Rapidan River about 30 miles above Fredericksburg where we quartered last winter. Everything has been remarkably quiet since our return from that trip of invasion. Scarcely a skirmish has occurred and there is no telling how long before this quiet repose may be broken. The army here is in excellent health and spirits and wo[u]ld fight a much harder fight tomorrow than they would have done before the retreat from Penn. All of the convalescents have returned to their post and army is much recruited. My company has now between 50 & sixty men present for Duty. All of them are in the best of health and can whip twice their number of yankees any day. There has been a considerable revival going on in the army of late and thousands of the men are joining the church.[56] The following of Co. "C" Monroe Thomas & Smith Scogin have joined the Baptist church and George Whitley the Methodist. They all are quite consistent and I have very little doubt of their reality. I have been considering the propriety of uniting myself to some Christian denomination but I feel too unworthy to connect myself with God[']s people. I fear that I might prove a stumbling stone to others. However I am not satisfied in my present condition. Would to God that I might be with and consult you on this subject. I feel my incompetency to arrive at any satisfactory conclusion. I shall be governed by my conscience for everything is all mystery and darkness with me. I pray God will right me, and I may once be brought to see light for my case is a terrible one. I must drop this tender but pleasant theme.

I have not heard a word from Henry or Dave since the fall of Vicksburg. I see that Dave was paroled with 200 men on duty. I think he might have written to me ere this but not a word. I sincerely hope they are all safe but shall be uneasy till I hear from them. I have no news of interest to write. Maj. Williams & Adj. Crawford were both killed at Gettysburg. Robert Smith who was severely wounded is in New York and doing fine. He belongs to Co. "G" 8th La. His Capt. received a letter from him the other day. All our boys are kindly treated by the enemy. I hear that many of the wealthy farmers of our State (on the river) are taking the oath. This I cannot believe but should such be the case they ought to be considered as registered enemies and all of their property confis-

56. Two great revivals swept the Army of Northern Virginia. The first climaxed in the autumn and winter of 1862–63 on the heels of the retreat from Sharpsburg and the second in August, 1863, following the Gettysburg campaign. In both cases, southern soldiers perceived God's wrath as revealed in their defeats and so strove to reclaim divine favor. Too, with death so near, many men naturally had thoughts of the afterlife and wished to assure themselves of eternal salvation. In an outpouring of religious fervor, forty chapels were constructed along the Rapidan River in August and September, 1863, where chaplains and missionaries conducted daily prayer meetings and church services. An estimated one thousand men joined the church—most often as Baptists, Methodists, or Presbyterians—in September, 1863, alone. See W. W. Bennett, *A Narrative of the Great Revival Which Prevailed in the Southern Armies* (Philadelphia, 1877); J. W. Jones, *Christ in the Camp* (Richmond, 1888).

cated at the earliest opportunity. I have no patience with such men. God will never suffer a determined and united people to be enslaved and though many of us may never live to see the day I feel assured that our separation from and freedom of the yanks is sure. I never have felt desponding a moment yet but had soon die than see my relatives domineered over by such a merciless foe. Our fore fathers endured the revolution for 7 years under far more advantages than we have to endure. Why may we not with their examples before us go on & take courage at our past successes?

Give my love and regards to all to whom it is due.

Accept the love of your absent & affectionate Son
R. A. Pierson

> <

REUBEN ALLEN PIERSON TO WILLIAM H. PIERSON
Camp in Orange County, Va.
Novr. 20th, 1863

W. H. Pierson, Esqr.
Mt. Lebanon, Bienville Par., La.
Dear Father & Brothers

As I have an opportunity of sending a letter direct to Miss. & the bearer promises to make all endeavors to forward it over the river I shall certainly write. I have been in fine health most of this year having a few light chills continue. I have not been absent from my command longer than one day at a time, and only once at that since Sept. 1862. I am now the only Commissioned officer present in the company. Lt. Melvin was captured while on picket on the north bank of the Rappahannock River, on Saturday the 1st of this month, so I am left alone with the company which numbers only 32 men, 20 having been captured at the same time with Lt. Melvin.

The particulars of the capture are as follows.[57] Our Brig. was on guard at the time on the north bank of the Rappahannock River and in a strongly fortified

57. On November 5, 1864, elements of the Army of the Potomac attacked a Confederate bridgehead north of the Rapidan River at Rappahannock Station while a second Yankee column attempted to force a crossing at Raccoon Ford. Lee hoped to spoil Meade's pincer movement by holding the Rappahannock Station offensive in check and destroying the column moving across Raccoon Ford. He therefore ordered Jubal Early to reinforce Robert Frederick Hoke's North Carolina brigade north of the Rapidan with Hays's Louisiana brigade. Hays, with artillery support from the Louisiana Guard Battery, assumed a defensive position in previously prepared breastworks. On November 7, two Federal corps concentrated on Hays's front, and Union artillery interdicted the single pontoon bridge that constituted the Rebel line of communication. Under cover of darkness, the Federals assaulted the Confederate position with bayonets,

position only about 200 yards distant from the river. On Saturday the 7th Inst. about 11 oclock the enemy appeared in heavy force directly in front of them & after deploying our Brig. as skirmishers they advanced slowly and cautiously. Col. Penn[58] who was then in command of our Brig. (Gen. Hays[59] being on duty on a Court of Inquiry) sent to the Maj. Gen. for reenforcements and about 4 P.M. received three regiments of N.C. troops which took position with us. With this small force not amounting to over 2500 men in all we were attacked by 2 Army Corps of the enemy, about dark. Our boys fought them killing nearly all of their first line and fighting the 2nd line with the butts of their guns until they were finally overpowered and compelled to surrender but few of them I think were killed as they fought behind good rifle works and of 63 men of my Company who made their escape not one saw a single one of our men killed and only about 2 wounded. I will here give you a list of those who were captured. Sergts. W. Ezra Denson & P. P. Maddox, Corp. Ambrose Walker, Privates G. T. Barnes,[60] W. H. Blount, F. M. & J. N. Candler, Daniel Carter, P. L. Collins, R. Colbert, A. Carlton, Z. Garrett, Moses Grant,[61] J. C. Lamar,

---

penetrating the Louisiana line in two places and cutting most of its defenders off from their line of retreat. Although the Federals reported 348 casualties in the assault, 1,600 Louisiana and North Carolina troops were captured, all but destroying Hays's brigade (Jones, *Lee's Tigers,* 181–87).

58. Davidson Bradfute Penn, a native of Lynchburg, Virginia, was a graduate of both the Virginia Military Institute and the University of Virginia. A New Orleans businessman at the time of the state's secession, he was first the captain of Company D and then elected major of the Seventh Louisiana Infantry. He was promoted to lieutenant colonel on June 22, 1862, and to colonel on July 25, 1862, when Harry T. Hays was made a brigadier general. Penn was twice captured, first at Chancellorsville and then at Rappahannock Station. After the war, he was elected lieutenant governor of Louisiana in 1872 and later served as the state's adjutant general.

59. Harry Thompson Hays was elected colonel of the Seventh Louisiana Infantry at the outbreak of the war, performed splendidly at First Manassas, and served with distinction in Jackson's Valley campaign of 1862. Wounded at Port Republic on June 9, 1862, Hays was promoted to brigadier general on July 25 while still recuperating. Given command of the Louisiana Brigade, Hays and his men further distinguished themselves in every battle of the Army of Northern Virginia from Sharpsburg to Spotsylvania, where Hays was again wounded. Upon recovering, Hays was transferred to the Trans-Mississippi, where he remained until the end of the war.

60. George Thomas Barnes of Mount Lebanon was exchanged from Point Lookout on March 10, 1864, but was recaptured on October 19, 1864, at Cedar Creek and returned to the same prison. Again exchanged early in 1865, he was on furlough when the war ended. He was promoted to corporal sometime after March, 1864 (Booth, comp., *Records,* I, 124).

61. Moses Grant of Ringgold enlisted in Company C on March 8, 1862, at Bienville. He was captured at Rappahannock Station on November 7, 1863, but exchanged from Point Lookout on March 15, 1864. He was promoted to corporal on August 1, 1864, but was absent without leave in Louisiana when the war ended (*ibid.,* Vol. III, Pt. 1, p. 79).

H. L. Rhodes, T. J. Sanders, J. S. Scogin, C. C. Talton,[62] G. W. Lewis[63] &
G. W. Whitley. This is a complete list of all killed, wounded & captured and we
have no idea as to who was killed or wounded but think that few was hurt. We
are now encamped on the Rapidan near Raccoon Ford in a strong position and
ready to repel any attack that [they] may make upon us. I received 2 letters
from home yesterday dated the 28th & 29th Ult.[,] one from David the other
from James brought across the river by Dr. Courtney. I was glad to hear from
you all &c.

You need not give yourselves any uneasiness about me for I shall endeavor to
look out for myself and Co. "C" the best I know how. I have had to write in
great haste as Shively[64] leaves in about ten minutes. I must close. Give my regards to all to whom regards are due. Receive the affection also to yourself and
family from

Your affectionate Son
R. A. Pierson

Give my regards specially to the negroes Jack, Mary & Adeline &c.

Excuse extreme haste if you please for I am now being quarreled at for delaying
&c. Yours

R. A. P.

62. Cullen C. Talton of Minden contracted smallpox at Point Lookout following his capture at Rappahannock Station but recovered in time to be exchanged on March 10, 1864. He was wounded and
again captured at Monocacy and admitted to the U.S. General Hospital at Frederick, Maryland, from
which he was transferred to a hospital in Baltimore and then to Point Lookout before being exchanged
in February, 1865 (*ibid.,* Pt. 2, pp. 764–65).

63. George Washington Lewis of Bienville Parish enlisted in Company C on March 8, 1862. Captured at Rappahannock Station, he was exchanged from Point Lookout on March 15, 1864, and remained
with his company until the war's end (*ibid.,* Pt. 1, p. 749).

64. Cornelius Shivley, a Brush Valley physician, enlisted in Company H, Ninth Louisiana Infantry,
as a private but was promoted to first lieutenant on April 15, 1862, and to captain after Grove Cook was
mortally wounded at Chancellorsville on May 3, 1863 (*ibid.,* Pt. 2, p. 552).

REUBEN ALLEN PIERSON TO DAVID PIERSON
Camp Hays['s] Brigade, Orange County, Va.
Novr. 26th, 1863

Maj. David Pierson
Mount Lebanon, La.

Dear brother

It has been some time since I received your late favor of the 29th Ult. and you may rest assured that I was quite anxious to hear from you all as the last word that I recd from home before was to the 30th of Aug. I have seen many ups and downs since I last wrote to you but by the blessings of Divine Providence I have been spared and still enjoy fine health. During the campaign into Pennsylvania I was arrested and that without any cause by Col. now Brig. Gen. L. A. Stafford. The circumstances were as follows: On the morning of the 28th of June an order was sent round to the company commanders not to permit any man to leave ranks with his gun. I forthwith had the order given to the men and charged the noncommissioned officers that they would see that no man left ranks with a gun. We had proceeded but a short distance on the march when I discovered that one of my men was somewhat intoxicated and I immediately put him in charge of a sober man to prevent any accident. But I had not gone exceeding half a mile before the said drunken man finding a muddy branch in the lane which we were traveling crossed the fence and went around the said mudhole for which crime I was arrested. On the day following my arrest the Col. sent me word that I could take command of my company and consider myself released; but I applied for a trial and would not accept the release intending to expose him on trial. The thing passed off till we arrived at a stationary camp about the first of Aug. when the charge was made out and sent up. It returned about the 20th of Aug. and was sent on to the Corps Court where it lay till about the 10th of the present month when I petitioned its withdrawal for the very good reason that my company was without a commander & my petition was forthwith granted because they well knew that it was utterly impossible for them to sustain the charge.

Well Dave I will endeavor to give you a kind of synopsis of our military maneuvers since we returned from Pennsylvania. We remained in the Valley of Va. but a few days after our return from Penn. till we fell back to the Rapid Ann [*i.e.,* Rapidan] River which we made our line having a cavalry force in front of us. We remained in a single camp all of Aug. and till the 14th of Sept. The enemy drove in our cavalry on the 13th and on the 14th we took our position on the bank of the river, which is quite small, to prevent their crossing. The enemy came up and opened on us as if they were determined to force a passage but being met rather warm soon ceased firing and endeavored to establish a picket line near the river which after about 2 days skirmishing our men allowed them to do. In this condition the two armies lay comparatively quiet till the 9th of Octr. when Gen. Lee for the purpose of dislodging Meade from his position flanked around the right of his lines thus forcing him to retire. Thus Meade continued his retreat till he reached the fortifications around Manassas. We lost [illegible] that no man [illegible] except a few pris[o]ners. Meade having made good his escape Gen. Lee next turned his attention to the destruction of the R.R. from Richmond to Washington. He tore up and destroyed over 20 miles of the road and burned both the ties and the railings. He then recrossed the Rhappahannock on the 19th of Octr. and took position but left the pontoon bridge standing across the river and continued to send a large train of wagons under a strong guard to haul as much of the iron across the river as possible to use in the iron works at Richmond. This soon brought on skirmishing as the enemy were slowly advancing and rebuilding the road. However we continued to [leave] one Brig. all the while as guard on the north bank of the river. On Friday the 6th of Novr. our (Hays['s] La.) Brig. went out on picket over the river as usual everything being then perfectly quiet, and as we were engaged in building winter quarters at that time some of the men [were left] in camp to complete the little huts by the [time] the rest returned. On Saturday about 11 O-clock A.M. the yankees appeared in heavy force [illegible] the charge [illegible] post [illegible].

⇒ ⇐

REUBEN ALLEN PIERSON TO JAMES F. PIERSON

Camp Hays['s] Brig. Orange Co., Va.
Decr. 9th, 1863

Mr. James F. Pierson
Mt. Lebanon, La.
Dear brother
    As it has been a long while since I have written to you I will now try and give you a few of the items of camp life in Va. The Army of Northern Va. is now encamped on the Rapid Ann River about 70 or 80 miles of Richmond. The weather is delightful—quite cold but clear and dry. We struck camp for the winter about the 1st of Novr. on the Rhappahannock River, had about completed nice comfortable log cabins when the enemy advanced, and the sad affair of the capture of a large portion of our Brig. occurred after which we retreated

to the South side of the Rapidan where we still remain. The yanks made a bold start again about the 27th of Novr.—crossed the Rapidan at Germana ford and advanced out some 12 miles above the old battle ground of Chancellorsville. We met their advance and after a short skirmish succeeded in driving them back upon the main force—when we formed line of battle and remained till about 12 oclock at night and then fell back to a strong position for the purpose of drawing them out. We fortified our position and awaited an attack, but alas! they had not the courage to bring on the assault and after lying in front of our line for 2 days they retreated across the river between dark and daylight. The following morning we pursued and captured several hundred of their strag[g]lers. Since that time we have been quietly encamped on the bank of the Rapidan River with no enemy in front of us except a few cavalry scouts and pickets. The enemy are said now to be on the North side of the Rhappahannock River. The yankee papers say that Meade has been superseded by Hooker in command of the Army of the Potomac. If this is true we will not be likely to have any more fighting before next spring as he (Hooker) is the same Genl. who stuck in the mud last winter and was unable to make his advance and again retreated from Chancellorsville (as he says) not because he was whipped but on account of a sudden rise in the river which rendered his communication difficult.[65] It is my opinion that we are to have an easy time in Va. the rest of this winter. Our picket duty is now very hard being on every other day but I [think] this will not long continue as some new troops are daily looked for from N.C. who it is rumored will take our place.

The general health of the company is as good as usual no complaints except colds & none of them confined to bed for that. I have sent a list of those who were captured in a letter some time since and consequently deem it entirely unnecessary to add the same in this letter. Jasper Hilbun who was wounded on the 7th Novr. (slightly) has received a 30 days['] leave of absence to visit Geo[rgia]. Wm. D. Mims has also received a furlough of 30 days to Miss. Cap Watts & John Palmore are in Jackson Hospital Richmond. Cap was nearly well the last I heard from him but John Palmore was suffering severely from a wound received at Gettysburg which was quite slight at first but owing to bad treatment is now a very bad leg. Frank Leatherman is a guard at the Division Ordnance train. He was in camp a few days since and in very good health. Tom Pittman is in fine health and as full of mischief as a kitten. Lieut. Colbert is just in from the coun-

---

65. This rumor was, of course, false. Meade remained in at least nominal command of the Army of the Potomac until the end of the war, although after March, 1864, Ulysses S. Grant conducted its field operations. Hooker, on the other hand, left the Army of the Potomac to take part in the raising of the siege of Chattanooga and remained in the western theater for the remainder of his active wartime career. The "general who got stuck in the mud" was Ambrose Burnside.

try and looks quite well and hearty. Pat Candler is in fine health. J. M. Thomas is well and hearty. John Evans d[itt]o, Tom Page, Henry King,[66] Frank Lewis,[67] Mobley, Boylston,[68] Ed Stephens, Joseph Stewart,[69] Joseph Martin,[70] F. F. Rolinson, J. H. Cox, C. K. Chesnutt, A. J. Evans, Jim Andy Williamson, R. H. McGouldrick, J. A. Norrid, R. L. Price,[71] Richard Reeve, J. D. Spears, H. T. Tooke, B. F. Harrison, J. D. Watts[72] & L. J. Wallace & I. M. Bryant, E. N. Hartwell is very fat, E. H. King,[73] J. D. Lassiter,[74] W. T. Loftin, W. H. Logan,[75] E. H. McCarty,[76] all of the above named are in camp & well. I hope that I have not left out any name as Pat is on picket and I have to give the names from memory. You are at liberty to say to the friends of any of the within named that they are all right side up with care. Give my love to all enquirers &c. Excuse haste. Your brother

R. A. Pierson

Address Co. "C" 9th La. Regt. Hays['s] Brig. Army Northern Va. hereafter.

66. Henry M. King, a farmer from Salt Springs, Louisiana, was promoted to third corporal of Company C on September 1, 1861. He served throughout the war, surrendering at Appomattox (*ibid.,* Pt. 1, p. 567).

67. Frank E. Lewis was a farmer from Sparta. He was killed at the third battle of Winchester on September 19, 1864 (*ibid.,* 748).

68. William A. Boylston was a seventeen-year-old farmer at Saline, Louisiana, when he enlisted in Company C on March 8, 1862. He was wounded and captured at Winchester on September 19, 1864, and held at Point Lookout until October 29. At some point, he was promoted to sergeant (*ibid.,* II, 78).

69. Joseph H. Stewart of Bossier Parish was on furlough in Louisiana when the war ended and was paroled at Shreveport on June 19, 1865 (*ibid.,* Vol. III, Pt. 2, pp. 703, 704–705).

70. Joseph P. Martin, a Minden farmer, was wounded at the battle of Fredericksburg (*ibid.,* Pt. 1, p. 895).

71. Reuben L. Price, a Natchitoches farmer, enlisted in Company C on March 10, 1862. At the end of the war, he was paroled at Jackson, Mississippi, among the "unattached men" of the Confederate army (*ibid.,* Pt. 2, p. 203).

72. John D. Watts of Buck Horn enlisted in Company C on March 8, 1862. He was severely wounded at the battle of Spotsylvania but served until the war's end, surrendering with his unit at Appomattox (*ibid.,* 1011).

73. E. H. King of Buck Horn was present on all of Company C's rolls until 1864, when he "deserted to the cavalry" (*ibid.,* Pt. 1, p. 567).

74. James D. Lasiter of Buck Horn was one of Company C's original members. He was present on every roll without an illness or injury until May 5, 1865, when he was killed in action at the Wilderness (*ibid.,* 665–66).

75. William H. Logan of Mount Lebanon was forty years old when he enlisted in Company C on July 7, 1861. He was detailed as assistant commissary for the Ninth Louisiana on August 1, 1861, and served in that capacity until captured at Petersburg on March 25, 1865. He spent the remainder of the war at Point Lookout (*ibid.,* 782).

76. Little is known of E. H. McCarty save that he was paroled at Appomattox (*ibid.,* 1139).

⇒ ⇐

REUBEN ALLEN PIERSON TO MARY CATHERINE PIERSON

Camp Hays'[s] Brig. Orange Co., Va.
Decr. 15th, 1863

Miss M. C. Pierson
Mount Lebanon, La.
Dear Sister

Having an opportunity of sending a letter by hand to Miss. I will write you
a short one. I am in very good health and have no reason of complaining about
my fare. I get plenty to eat, have a good comfortable fire place to my tent and
enjoy camp life far better than I ever anticipated I should at the commencement
of the war. The general health of all the boys is quite good; no complaint in
camp except colds & they are of seldom occurrence. Only one man reported on
the sicklist this morning and he is not confined to bed. Everything has been unusually quiet here for the past two weeks. No yankees in sight except a few
mounted men who always take care to keep a safe distance, beyond musket
range from our boys. We are encamped on a high position on the south bank of
the Rapid Ann River, within four hundred yards of the front picket line. I can
sit in my tent & see the scouts and couriers of the enemy riding up and down
the river on the opposite side almost any day. From present indications I do not
believe that there will be another general engagement between the two oppos-
ing armies of Northern Va. this winter. A great many of the men are getting furloughs of indulgence. Three men of Co. "C" have received furloughs in the last
month viz[.] Jasper Hilbun wounded furlough, W. D. Mims and C. J. Watts
both sick furloughs. It is more than probable that Mims will cross the river as
he had a furlough to Woodville Miss. I send letters by every opportunity and
hope you may hear from me often. The spirit of this army is excellent. No sign
of despondancy among the men. They are all willing and ready to do their duty
and will fight the enemy wherever they attempt to advance into our country.
Thomas J. Pittman has just drawn a furlough and will get off about Christmas.
He will go to some of his relatives in Geo. We have heard definitely that our
boys who were captured are at Point Lookout, Maryland;[77] we have not heard
from any of the members of our Co. but infer from the light loss of those heard
from that but few if any of our boys were hurt. There is some talk of our being
transferred to the trans-Mississippi department, and the officers of our Brig.
sent a petition today to the Senators and representatives of our State to use their

77. Point Lookout, located on Maryland's lower peninsula, was founded on August 1, 1863, and became the North's largest camp for prisoners-of-war. At times, as many as twenty thousand inmates were
crammed into its forty acres.

influence to that effect. I do hope that we may be sent back as our Brig. is now reduced to less than a good regiment and all of the men are bitterly opposed to being consolidated with the second La. Brig. for many of the regiments are composed of foreigners, and hence the difficulties arising out of consolidation. The weather has been remarkably good all this fall and still continues quite favorable for camp life. I received a letter from Cousin George Williams today. He is in good health. He writes me that James Pittman [Pitman],[78] was wounded both in the body and foot and supposed to be mortal. He was left on the battle ground and fell into the hands of the enemy. I fear he was killed. A. J. Koonce[79] was killed in the last battle of Lookout Mountain[80] and Blake Braswell[81] was missing. Cousin J. S. Scogin was not hurt. This is all the news from Tenn. The boys of Co. "C" are generally in fine health. Give my regards to all enquiring friends especially the young ladies who are still left in Mt. Lebanon. My love to all the relatives and family.

Your brother as ever
R. A. Pierson

Direct your letters hereafter to Army Northern Virginia instead of Richmond as we now have an army Post Office.
Yours

R. A. P.

78. James S. Pitman, a sergeant of Company I, Sixteenth Louisiana Infantry (the "Castor Guards" of Bienville Parish) apparently died of his wounds, for he does not appear on his company's rolls after October, 1863 (*ibid.,* Vol. III, Pt. 2, p. 154).

79. Andrew Jackson Koonce was a sergeant in Company I, Sixteenth Louisiana Infantry (*ibid.,* Vol. III, Pt. 1, p. 593).

80. The Confederate Army of Tennessee defeated William S. Rosecrans' Army of the Cumberland at Chickamauga, Georgia, on September 19–20, 1863, allowing Braxton Bragg to besiege the Federal army in Chattanooga. On November 23–25, 1863, however, Ulysses S. Grant broke the Confederate siege in a fierce three-day battle, which included fighting on Lookout Mountain, and sent Bragg's demoralized Army of Tennessee streaming back into Georgia. See Peter Cozzens, *This Terrible Sound: The Battle of Chickamauga* (Urbana, 1992); Peter Cozzens, *The Shipwreck of Their Hopes: The Battles for Chattanooga* (Urbana, 1994).

81. Blake W. Braswell, a corporal in Company I, Sixteenth Louisiana Infantry, was captured at Murfreesboro on December 31, 1862, and again at Missionary Ridge on November 25, 1863 (Booth, comp., *Records,* II, 96).

7

TELL THE GIRLS TO WAIT

REUBEN ALLEN PIERSON TO WILLIAM H. PIERSON

Camp Hays'[s] Brig.
Orange County, Va.
Jany. 5th, 1863 [i.e., *1864*]

W. H. Pierson and others
Mt. Lebanon, Bienville Parish, La.

Dear father

Once more by the kind mercies of Divine Providence I am permitted to seat myself by a warm fire in my comfortable little quarters to pen you a few of the latest of news from our gallant little band who still remain together as a company. We have just completed our winter quarters and may now be said to be comfortably situated for the time being and I hope will remain stationary till the rigors of hoary winter have passed away. All of the boys have rough log cabins covered with good oak boards—well chinked and daubed with mud and have also good chimneys and warm fire places. As for news there seems to be a general dearth at present from all q[u]arters of the Confederacy. We receive the Richmond papers daily and hence we keep well posted as to what is going on throughout our whole country. We have just received a letter from Sergt. P. P. Maddox who is now a pris[o]ner at Point Lookout, Maryland; from this we learn that all of our Co. who were captured at the battle of Rhappahannock Station on the 7th of Novr. last are safely guarded by the enemy at that place. Out of the 21 who were missing at that fight there is but one from whom we hear nothing and that is G. W. Whitley. I fear that he was either killed by the enemy in the fight or drowned in the river in endeavoring to escape. I also learn from the above mentioned letter that the boys' treatment is anything but good—he writes "our rations are short and we are very much in need of clothing. I thought that I had seen hard times before but I have never known what hard times were before. I would give my right arm to get away &c." He also writes that "none of our brigade are taking the oath." Poor fellows. I feel for them and wish I could share my clothing, blankets and food with them as scanty as my supply is; I would willingly divide the last thing I have on earth with them if it were in my power to do such a thing, but alas I cannot, no not even speak a consoling word to them. The weather is very bad—the ground is now covered with snow and the sleet is falling very fast tonight. I think that all military operations are over here till spring and I hope forever.

The boys are all in excellent health and much more cheerful than any one could expect when we consider their condition. Many of them are as good as barefooted, otherwise their clothing is very good—they get ¼ pound of bacon or 1 pound of beef; and 1 pound of flour per day which you know is a very slim allowance for a stout hearty man—notwithstanding all this they are very cheerful and merry all the while. They will vie with most gallant and patriotic nation of the earth in their devotion to the cause of liberty and the rights of their country. Our congress is now in session and appear to be taking one step in the right direction. They have repealed the Substitute act and passed another, putting into the field all those who have already furnished substitutes and who now come within the conscript age.[1] This throws all classes upon an equal footing giving to the poor man the same chance as his wealthy neighbor and it will doubtless rid our country of many fat saucy extortioners and speculators who have been striving to make fortunes off of the necessities of human sustenance not caring if the widowed wives and orphaned children of the soldier perished for want of food. I am in fine health as usual. Thank God for my good fortune and for preserving my life through so many dangers and have hopes that I may yet live to see the termination of this cruel strife.

We have prayer meetings every night in several of the companies of this regiment and in justice to those who pray in public (of whom there is a goodly

---

1. Substitution, a system designed to free skilled labor and businessmen to develop crucial war industries and to keep conscription to a minimum, allowed a man to avoid military service by supplying an able-bodied replacement. The system, however, was considered by many, both North and South, to be a legal form of draft evasion. It harmed army morale, since soldiers saw substitution as a confirmation that this was "a rich man's war and poor man's fight." As the war dragged on and military service became increasingly less desirable, the supply of able-bodied substitutes declined, and prices rose from a few hundred dollars early in the war to several thousand dollars by 1863. Too many substitutes were physically defective, while others accepted draft evaders' fees and then deserted to offer themselves as replacements elsewhere. In the South, healthy men out of uniform drew heavy criticism, especially from the ladies. By 1863 a law was passed making substitution illegal in the Confederacy.

number) I must say that the meetings are very interesting and instructive. There are but few men in Co. "C" who ever swear an oath and I believe the day soon will be when none can be found to blaspheme the name of the Lord. F. M. Leatherman wants me to write in my letter how he is getting along as he is guard for the Reserve Ord. train and absent from the company. I received a letter from him dated the 24th Dec. He is well and very comfortably situated. Please tell John Candler that his wife may hear from him. I spent quite a dull Christmas, was at work all day on my quarters preparing for bad weather &c. Give my regards to all enquiring friends. Tell Mrs. Randle I saw some of Walter[']s company yesterday morning who told me he was in fine health. Tom Pittman and Pat Candler are both down in Geo. on furlough of indulgence but will return about the last of this month. My love to all the family and to my lady friends. Your Son as ever

R. A. Pierson

⇒ ⇐

DAVID PIERSON TO WILLIAM H. PIERSON
Alexandria, La., Jany. 11th, 1864[2]

Dear Pa,

Your letter and money sent for Mr. Baber[?] by Dr. Cawthon are received. Money all right as to am^t. I fear I will not be able to get the Cards with the Bank Notes. They are scarcely worth anything here. The cards will be here in two weeks when I will do the best I can. I am very glad to hear that you found the horses. It is more luck than I could have had if I had hunted a month. I don't need the pony just now (am keeping a mule belonging to one of the men), but if you had rather not feed him at home, you can send him by first opportunity. I will have no chance to send for him that I now know of.

Jim is on the same guard duty that he was when he went home, but will be relieved in a few days by some other Se[r]gt. I have been in a terrible fix since I came back about a Cook (my free negro has not come yet). The Maj.'s boy had gone home to take Christmas and I had to do the best I could, and Jim the same. I have hired another at $50 per month with the understanding that I am to give him up if my boy comes.

The Maj.'s Boy came yesterday, and so we are now very pleasantly situated. I received a letter from Henry this morning. He is about to make application for appointment as member of the Military Court of the Trans-Miss. Dept. with the rank of Col. It is an easy place, but I fear too much coveted by others for

2. By December 1, 1863, Pierson had rejoined his regiment at Natchitoches, Louisiana, and spent the holidays there at the home of Dr. J. W. Butler, the father of Capt. Woodson B. Butler of Company G (Willie H. Tunnard, *A Southern Record: The Story of the Third Regiment Louisiana Infantry* [1866; rpr. Dayton, Ohio, 1970], 312).

him to get it. I shall try to get him appointed, however, as he has already sent me several recommendations. It will do no harm to make an effort, at all events.

I presume you have heard all the bad news that was on hand about a week ago about Sherman's taking Savannah[3] and Hood's defeat in Tenn.[4] It was the worst of the war, and spread gloom and dismay hereabouts. Men of sense and position were freely talking on the streets of our being whipped. Such has never been the case before, and it clearly shows the ominous state of affairs. We are in a bad fix, and everybody knows and feels it. If something is not done, and that speedily, all must be lost. I think our present Congress will make a desperate effort to obtain assistance from Europe by abolishing slavery. In anticipation of something of that kind, some parties are hurrying off their negroes to West[n] Tex. to sell for gold. I would do the same if I had such property. I sent you a paper of yesterday's date from which you can get the latest news. There is some talk of Federals coming up Red River, but I think it is only their boats. I have not drawn any wages since I came. When I do, I will send you what you loaned me & c.

Your Affectionate Son,
Dave

➥ ⋲

REUBEN ALLEN PIERSON TO WILLIAM H. PIERSON
Camp Hays[s] Brig. Orange Co., Va.
January 15th, 1864

Wm. H. Pierson, Esqr.
Mt. Lebanon, La.
Dearest father

Having another opportunity of sending letters across the great river I take my leisure and will try to give you a short history of how things are here near the Confederate Capitol.

---

3. Savannah, the largest city in Georgia and one of the Confederacy's few remaining ports, was the final objective of William T. Sherman's March to the Sea. It fell on December 21, 1864, after sustaining a siege of twelve days. Lt. Gen. William J. Hardee, however, was able to evacuate his 10,000-man garrison by way of a makeshift pontoon bridge across the Savannah River (Burke Davis, *Sherman's March* [New York, 1980], 102–20).

4. With the fall of Atlanta, John Bell Hood moved his army back into Tennessee, drawing George H. Thomas' Army of the Cumberland after him. Hood's hope of defeating Thomas and pulling Sherman back out of Georgia was a forlorn one, for Hood, although invincibly brave, was an unimaginative and unrealistic tactician. Hurling his depleted army against Federal entrenchments at Franklin, Tennessee, on November 30, he lost 7,250 irreplaceable veteran soldiers, and six generals were killed. On December 15 and 16, Thomas' army broke Hood's ineffective siege of Nashville, virtually destroying the once-mighty Army of Tennessee. See James Lee McDonough, *Five Tragic Hours: The Battle of Franklin* (Knoxville, 1983); Stanley F. Horn, *The Decisive Battle of Nashville* (1956; rpr. Baton Rouge, 1991).

The prices of all the necessaries of life are enormously dear as you will see from a prices current which I shall enclose. Everything in the line of clothing is almost beyond reach. Only think of paying fifty ($50.00) Dollars for a course hat or pair of shoes, one hundred ($100.00) Dollars for a common pair of pants & two hundred fifty (250) for a neat coat. Yet sir these figures are by no means exaggerated and the whole country is running wild with the idea of making money. However the spirit is destined to meet with a considerable check now as many of the athletic young men who have furnished substitutes, and are now lying around the various little vil[l]ages, towns, and cities scattered throughout the Confederacy, speculating on the sustenance that feeds the widowed wives and orphan children of soldiers who have sacrificed their lives upon the altar of Southern rights and Southern liberty, will be forced into the army in a very short time by a late act of Congress making those who have furnished substitutes liable to conscription, only giving them till the 1st of February to choose their companies. This law gives to every man the same chance the millionaire as the poorest laborer has to shoulder his musket in defense of his home, his property and his rights. This I look upon as a token of the wisdom and prudence that are to govern our legislators in the future. Congress is now spending much of their time in secret session endeavoring to bolster up the weakness of our fast failing currency and I hope they may succeed in devising means by which the Confederate notes may again be brought into a healthful condition. It is my opinion that the best thing that can be done will be to make the currency a legal tender. I am well aware that this would be very hard on those who sold property prior to the war but I see no other means of making the money what the exigencies of the times now demand it should be. In war times many sacrifices are demanded on the part of all true patriots. Everything remains unchanged here for the last two months. The two armies picket within sight of each other on the opposite sides of the banks of the Rapidan River, a small stream not larger than Black Lake at McDaniel[']s but differing in this that the Rapidan has steep banks & is cleared up all the way along its banks. This river is a very rapid stream as will appear from its name. The yankees are said to be in heavy force in Culpepper County on the north side of the river but as the weather is quite unfavorable for military operations I do not imagine that we shall have any fighting before late in the spring and by that time the status of affairs will most likely be materially changed from what it is at the present. At least twenty five thousand men will be added to our present force by the late acts of Congress and then I feel certain that we can cope with any force the enemy can raise.

I have nothing late from the boys who are in the enemies['] hands. They were all there except George Whitley and I very much fear that he was killed. The letter was from Sergt. Maddox dated the 16th of Dec. W. H. Blount had the small pox and was in the hospital. Cullen Talton had the dysentery but was able to be up. The health of all the boys is unexceptional. I have never known a heartier or hardier set of men in my experience than the members of Co. "C" are. They live on 1/4 lb. of bacon and one pound of flour and never murmer and while we have such men as these and fight in a holy and just cause we need have no fears of being enslaved by so brutal and cruel enemies as those against whom we are fighting. God who rules the destiny of all things and is a God of wisdom and of justice will never suffer a determined and Christian people to be overcome by a cruel Tyrant but will be their deliver[er] as in the days of old. He led the children of Israel dry-shod through the Red Sea. Since last August there has been a system of furloughing men in operation in this army and three of Co. "C" have had furloughs. The two last in December—Corp. Pittman and Sergt. Candler—are both absent on furlough of indulgence now. They went to Georgia and will be back I guess about the last of this month. Their time is out the 26th of this month. For the information of all concerned I will give the names of all those who have been disabled by wounds in Co. "C" and are still on this side of the river. C. K. Chesnutt wound in left shoulder now present though unable to bear arms. J. A. Colbert in right arm, now at Macon Miss. W. J. Heflin leg amputated now in Putnam Co. Geo. Jno. Palmore in leg and could not walk, the last I heard from him he is in Geo. also. These are the only cases of disabled men who have not crossed the river except John E. Stewart who I had like to have forgotten. He was wounded in leg and is now in Montgomery Co. Ala. The following is a list of men who have been sent to hospitals and never heard from since. Jessy Carter[5] who was left at Gordonsville in the spring of '62. J. S. Cabaniss[6] who was last heard from at Richmond in Feb. '63 and W. B. Greer[7] who was sent to White Sulphur Springs Va. in Feb. '63. None of the above named men have ever been heard from since the time mentioned and I fear they are all long since dead.

5. Jesse Carter of Mount Lebanon enlisted at Bienville on March 15, 1862, and was sent to the hospital at Gordonsville in April. He never returned to his company and was assumed to be dead (Andrew B[radford] Booth, comp., *Records of Louisiana Confederate Soldiers and Louisiana Confederate Commands* [New Orleans, 1920], II, 275).

6. James S. Cabaniss of Mount Lebanon enlisted at Bienville on March 8, 1862. He entered the Louisiana Hospital at Richmond in the summer of 1862, and Company C never heard of him again (*ibid.,* 212).

7. Two men named Greer serving with Company C were sent to hospitals in the rear and were not again heard of. Charles A. Greer of Homer left the company sometime in 1862. James B. Greer was left sick at Gordonsville on August 20, 1862, and, after being transferred to the Louisiana Hospital at Richmond, was "supposed to be dead as his family heard nothing from him." W. B. Greer, however, is not listed in Booth (*ibid.,* Vol. III, Pt. 1, pp. 97, 98).

There is considerable talk now of all the skeleton regiments being consolidated but I think Congress appreciates the feelings of the army too much to pass such a bill. The talk of our going back to La. has about played out and I now think that we will remain in Va. another campaign and by that time we will be reduced to a mere Company as all the men who get off on sick furlough generally cross the river and never will return.

I think that our brigade will soon be well supplied with clothing as I hear that there has been twenty thousand dollars contributed for that purpose by the citizens of Lynchburg & Richmond. This will provide all the necessary clothing to make the brigade comfortable through the winter as it will not now number over one thousand men now present. I shall try and get a leave of absence of thirty days about the 1st of Feb. to go down in Geo. but unless something turns up more than I now know of I shall not attempt to come west of the Miss. River. The trip besides being a very expensive one would be attended with many dangers and hardships and if I live till the close of this war I will then return home, while on the other hand if I fall a victim to the ravages of war I shall never be permitted to see those I dearly love on earth again but there is a sweet consolation in the thought that life is but a day when compared with the vastness of eternity and there we may all meet if we but do our duty as intelligent beings possessed of immortal souls. We have but to resist the temptations of the world, the flesh and the Devil and walk according to the dictates of a pure and upright conscience implanted in our breasts by the Author of our nature. The road to happiness is just as plain & much more pleasant than that to misery. Therefore I for one cannot see the consistency of thousands of such great numbers of the human pursuing the latter. I beg pardon for being so lengthy on a subject that you might teach me for years to come but I must soon close and permit me through you to present my love to all the family & near and dear friends. May heaven bless and protect you all through every scene and trial of life. May peace crown your last hours on earth and angels convey your spirit to real[m]s of eternal bliss after death. Remember me kindly to Jonathan as he is one to be pitied and as long as I live I will care for him if the fates do not separate our lots.

Do as you think best with my negroes. I leave them entirely in your charge. Tell old Jack I have not forgotten him. Few men so honest and faithful are to be found in these trying times. Tell him I look upon him as a protector to you all and feel that he will do a faithful part by you all. Tell sister my love for her is unchanging. I pray she may do well through life. Your affectionate Son
R. A. Pierson

⇒ ⇐

REUBEN ALLEN PIERSON TO WILLIAM H. PIERSON
Camp Taylor Orange Co., Va.
[ca. January 30, 1864]

W. H. Pierson, Esqr.
Mt. Lebanon, La.
My dear father

Think not strange of my writing so often to you during the winter and so seldom during the summer. As furloughs are being constantly granted to some of the regiment while we are lying in camp I have every opportunity to send letters across the Miss. River and this accounts for the difference of my writing. I have had no late news from the poor boys who were captured last fall. All I know about them is that they were all carried to Pt. Lookout, Maryland and that only one man was missing who has never been heard from viz: George Whitley. Our Congress is now in session but appear to be working very slow. They are now deliberating on the state of the currency in secret session and it is to be hoped that that they will greatly add to its present value as it is now quite low down.

My latest news from home is to the 6th of Dec. Was quite proud to hear that you all were enjoying good health and had plenty to eat, and I have no right to complain of either my health or rations. It is true I live on very little but our forefathers suffered in the war of the revolution that we might be a free nation and it is but our duty to face every danger that we may hand down to our posterity a government unsubdued by our cruel enemies. I am one who believes that God is with us & will carry us through safe if we will only prove ourselves worthy of the cause and freedom for which we are fighting. All the boys are in fine health and cheerful spirits. Do not think that because we are far from home that we are very despondent for I assure you that it is quite the reverse with us.

We hear very bad rumors from home sometimes such as our old playmates deserting and being held in prison under sentence of death. This of course grieves us very much and makes us wish that we could be back there to set before them a good and noble example of unselfish devotion to the cause of justice and right. I imagine that if we were there our presence would give new life to the desponding and rally the faint hearted from the dull stupor into which they have plunged themselves. How can those who have constant communication with home think of giving up their all? It is a mystery inexplicable to me. I had sooner die than see any of my kindred insulted for one moment by such a band of ruffians as compose the yankee army much more to see them domineered over for life. Who would not protect an aged parent or a loving sister from the abuses of the rabble? Let such an one die for he is unworthy [of] the blessings of his Creator and not fit to live among an enlightened people. I have no sympathy with skulkers and cowards. Now the times has come when we need but true and gallant men to stand in front of enemies' advancing columns and win or die by the power of their arms. There is no prospect of any fighting up here soon. I think we will remain in our present quarters till spring[,] say April. I received a letter from Cousin George Williams a few days since. He was in fine health &c. You must all write often to me and be sure to give all the news of the country. Give my regards to all enquiring friends &c. Receive the love of an absent Son

R. A. Pierson

Special. Write to me what has become of Lieut. Arbuckle and what he is doing in your [*illegible*].

> ⋑ ⋐

REUBEN ALLEN PIERSON TO WILLIAM H. PIERSON
Camp 9th La. Regt. Orange Co., Va.
March 22nd, 1864

W. H. Pierson, Esqr.
Mt. Lebanon, La.
Dearest father
    Notwithstanding that it has been a long time since I last wrote to you yet I never omit writing at every favorable opportunity. I have just received a letter from Henry Tomlinson [8] who is stationed in Mississippi and he says he will forward all my letters by hand across the river if I will send them to him. So I hasten to let you know that I am yet in the land of the living and doing much better than I have any right to expect. The health of all the boys is most excellent, only 2 men in the company complaining viz. John Palmore & F. E. Lewis. The former is suffering from an old wound and the latter has some chronic affliction. I have now about 40 men present in all and 18 of the company who were

8. This is most likely Benjamin H. Tomlinson, Company B, Twelfth Louisiana Infantry. This company, locally known as the "Arcadia Invincibles," was recruited in Bienville Parish and served in Kentucky, Tennessee, and Mississippi until ordered to the Army of Tennessee in May, 1864. Tomlinson was killed in action at Kennesaw Mountain, Georgia, on June 15, 1864 (*ibid.*, Pt. 2, p. 845; Arthur W. Bergeron, Jr., *Guide to Louisiana Confederate Military Units, 1861–1865* [Baton Rouge, 1989], 100–101).

captured at Rhappahannock Station last Nov. have been paroled and sent round by flag of truce to Richmond, where they were given furloughs for 30 days and they have all gone to where they have relatives or friends on this side of the river. I have only 2 deaths to record since last summer. George Whitley was missing at the battle of Rhappahannock Station and has never been heard of from that time hence. He is supposed to be dead. W. H. Blount died of small pox on the 30th day of Dec. last at Point Lookout, Maryland while a pris[o]ner. Two nobler or [more] gallant boys never raised arms in defense of the South than these boys were. I mourn their loss as I would that of my brothers; but this should only make those of us who still survive press forward with renewed vigor and resolve to die like men or establish our independence. I for one am unwilling to accept anything short of a final separation from the fiendish barbarians with whom we have been so long associated. It is true I love peace but give me an everlasting war in preference to a union with a people who condescend to equalize themselves with the poor, ignorant & only half civilized negro. Such a people is base, vile, & altogether unworthy of the honorable and once proud name of Americans. I will not dwell upon this theme. Such thoughts are always exciting my passions of revenge and veng[e]ance.

I have just returned from quite a pleasant trip down in Georgia and as you might justly suppose I enjoyed it amazingly well. I visited Griffin where Uncle James Perdue lives, spent one week with his family, during which time I was treated with every kindness that I could have desired. All his family was in fine health. Aunt Elizabeth looks very much like my kind and noble mother and of cours[e] I could not but adore her. She has four children—2 girls and 2 boys— none of whom have ever married. The youngest is a boy about 15 years of age. The girls have very good educations and are quite intelligent. The youngest is possessed of many rare qualities and has considerable experience in the world though but 17 years of age. But for fear you think I am taking on about my cousin let me assure you that I regard them all as I would my adored sister. Well I next visited Uncle Tom and Aunt Lucy at Lumpkin and if I had not known that I was many hundred miles from home when Aunt found out who I was, and began to take on I should have thought that Aunt Nan had hold of me. Well I enjoyed myself here as well as I could. I went out and paid a visit to old Uncle Daniel Richardson who still lives where he did when you left Stewart. His wife who I learned was your own cousin is still living and they were both very kind to me and asked me many questions. They both requested that I should present their warmest regards to you whenever I wrote to you. All of their children are grown and married or in the army except one son who had been discharged for disability. I promised to write to him and shall hear from there occasionally.

I also met 2 ladies, daughters of Mr. Crocker though they have both been married (one of them being now a widow). They were also your cousin's daughters. I found a host of relatives around old Lumpkin and you may tell Aunt Nan that I saw Uncle Jonathan Collins. He lives in Macon Georgia. Well Pa while in Georgia I did not visit any of your brothers not because I did not want to see them but for the following reasons. I had but 24 days leave of absence and not knowing exactly where to go to find them I of course went where I knew that some of my relatives lived; and before I had found out where any of my uncles were my time was so near out that I was forced to hasten back or be behind time which you well know was the last thing I should have thought of. I heard direct from Uncle Randle the other day. He lives in Thomas Co. Geo. and is doing well. Uncle John and Littleton are both in Talbot and Uncle Jerry is in Harris. Well this is about all I know about my relatives.

We are receiving tolerable good rations at present and taking everything into consideration I flatter myself that we are doing better here than any troops in the service. I never had the most distant idea of the honors that our army had gained till I visited Georgia; the mere name of being one of the Army of Northern Virginia is sufficient to pass one into the best circles of society down in Ga. Well Pa I have just received a letter from David of the 4th of Feb. and he gives a sad and distressing account of the state of things in that department. Can it be that the noble and generous people of our State are ready to submit to the yolk of our opprésers? Surely not. Oh! what a dark chapter in the history of the State from which we, a little few in Va. boast with pride that we come. Nothing is shurer than our ultimate success and why prolong the struggle by giving encouragement to our enemies. "There is a just God who presides over the destinies of Nations" and He will never suffer a noble and determined people to be trodden under foot by such a people as we are now fighting. I think the day dawn of peace is near at hand by the blessings of Almighty God. I believe that this will be the closing year of our struggles and it pains me to hear of the despondency of a country that I adore and worship more than all earthly objects. Were I possessed of the oratorical powers of a Demosthenes or Cicero I would in the most imploring manner beseech all my countrymen to stop their evil course and gird on their armor for Liberty, Justice and right. It makes my blood chill in me to think that I must forsake all my State pride; and look upon her as the only one that grew faint and despaired for want of true gallantry during the struggle for all that makes life endurable. I hope and trust that most of the accounts which of late has reached our ears are quite exaggerated but I fear that there is too much truth in them. Our army here is in the highest spirits and ready to meet the enemy at any day that we may be called on by our leaders.

Well father in several former letters I have referred to my condition as an immortal being one who was daily nearing to the grave and must give an account of my earthly career at the judgment bar of God. Let me now tell you that I have a hope that my sins have been forgiven through the mediation of "Him who spake as never man before spake, of Him who was crucified that poor wretched, sinful mortals might find acceptance to a throne of grace." I have not connected myself with any church nor do I think that I shall at any early day, because I do not find any church that complies with what I believe to be the duties of a Christain church. Mere formalities are too often substituted in place of real heartfelt repentance for sins. I am well aware that my case is a droll one and it often troubles me yet I intend to be guided by the dictates of conscience as my whole mind is now bent on complying with what I deem my duty. I have but room to hint at my feelings on the above subject. Give my warmes[t] regards and love to the family, relations and old friends. Remember me kindly to Mr. & Mrs. Randle and family as they always seem like home folks when I think of them. Do as you see fit with my property and I shall be pleased with your judgment. I leave all in your hands &c. Now hoping we may soon be permitted to meet again I remain as ever

Your affectionate Son
R. A. Pierson

⇒ ⇐

REUBEN ALLEN PIERSON TO MARY CATHERINE PIERSON
Camp 9th La. Regt. Orange Co., Va.
March 28th, 1864

Miss M. C. Pierson
My adored Sister
Having not heard from you in a long while and deeming it my duty to write home every opportunity I now pen you a few lines though with but a faint hope that they will ever reach your loving eyes. There are so many obstacles intervening between us that reason would say to me, lay aside your pen and cease to write for your missive will never reach those to whom it is addressed. Yet I can never despair of hearing now and then from my home. I am in fine health as usual. Yes I thank God that health and strength has been granted me to fulfil[l] my every duty and it is a source of pleasure to me to perform my duties no difference how hard or patience trying they may be. The general health and spirits of this army are altogether unsurpassed by any band of soldiers that his-

tory either modern or ancient gives an account of and all are eager for the opening of the spring campaign in the full belief that we will be blessed with some grand and glorious victories.

Well Cassie I know that you have heard of the sad misfortune that befell our brigade last Novr. on the Rhappahannock River in which a large number of the boys were captured. I have the cheering news that they have all been paroled and are now in the land of Dixie. I was at Richmond the day after they all arrived and spent most of the day with them. They were in fine health and looked much better than I could have anticipated. And oh! how proud they were to arrive at Dixie's land after a long winter confinement in that bleak island of Pt. Lookout. While in prison one of Co. "C" died of small pox viz[.] Wm. H. Blount. Lt. Melvin who was sent to Johnson's Island has not been sent round and paroled yet but I am looking for him daily. All of the boys have been given 30 days['] furlough and have gone to visit their relatives in the different States on this side of the river. I fear that some of them will try to cross the river and be captured again.

I had quite a pleasant furlough of 24 days in Feb. & March returning on the 17th Inst. I visited Uncle James Perdue at Griffin Ga. and Uncle Tom Simpson at Lumpkin. The former has four children 2 girls and 2 boys. They were all well and at home. One of his sons is old enough to be in service and has been in one year after which he was discharged. He then joined a battalion who were doing Provost duty at Macon. This organization was broken up while I was in Ga. and he was talking of going into a printing office, that being his profession. The youngest of the girls a blooming lass of "sweet seventeen" was very interesting and had the most amiable disposition I almost ever saw. She reminded me very much of Aunt Araminda. The oldest of the girls is fine looking but has a boisterous temper. Aunt Betsie reminded [me] of my own dear Mother. Her and uncle are both good hands to spoil children and consequently all the children are very bad pets. Well Aunt Lucy and Uncle Tom have five living children 4 boys and one girl. The oldest of the boys has a wife and one child. The boys are all in the army. 2 of them were at home on furlough while I was there. One had been slightly wounded in a fight down in Florida. The other like myself was on furlough of indulgence and had not been home in near 3 years. All the family were very kind to me as was every body I met while in Ga. Well Cassie I made the acquaintance of many fascinating young Ladies while on furlough; but I tell you that some of the Ga. girls are worthy of the affections, confidence, yes the love and hand of the most valliant [sic] and noble Confederate boys. I saw one young widow whom I particularly admired. She lives at Griffin, has cold [sic] black hair and eyes, and she was as eloquent as a Demosthenes. Her words were uttered in such a sweet tone till he who listened to them instantly fell a captive to their electrical influence. But I must cease my foolishness. I know it does interest you and therefore beg your pardon. Do not show this out of the family if you please. We separated many hundred miles from each other but let us live in hopes that this cruel war with all its ravages may soon cease and we may meet and talk over the mysteries of the past. Give my regards to all enquiring friends—my love to the young ladies, my hatred to those who are staying in the woods and shirking their duty in this war, and last though not least my tenderest regards to my brothers, my aged father and mother. Ah I often think of you all when lying on my bed of straw at night and all nature is wrapped in the arms of sweet sleep. Think not that I have forgotten you all for I never can desire to eradicate those dear emotions of the mind which were instilled into my youthful mind as I grew up under the training of my pious parents. Well Sissy I hope and pray that you that you may not suffer yourself captivated and led to the hymenial altar by the conscript gentry, who cover themselves with gilt lace and brass buttons, support a huge mustache and imperial but all the while take care to keep their precious carcasses beyond the reach of the death dealing missiles of our heartless enemies. Never marry any young man who puts in a substitute in the army nor one who has to be dragged into service by law, but I would not say refuse a good and gallant soldier provided you fancy him and know his character; though I don't know why I feel so much interest in your marriage only that I wish you well through life and nothing gives me more pleasure than to hear of your being in fine spirits. I remain your affectionate Brother

R. A. P.—

REUBEN ALLEN PIERSON TO WILLIAM H. PIERSON
Camp Hays[s] La. Brig.
April 19th, 1864

Mr. W. H. Pierson
Mt. Lebanon, La.

As it has been a long while since I received any news direct from home I of course cannot feel at all assured that my letters get safely through and reach you. And while I pen these lines I have but a fe[e]ble hope that they will ever reach the eyes of those for whom they are intended; however be this as it may some letters are coming across daily and why not mine as well as others? The path of duty is plainly before me. I ought to write to my absent father, for whose welfare and prosperity I would endure every suffering, brave every danger, and shrink not from the firey darts of war[']s dreadful missiles.

Would to God that I was among the few of Louisiana's sons who are now battling with the enemy to prevent his merciless hordes from over running my loved home.[9] Sooner would I die and leave my bones to bleach in the sunshine on the battle plains of the state of La. than have my adored father and mother, my amiable and proud hearted sister and my crippled and wandering minded brother, insulted by the brutish and inhuman wretches who now march beneath the folds of the once proud but now dishonored and degraded emblem of American freedom. Think not because the decrees of fate have separated me from my home and loving friends that I am so undutiful as to forget even for one short moment those who nursed and fed me in my infancy and made me what I now am. Your examples, your precepts and your Christian character all are still fresh in my memory as they were when I was with you daily and had the benefit of your counsel in everything that I had to do.

My health is not as good as it usually has been but still I am able to keep up. I have been troubled for sometime past with a severe cold but I think I shall be all right in a few days. Those of the boys who are present are all in very good health. The boys who were captured have all been paroled and given furloughs for 30 days and there time was out yesterday though none of them have reported yet. I understand that a majority of them intended to cross the river and visit home before they returned and if this be true they will not be apt to come back soon if ever. I expect some hard fighting here by the 1st of May but all the troops believe that victory will be ours and that the present year will close this bloody and heartsickening war. The federals are all ready too far gone into the malestrom of financial ruin to ever return and every moment brings them nearer to the fatal whirlpool, that is to wreck their already shackling ship of state. They cannot retreat from the position they have chosen and to remain where they are or attempt to go forward is certain death.

9. Following the fall of Vicksburg, the Union high command sought once again to subdivide the South, this time sending a joint land and naval expedition under Nathaniel P. Banks up the Red River to cut Louisiana in two, invade Texas, and capture as much Confederate cotton as could be had in the region. The campaign began in early March, 1864, but on April 8, Richard Taylor defeated Banks at Pleasant Hill, Louisiana, sending him in retreat down the Red River. Although Banks won a tactical victory at Pleasant Hill, Louisiana, the following day, he continued his retreat. By May 27, his badly-used command was back on the Mississippi River, having accomplished none of its objectives and delaying Grant's intended campaign against Mobile by several vital weeks. See Ludwell H. Johnson, *Red River Campaign: Politics and Cotton in the Civil War* (Baltimore, 1958); T. Michael Parrish, *Richard Taylor: Soldier Prince of Dixie* (Chapel Hill, 1992), 317–404.

I have already given you in a former letter a history of my trip (on furlough) down in Ga. last winter & for fear you may not have gotten that letter I will state here that I spent one day with Uncle Danl. Richardson, who married your cousin and lived near you in Stewart. They are both still stout and hearty though very old. The old man had a thousand questions to ask me about you and appeared to be as proud to see me as if he had met one of his own children. He still lives in three miles of Lumpkin and all his children are grown and scattered off. I heard direct from Uncle Randle only a few days since. He lives in Thomas County Ga. I also heard from Uncles Littleton and John. They both live in Talbot County and Uncle Jerry lives in Harris. I went to Griffin & Lumpkin and saw Aunt Elizabeth and Lucy. They were both well but looking quite broken. All their children are grown and many of them in the army. I spent a very agreeable time while on furlough and was treated with every kindness that I could wish. A good Soldier meets with friends wherever he goes & well may the people at home deal kindly with them for the soldiers are protecting the wealth, honor & liberties of this Confederacy. I hear glorious news from the Trans-Mississippi department during the last few days. It is reported that Banks has met with a severe defeat on Cane River which I suppose to be near Natchitoches and that Dick Taylor and Smith were pursuing him. The yankee papers say that the Red River expedition is a complete failure. I do hope that these reports may all be true and that the soil of Bienville Parish may never be polluted by the foot of one of the heartless wretches who are striving to enslave us. With the many peculiar advantages of swamps and thickets, which is so common in our country a very small cavalry force can operate against vast numbers of the enemy and so impede their progress as to check them effectually and force them to retire. Now if our people are only true Confederates they may forever protect their homes and thrash any yankee force that attempts to penetrate into the inland country. As long as Gen. Smith has no abler commander than Banks to contend with he may think himself blessed, for I have an idea of how Mr. or rather Commissary Banks fights. I was with Jackson when he chased him through the Valley of Va. in May 1862, and have never met with a set of men so ready to take to their heels since that day.

Well as I have not heard from home in so long a time till I do not have but little idea as to what the state of the country is at present, however I have no little missives to send to the fair sex nor have I any ties that in any way claim my attention. I am free from the influences of Cupid[']s darts and can say with a clear conscience that no woman on earth can claim the least promise on my part of a *love* when I shall have finished my days of soldiering. As for what property I may possess I will leave it entirely to your government till I return. And if I should never return you can keep it through your lifetime and then turn it over to Sister Cassie for she is the only one of my relatives but what I think is able to take care of themselves, Jonathan excepted and I know you will leave him a competency and he shall be taken every care of as long as I live.

I have not been in a fight since last July at Gettysburg but do not know how long before I shall be called upon and then I shall do my duty though it be at the risk of my life. Three of Co. "C" has crossed the river on furlough this winter and two of them I am sorry to say signed an oath before leaving here not to go into or through the enemies['] lines. I refer to Chas. E. Prothro and W. C. McCoy. W. D. Mims I learn has joined a cavalry company in La. Lieut. Arbuckle will not return though he has been ordered specially to do so. James A. Williamson desires me to request you to visit his family and write in your next letter how they are getting along.

Give my regards to all enquiring friends &c. Tom Pitman, Pat Candler, Cap Key, Proff. Lindon, John Norrid and Jasper Hilbun are all present and well. Ed Stephens and John Evans from Sparta are both well. Monroe Thomas, Tom Page and J. D. Lassiter are all well. There is but one sick man in Co. "C" viz: F. E. Lewis nephew of Ben Pearce. He will get a furlough in a few days to go to Ala.

I hear occasionally from Cousin George Williams. He was well in March. I have been rather tedious and uninteresting in this letter—hope you will excuse it all as I am a little unwell. Tell Jonathan I have not forgotten him. I will bring him a yankee trick when I come home. Tell Sister to write to me and not forget. Tell Aunt Nan not to take the hystericks when you read this letter. Tell Joseph to go to School and study his books and get an education. Give my regards to Dave, Henry & Jim when you write to them &c. Learn Adeline and Bob to be smart children and useful to all the family. With my warmest regards and affections—hoping we may both be spared to meet again on earth
I remain your devoted Son
R. A. Pierson

⇒ ⇐

REUBEN ALLEN PIERSON TO DAVID PIERSON

Boston, Thomas Co., Ga.
May 22nd, 1864

Col. David Pierson
3rd Regt. La. Vols.
Dear David
Having but little to do I have concluded to write you a short letter to let you know that I am safe. I was slightly wounded in the right hand on 5th Inst.

the first day[']s fighting of the grand armies of Gens. Lee & Grant.[10] We have been quite successful in all the fights on this side of the Miss. River this spring & the general impression here now is that the present campaign will close the war. The yankee armies in this department has been greatly reduced by desertion & the going out of a large number of their old troops, whose time of enlistments have expired. As I was wounded at the very beginning of the fight I know but little about the casualties of my company. James D. Lassiter was killed and E. L. Stephens was severely if not mortally wounded. I hope he may recover. These are all the two that I saw of the company who were hurt. I hope they may all come out safely, though I see that our Brig. Gen. has been wounded since I left.

I am now at Uncle Randle Pierson[']s and faring splendidly—have only been here five days & have been fishing twice. Uncle is very healthy & stout for a man of his age, and has plenty of everything around him to enjoy life well. Aunt Martha is in quite feeble health. She has spells of fits every now & then but still she keeps up. I shall probably return to my command about the first of June. I have a furlough for thirty (30) days which will be out the 10th of June—my hand is improving very fast but is quite sore yet. The ball cut a gash across the back about 2½ inches long and the depth of a large minnie bullet. At the same time I had one hole through my coat & four through my pants so you may judge that I feel very thankful that I escaped as well as I did. I now have a scar that will show the battle mark as long as I live & hope this may be the last one I ever shall receive. My health is very good & I have nothing to fear now from sickness. The health of the army was fine when I left it & scarcely any sickness known in the army. Gen. Lee's army was in the best of spirits and were driving the enemy when I left the field. The yankees report their loss as being the heaviest of any battle of the war—between 50 & 75 thousand in all & over ten Gens. in all. In north Georgia fighting has been growing for several days but without any definite result.[11] I very much fear

10. On May 4, 1864, the Federal Army of the Potomac, nominally commanded by George Gordon Meade but in fact closely overseen by Ulysses S. Grant, crossed the Rapidan River in northern Virginia and instigated the longest and costliest Civil War campaign. The 120,000 Union soldiers met Lee's 60,000-man army in the battle of the Wilderness on May 5. For forty consecutive days, the two sides were in constant and brutal contact. Although the southerners were able to inflict twice as many casualties on their enemies as they themselves sustained—killing and wounding an average of two thousand Federals a day in the fighting at the Wilderness (May 5–7), Spotsylvania Courthouse (May 8–21), on the North Anna River (May 23–26), and at Cold Harbor (May 27–June 12)—Grant's losses were replaceable, while Lee's were not. See Gordon C. Rhea, *The Battle of the Wilderness, May 5–6, 1864* (Baton Rouge, 1994); William D. Matter, *"If It Takes All Summer": The Battle of Spotsylvania* (Chapel Hill, 1988).

11. From the first week in May through the first week of September, 1864, William T. Sherman's 98,000-man army group advanced inexorably toward Atlanta against the determined resistance of Joseph

that we are destined to meet with a slight if not a [*two words illegible*] at that point. I fear that Gen. Johnston is too slow for the emergency; but I shall hope that our next news will be of a grand victory. From the Trans-Miss. Department we have the most cheering news. Report says Price has captured Steele in Ark. with about 10,000.[12] Another report says that Banks surrendered to Dick Taylor, and that a large fleet has been cut off above the falls and will be either destroyed or captured. It seems that the yankees have met with defeats on every side this spring. Their campaign against Charleston S.C. was a complete failure. Sherman[']s advance into Miss. was of no value.[13] In N.C. they lost about 3,000 men, 25 pieces of artillery & a vast amount of stores by advancing out too far.[14] Gen. Forrest captured Fort Pillow & made a successful raid into Kentucky and has returned safely.[15] In Florida they were shamefully

E. Johnston's 53,000-man Army of Tennessee. Although primarily a campaign of maneuver, the campaign was punctuated by the battles of Resaca (May 14–15), New Hope Church (May 25–27), and Kennesaw Mountain (June 27), none of which proved decisive. See Albert Castel, *Decision in the West: The Atlanta Campaign of 1864* (Lawrence, Kans., 1992).

12. Following the repulse of Banks's Red River campaign, Confederate forces under Edmund Kirby Smith turned their attention to the second prong of the Federal offensive—Frederick Steele's column approaching northwest Louisiana across Arkansas. Upon learning of Banks's defeat and the approach of a sizable Confederate force, Steele began a retreat from Camden, Arkansas. The Yankees were brought to bay, however, as they attempted to cross the Saline River on April 30. The resulting battle of Jenkins' Ferry was a relatively bloodless affair, allowing Steele to recross the Saline unharmed. Smith had, however, forced the evacuation of Arkansas and ended the last Union threat of an overland invasion of Texas.

13. In January, 1864, following the battle of Chattanooga, William T. Sherman was given command of the Department of Tennessee, which included the left bank of the Mississippi from Cairo to Natchez. Fearing Rebel interference with the navigation of the river, Sherman led twenty thousand men to Meridian, Mississippi, there to interdict the Mobile and Ohio railroad and to destroy Bedford Forrest's cavalry command. Leaving Vicksburg on February 3, Sherman's column entered Meridian on February 14, remaining five days and destroying the arsenal and rail yard. Sherman was forced to retire, however, when the second Union column, under Brig. Gen. William Sooy Smith, was defeated by Forrest's troopers at West Point, Mississippi, on February 21 and at Okolona on February 22. Sherman himself came very near being captured by Confederate cavalry at Decatur on February 12 (William T. Sherman, *The Memoirs of General William T. Sherman by Himself* [1875; rpr. Bloomington, 1957], 387–95).

14. On April 20, 1864, Confederate forces under Robert F. Hoke, with the assistance of the C.S.S. *Albemarle*, captured Plymouth, North Carolina, seizing 2,800 prisoners and a large trove of weapons and ammunition and raising Rebel hopes of breaking the Union stranglehold on the Atlantic coast.

15. On April 12, 1864, elements of Nathan Bedford Forrest's cavalry corps surrounded Fort Pillow, located on the Mississippi River about forty miles north of Memphis and, after heavy fighting, demanded the surrender of its garrison—a regiment of Tennessee Unionists and one of African-American soldiers. When the Union commander, Maj. William F. Bradford, refused Forrest's terms, the Confederates attacked, overrunning the Union position and driving the survivors back to the river. Union survivors claimed that Forrest's men massacred prisoners and the wounded—a charge that the Confederates stoutly denied. Given their extreme animosity toward both black and southern Unionist troops, however, some excesses are almost certain to have occurred. (Brian Steele Wills, *A Battle from the Start: The Life of*

beatten.[16] From every quarter the news of victory is constantly pouring in & if it continues through the present campaign this "cruel war will then be over."

Well Dave one word now about the fair sex of La. I hope they have escaped the dreadful demoralization that is so prevalent in this country. For let me assure you that I never read or heard of such prostitution as I find in some parts of this country.[17] Tell the girls to wait with patience for there is plenty of men yet left. I do abhor & detest to see a woman throw herself upon a level with the brutes. When they do this they are truly the lowest of God[']s creation. Give my regards to all enquiring friends, particularly the family. Excuse bad writing as I am writing with a wounded hand & it quite sore. With my regards & best wishes for your prosperity through life I remain
Yours Fraternally
R. A. Pierson

⇒ ⇐

PHILIP L. COLLINS TO WILLIAM H. PIERSON
Line of Battle   Hays['s] Brigade   June the 5th 1864
Mr. W. H. Pierson

Dear uncle

I take the present opportunity of writing you a few lines as I hav an opportunity of sending it a cross the River by hand and Allen is not present. I hav received for Al one letter from you on May the 1st and one from Cas[s]ie of Feb. the 7th since he left. He was wounded on the fifth of May, slight across the back of the right hand and I was just coming in from Richmond and met him on the 6th on his way to Richmond where he got a furlow of thirty days to go to Thomasville, Ga. to see some of his relatives. I arrived at Camps on the night

---

Nathan Bedford Forrest (New York, 1992), 179–96; Jack Hurst, *Nathan Bedford Forrest: A Biography* (New York, 1993), 165–81.

16. On February 7, 1864, a Union division under Brig. Gen. Truman Seymour landed at Jacksonville, Florida, and marched inland until checked at the battle of Ocean Pond on February 20. In this engagement on the Olustee River, Brig. Gen. Joseph Finigan, with nearly 5,200 men, delivered a stinging blow to the 9,400 raiders and sent them scurrying back to the safety of Jacksonville.

17. Virtually every city, north or south, where large numbers of soldiers were encamped became the home of great numbers of prostitutes. Chicago, Cincinnati, New York, Boston, and especially Washington were Unionist meccas for what soldiers referred to as "horizontal refreshment." In Richmond, enterprising prostitutes worked out of houses opposite military hospitals, much to the distress of the doctors. Some even solicited on the grounds of the Confederate capitol (Thomas P. Lowry, *The Story the Soldiers Wouldn't Tell: Sex in the Civil War* [Harrisburg, Pa., 1994], 61–87; James I. Robertson, Jr., *Soldiers Blue and Gray* [Columbia, S.C., 1988], 116–21).

of the 6th of May and found them all in line of battle and we hav been in line
or on the march ever since but we hav been ingaged in regular battle but one
day since the 5th and that was on the 12th of May, where we sustained considerable loss from our Brigade on account of our line beeing broken on our right
which let the yankees in on our flank and rear which compelled us to fall back
under a most terrific fire of musketry and shells, but our gallant little Brigade
rallied and at the propper place and repelled the advance of the enemy and held
them in check until reinforcements came up and drove them back which saved
the day and gave us some rest for a few days.[18] The loss of our company was
light on the 12th as we were on the left of the Brigade and where we ral[l]ied we
had temperary breastworks. There has been some of the most desperate charges
made by the yankees this Campeign that I hav ever known them to make before
but they hav been handsomely repulsed on every occasion with great slaughter
as our army has don the most of their fighting behind breastworks. Grant finding that he could not whip our army at the wilderness he marched his forces to
our right to flank us compelling the army to march to Spotsylvania C[ourt]
H[ouse] where we met him a gain and fought him several days and he a gain
marched to our right and then we taken position at Hanover Junction but he
would not fight much there but kept marching to our right until he reached his
present position which is near Gaynese Mill[19] the noted battle field of the 27th
of June 1862, where Jackson routed Mclelon and we hav a strong position in
front of him and there is occasional fighting along the lines. I heard heavy
canonading and musketry last night and we heard that they attacked
Longstreet[']s corps and was repulsed with great slaughter. Grant has got a good
deal nearer Richmond than he was when he fought us in the wilderness but our
army is just as far from being whipped now as it was then and from all accounts
the yankees are pretty badly whipped now and if they dont mind they will bee
whipped wors than they hav ever been before they get out of this. Grant leaves
his dead on the battle field to rot like buts[?] to rot on top of the ground. I hav
seen a great many of them myself after they had decayed so much that the flesh
had left their faces. I must give you the casualties of our Company as I do not

18. This action was part of the defense of the "Bloody Angle," a salient in Lee's line at Spotsylvania
overrun on May 12 by Winfield Scott Hancock's corps of the Army of the Potomac. Edward Johnson's division of Ewell's corps, of which the Louisiana Brigade was a component, was badly hurt in the day's
fighting. See Matter, *If It Takes All Summer.*

19. The second battle of Gaines's Mill, better known as the battle of Cold Harbor, was fought on
June 1–3, 1864. In an ill-conceived attempt to rupture the Confederate line, Grant launched a 40,000-
man frontal attack against Lee's well-entrenched army. Within half an hour, he suffered seven thousand
casualties with no compensating damage to his enemy.

know how long it may bee before my priveldige of writing will bee closed. On the 5th of May was killed James D. Lasiter, wounded Ed. Stephens mortally, since died at Sta[u]nton, and R. A. Pierson slight, on the 12th wounded T. J. Sanders sevearly, J. D. Watts sevearly in the side, J. C. Watts slight, John Evans slight in the face, D. Carter slight in the head, and Lieut. Ed. Arbuckle slight, and on the first of June Corpral A. N. Walker was wounded in the hand from the enemies['] skirmishers and on the third Smith [*illegible*] was wounded in the head in a skirmish with the enemies. T. J. Key was slightly wounded on the first of June but never left the field. I came very near forgetting him as he does not stay with the Company. You must excuse me for putting it down in the way I have as I am in a great hurry and hav to put it down as it comes to my mind. I spent a thirty day furlow in Geo[r]gia this spring mostly in Lumpkin and Griffin and Lousy [*i.e.,* Lucy] and aunt Betsy were in good health when I was there. You can put the casualties in a regular form and hav it put in the Baptist if you choose. I neglected to state the missing. H. L. Rhod[e]s and William Candler were taken prisoners on the 12th and James Speers missing and supposed to be killed but not known. If I hav time I will give you a [*illegible*] list separate. Give my respects to all your family and to all inquiring friends.

I remain yours with respect

Philip L. Collins

P.S. Tell Charity that Monroe is well.

⇒ ⇐

REUBEN ALLEN PIERSON TO WILLIAM H. PIERSON

Macon, Ga.
June 22nd, 1864

W. H. Pierson, Esqr.

Mt. Lebanon, La.

Dearest Father

Having a faint hope that you may get this and learn that I am still living and doing well I now proceed to give you a few of the ups and downs through which I have passed in the last few months. [In the battle of] the 5th of May [I was wounded] in the right hand. I was sent to the hospital at [Richmond.] I was furloughed and went [to Thomasville, Georgia]

[*remainder of letter illegible*]

⇒ ⇐

PHILIP L. COLLINS TO WILLIAM H. PIERSON
Camp Hays[']s Brigade Near Montainsburg, Va.
July the 28th 1864

Mr. W. H. Pierson

Dear uncle

    I take the present opportunity of writing you a few lines to communicate to you the very unpleasant news of the death of R. A. Pierson. He was killed on the morning of July the 18th by a Minnie ball from the yankee sharpshooters. He was shot dead. He only spoke twice after he fell. He spoke to me and sayed he was killed dead to take him out and he died immediately. The ball passed threw his Rite arm just below the shoulder and went threw his side and lodged in his clothes on the opposite side. He had just taken command of the skermish line that morning and was passing down the line which was on the west bank of the Shannandoah River and the yankees were in ambush on the opposite bank. He had just returned from furlough and joined us on the night of the 16th of July. I got a pass from the General and went and got permission from a Farmer and buried him in a private Family grave yard. He was buried as deasent as we could bury him. We had a coffin made for him. He was buried in the grave yard of Mr. P. D. Shepherd near Berryville Clarke County, Va. I should have wrote to you sooner but I have been waiting for an opportunity to send it a cross the River but I do not see any prospect of chance of sending it so I shall trust it by mail. He left his business unsettled. He had no money except two dollars in gold and ten cts. in silver but the government owes him about seven hundred dollars which can be collected by a regular process and he is owing some of the Company. He owes one man one hundred dollars W. A. Bailston,[20] and he owes F. F. Rolinson fifty five dollars is all that I know of. He was buried in his unaform suit, and the remainder of his clothes I could not do anything with them as there is no wagon allowed here for line officers so the Company taken them. There was nothing of importance. I hav his pocket book and the money he left and I have his gold pen and I hav allso some buttons which were taken off of his coat after he was shot and a small lock of his hair to send home by the request of the Colonel. If I have an opportunity I will send them home or if it should be my fate to fall some of the boys will send them. We hav had a very hard Campeign this year. We had a battle at Frederic[k] City on the 9th of July where our Co. lost 9 men killed and wounded.[21]

20. This is Sgt. William A. Boylston.

21. What Collins refers to as the battle at Frederick City is better known as the battle of Monocacy, Maryland, fought on July 9, 1864.

The killed were E. W. Denson and John Graham. Wounded Ed. Hartwell severly C. J. Watts severaly and C. C. Talton severaly. These three were left in the enemies['] hands. The rest were slightly wounded and came across the River. They were J. M. Thomas, H. Cox, J. R. Reynolds,[22] W. Loftin. We then marched on Washington City but was a little to[o] late to take it. We got in sight but we then had to fall back. We have just heard some good news from the west if it is true. The soldiers are generally in good spirits. I would like to hear from you some time as you can hav an opportunity of sending letters across.

I hav nothing more of importance to write at present. Give my respects to all your family and inquiring friends. I remain as Ever

Philip L. Collins

P. S. Capt Pearson reached Camps on the 16th—went with us on picket yesterday morning. While posting us, four or five yankees fired from the opposite bank of the river—not more than one hundred yards across. The Yankees were behind trees—in the bushes and grass so that we could only now and then get the glimpse of one. We all fell upon the ground, and then sought trees upon the bank of the river. Except Capt P. He walked along perfectly regardless of dangers and exclaimed "Boys see those Yankees behind that clay root—shoot them." 25 Yankees were within 100 & 150 yards of him. Several Yankees show themselves—we begin to fire. Pearson stops in open view of the enemy giving orders speaking in his usual loud tone—this attracting the enemy['s] attention. Just then a Minnie ball pierced him through. He fell and said to one of his Co. "Collins, I'm killed take me out." One of the boys started to him—but found that it would be rashness to attempt it. These were all the words he uttered and in a few minutes expired. We sent some of the men up the river to give them a cross fire while we in front made them lie low. We soon forced them to fall back. Capt P was a brave officer & much beloved by his company. He was true as steel—good and kind to his men. His bravery suited him well for the battlefield—while he was too boisterous and too much destitute of caution and craftiness to fight the Snake in the grass. His loss is felt greatly—

Thus we pass away.

F. A. Bledsoe

22. Corp. John R. Reynolds, a Mount Lebanon druggist, was captured in Loudon County, Virginia, on July 15, 1864, and spent three months in New York's Elmira Prison (Booth, comp., *Records*, Vol. III, Pt. 2, p. 293).

⇒ ⇐

DAVID PIERSON TO WILLIAM H. PIERSON

Camp near Alexandria, July 18th/64

Wᵐ H. Pierson
  Mᵗ Lebanon,
    La.

Dear Pa,

The wagon came to hand this morning with bacon and coat all right. Many thanks for the same. My health is very good, but there is much sickness in our camp. The men of the 3ʳᵈ Regᵗ are nearly all here except for those companies from the swamp engaged in guerilla service.[23] Genˡ Walker's[24] orders and the cavalry are bringing the boys into camp better than anybody had supposed. Jim ought not to have remained over his leave for we are compelled to be very strict. If he is punished at all, it will only be a few days' imprisonment in the guard house. I hope not even that. I send ½ lb. indigo to Aunt Nan and as much to Charity, a part belonging to Henry. If you can get Stall to make me a pair of boots, do so at any price. My old pair are nearly gone. My horse is quite poor. I get very little corn to feed him. I will try to get a leave of absence before long.

Truly and Affectionately Yours,

D. Pierson

23. Not until July 21, 1864, by Edmund Kirby Smith's General Order No. 56, were the men of the Third Louisiana Infantry officially exchanged and legally eligible for active duty against the enemy (Tunnard, *A Southern Record,* 319–20).

24. John George Walker resigned from the U.S. Army on July 31, 1861, and accepted a commission as major of cavalry in the Confederate army. Walker raised and commanded Company K of the Eighth Texas Cavalry until he was elected the regiment's lieutenant colonel. On January 9, 1862, he was promoted to brigadier general and transferred to the Army of Northern Virginia, where he led a brigade in the Sharpsburg campaign. On November 8, 1862, he was promoted to major general and transferred to the Trans-Mississippi theater. There he took command of the Texas division, which he led during the Red River campaign of 1864. After the battles of Mansfield and Pleasant Hill, Walker superseded Richard Taylor as commander of the District of West Louisiana. At the end of the war, Walker was commanding a division of cavalry in the District of Texas, New Mexico, and Arizona. See *The War of the Rebellion: A Compilation of the Official Records of the Union and Confederate Armies* (130 parts in 70 vols.; Washington, D.C., 1880–1901), Ser. I, Vol. XXII, pp. 903–904; J. P. Blessington, *The Campaigns of Walter's Texas Division* (1875; rpr. Austin, 1994).

⇾ ⇽

JAMES F. PIERSON TO WILLIAM H. PIERSON

Camp near Alexandria, La., Aug 5th/64

Mr. Wm H. Pierson

Dear Father

As I have not had the opportunity of sending a letter, I have not written, but not knowing how long before I will have a chance I write this to send by the first chance. I have been in good health ever since I left home. I was not troubled when I got back to the Regt. as was reported I would be. We are all in service again. I have just come off of guard this morning. We have only a few guns yet, but are expecting to be armed and equipped soon. Gen. Mouton's[25] old Divis[i]on passed here a day or two ago, marching towards Black River. The whole army on this side is concentrating on Black River, for what purpose no [one] knows, but everybody conjectures that it is for the purpose of crossing the Miss. River. There is no little excitement in our camp about the matter. We are expecting to go with the rest. Nearly all of the army has crossed. I do not think that there are any west of here or south of Red River. An immense train passed here yesterday evening after the army. Two officers were arrested yesterday in Alexandria for spending their opinions of the movements of our army in this section. The Gen. refused Col. Russell a furlough yesterday, which he promised to grant him a few days ago. The Gen. said that he could not furlough a man under any circumstances now, and but a few days ago he was granting 15 day leave of absence to a good many of our Regt. But there is nothing certain about it any way yet. It may be for the purpose of making a raid on the Miss. River somewhere, but I am under the impression that it is for the purpose of crossing the river, but you will know as soon as we do.

I got here safely with all my things, but the most of the provisions that was in my box was molded and consequently I did not eat a great deal of it. The biskets were nearly all spoiled. The cake was not injured but little. The wine nearly all leaked out which ruined most of the biscuits. However, we have had plenty of bacon, which we feast on very heartily. We are doing our own cooking now as the negro is off sick in the country. We are having a great deal of sickness here now, especially among the Parole men. The weather dry and hot.

---

25. Jean-Jacques Alfred Alexander Mouton, the son of former Louisiana governor and senator Alexander Mouton, was elected colonel of the Eighteenth Louisiana Infantry. He was severely wounded at Shiloh but upon recovery was promoted to brigadier general and reassigned to duty under Richard Taylor in the Trans-Mississippi Department. Mouton was killed at the battle of Mansfield while leading his division in the attack that broke the Federal center.

Nothing more for the present.

I am your son till death,

James F. Pierson

P.S. If you have a chance before we leave here, send me some paper for I cannot get a scrap and this is all I have.

Yours & c.,

J. F. Pierson

⇒ ⇐

DAVID PIERSON TO WILLIAM H. PIERSON

Pineville, La., Aug. 7th, 1864

Wm H. Pierson

Mt Lebanon,

La.

Dear Pa,

I send you a note by Mr. Radcliff[?], who leaves tomorrow, to say that we are well. Jim's box came in yesterday and was sent to our camp this morning all right I suppose, though I have not seen it. Co^l Russel leaves tomorrow on recruiting service which nails me to camp for some time to come. I had hoped to get a leave of absence, but now there is no chance. My negro cook is sick with slow camp fever, and I am in quite a fix about a servant, but will get along somehow until he gets well, if ever. Jim was excused by the Co^l for staying over his time on my account, I suppose, for others are punished for like offenses. I got a letter from Al five days ago, the date of which I do not now remember. He was at Uncle Randle's, Boston, Ga., & recovering fast from his wound. He wrote that he would return to his command on the first of June. We have the promise of the Genl that we will be filled up to a full Reg^t and avoid consolidation. No arms yet, and no immediate prospect of taking the field. Polinacks[26]

26. Camille Armand Jules Marie, prince de Polignac, was born in Millemont, Seine-et-Oise, France, and in 1861 offered his sword to the Confederate States Army. He was commissioned a lieutenant colonel and appointed chief of staff to P.G.T. Beauregard. After distinguishing himself at the battles of Shiloh and Corinth, Polignac was promoted to brigadier general and transferred to Richard Taylor's command in Louisiana. Following the death of his division commander, Brig. Gen. Alfred A. Mouton, at the battle of Mansfield, Polignac assumed command of the division and led it to a spectacular victory over the Union forces. For this exploit, he was promoted to major general. In March, 1865, he returned to France to seek aid for the doomed Confederacy and retired to his estate when he received word of Lee's surrender. See Alwyn Barr, *Polignac's Texas Brigade* (Houston, 1964).

Division is here on its march to the Ouchita, it is said. Walker's Division [27] is at Harrisonburg, for what purpose it is not known. My own impression is that an effort will be made to put these two Divisions on the east side of the Miss. R. I was at Genl Gray's [Gano's?] [28] H^d Q^trs yesterday. None of his officers seemed to understand why it was that they were being sent to the Ouchita, but none believed they would be sent to the other side of the river. Our men are all in camp except those engaged in the guerilla service. Cavalry has been sent for them, and the officers dropt from the rolls.

River very low and falling still. We will perhaps be sent from here in a few weeks to some point more convenient to supplies. Don't forget to urge Stall to make me a pair of winter boots. I will use them very much, & it is my only chance to get them. No [need] for horses yet. Excuse this hastily written note.

Affectionately Yours,
D. Pierson

⇒ ⇐

JAMES F. PIERSON TO WILLIAM H. PIERSON

Shreveport, La., Dec. 3rd, 1864

Wm H. Pierson

Dear Father,

As Mr. Hays starts back with his wagon tomorrow, I will send by him a pair of cotton pants that I drew from the Governor's store and a shirt that I got from one of the men on guard here with me. I do not think that I will need them this winter. I would have sent them by Dave, but I never thought of them while he was here. I also send you some cartridges which one of the company gave me

27. Walker's Texas Division was the largest unit of Texans to serve the Confederacy and the only Rebel division comprised of troops from a single state. The division saw action in Texas, Arkansas, and Louisiana, taking an especially crucial role in Taylor's repulse of Banks's Red River expedition. In June, 1864, Walker was transferred to the command of the District of West Louisiana, and his division passed to the leadership of Maj. Gen. John Henry Forney. For the rest of the war, the division was stationed at Hempstead, Texas, where it disbanded on May 19, 1865. See Norman D. Brown, ed., *Journey to Pleasant Hill: The Civil War Letters of Captain Elija P. Petty* (San Antonio, 1982); Blessington, *Walker's Texas Division;* Thomas W. Cutrer, ed., "'Bully for Flournoy's Regiment, We Are Some Punkins, You'll Bet': The Civil War Letters of Virgil Sullivan Rabb, Captain, Company 'I,' Sixteenth Texas Infantry, C.S.A.," *Military History of the Southwest,* XIX (Fall, 1989), 161–90 and XX (Spring, 1990), 61–96.

28. This name is illegible in the Pierson manuscript. It may refer to either Gano or Gray, both of whom commanded brigades in the Trans-Mississippi. Richard Montgomery Gano was assigned to Indian Territory after the April 29–30 battle of Jenkins' Ferry, however, and Henry Gray was not yet a general in August, 1864.

and also a few caps.[29] They may be of some use to you. I would send you the saddle bags, but I have nothing in the world to keep my clothing in if I sent them back. I have some hope of getting off home about Christmas, but I do not know for certain. If I do not, I will see some chance of sending them home some other time. I am very well pleased with my new knife that you sent me. I was greatly in need of such a thing. Tell Cassie I am the best pleased in the world with my gloves. They are just the thing for camps. Also, many thanks to Aunt Nan for sending me a bottle of wine, if I didn't get to taste it. Capt. Russell[30] and Dave leaked it all out before they got here with it. Nevertheless, I am as thankful to Aunt Nan as if I had received it all right.

I've nothing more at present. I will send this by Mr. Hays. I am as ever,

Your son till Death,
James F. Pierson

➜ ⬅

JAMES F. PIERSON TO WILLIAM H. PIERSON
Shreveport Hospital, Dec. 8th, 1864

Wm H. Pierson
Dear Father,

As I have not written you since I have been here, I write this morning. I came here day before yesterday with inflammation of the Glan[d]s and mouth, and since I have been here my face has swollen so that I can scarcely eat anything. The Doctor pronounces it the Scrofillas,[31] but I am yet in hopes that it is not. I am not allowed to leave the room at all and not allowed to sit up but a little while at a time. I get as good attention as I could expect at such a place. I get a little piece of light bread and coffee three times a day, but I have not been

29. The percussion cap, an 1805 invention of Reverend Alexander John Forsyth of Scotland, is a crimped metal disc filled with fulminate of mercury. Fitted over the nipple of a gunlock and struck with the rifle or musket hammer, it produced a small explosion that communicated a spark to the weapon's chamber, firing the cartridge's powder charge. The percussion lock quickly replaced the flintlock in northern inventories after 1861. In the South this technologically sophisticated system was more difficult to manufacture, and the Union blockade hindered its importation (Trevor N. Dupuy, *The Evolution of Weapons and Warfare* [London, 1982], 177, 190–92, 296).

30. William E. Russell was elected third lieutenant of Company D, Third Louisiana Infantry, at Camp Moore and was promoted to captain when the unit was reorganized at Corinth on May 10, 1862 (Booth, comp., *Records*, Vol. III, Pt. 2, p. 420).

31. Scrofula is a tuberculosis of the lymph glands, especially of the neck, characterized by a painful swelling. This disease was, by 1864, one of the few remaining medical reasons for exempting Confederate soldiers from further military service (H. H. Cunningham, *Doctors in Gray: The Confederate Medical Service* [1958; rpr. Baton Rouge, 1993], 164).

in a condition to want anything. I have not tried to get a transfer because I am not able to make the trip on horse back. I think that I will be able to get a transfer sometime between now and Christmas if I get able to travel. The swelling has never been checked on me yet. My face will be a sight in a day or two longer if it runs on. I see a great deal of trouble with it of a night. The nurses all go to bed, and I am left all alone. I have nothing more at present.

I will try and write you again by next mail.

As ever, Your Son till Death,

James F. Pierson

⇒ ⇐

JAMES F. PIERSON TO WILLIAM H. PIERSON
Camp Boggs,[32] La., Dec. 16th, 1864

Mr. Wm H. Pierson

Dear Father,

I write you this note that you may know how I am getting on with my sore mouth that I wrote to you about last week. I am not entirely well of it yet, but it does not give me any trouble now. I think that I will be entirely well of it in a few days. Col. Russell promised me a pass this morning to go home on Christmas. I will be at home either on the night of the 23rd or 24th. I will not remain longer than three days at home. I did think I would not come if I could not get to stay longer, but I can't possibly get any longer a time so I think that I had better take any length that I could get it for. I have a horse here that I can ride when I get it, so I will make it home in one day when I start. The duty is very heavy, and I am on guard two or three times a week. I will expect to bring my pony back with me. I hope that he is in good order by this time. I will have to give up this pony that I have got about tomorrow as the man will [be] coming after him, or rather, he is coming back to the company, but I think that he will let me have him to ride. If he does not, I can get one in the Regt.

Nothing more now. Your Son till Death,

James F. Pierson

32. Camp Boggs, one and a half miles south of Shreveport, was the third and largest of the Louisiana camps named in honor of Brig. Gen. William Robertson Boggs, chief of staff of the Trans-Mississippi Department under Gen. Edmund Kirby Smith. The Third Louisiana garrisoned Camp Boggs on August 16, 1864, replacing the Crescent Regiment, and remained on duty there until the close of the war (Powell A. Casey, *Encyclopedia of Forts, Posts, Named Camps, and Other Military Installations in Louisiana, 1700–1981* [Baton Rouge, 1983], 28).

⇒ ⇐

JAMES F. PIERSON TO JOSEPH PIERSON

Shreveport, La., Feb. 3rd, 1865

Master Joseph Pierson
  Mt. Lebanon, La.

Dear Brother,

Your esteemed favor of the 26th ultimo came duly to hand and found me just in time to give me some news from home as I had not heard from you since Dr. Powell left there. I am as usual in good health and am enjoying myself hugely in the fast city of Shreveport of which you have doubtless heard numbers of times.

We have been recently flushed with officers from Walker's Division that came over here last Sunday. The report is that they are ordered to Houston, but some say that the order is countermanded. They are camped in about a mile from us and two from town.[33] I am on permanent guard in town again but not at the Sugar House now. I am at the Magazine, the place that they keep the powder in. I was sent back to the Sugar House again, but I exchanged posts with another Seargt. and went to the Magazine. I sent 4 ½ Yds. of blue cloth to Charity last Sunday by Mr. Simmes of Winn Parish, and I wrote to her to send it home for me the first chance she got, but the letter was not sent by Mr. Herd[?] who leaves here in a few days. If you get the cloth at home, you must write to me. I bought the cloth from one of the Regt. I have been in a very good place to make money. I made 50 dollars pr. night for watching some property landed on the wharf in town. I am again out of business, but I expect to have some more guarding to do for the Speculators. They give me a good price to watch for them of a night on the wharf. I won't do it for less than 50 dollars a night.

You must write soon and as often as you can conveniently.

Yrs. & c.,
J^{as} F. Pierson

33. On October 28, 1864, the Texas Division entered winter quarters at Camp Magruder near Minden, Louisiana. It remained there until January 26, 1865, when it took up the line of march to Shreveport, arriving there on the twenty-eighth. After a "sham battle," fought on February 18, the Texas Division was formally presented to "that gallant band," the Third Louisiana Infantry, then numbering only 130 men. Each unit saluted the other and then stacked arms and "repaired to the tables where a bountiful and substantial repast was spread." On February 19, the Texas Division was ordered to Nacogdoches, Texas (Cutrer, ed., "Bully for Flornoy's Regiment," 85–86; Blessington, *Walker's Texas Division*, 281, 285–86, 289–90).

⇒ ⇐

JAMES F. PIERSON TO JOSEPH PIERSON

Shreveport, La., Feb. 20th/65

Master Joseph Pierson
  Mt. Lebanon, La.

Dear Joe,

Your welcome favor of the 14th came duly to hand. I was glad to hear from home. But I was very sorry to hear of the Small Pox raging to such an extent in that country. I am also sorry to hear that you had not received the cloth that I sent. You must make some inquiry about it for me. I will write to Mr. Simmes to know where he left it. I was at one of the grandest barbeques last Saturday that I ever saw. There was the largest crowd that I ever saw assembled together. The dinner was given to Gen. Forney's Division,[34] and our Regt. was invited to partake with them. We had a sham battle and many pretty maneuvers that you would have been glad to have seen. I may possibly get a furlough in the course of next month. I do not know, though, now.

You must write soon.

Dave & I are both well.

Your brother,
James F. Pierson

⇒ ⇐

JAMES F. PIERSON TO WILLIAM H. PIERSON

Shreveport, La., Feb. 20th, 1865

Mr. Wm H. Pierson

Dear father,

I mailed a letter to Joseph this morning, but as Dr. Mathis leaves here for Mt. Lebanon this evening, I drop you a short note. I have been uneasy for some time about home, as I hear that the Small Pox is raging so in Bienville. But I hope that it will not reach Mt. Lebanon.

I was at the grand festival given in honor of Genl Forney's Division last Saturday. It was a grand scene. There was as much as twice that number of men could eat on the ground. There was plenty of whiskey given to all the

---

34. John Horace Forney entered Confederate service as colonel of the Tenth Alabama Infantry and saw action at First Manassas. He was promoted to brigadier general on March 10, 1862, and to major general on October 27—a rise in rank that probably outstripped his abilities. After brief service as commander of the Department of Southern Alabama and West Florida, he was given a division of John C. Pemberton's army defending Vicksburg and was captured there when the city fell. After exchange, Forney was sent to the Trans-Mississippi, where he superseded John G. Walker as commander of the Texas Division (Blessington, *Walker's Texas Division*, 271, 276–78, 285–87).

troops.[35] I have been a little afraid that you would not get the cloth that I sent by Mr. Simmes to Henry's about the first of this month. I hope that you will make some little inquiry about it for me. There was about 4¾ Yds. of double width blue cloth. I would not take anything for it if I can get it. I will write to Mr. Simmes in a few days to know where he left it, and then, if I find out, I will write to you where it is.

I am very much in need of that hat that you promised me when I was at home. But you need not put yourself to any extra trouble about it, for I can do very well for sometime yet. I have drawn a full uniform since I left home. The uniform consists of a gray jacket, blue pants, and then I have drawn one undershirt net, one top shirt, a pair of drawers, and a pair of socks, so I am very well off in the way of clothes. I also drew a pair of brogan shoes. I will watch the auctions here, and if I can I will buy you and me some shirting to wear next summer. They are auctioning off goods every day, and money is getting scarce, so I may get it on reasonable terms. Write soon. If I stay here I will get a furlough about the middle of April. Tell Cassie to write & Joe. Tell Aunt Nan that her pants will be very thankfully received, as I do not want to wear my pretty uniform every day.

As ever, Your Son till Death,
J^{as} F. Pierson

⇒ ⇐

DAVID PIERSON TO WILLIAM H. PIERSON
Shreveport, March 13th, 1865

Dear Pa,

Your letters by Mr. Coullinsworth[?] are received. I have collected your coupons and send your two-hundred and forty dollars though strongly tempted to keep a little as fees. I have no news except what is bad and I suppose you have had enough of that sort lately. I am glad to see Henry is a Candidate for the Judgeship.[36] He needs the office, and I hope will be elected. Tell Aunt Nan

---

35. The grand review, barbecue, and mock battle held in honor of Forney's Division or, more commonly, Walker's Texas Division, was held on February 18. To this review, the Third Louisiana was invited as a "guest of honor." It was here that the veteran regiment first appeared in new uniforms and under arms for the first time since the fall of Vicksburg and was presented with a new battle flag (Tunnard, *A Southern Record*, 332–35).

36. Henry Lewis Pierson lost the race for the judge's bench to William B. G. Egan, a son of Dr. Bartholomew Egan. Judge Egan went on to become an associate justice of the Louisiana Supreme Court. He died in New Orleans on March 30, 1878 (Letters in Egan Family Collection, Cammie G. Henry Research Center, Eugene P. Watson Library, Northwestern State University of Louisiana).

to send me my cottonade pants by the time summer [*illegible*] and some cotton socks, & c.

All well. Don't know how long we will remain here. We have nearly seven-hundred men in the Reg^t now, all told, and I hope we will escape consolidation.

My love to all at home & c.

Affectionately yours,
D. Pierson

DAVID PIERSON TO MARY CATHERINE PIERSON
Shreveport, La., March 20th/65

My Dear Sister,

Being somewhat idle tonight and thinking the time could not be better employed, I seat myself to write you, though I suppose you all at home must think that Jim and I have nothing else to do from the frequency with which we trouble you with our nonsense. And in that respect you are not far wrong so far as I am concerned, for, in truth, my duties are neither severe or arduous. Indeed, time has glided on more smoothly with me here than at any other time since I have been soldiering. Having plenty of candles, I sit up late at night reading whatever book I can lay my hands on, rise late in the morning, breakfast at eight o'clock, dine at four (we eat two meals only), attend drill two hours during the day, and occasionally ride to town in the evening to hear the news and see who can be found. Altogether it is a lazy life, but something is learned almost every day—of human nature if nothing else. Speaking of eating, let me tell you we had a magnificent dinner today. My Cook having killed a fine wild turkey (it would not do for officers to eat tame ones) we bought some extra luxuries, set the kitchen in busy uproar, and produced a meal of which home itself might not be ashamed. Like true soldiers, we shared it with our friends who partook of our hospitalities with good cheer as well as *Appetite*. We are all in good health and doing very well. There is no talk of our leaving here soon, the Post Commandant is our friend and will retain us as long as possible. Let me tell you a good joke on myself. I went to a party in town the other night—was introduced to a pretty lady whom I took to be a widow—was very gallant and thought I had made an impression when, lo! I am told that her husband is present. To crown my misfortune, I entered into conversation with another from whose diminutive size and innocent face I take to be a child—addressed her as "Little Miss" when I am indignantly told by her that she is eighteen years of age. You can imagine how I must have felt. I shall try to get a leave of absence in June to attend court in Winnfield. Ten per cent of the men are allowed to be furloughed at a time now by Orders from Genl. Smith. Jim's time will come around some time in the summer, but he is making too much money now to think about it.

Well, sister, I must tax your kindness for a pair of gloves. My buckskin ones are nearly worn out. Let them be plain and thin—no gauntlets to them. Another article I will want early in the spring—my mosquito bar. Send it by first opportunity. They are terrible here, they say, as soon as the river falls, which is now receding very fast. If you want anything out of the stores here, let me know and I will get it for you—that is, when the Gov^t pays me, and I suppose it will be for much longer.

No news. Love to all.

Your Affectionate Bro.,
Dave

P.S. I had forgotten to say that I am again appointed on a Genl Court Martial which convenes next week to try Co^l Guess for some crime about Cotton.[37]

Dave

>⋲<

DAVID PIERSON TO WILLIAM H. PIERSON

Shreveport, La., March 25th, 1865

Dear Pa,

Mr. Bob Key[38] informs me that his wagon is going to start to Mt. Lebanon tomorrow and will return to this place in a few days. Please send my Mosquito-Bar and summer pants when it returns. No soldiers['] cards have come yet, else I would send a pair home. An inferior article of Cotton Cards are in the State Store at seventy (75) five dollars.[39] The Quartermasters' Dep^t has received a large amt. of money lately, and I suppose we will be paid soon. I have only drawn one month's wages since I came here, and, of course, have been scarce of

37. This is presumably Lt. Col. George W. Guess of the Thirty-first Texas Cavalry (Marcus J. Wright, comp., *Texas in the War, 1861–1865*, ed. Harold B. Simpson [Hillsboro, Tex., 1965], 120).

38. This is Robert A. Key of Mount Lebanon, the son of Tandy A. Key.

39. Cotton cards are wire-tooth brushes used, in the absence of a proper cotton gin, to prepare lint cotton for spinning into cloth. As part of his program to bring relief to the impoverished citizens of north and west Louisiana, Governor Allen persuaded the state legislature to appropriate money to purchase cotton cards for distribution either at cost or free of charge.

money all the while, but have not needed much and have managed to get along with little. I now begin to doubt the Govm^t will ever send money enough this side of the river to pay off all that it is due the Soldiers. The best we can expect will be to draw one or two month's at a time. It is now due me over fifteen ($1500) hundred dollars which, if I could get now, would pay up all my debts and enable me to get along handsomely in the future.

I sent you a pound of very fine powder by Mr. Head. Did you get it? We no longer get half rations, but bacon and plenty of it. I don't know how long it will last.

I send you the latest papers by mail from which you can obtain the news. As soon as the election for Judge comes off, let me know the result. I have some hope of Henry's election. Eagan will be hard to beat [*corner of page torn*] only one in the [*end of page torn*].

> <

DAVID PIERSON TO WILLIAM H. PIERSON
Shreveport, La., Mar., 26th, 1865

Dear Pa.,

Send my Mosquito Bar and Summer pants by the return of Mr. Bob Key's wagon which leaves here tomorrow for Mt. Lebanon. I have mailed a letter with the same request which I hope will reach you before the wagon arrives.

I send this by the driver & c. All well. I send you a paper from which you can get the news. I have been detailed on Genl Court Martial duty again, which meets in town tomorrow. Lieut. Col. Guess is to be tried first for some crime in regard to his cotton dealings.

The celebrated Colonel McRae[40] left here a few days ago for Natchitoches where he is to be tried. Genl Churchill's Division[41] still here, though I hear that it will soon march to Texas. The Dist. of Ark. has been abandoned for want of supplies, and if reports be true from Alexandria, I should think this

---

40. Dandridge McRae raised the Third Arkansas Infantry Battalion, which he commanded as a lieutenant colonel at the battle of Oak Hills or Wilson's Creek. After commanding the Twenty-first Arkansas Infantry at Pea Ridge, he was promoted to brigadier general on November 5, 1862. He led his brigade at the battle of Prairie Grove in December, 1862, but the following July drew the wrath of his commanding officer, Theophilus H. Holmes, when he failed to follow orders at the battle of Helena. McRae requested a court of inquiry which, after numerous delays, at last convened at Camden, Arkansas, on June 7, 1864. Although the court found that McRae's actions "were obnoxious to no charge of misbehavior before the enemy," he resigned from the army in 1864.

41. Thomas James Churchill was elected colonel of the First Arkansas Mounted Rifles, which he led at the battle of Oak Hills. On March 4, 1862, he was promoted to brigadier general and served for a time under Edmund Kirby Smith in Kentucky. Late in 1862, he was given command of Arkansas Post, which,

Dist. will soon share the same fate. It is truly alarming to see how the resources of the Country are being exhausted. All accounts agree that the army at Alexandria is on the point of suffering for want of provisions. Forney's Division is in Texas, somewhere about Houston or below. Our Red River Fleet of Gunboats left here two days ago bound for Alexandria. There seems to be some apprehension of an advance of the enemy in that direction. If the Yankees attempt the invasion of this Dep^r, it will be prompted solely by the fear of French interference. If they come again, I shall have hopes of Foreign Intervention.

Yours & c.,

Dave

>⋅ ⋅<

JAMES F. PIERSON TO MARY CATHERINE PIERSON

Shreveport, La., Apr., 11th, 1865

Miss M. C. Pierson

    Mt. Lebanon, La.

Dear Sister,

Your welcome favor sent by Mr. Key's Boy came to hand and also the things which you sent by the wagon. I went to see Gov. Allen[42] this morning about exchanging the calico for the clothes that you sent. He told me to come again next Saturday, and he would attend to it for me. I suppose from what he said that he was willing to make the exchange. I will not get it in time to send it by Dr. Mathis, as he leaves tomorrow morning [on the] Stage. I am truly sorry for the Dr. Mathis [*page torn at fold, making several words illegible*] afoot at last by his speculating schemes. He had his mule, bridle, and saddle stolen from him

---

after a spirited defense, he was forced to surrender on January 11, 1863. After his exchange, Churchill commanded an Arkansas infantry division in the Red River campaign. For this service, he was promoted to major general on March 18, 1865.

    42. Henry Watkins Allen was appointed lieutenant colonel of the Fourth Louisiana Infantry and in February, 1862, was promoted to colonel of the regiment that he led at Shiloh. He commanded a brigade at the battle of Baton Rouge, where he received a crippling wound to both legs that incapacitated him for field service. Allen was promoted to brigadier general on August 19, 1863, and posted to Shreveport, where he was in charge of paroled prisoners of war.

    Allen was elected governor on November 2, 1863, and did as much as his limited resources would allow to bring relief to the embattled people of Louisiana, distributing at state expense food, clothing, utensils, and medicines to those in need. He attempted with remarkable success to control the state's runaway inflation and, to some degree, restored the state's economy by exporting Louisiana cotton and sugar to Mexico in exchange for munitions and machinery. See Vincent H. Cassidy and Amos E. Simpson, *Henry Watkins Allen of Louisiana* (Baton Rouge, 1964).

three miles from this place. He is now returning home a broken merchant. The
cotton cards that the Dr. gave to you for me belongs to Mr. Bob Key who sent
them to his father-in-law by the Dr. You may turn them over to the Dr. again. I
have been intending to send you a pair, but am just waiting for my furlough,
and then I can bring them myself. I guess from the tenor of your letter that you
think that I am becoming rich off of a small spur[?] speculation. I can scarcely
bear mine and Dave's expenses which are very economical. But if I can even do
that, it is very well to do it.

[*letter unsigned*]

➤ ⋲

David Pierson to William H. Pierson

Shreveport, La., Apr. 27ᵗʰ, 1865

Wᵐ H. Pierson
  Mt. Lebanon
    La.

Dear Pa,

I have delayed writing to you several days because of the uncertainty of the
mails and the want of any opportunity to send a letter by hand. The appropria-
tion for the payment of interest is out and no collections of that kind are now
being made. There is but little money in any of the Departments here now.
What little there is will be reserved to pay disabled soldiers. Don't send your
coupons now. When any money arrives (which is not likely soon to be) I will let
you know. We have had a host of bad news of late, some of which has been con-
tradicted, but enough has been confirmed to render our affairs as a nation almost desperate. The capture of Genˡ Lee with a portion of his army is enough
to make the most sanguine among us tremble for the result. Johns[t]on must
now accomplish wonders to extricate himself and army from their perilous situation. All depends upon him now, unless Genˡ Smith should cross the army of
this Depᵗ to the other side. A few more weeks may decide the war. The latest
news is that Johns[t]on's army is in good condition and still hopeful. It is reported this morning that Mobile has fallen. A mass meeting is to be held here
on Saturday next. Speeches are to be made by Genˡ Hays and others, the object
being to start a patriotic party and to give confidence to the doubting and despondent—in other words, to bind up the wounds of the mangled Confederacy
with plausible reasonings and sweet words. I happened to be present at a pre-
liminary meeting yesterday to arrange the affair, and much to my regret was put
upon one of the Committees. I expect to be as patriotic as anybody and to stay

in our army as long as anybody, but I have a perfect disgust for public meetings gotten up by men out of the army to dictate to our soldiers what they should do. They could do immeasurably more good by taking a gun and becoming soldiers themselves. It is in bad taste, to say the least of it, for able bodied men who never have fired a gun at the enemy to be ever boasting of their patriotism and urging a spirit of desperate resistance to the soldiers. I am now writing from the Court house where our Court Martial holds its sittings. We are now trying one Lt. Col. Guess for some unlawful Cotton dealings with the enemy. It is an interesting case and will perhaps occupy the court for over a month. The Dept. Court has been ordered to Houston, and ours is the only one left here. We are therefore likely to remain here the balance of the summer in our present capacity. It is reported that the Reg[t] will soon be ordered to Alexandria and its place filled by another from Thomas's Brigade.[43] If such should be the case, I shall try to get Jim detailed as orderly for the Court Martial and keep him with me.

I have done nothing as yet with your Int[erest] Notes. I could have sold them for twenty (25) five dollars a piece when you sent them, but that looked so much like giving them away that I refused to take it. Now they are worth nothing. I don't suppose they would command over five dollars in the market. New Issue is almost as worthless. Corn meal is one hundred dollars per bushel, and I saw an ordinary cow sell here for the enormous price of $1,500 dollars. Confidence has been to some extent restored since the reported death of Lincoln and Seward and the contradiction of the capture of Lee's whole army. It is bad enough, still, and may on the receipt of any bad news get worse.

I am still unfortunate with horses. My black has, or is taking, the Swiney. His shoulder is shrinking, and he is quite lame, and I [am] very much afraid that he will in a short time be useless. All's well. No further news.

Yours Affectionately,
Dave

43. Allen Thomas was elected to command of a battalion that later expanded into the Twenty-ninth Louisiana Infantry. This regiment served in the Vicksburg campaign and was captured on July 4, 1863. After his exchange, Thomas was assigned to reorganize paroled prisoners in his brother-in-law Richard Taylor's District of West Louisiana. On February 4, 1864, he was promoted to brigadier general and assigned to the command of Henry Watkins Allen's old brigade. When Maj. Gen. Camille Armand de Polignac returned to Europe, Thomas was assigned to the command of his division.

>≈ ≈<

JAMES F. PIERSON TO MARY CATHERINE PIERSON

Shreveport, La., Apr 28ᵗʰ, 1865

Miss M. C. Pierson

Dear Cassie,

I reᶜᵈ your letter sent by Mr. Key's wagon and also the clothing with directions what to do with them. I went to Gov. Allen's office three times before I effected a trade with him. I am afraid that you will not fancy it much now, but it is the best that I can do. There is no calico in the store now. This was one of the remnants that was left off of a bolt, and was the only piece that was any way suitable. I have been very sick in the last few days. I was first taken with a very severe fever which I succeeded in weakening, and while I was getting up out of that spell I was taken with a hard spell of the flux which I could not check under three days which reduced me almost to a skeleton. I am now getting over it very fast. I will be stout again in a few days if I have no back set now. I will send you the calico as soon as I can see a chance. I have not seen any person going there since I got the calico. The people are all very much demoralized about Shreveport—a great deal worse than the soldiers. I can't see what will be our next mishap. Everybody is listening for Gen. Johnston to give up with his army, but I think that it will end in the course of the summer.

I have not been able to get my furlough as I expected to have gotten it. I was not able to go at the time, and consequently another was furloughed, so I will not be able to get my furlough until about the 20ᵗʰ of May, but I don't care a great deal though I would like very much to be at home. I may not get home before the 1ˢᵗ of June as the men are not very prompt in reporting back when their time is out. It is thought that the Regt. will leave here in a few days. They say that the 17ᵗʰ Regt.⁴⁴ is ordered here to fill our place. Dave told me secretly that Col. Shivers⁴⁵ told him that we would soon be ordered off from here. Dave

44. The Seventeenth Louisiana Infantry was recruited from Caddo, Catahoula, Claiborne, Ouachita, Morehouse, and Sabine parishes and organized at Camp Moore on September 29, 1861. Under its first colonel, S. S. Heard, the unit fought in the battle of Shiloh and was ordered into the defenses at Vicksburg in May, 1862. Under Col. Robert Richardson, the regiment saw heavy fighting at Port Gibson on May 1, 1863, and surrendered with the rest of Vicksburg's garrison on July 4. The regiment reassembled at a parole camp near Shreveport in January, 1864, and was then ordered to Pineville as a component of Thomas Allen's brigade. In May, 1865, the regiment marched to Mansfield, where it disbanded on or about the nineteenth (Bergeron, *Guide,* 115–16).

45. William R. Shivers, a native of Georgia and a Shreveport merchant before the war, was elected captain of Company A of the First Louisiana Infantry and then as major when the regiment was organized at New Orleans on April 28, 1861. He served with his regiment in the Army of Northern Virginia, receiving promotions to lieutenant colonel on September 27, 1861, and to colonel on or about April 28,

is on Genl. Court Martial and consequently will be left here when we leave here. I am going to try to get to be orderly for the court to stay with Dave.

You must write often as you can.

Your brother till Death,

Jas. F. Pierson

≫ ≪

DAVID PIERSON TO WILLIAM H. PIERSON

Shreveport, La., May 9th*, 1865*

Wm H. Pierson

Mt. Lebanon,

La.

Dear Pa,

At last we have some definite news in regard to the situation of affairs East of the Miss. River. There is now but little doubt that the Confederacy is fast collapsing. Scarcely one item of bad news is digested until others more startling reach us. It is officially stated that Genl Johns[t]on has surrendered his army on the same terms given to Lee and that For[r]est's command is demoralized and scattering through the country to their homes. Also that Jef[f] Davis is making his way to this Dept. with all the specie he could get and the Federal Cavalry trying to cut him off. The Federal Commissioner sent by Grant to this Dept. to demand its surrender arrived here last night and is in council with Genl Smith today. Street reports say that Genl Smith will surrender the Dept. on the terms offered, which are to surrender and be paroled, the Federals transporting the troops to their homes and sending rations to the destitute of the army and people. I cannot believe that Smith will accept the terms immediately but that he will get all the delay in his power so as to hear from the President who, it is thought, will soon arrive in the Dept. If Mr. Davis does not arrive here before long, then I believe that Smith will accept the terms offered. My last hope died within me when Genl Lee surrendered, but up to this time I have tried to keep quiet. Now the last prop of the Government is broken and there is no longer any room for hope. This Dept. might hold out for a year longer by falling back into Texas, but neither the people nor the army will sustain such an undertaking. If Mr. Davis gets into this Dept., he will make a last effort to sustain himself, but his efforts will all be in vain. The soldiers are disheartened & disgusted and determined not to sacrifice their lives to gratify

---

1862. Wounded in the right arm during the Seven Days' Battles, he left the regiment and was assigned to duty at Shreveport (*ibid.,* 71–72).

anybody's ambition. All well. This written in great haste so as to get it in the Mail. A few more days and all will be over. What the consequences will be, I cannot surmise.

Yours & c.,
Dave

[On May 16, with rumors rife that Shreveport would be sacked and burned by soldiers of the Third Louisiana, David Pierson assembled his regiment and informed it that "he expected every man to do his duty as a soldier, and the people of the town were looking to them for protection." According to Sgt. Willie H. Tunnard, Pierson insisted that "they must not, should not be disappointed. He hoped that the men would uphold their former honor and reputation, and be as firm and true as steel." Four days later, the men of the Third Louisiana Infantry were discharged from the Confederate army. Tunnard recalled the parting as "most affecting." The veterans of Oak Hills, Elkhorn Tavern, Corinth, Iuka, and Vicksburg "put their arms around each other and sobbed like children; others gave the strong grasp of the hand, and silently went away with hearts too full for utterance, while still others would mutter a huskily spoken 'good-bye' or deep oath." David Pierson remained with his regiment until the last man had departed on the twenty-first.[46]]

46. Tunnard, A Southern Record, 336–37. Interestingly, exactly this same phraseology is found in John P. Blessington's description of the breakup of the Sixteenth Texas Infantry (Blessington, Walker's Texas Division, 307).

☞ INDEX ☜